D0946635

Principles of Operating Systems

Principles of Operating Systems

Sacha Krakowiak

translated by
David Beeson

The MIT Press
Cambridge, Massachusetts, London, England

Original edition © 1987 by Bordas, Paris, published under the title *Principes des systèmes d'exploitation des ordinateurs*.

This book was typeset in Oxford by Cotswold Press Ltd. and printed and bound in the United States of America.

Library of Congress Cataloging-in-Publication Data

Krakowiak, Sacha.
Principles of operating systems.

Translation of: Principes des systèmes d'exploitation des ordinateurs.
Bibliography: p.
Includes index.
1. Operating systems (Computers) I. Title.
QA76.76.063K7313 1988 005.4'3 87-5676
ISBN 0-262-11122-5

Contents

Preface

The operating system in a computer, or a computer installation, is a set of programs carrying out two main functions:

- managing an installation's resources, ensuring, if necessary, that they are shared between several users and controlling their distribution over the many tasks submitted to an installation, and
- providing a series of services by presenting users with an interface that is more adapted to their requirements than that of the physical machine; this interface is that of a 'virtual machine' made up of a set of functions to manage and communicate information and to implement the application software.

Recent developments in computer science have been marked by the emergence of microcomputers and telematics services, alongside distributed computer systems and individual workstations, and the integration of computers both into complex industrial processes and into equipment for the mass market. Although these developments have led to changes in the form and function of computer systems, their design is still based on a set of principles that have been gradually elaborated over the years, supported by theoretical research and validated by their application to the construction of actual systems.

This book has two aims:

- to describe the main principles underlying computer operating systems: management of parallelism and synchronization; naming, storage, and protection of information; and resource allocation; and
- to illustrate the application of these principles to the actual design of systems, taking account of recent developments in computer technology and its fields of application.

To meet the latter objective, several sections (3.3, 5.3, 10.1, and 10.2) will deal with specific examples, for which simplified systems based on existing implementations have been drawn on. A faithful and complete description of a real system would have overloaded this book with details that would not have contributed to an understanding of the principles underlying system design. Nonetheless it is hoped that the discussion of simplified examples will assist in the detailed study of real systems by providing guidelines to their structure and highlighting their essential aspects. It is strongly recommended that such a study be carried out in order to supplement the lessons given in this book, particularly by teachers who draw on it for course material. Bibliographic references to guide a study of this kind are given at the end of chapter 1.

The field covered is essentially that of systems using a common memory, so-called centralized systems, whose design principles are now fairly stable. A letter dated 21 May 1987 from M. Vitry, Foreign Rights, Bordas, states, "We have just put in production the second French edition which contains minor corrections and the additional chapter 11 ... It's due to be published early in October 1987."

This book contains material corresponding to preparation for a master's degree or the equivalent. It is principally directed at computer scientists who want to improve their knowledge in the operating system field.

It shall be assumed that readers are familiar with

- the general principles of computer architecture and
- the principles underlying the design of algorithms and programs; a programming language, including its practical use; and the general functions and organization of a compiler.

It is always difficult to select a language in which to present algorithms when discussing operating systems. As well as the difficulty of giving an overall view of complex programs, there is that of dealing with problems of hardware. Since this book is concerned with illustrating the methods used, rather than the details of their implementation, a Pascal-based notation that is quite common with any local extensions felt to be necessary has been chosen.

The end of each chapter gives an annotated list of bibliographic references and a set of exercises. Some of these exercises represent a direct application of concepts discussed; others require a certain amount of design work and could form the basis for a project; others are intended to encourage students to consider questions that have not been discussed and include references to guide further study in these areas.

Acknowledgements

The general approach in this book was heavily influenced by the work published by the Crocus[1] group: *Systèmes d'exploitation des ordinateurs* (*Computer Operating Systems*), published by Dunod in 1975. The task is easier now, as the essential concepts that at the time were still being elaborated or were changing rapidly are now more stable. But without the clarification and survey work carried out by that group, this book would never have been written; my cordial recognition is therefore due to my colleagues in the Crocus group.

Although in this case it was more indirect, another influence on this book was that exerted by the work since 1976 of the Cornafion group. The presentation given here of the questions of synchronization and object management, in particular, owes a great deal to the Rennes sub-group: Françoise André, Daniel Herman, and Jean-Pierre Verjus.

This book emerged from courses taught since 1973 in various departments of the Université Scientifique et Médicale and the Institut National Polytechnique, both in Grenoble, France. Many people, both teachers and students, have contributed over the years to the development of these courses. The way in which concepts are presented here, as well as the preparation of example applications and exercises, draws heavily on long-standing work in collaboration with Jacques Briat, Joëlle Coutaz, Guy Mazaré, Jacques Mossière, and Xavier Rousset de Pina. I naturally remain responsible for any errors there may be (which I invite readers to point out to me, for correction in any subsequent edition).

The original edition of this book was published with the support of the French Ministry of Education, Industry and Research, as part of the programme to assist the publication of scientific and technical books in French.

(1) Crocus: a collective name for J. Bellino, C. Bétourné, J. Briat, B. Canet, E. Cleeman, J.-C. Derniame, J. Ferrié, C. Kaiser, S. Krakowiak, J. Mossière and J.-P. Verjus.

Principles of Operating Systems

Chapter 1
Introduction

Programs executed on a computer are generally classified, according to their functions, under two headings: *system software* and *application software*. The operating system is an important component of system software. The aim of this introduction is to explain precisely what is meant by these terms, to define the main functions of operating systems with a few examples as illustrations, and finally to describe their common characteristics.

1.1 Functions of an operating system

A computer system is a combination of hardware and software intended to carry out tasks involving the automatic processing of information. Such a system is linked to the outside world by input-output mechanisms, allowing it to communicate with human users or to interact with the physical devices it is intended to control or to supervise.

The function of a computer system is to provide services suitable for the resolution of common problems:

- Information management: storage, naming, retrieval, communication
- Preparation and debugging of programs
- Execution of programs

It is convenient to regard the services provided by a computer system as defining, for the user, a new machine that is often called *abstract* or *virtual* as opposed to the physical machine formed by the components of the hardware. The description and operating instructions for these services form the **interface** of the computer system. We can therefore say that this interface defines a language, which is that of the abstract machine, and which allows users to communicate with the system. All the information necessary for the proper use of the system by a user (or by a connected physical device) is contained in the interface.

The level of abstraction of the means of expression provided in this way tends to increase with technical advances, i.e. the objects and operations considered as elementary on the abstract machine are implemented by more and more complex sets of objects and operations on the physical machine. Furthermore, different users of a single computer system may require different abstract machines. To simplify the design of the system, it is convenient to decompose the task to be carried out: in very broad terms, functions common to many applications are implemented by a set of programs called

system software; application software, on the other hand, implements a specific application by calling on the services provided by system software. Figure 1.1 shows this form of organization by means of a hierarchical schema where each *layer* uses the resources provided by the layer immediately below and presents the layer above with an interface describing the resources it offers; the interface of the highest layer is that of the whole computer system. The concepts associated with the decomposition of systems are discussed in detail in chapter 3.

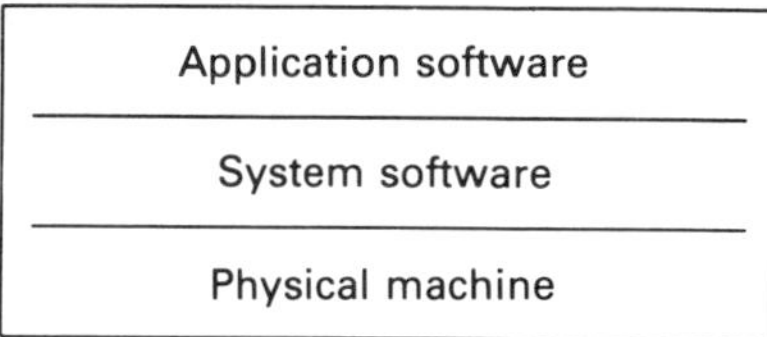

Fig. 1.1. Structure of a computer system

This structure should not be interpreted too strictly; in particular, the boundaries between layers are often imprecise and moving: a program initially developed as an application program may be built into system software if it turns out to be a commonly used tool for a class of users; in the same way, system software functions initially implemented by a program may be implemented by a microprogram or by an electronic circuit if savings or improved performance justify this step. Within system software itself, it is common to distinguish two levels (fig. 1.2).

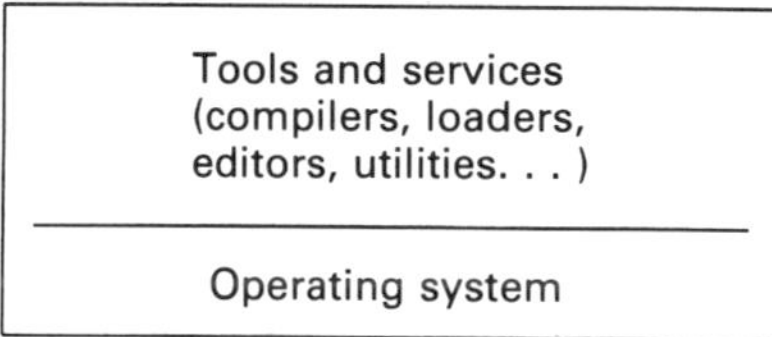

Fig. 1.2. Components of system software

Here again, the boundary cannot be strictly defined. The main functions of the lower layer of the system software, the **operating system**, can be classified under two main headings.

1. Definition and implementation of a virtual machine

a. Information management: structuring, storage, naming (virtual memory, files); transfer (input-output).

b. Execution control: execution of programs in sequence, in parallel, program composition, etc.

c. Miscellaneous services: assistance to debugging, fault handling, time measurement, etc.

2. Resource management and sharing

a. Management of physical resources: allocation of main memory, of secondary memory, of input/output devices
b. Information sharing and exchange between users
c. Mutual protection of users
d. Miscellaneous services: resource usage accounting, usage statistics, performance measurement, etc.

Decomposition into layers as a structuring tool occurs again within operating systems.

1.2 Examples of operating systems

The four examples below illustrate the variety of functions that an operating system must carry out. These examples are characteristic of several major classes of systems, but are not intended to be an exhaustive list. For each example, we indicate the functions to be carried out and the major characteristics required. Common characteristics of operating systems are summarized in section 1.4.1.

1.2.1 Personal computers

A personal computer, in its simplest configuration, is made up of a central processing unit, main memory and a terminal (screen and keyboard, possibly a mouse). This configuration is generally supplemented by secondary memory (floppy disk) and a printer (fig. 1.3).

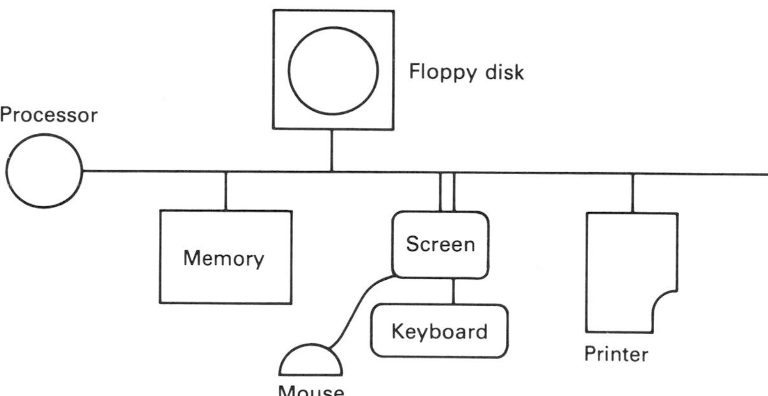

Fig. 1.3. Personal computer

Users of such systems essentially require two types of service:

- Creating and naming files, or structured sets of information; storage of these files in secondary memory; transfer of information between files and input/output devices (screen, keyboard, printer).
- Execution of programs which may be part of the system or be introduced in the form of files; data are entered through the keyboard or provided in a file; the results are displayed on the screen, listed on a printer, or copied to a file.

The interface presented by the system to a user is a **command language**. A command is a construction of the form

< action > <parameters >

input via the keyboard, or using a mouse, and immediately interpreted by the system.

Here are two examples of typical sequences of actions:

1. Debugging programs

- Write a program at the keyboard (using a text editor)
- Execute of the program providing data through the keyboard
- Modify of the program if results are not satisfactory, and reexecute it
- Store the final version of the program

2. Operation

- Request the execution of a pre-existing program, or a program written as above, using a set of data contained in a file or input on demand to the keyboard. Results are displayed on the screen, listed on a printer or copied to a file to be reused.

In such a system, there is no resource sharing, since the machine is being used by a single user who has total control over it. Resource allocation occurs for memory management and file loading. The main functions of the operating system are file management, implementation of input/output and interpretation of the command language.

For this type of system, the most important qualities are:

- Reliability
- Efficiency (as the performance of the hardware is often low, it is important to make the best possible use of it)
- Simplicity in use
- Ease of extension by adding new utility programs, or adapting to new peripherals

The latter two aspects highlight the importance of a careful design of the interfaces provided by the system, both for the command language and the file management system.

The organization of a simple operating system for a personal computer is discussed in chapter 3.

1.2.2 Control of industrial processes

In a chemical products factory, a reactor is used to synthesize product C from two products A and B (fig. 1.4).

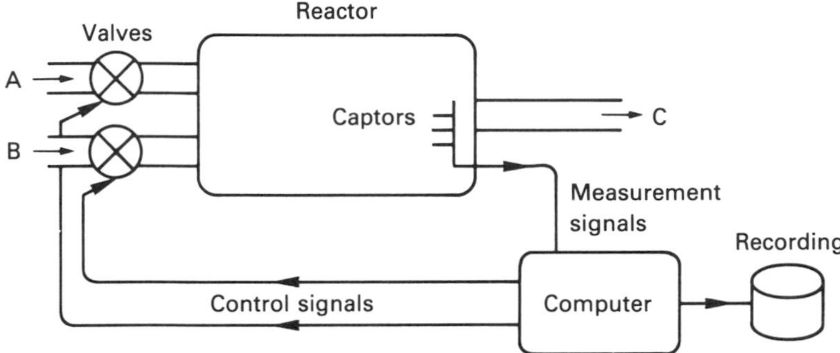

Fig. 1.4. Control of a chemical reactor

This manufacturing process is controlled by a computer, which carries out three functions.

- *Regulation*. For the process to take place correctly, operating parameters (temperature, pressure, concentration, etc.) must be maintained within fixed limits. This means regulating the input rate of products. Operating parameters are measured using sensors; the computer collects these measurements and acts in consequence on the input valves, as specified in a regulation program.
- *Recording*. The various results obtained by measurements are recorded periodically, their values displayed on a control panel and copied into a file (or 'log') with a view to additional processing later (operating statistics).
- *Security*. If certain measured parameters exceed a predefined critical value (as would be the case in an accident), emergency shutdown of the reactor must take place.

Let us now examine the constraints introduced by this mode of operations.

1. Measurements are taken periodically; let T be the sampling period and let t be the total time necessary for the computer to process a set of measure-

ments (collection, recording, determination and execution of valve commands).

The system can only operate if

$$t \leqslant T$$

2. The security function must be given priority over all others; in other words, it must be possible at any moment to detect that a critical value has been exceeded and procedures for handling such an occurrence must interrupt operations that are under way.

The main functions of the operating system are the following.

- To act on external devices (reading of sensors, control of valves)
- To schedule events in physical time (periodic triggering of the processing cycle)
- To react to external events (emergency shutdown)
- To manage information (storage and maintenance of the log file)

The specification of a physical limit to the duration of a computer process, the existence of scheduling periods, the concept of priority handling and the connection to equipment for the control or measurement of an external device are characteristic of computer processes known as **real time** applications.

As well as process control, examples of the use of these systems are: the management of telephone switchboards; automatic pilots for aircraft, missiles or satellites; medical monitoring, robot control; etc.

For these systems, the major requirement is reliability. As the consequences of a failure may be catastrophic, the system must be able to guarantee the safety of the device it controls at any time: it must therefore be able to guarantee a minimal service even in the case of a hardware breakdown, an accident or a human error.

An example of a system kernel suitable for programming real time systems is described in chapter 5.

1.2.3 Transaction systems

Transaction systems are characterized by the following properties.

1. The system manages a set of information, or database, which may be very large (billions of bytes).

2. A certain number of predefined operations, or transactions, which are often interactive, can be applied to this information.

3. The system has a large number of access points (terminals) and many transactions can take place simultaneously.

Systems used to handle rail or air seat reservation, to manage bank accounts or to retrieve documents, are all examples of transaction systems.

Information contained in the system database is subject to integrity constraints expressing its internal consistency. These constraints obviously depend on the application: e.g. the number of seats reserved in a train may not exceed the number of seats available, the same seat cannot be assigned to more than one person, etc. Execution of a transaction must maintain the consistency of the information.

The qualities required of a transaction system are availability and reliability; for certain systems, fault-tolerance is also essential. Important characteristics of transaction systems are that they cater to many parallel activities, and, in many cases, components are widely spread geographic ally, which leads to specific problems (see section 1.3.3).

1.2.4 Time-sharing systems

The function of a time-sharing system is to provide services to a group of users; each of them may use:

- Services equivalent to those available on a personal computer
- Services associated with the existence of a community of users: sharing of information, communication between users

Moreover, thanks to the sharing of costs between a large number of users, it is possible to offer each of them common services that would not be available individually, such as access to special peripherals (graphics output, etc.) or to complex software requiring large amounts of memory.

The problems involved in designing time-sharing systems therefore combine those of personal computers and those of transaction systems. They can be classified as follows:

- Definition of the virtual machine offered to each user
- Sharing and allocation of common physical resources: processors, memory, input output devices
- Management of shared information (files) and of communication

The qualities required of a time-sharing system also cover those of a personal machine and of a transaction system: availability, reliability, security; efficient use of the hardware; quality of the interface and of the services provided to users; ease of extension and adaptation.

1.3 Historical development of operating systems

A rapid description of the way operating systems have evolved will give a clear idea of their characteristics today and help to introduce some common terms.

1.3.1 From 'hands on' to batch processing

The first computers built included no real operating system. Each user took over the machine alone for a given period, and consequently had access to all its resources. Direct interaction (step by step execution, direct modification of memory) was the main tool for program debugging. The earliest forms of system software included tools to assist in program development (assemblers, compilers, debuggers) and input-output subroutines.

This form of operation, called hands-on operations, was uneconomical, since expensive hardware was being underused. Consequently, towards the end of the 1950s, the first 'job sequencing monitors' began to appear. These programs made it possible to execute sequentially a series of jobs (programs and data) prepared in advance, with automatic transition from one job to the next.

The main function of such a system was resource management: memory, processor and input-output. Automation of management procedures implies a **protection** function for all tasks against perturbation if errors occur:

- Limitation on processor occupation time, to prevent an endless loop in a program from blocking the whole system
- Supervision of input-output, in particular to prevent loops in the use of devices
- Protection of the memory area reserved for the monitor, to avoid accidental modifications by an addressing error in a user program

The need to provide these functions was the source of various hardware extensions: clock management, restrictions on the use of certain instructions, memory protection.

The use of job sequencing monitors led, in particular, to improvements in the utilization of the processor. Productivity was nonetheless limited by the fact that the processor was wholly occupied during execution of input-output operations. One solution was to use two computers in tandem. Programs were executed on the main computer, while input-output took place on a magnetic tape with a high transfer rate. An auxiliary computer was responsible for producing input tapes from punched cards and for listing out on paper the contents of output tapes. Careful planning of task submission made it possible to operate the two computers in parallel and therefore to make full-time use of the processing capacity of the main computer; on the other hand, it led to a certain rigidity in operations (time constraints on job input, poor response times) which were inconvenient for users. These

batch processing systems were being widely used at the beginning of the 1960s.

1.3.2 Multiprogramming and time-sharing

Between 1960 and 1970, important advances, both in hardware technology and in understanding of system design principles, made it possible to break free from the limitations of batch processing.

1. The introduction of autonomous specialized processors for information transfer (exchange units or input-output channels) made it possible to free the central processor of detailed management of input-output.
2. Multiprogramming, or sharing of memory between several jobs, allowed better use to be made of the central processor by taking advantage of the possibility of carrying out input-output operations concurrently with processing.
3. Time-sharing systems gave back the users the interactive mode of operation provided by individual machines, while allowing them to take advantage of common services at low cost.

We shall now consider the consequences of each of these developments on the organization of operating systems.

1. Buffered input-output

A channel, or exchange unit, is a processor capable of executing input-output in an autonomous way, in parallel to processing as such. The cpu and channels therefore access common information in central memory, and the relative speeds of processing and transfer operations become an important factor. It may be noted that the throughput of peripheral devices such as a card reader or printer, based on mechanical operations, is very low compared to the processing capacity of the cpu. For example, the mean time it takes to process one card in the central processing unit is very much lower (by a factor of 1,000 or 10,000) than the time it takes to read that card; similarly, the cpu can produce many lines of results in the time it takes to print a single line. This leads to two consequences for the organization of the operating system:

a. A large number of jobs should be read in advance in order to maintain a high rate of activity in the cpu.

b. A large amount if output data must be stored in memory while awaiting printing.

Consequently, the introduction of simultaneous transfer leads to an accumulation of information in memory in the form of input or output buffers. This is the situation shown in fig. 1.5.

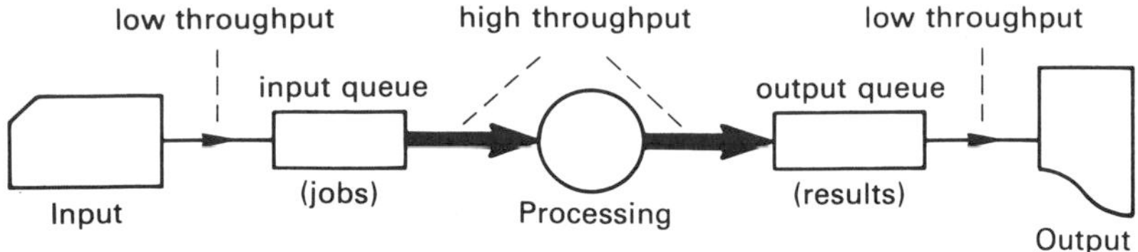

Fig. 1.5. Buffering slow input-output

To limit the load on central memory, input output buffers are implemented on secondary memory, so that the transfer rate between central memory and secondary memory is high with respect to slow input output. Transfers between the two storage levels are also handled by channels. The consequences for system structure for this form of organization of input-output will be examined next.

2. Multiprogramming

In an operating system using simultaneous input output, memory is shared between an input buffer zone, an output buffer zone and a zone reserved for the job currently being processed. Jobs are executed in sequence, with input, output and processing taking place simultaneously.

In this mode of operation, two undesirable events may occur:

a. If the job under way has to read data needed for its execution, the cpu remains inactive while reading takes place.

b. A short job arriving during the execution of a very long job is delayed until the latter is over.

These observations lead us to consider a mode of operation in which:

a. A job awaiting execution can use the cpu while the last active job is waiting for input data.

b. The cpu can be reassigned before the end of a job, to meet response time constraints.

In both cases, it is necessary to keep the cpu reassignment time short with respect to the transfer time between memory levels, which implies the simultaneous presence, in main memory, of several programs or parts of programs. This mode of operation is called **multiprogramming**.

The flow of information in an operating system designed in this way is shown in fig. 1.6.

This diagram highlights two major points: the central role played by main memory (while early systems were organized around the processor) and the importance of information flow between main memory and secondary memory. Consequently, the size of main memory and the transfer rate between the two memory levels become crucial parameters for system

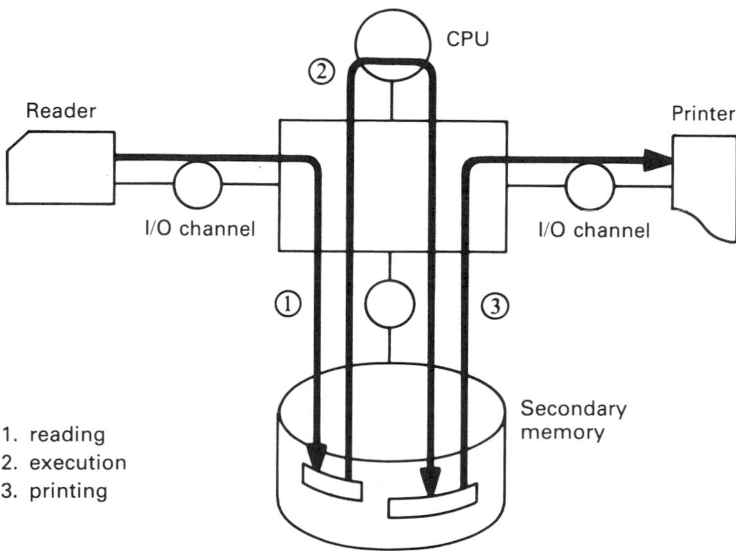

Fig. 1.6. Flow of information in a multiprogrammed system

efficiency. A detailed study of multiprogrammed systems appears in chapters 9 and 10.

The main advantages and constraints of multiprogramming are as follows.

1. System complexity: a multiprogrammed system is more complex as it is necessary to provide for memory sharing and mutual protection of programs.

2. Hardware characteristics: multiprogramming requires special devices to relocate programs and to protect memory.

3. Use of resources: a multiprogrammed system allows a better balance of the load of the various resources cpu, memory, input output devices.

4. Efficiency for the user: multiprogramming makes it possible to reduce response times for short jobs in a sequential processing system; moreover it provides for acceptable response times for interactive jobs (time-sharing). In a monoprogrammed system, response time is determined by the longest jobs or by loading times from secondary memory.

Note that these considerations are closely dependent on the one hand on the state of technology, and on the other hand on the assumption that hardware is being shared. Multiprogrammed systems are therefore still evolving, in particular because of:

- Falling costs of main memory
- The development of rapid access secondary memory

- The development of distributed systems and personal computers (see section 1.3.3)

3. Time-sharing sytems

The function of a time-sharing system, described in section 1.2.4., is to offer the user the equivalent of a personal machine and also the possibility of taking advantage of common services. Users access the system through terminals and use it interactively. The system must therefore guarantee an acceptable response time to each user (of the order of a second) for the execution of elementary jobs, such as editing and interactive program debugging. This is obtained by allocating the processor in turn, in very short time slices, to the user programs.

The viability of this technique is linked to the characteristics of interactive work: user activity is divided into *thinking time* where a request is being prepared and typed in, and *waiting time* during which the system executes the corresponding service. Experience shows that thinking time is much longer, on average, than acceptable waiting time: the system can therefore serve many users by taking advantage of the idle time taken for thinking.

An approximate calculation yields order of magnitude figures, but the estimate is poor as it is based only on mean values while fluctuations around the mean play a major role. More reliable models will be introduced in chapter 8.

Let us consider a time-sharing system serving 100 users, whose mean behavior is identical. Let us assume that thinking time is on average 9 times longer than waiting time. The latter therefore represents 10% of total time, and they are therefore on average ten 'active' users, i.e. users waiting for a requested service to be executed. Assume that the cpu is divided into 50 ms time slices: if the execution of an elementary request uses at most 1 time slice, the response time will therefore be of the order of 0.5 second.

In this calculation, we have implicitly assumed that all programs submitted by active users are in main memory: switching time between two user programs is therefore reduced to the time taken for cpu switching, which is negligible with respect to the length of a time slice. Given the relation between this time and the loading time for a program from disk, multiprogramming is clearly necessary for operating a time-sharing system. But the situation is in fact more complex: the size of main memory does not allow it to contain all programs submitted by active users at the same time. It is therefore possible that some information (a program or data) is missing from main memory at the moment the cpu needs to access it. The role of the memory management system is to reduce as far as possible the probability of this event. The techniques studied in chapters 9 and 10 make this possible.

The development of time-sharing systems highlights the importance of man-machine interaction and in particular of the command language, which is the interface presented by the system to its users. This aspect was neglected for a long time: command languages, designed empirically, were often rigid, inconvenient or even esoteric. The Unix([1]) system, designed in 1970–71 and now widespread, owes a large part of its success to its flexibility, its power and the ease of use of its command language. The emergence and the foreseeable extension of graphics terminals, allowing simultaneous monitoring (in separate 'windows') of the operation of multiple activities as well as making it possible to combine text, images and perhaps even voice input and output, suggest that there may well be profound modifications in this area, and that the very concept of a command language may be transformed by the power of interactive tools.

1.3.3 Networks, distributed systems, personal computers

The 1970s and the beginning of the 1980s were marked by two phenomena:

- The appearance of microprocessors and the increase in their performance levels, making considerable processing power at lower and lower cost available
- The development of data transmission techniques (remote processing) and the gradual integration of the communication function into computer systems computer networks and distributed systems

At the same time, the users of computer systems are expressing new requirements:

- There is a requirement for resource sharing, both for economic reasons and because of the need to access shared information
- Resources and information may be distributed geographically
- There is a need for better adaptation of system structure to the applications handled, leading to decentralization of the system and the geographic distribution of its elements
- There is a need to bring togethere previously separate applications within a single framework

New types of computer system are therefore gradually emerging:

1. Wide area networks, allowing existing systems to be connected together, making it possible to transmit data between these systems and to access remote services

2. Local area networks, built around a high throughput communication channel (10Mbit/s); these are geographically concentrated and designed for a particular application:

([1]) Unix is a registered trademark of ATT Bell laboratories.

- Process control systems (or *real time* systems, as defined in section 1.2.2)
- Document communication and storage systems (or office information systems), which are oriented towards exchanging information or producing and storing documents
- General purpose systems, in particular for the production of software

Local networks for general purposes are tending to take over from time sharing systems: each user has an individual machine, whose performance is now sufficient for most applications, and the network has two functions:

- To allow communication between users
- To allow users to access common services that are too costly to be provided on an individual basis: storage of large quantities of information, document printing, very fast processors, etc. These services are managed by specialized systems or *servers*, to which clients address their requests for service

The concepts and techniques developed for centralized systems remain valid for the design of servers and for the operating systems of personal computers. The distribution and communication of information introduce new problems such as coordination of remote activities and maintenance of consistency between distributed data.

Foreseeable developments in networks and personal computers will not, however, lead to the disappearance of large centralized systems and time-sharing access, as they remain economically valid for many applications. Requirements for numerical computation in specialized applications (aerodynamics, meteorology, etc.) are also encouraging the development of very powerful systems including specialized multiprocessors (anay processors), for which new operating system architectures have still to be developed.

1.3.4 Conceptual progress

The brief overview of the development of systems given above was primarily based on their technical and functional aspects. At the same time, major conceptual developments have led progressively to a better understanding of the functioning of operating systems and have allowed methods to emerge making their design easier. We shall here consider the most important steps in this development.

In general terms, we can date the beginning of a scientific approach of operating systems to the period 1964–65. This period immediately followed a time of major technical developments: the first time-sharing systems

(Thor, CTSS); the announcement of the IBM 360 series and the introduction of input-output channels; the first paging memory (Atlas). Taking this period as our starting point, we shall consider the development of the main concepts and the consequences for later implementations. The corresponding bibliography appears at the end of this chapter.

1.3.4.1 Processes and synchronization

The management of physically or conceptually parallel activities was an idea that failed to be understood for a long time. The operation of certain input output programs, for example, was based on numeric evaluation of the transfer time: this operation failed if there was a hardware fault or if a program was modified too hastily. Systems were liable to breakdowns of unknown origin, which seemed to defy analysis as it was impossible to reproduce them.

From 1965 to 1968, the necessary concepts were elaborated: the concept of a sequential process; the formulation and solution of the mutual exclusion problem; the concept of synchronization and the invention of semaphores, an elementary tool for synchronization. They were applied successfully to the design of actual systems: the THE system (1967) used semaphores; the Multics system (1964–70) included a process management kernel.

Later progress has been slower. Around 1974–75, various mechanisms were proposed to replace semaphores: monitors, which allow a more global expression of synchronization, are the only ones applied in real systems. Methods and tools adapted to distributed systems were developed towards the end of the 1970s; this development is still going on. Tools for the expression of synchronization are beginning to appear in programming languages. Much work remains, however, to be done on the specification and proofs of synchronization.

1.3.4.2 Naming and management of information

The problems of naming information were initially tackled by means of programming languages: each language defines the universe of objects accessible to a program and the operations on these objects. From the point of view of the operating system, the problems of naming were simply reduced to allocating the objects defined by the language in a physical memory, which was directly addressable.

Limitations on main memory very quickly made clear the need for secondary storage and mechanisms of exchange between the two levels of memory. The first paging memory appeared in 1962 (Atlas); at about the same time, compilers (Algol 60) used software paging for run-time program management. In fact, concepts related to the naming of information and those associated with the management of physical space (primary and secondary memory) were not clearly distinguished for a long time, as it was only in 1965 that the concept of segmentation, as a means of structuring and naming information, was clearly elaborated. There were several steps in the process:

- The Burroughs B5000 system (1962) introduced a logical addressing mechanism for variable size units or segments. The mechanism was used for the run-time management of Algo 60 programs.
- The main concepts underlying segmentation emerged in 1965, based on experiments carried out on the first time-sharing systems. The Multics system, whose design was launched in 1964–65 following experiments carried out at MIT or CTSS, provided a field of application: the machine, designed at the same time as the operating system, included segmented addressing; the pursuit of a high level of generality, which was one of the objectives of the system, led to the development of all the extensions to this concept, notably that of dynamic linking. The system only became operational in around 1970.
- A study carried out in 1966 developed a machine architecture adapted to time-sharing. The results of this study provided the basis for the design of the 67 model in the IBM 360 series; the machine did not in fact have segmented addressing, but two-level paging which was used to simulate segments.

In fact, the example of the IBM 360/67 is typical: the concept of segmentation was misunderstood for a long time in the computer community as very few systems genuinely implemented it, and machine manufacturers maintained the confusion by using the term segmentation for physical memory management mechanisms.

Around 1971–72, the development of a time-sharing systems highlighted the importance of problems concerned with information sharing and protection, and their close connections with the issue of naming. The concept of a segment, even if it is supplemented with the *protection rings* of Multics, is insufficient to provide a solution. The first models used for the study of protection gave rise to the concepts of objects, capabilities and domains, which became the basis for several experimental systems. The subject is still very much open (see section 1.3.4.4.).

1.3.4.3 Resource allocation

The problems of resource allocation began to appear with the introduction of multiprogramming. They took on a particular importance with the introduction of paging and the appearance of the first virtual memory system. The concept of virtual memory makes it possible to hide the management mechanisms for a two-level storage system while presenting users with an apparently uniform addressing space. The first virtual memory systems were subject to unexpected losses in performance: the system could not cope with the load for which it was designed and *thrashed*, while response times reached unacceptable levels. The phenomenon was more or less explained around 1968–69 by the behavior characteristics of programs.

Satisfactory solutions (load control) were progressively developed; better theoretical understanding of the wait and congestion phenomena and the development of simulation and measurement tools, made it possible to adjust the characteristics of a configuration to the desired performance levels. Complete control of performance, and more precisely *fine tuning* of a system, remains a question of experience and practice, because of the complexity of the phenomena involved.

1.3.4.4 System structuring and protection of objects

Operating systems are complex and large programs, and all software decomposition and structuring techniques may be applied to them. Here we shall consider two important aspects.

1. Modularity and hierarchical structuring

The modular decomposition method involves breaking a system down into elements, or modules, each of which has its own functional specification describing its behavior without reference to implementation details. A module depends on another module if it uses resources provided by the latter. If a system is organized into modules in such a way that the dependence relation has an acyclic graph, the system can be described hierarchically, as a set of *layers* each of which only uses resources from the layers below; the lowest layer is the physical machine. The essential advantage of this method of structuring is the separation that it allows between modules or layers by restricting their mutual dependence to a clearly specified interface. The recent development of languages including the module concept and adapted to system writing (Mesa, Modula-2, Ada) should make the use of these methods more widespread.

2. The object concept; protection

The concept of an object is a structuring tool generalizing the concept of types drawn from programming languages. This concept allows global definition of classes of objects by a set of common properties (access functions, state specification) and makes it possible to generate instances of these classes. The protection mechanisms associated with objects allow the definition of access restrictions which must be respected for each object, depending on the type of user or the current context. The concept of an object was first implemented in experimental systems (CAL-TSS, Hydra), and then introduced into some machine architectures (Plessey 250, CAP, IBM 38, Intel iAPX-432). It is still more used as a design tool than as a mechanism for the actual structuring of systems.

1.4 Structure of this book

We have decided to base our approach on the main concepts whose development we have been discussing here, each of which occurs in the main classes of systems used:

- Structuring and modularity
- Management of parallel activities
- Management, communication, and protection of information
- Allocation and sharing of resources

For each of these fields, we shall consider methods and tools making it possible to resolve the problems posed, as well as specific examples of applications. Moreover, two chapters (3 and 10) are entirely devoted to more detailed application examples, summarizing the discussions in the previous chapters.

Chapter 2 describes mechanisms for executing programs and for communicating information within computers. These mechanisms, in particular interrupts and input output operations, are directly managed by the operating system kernel, which prevents direct access from the upper layers.

Chapter 3 reviews the organizational principles underlying software systems: hierarchical and modular structuring, abstraction levels and interfaces, the concept of an object. These concepts are illustrated by a description of the overall structure of an elementary operating system.

Chapter 4 is dedicated to the concepts and mechanisms used in programming parallel activities. The concept of a *process* is the key to a systematic presentation. The main concepts associated with process management are introduced: mutual exclusion, synchronization and communication. The chapter describes a synchronization tool, monitors, as well as the constructs allowing parallelism to be expressed in programming languages.

Chapter 5 describes the design principles for the implementation of a synchronization kernel, allowing parallel process management and synchronization primitives to be implemented on a machine.

Chapter 6 introduces the main concepts associated with the management of information in an operating system: naming, linking and representation of objects. The hardware and software mechanisms used for segmentation and protection are discussed and illustrated by means of examples.

Chapter 7 describes the organization of file management systems: logical structure, physical implementation, access functions, information representation, security and protection.

Chapter 8 is an introduction to a study of general problems of resource allocation: waiting phenomena, queueing networks, deadlocks and starvation. In particular, the main approaches to the allocation of a single class of resources is discussed, with an application to the allocation of a processor and the management of memory-disk exchanges.

Chapter 9 deals with memory allocation and memory hierarchy management problems. It starts by introducing concepts associated with the use of the memory resource: the concept of virtual memory, the behavior of programs in their addressing space, as well as mechanisms making the implementation of virtual memory easier (paging).

Chapter 10 describes the general structure of a multiprogrammed system, stressing global management of resources and the structure of programs and tables that make up an operating system. This description is based on two examples: a fixed partition system and a paging virtual memory system.

Chapter 11 studies distributed computer systems, where processors communicate with each other over a network. This is a field in which considerable research work is taking place, and the discussion here is intended to provide an introduction to the study of the problems involved.

1.5 Bibliographic notes

Information on the historical development of computers and of operating systems respectively appear in [Rosen 69, Rosin 69]; a discussion of the history of systems is also given in [Weizer 81].

A large number of books on operating systems is now available. Such books come in three categories.

1. Introduction to the main aspects of operating systems, intended in principle to give an overall view of the field to non-specialists: [Bull 71, Colin 71, Wilkes 75, Lister 79, Calingaert 82, Theaker 83]

2. A more detailed description based on design principles [Watson 70, Brinch Hansen 73, Shaw 74, Tsichritzis 74, Crocus 75, Habermann 76a, Peterson 83, Janson 85, Tanenbaum 87]

3. A more descriptive discussion, generally oriented towards technical aspects [Madnick 74, Deitel 83]

Older books are principally of historical interest, given the rapid development of this field.

There are also monographs on various more specific aspects of operating systems: models, synchronization, protection, etc. They are mentioned in the bibliographic notes to the chapters dealing with those subjects.

Case studies are an indispensable supplement to any course on operating systems. They come in two great classes:

1. A logical presentation of design decisions and implementation techniques in a real system; critical study of practical experience with such a system

2. Description of a 'model' system constructed essentially for didactic purposes, sometimes based on an existing real system

In class 1, we might mention: Multics [Organick 72, Corbatò 72, Banino 78], Unix [Ritchie 74, Thompson 78, Bach 86], Tenex [Bobrow 72], Thoth [Cheriton 79], OS/360 [Mealy 66], MVS/370 [Scherr 73, Lynch 74, Auslander 81], Pilot [Redell 82], VAX/VMS [Kenah 84]. The monograph [McKeag 76] brings together four case studies of historical interest: Burroughs MCP, CDC Scope 3, THE, Atlas Titan. Other references appear in chapters 3, 5 and 10.

In class 2, there are: OS6 [Stoy 72], Solo [Brinch Hansen 76 and 77], Tunis [Holt 83], Xinu [Comer 84], Minix [Tanenbaum 87]. The last three systems are based on Unix.

Exercise

Exercise 1.1 [Brinch Hansen 73] for questions 1 and 2

The aim of this exercise is to highlight, by means of an extremely simplified example, the influence of the historical development of operating systems on certain quantities characteristic of performance.

Consider a computer whose input output devices are a card reader (1000 cards/min) and a printer (1000 lines/min). An *average job* is defined as:

- Read 300 cards
- Use the processor for 1 minute
- Print 500 lines

We assume that all jobs submitted by users have exactly the characteristics of this average job.

We define two means of measuring system performance:

- Mean throughput of jobs T: number of jobs executed in an hour
- Efficiency η of the cpu: the fraction of the total cpu usage time during which the cpu is executing useful work (other than I/O devices management)

1. We assume to start with that I/O devices are managed by the cpu. Calculate η and T under the following operating hypotheses:

a. The system is being used in hands-on mode; sessions may not last more than 15 minutes

b. The system is being used with a job sequencing monitor for jobs

2. Now assume that I/O devices are managed by a separate computer, which is dedicated to card-to-tape and tape-to printer transfers. The input tape is fed into the main computer and results are written on the output tape; we can ignore the tape read and write times. The transfer time for tapes from one computer to another is 5 minutes in each direction; we assume that a tape holds a batch of 50 jobs (see diagram).

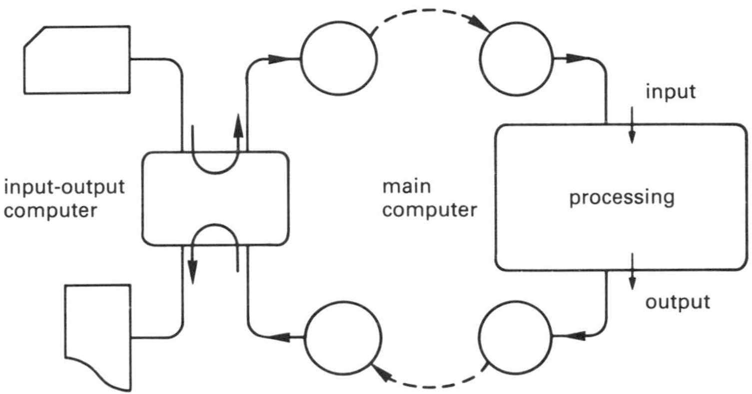

a. Assume that the jobs are being submitted at a sufficient rate to occupy the central computer full-time. Calculate the values of η and T.

b. Establish a schedule for job submission and calculate the mean waiting time for a user (time between submission of a job and reception of the result). Assume that jobs arrive at a regular rate, that the time taken to make up a batch (preparation of a set of cards) is 10 minutes and that the time to distribute results from a batch (cutting up and sorting listings) is also 10 minutes.

3. I/O devices are now being managed by an input output channel. The system is monoprogrammed, and the linkage monitor allows the central unit to process one job while reading the next and printing the last. Calculate η and T under these conditions. Carry out the same calculations on the assumption that the average job reads 1200 cards and prints 1500 lines per minute of use of the central unit.

4. Input output is now being buffered on disk (read and print spooler). The average job is as defined in 3) (1200 cards, 1 minute, 1500 lines).

a. Assume that a card image and a printer line take up 80 and 100 bytes respectively. What is the minimum size necessary for input and output buffers on the disk if the cpu is to be used at maximum efficiency? What will then be the job throughput rate?

b. The rate of arrival of jobs and the size of the input buffer are as calculated in a), and the size of the output buffer on the disk is 2 Megabytes. What is the efficiency of the cpu?

Chapter 2

Execution and communication mechanisms

This chapter is devoted to a study of the mechanisms allowing a computer, on the one hand, to divide its activity between multiple tasks, and on the other hand to interact with the external world and to exchange information with it. Management programs for these mechanisms stand at the heart of operating systems; a detailed knowledge of their structure and their operations is therefore indispensible to a system designer.

2.1 Sequential execution of a program

Let us start with the concepts involved in the sequential execution of a single program on a machine. We shall use a simplified model, but one that is representative of the most common cases.

The machine is made up of an addressable memory, which contains the instructions and data for a program, and of a processor, capable of interpreting instructions. Instructions and data are contained in distinct segments: a segment is a collection of information, that can be named and handled as a single unit, which is held in a series of adjacent memory locations. We assume that segments containing the instructions (the procedure segments) are not modified during execution.

A sequential program is made up of a sequence of instructions, whose execution causes the state of the machine to change. This evolution is discrete: the machine's state can only be observed at particular moments (observable points) which generally correspond to the beginning and end of instructions. Certain long and complex instructions, whose execution takes place in several stages, may include further intermediate observable points. The state of the machine is defined, at these moments, by the state of the processor and the state of the memory.

The state of the memory is defined by the contents of all segments loaded into it. The state of the processor is defined by the contents of a set of programmable or internal registers; for a detailed discussion, see section 2.1.2.

2.1.1 Procedure, activity, context

2.1.1.1 Definitions

A sequential program is made up of a set of procedures which call each other. Each of these procedures is associated with a distinct procedure segment; a data segment can belong to a procedure or be shared between several procedures.

We use the term **activity** for the uninterrupted execution of a single procedure. The execution of a sequential program is therefore a series of activities. We use the term **context** of an activity for the information accessible to the processor during that activity. The context therefore includes a processor context (programmable and internal registers) and a memory context (procedure segment, data segment). Transition from one activity to another takes place by way of special instructions, procedure calls and returns, which lead to context switching. The following are two examples.

1. Procedure call and return

A procedure *p* (the calling procedure) invokes a procedure *q* (the called procedure) by a calling sequence, which includes the following stages:

- Preparation of the parameters transmitted by *p* to *q*
- Saving part of the context of *p*, to be restored on return
- Replacement of the context of *p* by the context of *q*

Return follows a more or less symmetrical pattern, but the context of *q* is lost:

- Preparation of results transmitted from *q* to *p*
- Restoration of the context of *p* to its state before the call

2. Operations based on coroutines

When using **coroutines**, the calling and called procedures play a symmetrical role: the return sequence is identical to the calling sequence. The activity occurring as a result of a call to procedure *p* takes as its initial context the context saved during the last call executed by *p*. The first call to a procedure must specify the initial value of its context.

The single context change sequence (resume) includes the following steps (*p* is the coroutine being exited, *q* the coroutine being resumed):

- Preparation of parameters transmitted by *p* to *q*
- Saving that part of the context of *p* which must be restored on resumption
- Restoration of the saved context when *q* was last exited (or establishment of the initial context if we are dealing with a first call)

2.1.1.2 Sequential execution mechanisms

The general mechanism described here allows sequential execution of a program as a sequence of activities resulting from the execution of procedures or coroutines. It carries out the following functions:

- Saving and restoration of call and return contexts
- Transmission of parameters between calling and called procedures
- Management of a work area specific to each procedure: it allows recursive calls

1. Procedures

The data structure used is an **execution stack**. Different variants are used, distinguished essentially by the detailed specification of the context and its modifications on procedure calls and returns. The execution pattern may be directly programmed (e.g. in assembly language) or it can be induced from the execution structure defined by a programming language. In the latter case, the context is the set of accessible variables given the rules of visibility for identifiers defined by the language (block structure, modules, etc.). The organization we shall define is one of the simplest possible; it corresponds more or less to the execution pattern for language C. Please refer to the bibliography at the end of this chapter for a description of more complex patterns which require languages using block structures or modular languages.

This model is based on the following assumptions:

- The parameters of a procedure are transmitted by value; a single result is returned
- Procedures can be called recursively (directly or indirectly)

On each procedure call, a data structure called the activation record of the procedure is created at the top of the execution stack. It disappears at the corresponding procedure return. A procedure called recursively therefore has as many activation records on the stack as there are non-terminated executions of that procedure. At any moment, the activation record at the top of the stack is that of the procedure *q* currently being executed, the record immediately below is that of procedure *p* which called *q*, etc. The stack is managed using two pointers (fig. 2.1):

bottom points to the bottom of the current activation record
top points to the first free location at which a new activation record can be created.

The activation record contains the following information:

a. saved information and return links

- Pointer to the bottom of the record of the calling procedure
- Return address

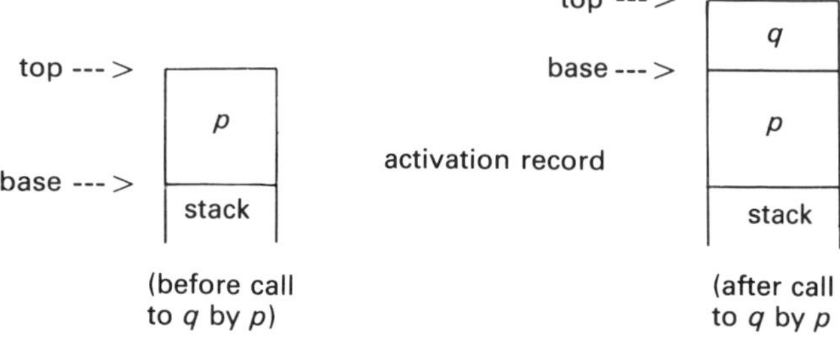

Fig. 2.1. Execution stack

- Location for the result

b. Parameters

- $n + 1$ locations, the first of which contains the number n of parameters, and the others the values of these parameters

c. Local variables and work space for the procedure

All this information (except for the work space) is stored in locations whose displacement with respect to the origin of the activation record is known at compile time; it can be addressed relatively to the bottom of that record. The work space is addressed starting from the top of the stack.

On calls to or returns from procedures, the following operations are executed:

Call

1. Allocate an area on the stack for the activation record (its size, apart from the work space, is known in advance)

```
temp:=bottom
bottom:=top
top:=top+size of activation record
```

2. Save return information

```
oldbottom:=temp
store return address
```

3. Store parameters

4. Execute a branch to the called procedure

Return

1. Store the result in the location prepared for it

2. Restore the return information and free the activation record

```
temp:=return address
top:=bottom
bottom:=oldbottom
```

3. Return

```
branch *temp     -- indirect branch
```

If registers have to be saved and restored, this is left to the calling procedure.

2. Coroutines

The stack model is directly applicable to the execution of coroutines only in the simplest cases: execution of two coroutines, for which the only information to preserve is return address. In more general cases, notably if a coroutine is itself made up of separate procedures, the single stack approach is not appropriate. Consider, for example, the following case:

```
coroutine p;            coroutine q;
  begin                   procedure q1;
          ---               ---
  resume q;                 resume p;
          ---               ---
  resume q;                   return
          ---             end q1;
  end p                 begin
                          ---
                          q1;
                          ---
                        end q
```

When q executes **resume** p, the stack contains the activation records of p, q

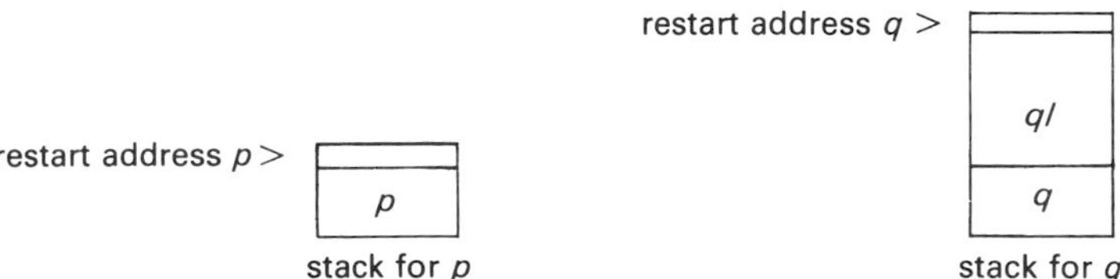

Fig. 2.2. Coroutine execution pattern

and *q1*, in that order. The activation record to restart is that of *p*, but the records *q* and *q1* must be preserved.

The solution is to set up a separate stack per coroutine (fig. 2.2).

At any moment, the current stack is that of the coroutine being executed. A *changestack* operation makes it possible to change the current stack while saving the resume address at the top of the current stack:

```
changestack (p):
  currentstack.top:=resume address;
  currentstack:=stack (p)
```

The resume sequence can then be written:

```
resume p:
  changestack (p);
  if first call then
    call (p)-- ordinary call sequence
else
    temp:=currentstack.top;
    store parameters on currentstack;
    branch *temp
endif
```

To summarize, an activity's context in memory at any moment contains not only the procedure segment being executed and its data segments, but also the current activation record on the execution stack. We shall now examine in detail how the processor context is made up.

2.1.2 State of a processor

The registers of the processor, whose contents define its state, include:

- Addressable registers, called **general registers**, manipulated by programs
- Specialized registers, generally expressed as a single record called the processor's **program status word**, abbreviated to *PSW*)

  The status word contains information that can be classified under three headings:

  1. Information on the state of the processor

  a. Execution state. The processor may be in the **active** state in which it is executing instructions, or in the **wait state**, where execution has been suspended. The transition *active* → *wait* takes place by loading the status word or by execution of a special construction; the transition *wait* → *active* can only take place as a result of an interrupt (see section 2.2.3).

b. Mode. For protection reasons, it is useful to be able to reserve the execution of certain instructions to operating system programs alone. On many computers, this is made possible by defining two functional modes for the processor, distinguished by an indicator bit in the status word: the **supervisor,** or system mode and the **user**, mode. The set of instructions that can be executed in user mode is a subset of the instructions corresponding to the supervisor mode. Instructions reserved to the supervisor mode are called **privileged**; they include in particular input output instructions, and those that concern interrupts or protection.

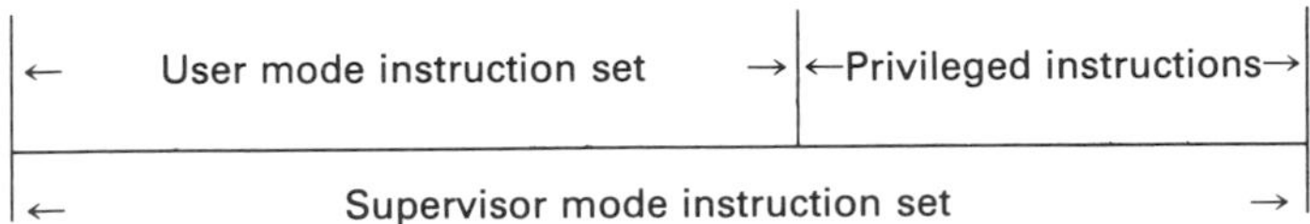

In certain machines (e.g. Motorola MC68000), a special *trace* mode makes it possible to execute instructions step by step for program debugging.

c. Interrupt masks. Detailed information is given in section 2.2.3.

2. Information on the context accessible in memory and associated access rights: segment table pointers, memory protection indicators, etc.

3. Information on the execution of the activity under way: condition code, program counter

Note: In certain machines, the program counter is a register that is distinct from the status word as such; on others, it is a field in the status word. If we are not referring to a particular machine, we shall take the term *status word* as applying to the information defined above, including the program counter.

2.2 Interrupts, traps, supervisor calls

2.2.1 Communication between asynchronous activities

The model described in section 2.1 applies to the execution of a single program on a processor, as a sequence of activities. The only communication mechanisms necessary between activities are procedure calls and returns, or coroutine resumes.

When it comes to programming operating systems, two considerations demonstrate the need for new mechanisms:

- **Asynchronism,** i.e. the effect on the execution of an activity of events external to it

- **Mutual protection** between activities, which makes it necessary, as we are moving from one activity to another, to modify the context more deeply than would occur in a simple procedure call

A typical case of asynchronism is that of the execution of input output operations simultaneously with the execution of a program. The program must be informed of the completion of the transfer. A first method of communication, which requires no special devices, is that of **busy waiting,** which we shall illustrate using an example, before discussing its limitations.

Example: Input output on the CDC Cyber 170. The architecture of computers in the CDC Cyber 170 series was based on that initially introduced on the CDC 6600. It includes a central processor *CP* and ten identical peripheral processors *PP*. The programs that make up the operating system execute on the latter: one of them, called *SP*, is assigned to job sequencing and resource allocation; the others, called *PIO[i]* are dedicated to input-output. Communication between the *CP* and the *PPs* takes place through common memory.([1]) In very simple terms, an input-output operation takes place as follows:

1. A user program, executed on *CP*, requests input output. The procedure used for this updates a pair of indicators *R* (request) and *E* (end). The request is made by setting *R:=1; E:=0*; the precise specification of the transfer requested is stored in a descriptor whose address is known to *SP*.

2. A supervisor program, executed on *SP*, periodically reads the indicator *R*. If it finds that it is set to 1, it chooses one of the *PIOs*, say *PIO[i]*, and asks it to execute the input output operation. To do so, it uses two indicators *REX[i]* and *EEX[i]*, which play the same role as *R* and *E*, and transmits the address of the input output descriptor to *PIO[i]*.

3. The input output program which executes on *PIO[i]* periodically tests its indicator *REX[i]*. If it finds it set to 1, it executes the information transfer requested, using information it finds in its descriptor. Once the transfer has been completed, the program signals the fact to *PIO* by setting the *EEX[i]* indicator to 1.

4. The supervisor periodically examines *EEX[i]*. If it finds it set to 1, it itself sets indicator *E* to 1, and this will be consulted by the user program to check whether the transfer has been completed.

([1]) A *PP* can also interrupt the *CP*, but the program described here does not use this possibility.

This mode of operation can be summarized as follows:

```
user program          supervisor program           input-output program

< I/O request >       loop                         loop
R:=1;                   if R=1 then                  if REX[i] = 1 then
E:=0;                     choose PIO[i];               execute I/O;
...                       EEX[i]:=0                    < synchronous >
                          REX[i]:=1                    EEX[i]:=1
                        endif                        endif
< test end I/O >        ...                        endloop
if F=1 then             < test end execution >
...                     if EEX[i] = 1 then
                          F:=1
                        endif
                      endloop
```

Further comments can be made about this mode of operations:

- The relations between the *CP* and *SP* on the one hand, and between *SP* and the *PIOs* on the other, follow the same pattern. Each indicator can only be set to 1 or read by *one processor*. We shall find this pattern again (chapter 4).
- The central processor is entirely freed of the need to execute the input output operation; it can, in particular, execute other tasks while the input output operation is taking place. However, the requesting program can only check whether input output has been completed by means of an explicit test.
- Input output tasks are themselves divided into two: supervision (choice of input output processor as a function of the occupation of the *PIOs* and the urgency of the operation, relations with the requesting program) and the transfer of information as such, which may be carried out more efficiently by a processor not responsible for the above functions. We shall meet this distribution of functions again (in section 2.3.1).

Communication between asynchronous activities by means of busy waiting however has its limitations, as the examples below show.

Example 1: Multiprocessor with common memory. Here we are dealing with a machine architecture consisting of a common memory to which several identical processors are linked; these processors are not specialized as in the CDC Cyber 170, but standardized, i.e. an activity can be carried out on any one of them.

Communication between activities executed on different processors may take place by periodic modification and testing of indicators in common memory. The advantage of busy waiting is limited here by efficiency considerations, as periodic consultation ties up the processor which might be employed on another task. We therefore only use this approach in specific cases where waiting lasts a very short time (see section 5.1.2).

Example 2: Measurement of time. The measurement of physical time may be involved in two ways in the execution of the program:

- Intrinsically: this is the case of so-called *real time* programs (see section 1.2.2): process control, data sampling, etc.
- Externally, for security reasons, e.g. halting another program if it is not completed within a given time, to avoid waiting in cases of infinite loops.

In all cases, time is measured by a clock, a device external to the processor. We can imagine this taking place by periodic consultation of the clock by the program, but this solution is expensive if consultation takes place frequently, and inaccurate otherwise. We therefore need a mechanism allowing the clock to act directly on the processor, at the specified time.

Example 3: External intervention. For various reasons (high priority actions, security), it is useful to be able to interrupt the execution of a program at any moment in order to make the processor carry out a specified action. This interrupt may be triggered by a human operator, an automatic measurement device, etc. This situation is similar to that mentioned for the clock; for the reasons given, programmed periodic consultation of an indicator is not acceptable. Again, a direct action mechanism is necessary.

2.2.2 Context switching mechanisms

Switching a processor's context causes the following two operations to be carried out in an **indivisible** way:

- Storing the current status word in a specified memory location
- Loading a new status word from a specified memory location

This operation is only possible if the processor is in a clearly defined state, i.e. at an observable point (generally between two instructions) or in a waiting state (see section 2.1.2). For this reason, the term *interruptible point* is used as a synonym of *observable point*.

As we shall see later, context switching can be triggered by various different causes. We shall assume that each of those causes is identified by an integer index. Different machines use one of two possible patterns.

1. Saving at fixed locations: each cause, with number *i*, is associated in a fixed way with two memory locations whose addresses we write *old_psw[i]* and *new_psw[i]*. Switching takes place as follows (the notation *Mp[addr]* stands for the contents of the memory i.e. location of address *addr*:

Mp[old_psw[i]: = <processor status word >
<processor status word>:= Mp[new_psw[i]]

There is also an instruction *load_psw(addr)* whose effect is as follows:

<processor status word>:= Mp[addr]

This instruction is always privileged.

2. Saving on a stack: this is an identical pattern to the preceding as far as the processor status word is concerned. The old status word, on the other hand, is no longer stored in a fixed location, but on a stack reserved for this purpose:

```
ptr:=ptr + 1
stack[ptr]:= <processor status word>
<processor status word >:= Mp[new_psw[i]]
```

The instruction *load_psw* is identical to the instruction in 1); there is also an instruction *pop_psw* which restores the processor status word taking the value from the top of the stack:

```
<processor status word>:= stack[ptr]
ptr:=ptr - 1
```

Context switching as described here is triggered depending on the state of a number of internal indicators that the processor consults as it is interpreting each instruction. According to the meaning of the indicators and the way in which they are modified, we can distinguish three mechanisms, whose characteristics are summarized in the table below.

Mechanism	Cause	Use
Interrupt	External to the execution of the current instruction	Reaction to an asynchronous external event
Trap	Associated with the execution of the current instruction	Handling of an error or an exceptional condition
Supervisor call	[as for traps] (explicit switching)	Call to an operating system function

Note: The generic term *interrupt* is often used for all three these mechanisms; we shall keep the three terms distinct in this book.

We shall now describe these three operations in detail, before we give examples of their use.

2.2.3 Interrupts

2.2.3.1 Basic principle

An **interrupt** is a processor context switch triggered by a cause external to the execution of the current instruction. Physically, the interrupt takes the form of a signal sent to the interrupted processor, which sets an indicator consulted during each instruction. It may originate from another processor, from an input output device, from an external device, from an operator call and more generally from any physical process external to the interrupted processor. An interrupt therefore makes it possible to force a processor to suspend execution of the current program, at the first interruptible point, and to execute a predefined program. This program is called the *interrupt handler*. It is executed in a context distinct from that of the interrupted program, in particular from the points of view of mode, protection, accessible information, etc.

2.2.3.2 Levels, priorities interrupt masks

1. Interrupt levels

A processor may be interrupted for various reasons, requiring the execution of different interrupt handlers.The interrupt mechanism must allow a distinction to be made between these causes. Two basic patterns are used:

A single indicator is used for all interrupts; a single handler is associated with it. Additional information (interrupt codes) contained in the processor status word or in a fixed memory location makes it possible to distinguish between possible causes. The first task of the interrupt handler is to consult that code to determine the origin of the interrupt and call the appropriate handling procedure.

A separate indicator is associated with each interrupt cause; we then say that the cause is associated with an interrupt **level**. A different handler program corresponds to each level, and it is automatically activated by the context switching mechanism.

2. Priority and interrupt masking

If there are several interrupt levels, two indicators corresponding to two different causes may be modified at the same time. Conflicts are resolved by establishing an order of priority between interrupt levels. This order is generally defined once and for all, or only modifiable by microprogramming.

Moreover, it may be useful to protect the execution of a series of instructions e.g. interrupt programs themselves (see section 2.3.4) against certain interrupts. This means delaying context switching caused by an interrupt signal on a certain level: we then say that that level has been **masked** (or inhibited). The removal of inhibition, or unmasking, allows context switching. The interrupt masks are part of the processor status word. Interrupt masking may therefore be modified by the effect of an interrupt.

3. Interrupt enabling

For certain interrupt levels, it is possible to suppress (rather than merely delay) the effect of the arrival of an interrupt signal. Everything takes place as though the cause of the interrupt had itself been eliminated: the interrupt level is said to be **disabled**. A disabled level can be re-enabled, i.e. put back into service.

4. Programmed triggering

On certain machines, notably those used in process control, there is a programmed triggering instruction making it possible to modify, within a program, the indicator associated with an interrupt level. In this way, one simulates the occurrence of the external cause of the interrupt. This instruction is particulary useful in the construction of interrupt handlers.

Once all the conditions necessary for dealing with an interrupt at a given level are met, the level is said to be **active**. This state corresponds to the execution of the interrupt handlers. Note that such execution may be suspended to allow execution of the handler for an interrupt with high priority. Exit from the active state takes place by **acknowledgment** of an interrupt. Acknowledgment is generally implemented by the *load_psw* instruction, which ends the handler by switching context.

The interrupt enabling, disabling, masking, unmasking and triggering operations are always carried out by privileged instruction.

Figure 2.3 shows the state transitions on an interrupt level.

2.2.3.3 Outline of an interrupt handler

An interrupt forces a processor to react to an event. The execution of the program under way is therefore suspended and an interrupt handler program is executed. The program restarted by the processor when handling is complete is not necessarily the interrupted program (the interrupt may specif-

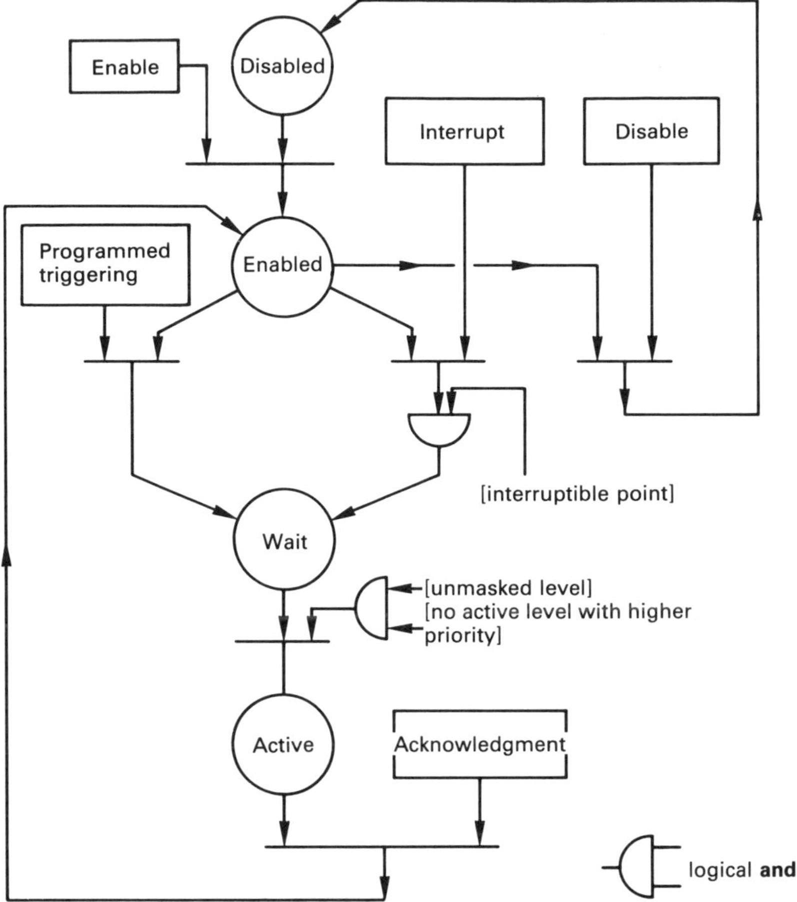

Fig. 2.3. States of an interrupt level

ically have the effect of reassigning the processor). The general pattern for interrupt handling is shown in fig. 2.4.

2.2.4 Traps and supervisor calls

Unlike an interrupt, a trap or a supervisor call is triggered by a cause directly associated with the execution of the current instruction.

1. Traps

A **trap** indicates that there is an anomaly in an instruction, preventing its being executed. Various sources are possible:

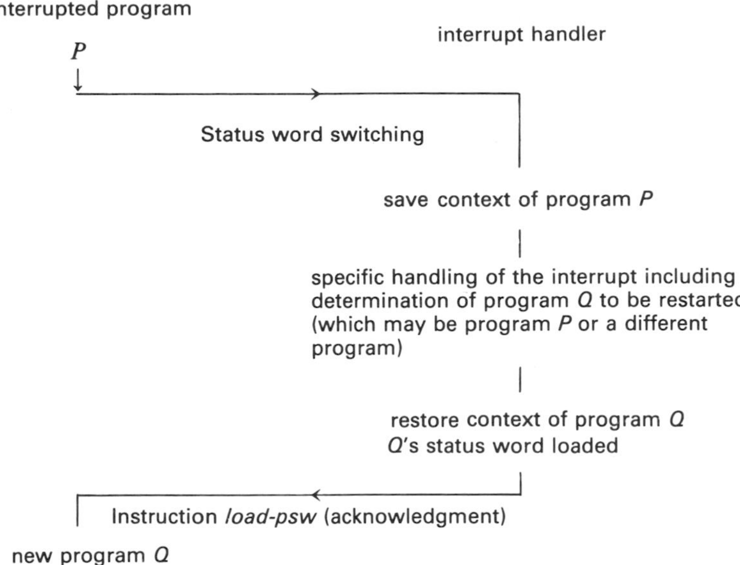

Fig. 2.4. General structure of an interrupt program

- Incorrect data making it impossible to execute the instruction correctly (arithmetic overflow, division by zero, etc.)
- Attempt to execute an operation forbidden by a protection device (memory protection violation, execution of a privileged instruction in user mode, etc.)
- Non-executable instruction (unassigned operation code, address outside existing memory, use of an optional device missing from the configuration being used, etc.)

These traps can be classified according to their causes, in the same way as interrupts; one may also eliminate the effect of certain of these causes (e.g. it is generally possible to suppress traps associated with arithmetic operations, with errors only being indicated by the value of their condition code). On the other hand, given the synchronous nature of a trap, the notion of masking does not apply: a trap may be eliminated, but not delayed.

2. Supervisor calls

A **supervisor call** (abbreviated to **SVC**) is an instruction whose effect is to produce a processor context switch; this effect is similar to that of a procedure call, but the context modification is deeper since it concerns the whole status word and not only the program counter.

The function of a supervisor call is to allow calls to be made from the user's program to an operating system procedure requiring extended rights (supervisor mode, masked interrupts, access rights, etc.). The context switching mechanism allows for protection, by imposing conditions on entry to the called procedure. Specifically:

- The new context (mode, masking, etc.) is specified in the new status word, stored in an area of memory inaccessible to users.
- The supervisor call handler starts with a sequence checking the user's right to execute that call and the validity of the parameters transmitted.

Parameter passing is governed by call conventions as in ordinary procedure calls. Return to the calling program takes place by restoring the status word saved during the call.

The choice of a procedure amongst those accessible by a supervisor call is generally specified by means of a supplementary parameter passed in a register or in the address part of the call instruction. The procedures accessible in this way to the users of an operating system may be regarded as an extension to the instruction set, which therefore implements a new machine. In this way, file access and input-output operations in a system are available to users in the form of supervisor calls.

The general pattern shown in fig. 2.4 for interrupts also applies to traps and supervisor calls.

2.2.5 Examples of interrupt systems

The operation of interrupt systems is illustrated by two representative examples, one on a mainframe, the other on a microprocessor.

Example 1: IBM 370. The status word (64 bits) includes the following fields:

<0–7>	interrupt mask	<16–31>	interrupt code
<8-11>	protection key	<32–33>	instruction size
<12>	character code	<34-35>	condition code
<13>	interrupt mask	<36–39>	trap disabling
<14>	1:waiting, 0:active	<40–63>	program counter
<15>	0:supervisor, 1:user		

The interrupt system includes five levels (in decreasing priority order): hardware error, trap, supervisor call, external, input-output. To each level corresponds a pair of low memory locations for the old and new status word. Given the small number of different levels, each covers many interrupt causes. They are distinguished by an interrupt code stored in bits 16–31 of the status word; that code is automatically updated when an interrupt occurs. For example, for an input-output interrupt, it contains the address of the channel and the device causing the interrupt; for an external interrupt, it makes it possible to determine if it comes from the clock, from an operator call, from an external device, etc. Bits 0–7 and 13 of the status word are interrupt masks; they allow masking of interrupt levels associated with external causes, hardware errors and (selectively) input-output interrupts from different channels (see section 2.3). Bits 36–39 make it possible to inhibit four causes of traps.

Note that traps and supervisor calls are treated as special cases of interrupts.

Example 2: Motorola MC68000. The status word (16 bits) includes the following fields:

<0–4>	condition code	<13>	1:supervisor, 0:user
<5–7>	unused	<14>	unused
<8–10>	interrupt mask	<15>	trace
<11–12>	unused		

The program counter (32 bits) is contained in a separate register.

The machine includes data registers *(D0..D7)* and address or pointer registers *(A0..A7)*. The interpretation of name *A7* depends on the mode: in supervisor mode, *A7* names a pointer to a *supervisor stack*; in slave mode, *A7* names a pointer to a *user stack*. Each user therefore has a separate execution stack, and the supervisor stack is inaccessible to user programs which execute in user mode.

The concept of *exception handling* covers interrupts, supervisor calls and execution in *trace* mode. There are three distinct groups of exceptions, each of which covers several cases:

Group 0: address errors, bus errors, reset

Group 1: trace, interrupts, protection violations

Group 2: arithmetic traps, supervisor calls

Group priority decreases from group 0 to group 2. To each of the different causes of exceptions there corresponds a fixed low memory locations for the program counter of the handler associated with that cause. Exception handling takes place as follows:

1. The status word of the processor and the program counter are stacked on the supervisor stack

2. The new status word is obtained by

- Setting the *supervisor mode* bit to 1
- Setting the *trace* bit to 0
- Loading the interrupt mask (which determines the current priority of the processor) with the level of the interrupt being handled; the handler is therefore masked against lower level interrupts

3. The program counter is loaded with the contents of the location associated with the exception being handled

Return to the interrupted program takes place by restoring the program counter and the status word from the supervisor stack. This approach makes it possible to deal with several nested exceptions.

In *trace* mode, a trap is caused by the execution of each instruction, whose effect can therefore be analysed step by step.

2.3 Implementation of context switching mechanisms

The implementation of mechanisms described in section 2.2 will be illustrated by a series of examples that are representative of the major uses made of them.

We shall use the following notation to denote the contents os a status word

<activity, mode, masking, program counter>

The first three fields can take the values, respectively: waiting/active, supervisor/user, masked/unmasked. If *loc* is used for a status word, its fields are *loc.act, loc.mode, loc.mask* and *loc.PC*.

- The operator **addr,** applied to the identifier for a variable or a procedure, indicates the address of the location where the variable is stored, or that of the first instruction in the procedure.
- The notation *Mp[addr]* is used for the contents of the location with address *addr*.
- The notations *old_svc, old_trap, old_it_x, new_svc, new_trap,* and *new_it_x* are used for the locations for storing or loading status words.

We shall also assume

- That supervisor calls take the form *SVC <code>* where *<code>* represents a number identifying the function requested
- That an indicator *cause* makes it possible to determine the cause of a trap

The segments of code presented include an initialization program, executed at system start up. Its function is to initialize the status words associated with the handling of interrupts, traps and supervisor calls.

2.3.1 Use of traps and supervisor calls

2.3.1.1 Simulation of unimplemented instructions

1. Description of the task

Certain instructions in a processor's set are only included as *options*, and are not available in certain machine configurations. An attempt to execute an optional instruction which is not available gives rise to a trap for a non-existent instruction. This mechanism may be used to simulate the effect of the missing instruction. For example, on a configuration where floating point arithmetic instructions are not available, their effect can be simulated by calling the corresponding procedures during trap handling. Note that these procedures must be executed in user mode, to allow, in particular, for error handling: they are therefore called by loading a status word. A return address must be provided by the trap program at the top of the user stack, to allow return to the instruction following the simulated arithmetic instruction.

2. *Programs*

```
procedure intialization;
  new_trap := <active,supervisor,masked,addr handle_trap>;
  psw[FL_ADD]:=<active,user,unmasked,addr float_add>;
    ...
  psw[FL_DIV]:=<active,user,unmasked,addr float_div>;

procedure handle_trap;
  begin
  save (area);
  case cause of
    ...
non-existant instr:
    op_code:=Mp[old_trap.PC].operation_code;
    case op_code of
     ...
  FL_ADD: determine operands;
          push(stack_user,old_trap.PC+1);
          load_psw(psw[FL_ADD])
     ...
    else    -- error
     <error handling>
    endcase;
  endcase;
  restore(area);
  load_psw(old_trap)
  end
```

Operands are retrieved analyzing the contents of the instruction, which contains their addresses; result transmission is based on conventions specific to the instruction handled (using a register etc.).

2.3.1.2 Measurement of memory size

1. Description of the task

An operating system is generally intended to be used on different configurations of the samc machine, which differ in the size of the memory available, the number and nature of peripherals, etc. The operating system must be adapted to the configuration used, as well as to particular usage conditions (number of users, priorities, etc.). The creation of a new specific version is called **generation** of the system. To reduce the number of generations, certain parameters in the configuration may be automatically determined when the system is initialized.

It is possible in this way to determine the size of main memory, using a trap for non-existent location addresses. Memory is made up of a number *nblocks*, to be determined, of blocks of *p* words. A program executed on system initialization attempts to access the first word in each block; the attempt to access the unimplemented block in the current configuration causes an exit from the loop, by means of a trap. The number of blocks is equal to the number of the first block unimplemented (blocks are numbered starting from 0).

2. Programs

```
  main program:
    begin
    new_trap:=<active,supervisor,masked,addr measurement>;
    i:=1;
    loop
      <access to a word with address i.p>;
      i:=i+1;
    endloop;
next: nblocks:=i;
    new_trap:=<active,supervisor,masked,addr trap_handler>
    end
  procedure measurement;     -- called by trap
    if cause = address not in memory then
    workloc:=<active,supervisor,masked,addr next>;
    load_psw(workloc)
    endif
```

Note that on exiting this measurement program, it is necessary to restore normal trap handling (procedure *trap_handler*).

2.3.1.3 Trap management by the user

1. Task description

The standard reaction to a trap during the execution of a user program is a call to a system procedure causing an error message to be sent, the program under execution to be halted and control to be transferred to the next user program.

What we want to do here is to provide the user with the possibility of associating a user-defined service procedure with each distinct trap cause *i* so that a call to that procedure will take place instead of standard handling if trap *i* occurs. However, to avoid infinite loops, a trap of cause *i* in this service procedure will itself be handled in the standard way.

Associating a service procedure *proc* with a cause of trapping *i* takes place by means of a supervisor call (the SVC *associate_trap*) whose parameters are *i* and *proc*.

The next user program is activated by means of a call to an operating system procedure; this call is implemented by loading a status word called *change*.

2. Programs

```
const ntrap = <number of causes of traps>
var C: array[0..ntrap-1] of boolean;
  handler_addr: array[0..ntrap-1] of address;

procedure initialization;
begin
  new_svc:=<active,supervisor,masked,addr handle_svc>;
  for i:=0 to ntrap-1 do   -- standard handling
    C[i]:= false;
  endfor;
  new_trap:=<active,supervisor,masked,addr handle_trap>
  end

procedure handle_svc;
  begin
  save (area);
  case code of
  ...
associate_trap:              -- parameters: i,proc
  C[i]:=true;
  handler_addr[i]:=addr proc;
  restore(area);
  load_psw(old_svc)
  ...
  endcase
  end

procedure handle_trap(i);
  start
  save(area);
  if C[i] then
    C[i]:= false;      -- restore standard handling
    push(user_stack,old_trap.PC);   -- for return
    old_trap.PC:=address[i];
    restore(area);
    load_psw(old_trap)
  else
    <standard handling[i]>;
    load_psw(change)     -- next program
  endif
  end
```

Note that the service procedure specified by the user executes in slave mode and return takes place by the standard procedure return mechanism, since the return address has been set up on the top of the execution stack.

2.3.2 Examples of the use of interrupts

The main applications of interrupts are time measurement and the management of input and output. We shall present a few examples of the use of a clock here; input-output is discussed in sections 2.4.3 and 2.4.6.

A clock is implemented by a quartz oscillator emitting periodic pulses. The period can be selected and is generally between 0.1 microsecond and 100 milliseconds. These pulses are used to decrement a counter, contained in a special register or in a reserved word in memory. When this counter reaches zero, an interrupt called the clock interrupt is triggered at a level reserved for this use.

In the applications below, we shall assume that each pulse decrements the contents of a memory location, denoted *clock*, by 1. The elementary *activation* mechanism involves initializing this location with a possible value q and enabling the clock interrupt level; the interrupt will occur after q clock periods.

2.3.2.1 Timeout

1. Task description

Assume that a procedure p is to be executed, in such a way that if p is not complete within a period q called a **timeout**, the execution of p will be interrupted and a specified procedure *error_handler* is called.

2. Programs

A *timed call* to p is implemented by a supervisor call whose parameters are p, the timeout q (expressed in clock cycles) and the restart procedure *error-handler*.

```
procedure initialization;
  new_clock_it:= <active,supervisor,masked,addr clock_it>;
  new_svc:= <active,supervisor,masked,addr handle_svc>;
  disable (clock_it);

procedure handle_svc;
  save(area);
  case code of
    ...
  timed_call:                     parameters:p,q,error_handler
    clock:=q;
    return_psw:=old_svc;          -- saved for return

    workpsw:= <active,user,unmasked,addr p>;
    errorpsw:= <active,user,unmasked,addr error_handle>;
    enable(clock_it);
    restore(area);
    load_psw(workpsw)
    ...
  return:                         -- must terminate procedure p
    disable(clock_it);
    load_psw(returnpsw);
    ...
  endcase

procedure clock_it                -- end of timeout
    disable(clock_it);
    load_psw(errorpsw);
```

These programs are based on a simple principle: whichever of the two events, end of timeout or return from *p*, occurs first, disables the clock and activates the appropriate procedure by passing it the current context as it stands. Note that a return from *p* must take place by means of a supervisor call reserved for this purpose and not by use of the usual return instruction. A return from *error_handler* must also use this supervisor call if we want to return to the initial call context for *p*.

2.3.2.2 Taking measurements

1. Task description

A computer is required to take measurements periodically from an industrial installation. The clock period is 5 μs. Measurements must be taken every 100 ms. As the duration of the measurements is very much less than this interval, the computer in the meantime carries out background work, which must therefore be periodically interrupted.

2. Programs

```
const q = 20000;     -- 100 ms/5μs
procedure intialization;
  begin
  new_clock_it:= <active,supervisor,masked,addr clock_it>;
  workpsw   := <active,user,unmasked, addr background>;
  measurepsw: = <active,user,unmasked, addr measurement>;
  clock:=q;
  load_psw(workpsw)
  end

procedure clock_it;
  begin
  save(area);                      -- background context
  savepsw:=old_clock_it;           -- save background context

  clock:=q;
  load_psw(measurepsw)             -- measurement program
  end
```

The measurement program must end with a supervisor call *SVC return* whose effect is to restore the context of the background work. This supervisor call executes the sequence:

```
restore(area);
load_psw(savepsw);
```

Operations can be represented as follows:

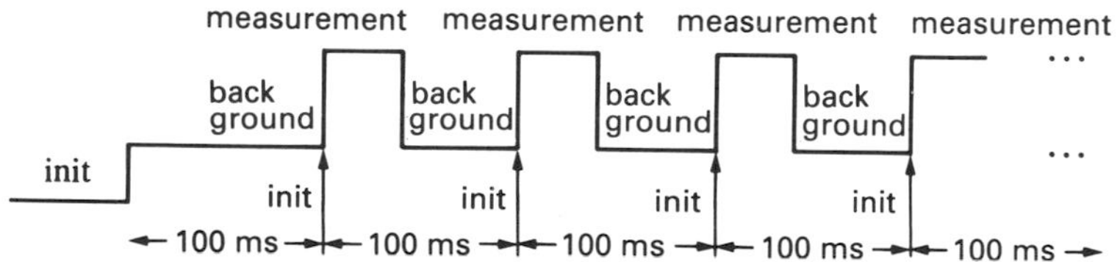

Note: We could have directly included procedure *measurement* in the interrupt program, which would then have had the form.

```
save(area);
clock:=q
measurement;
restore(area);
load_psw(old_clock_it)
```

But this would have had the disadvantage that the measurement program would have been executed in supervisor mode with masked interrupts, and would not have allowed its modification or replacement by a non-privileged user. This comment illustrates a general principle: interrupt handlers, which are short sequences executed with high privileges, should be separated from programs which may be activated by these handlers and which are called by loading a status word. These procedures are sometimes called primary and secondary interrupt handlers respectively. These concepts will be taken up again in chapter 4 when we consider process activation.

2.3.2.3 Time-shared job management

1. Task description

A set of programs, or jobs, must be executed on a computer, using the processor in shared time: the processor will be allocated in turn to jobs, in a fixed order, in time slices of fixed duration q. If a job terminates before the end of a time slice, the processor is immediately allocated to the next job.

Jobs are numbered from 0 to $n - 1$. For each job i a storage area *psw[i]* is defined for its status word, as well as a storage area *reg[i]* for its registers. These areas are used to save the user context each time a job is interrupted, to allow the job to be restarted later.

2. Programs

We shall start by assuming that jobs never terminate. We use a circular job queue, called *job_queue*, associated with three procedures, *insert, remove* and *next*.

```
procedure initialization;
  begin
  for i:=0 to n-1 do
    psw[i]:= <active,user,unmasked,addr job[i]>;
    insert(i,job_queue);
  endfor;
  new_clock_it:= <active,supervisor,masked,addr clock_it>;
  new_svc:= <active,supervisor,masked,addr handle_svc>;
  selected_job:=0;      -- we start with job 0
  load_psw(psw[selected_job]);
  end

procedure clock_it;
  begin
  psw[selected_job]:=old_clock_it;
  save_registers(reg[selected_job]);
  selected_job:=next(selected_job);
  clock:=q
  load_registers(reg[selected_job]);
  load_psw(psw[selected_job]);
  end
```

To take account of the termination of jobs, each job must tell the system that it has terminated, using a supervisor call *SVC end* for which the program is as follows:

```
procedure handle_svc;
    ...
  case code of
    ...
end:
    successor:=next(selected_job);
    remove(selected_job,job_queue);
    selected_job:= successor;
    clock:=q;
    load_registers(reg[selected_job]);
    load_psw(psw[selected_job]);
  endcase
```

We assume that the job queue never becomes empty; in practice, this is made possible by adding a background job, which may be reduced to a single loop.

2.3.3 Conclusion

The examples above illustrate the elementary modes of communication between the programs that make up an operating system and the external world. The system programs are activated:

1. Either by a user program, which indicates an anomaly (trap) or requests the execution of a service (supervisor call)
2. Or by an external device (clock, controlled external process, peripheral device or communication line), which reports the occurrence of an event requiring an immediate reaction by the system

This can be summarized by saying that an operating system is *event-driven*. Note too that internal communication between system programs uses supervisor calls if protection is needed (programs executed in user mode, for example) and ordinary procedure calls otherwise. The execution of a system program ends by loading the processor status word, making it possible to specify the restored context entirely.

2.4 Input-output programming

We shall use the general term **input-output,** abbreviated to I/O, for any transfer of information from or towards the set (processor(s), main memory). Input-output operations therefore include:

- Information transfer between various levels in the memory hierarchy
- Information transfers from or to the outside world (local or remote peripheral devices, sensors or activators, other computers, etc.)

In section 2.4.1, we describe the general organization of input-output operations, and in sections 2.4.2 to 2.4.4 we shall consider the principles on which their programming is based. Other descriptions of input-output subsystems appear in chapters 3 and 4.

2.4.1 General organization

2.4.1.1 Peripherals, controllers, channels

An input-output device is a unit capable of transferring information between the processor or memory of a computer and an external information medium. This transfer is controlled by the central processor. In the simplest case, a special instruction allows the transfer of information between the external medium and a processor register; the processor is busy throughout the transfer operation. As computers developed, a desire for better use of the processor led to increased autonomy of input-output devices and to their being entrusted with more and more complex sequencing and control operations, with the central processor remaining responsible only for initiating and controlling operations. Concern with economy then led to separating peripheral devices as such from their control devices, in order to share the latter between several peripherals.

Figure 2.5 shows certain currently used forms of organization. The configuration in (c) is that of a mainframe computer; (a) and (b) how micro-computer configurations. Let us consider the functions of the various devices shown.

1. A **channel**, or exchange unit, is a specialized processor for input-output operations. It can only be started by a central processor; it has no interrupts, but may itself interrupt a central processor. Its instruction set allows it to activate the controllers and peripherals connected to it. On mini and micro-computers, we find units called *direct memory access units* or DMA, which are simplified forms of channels. The operation of a channel or a DMA is described in greater detail in section 2.4.2.3.

2. A **controller** is a control device adapted to a given type of peripheral. Its autonomy is limited to very elementary operations. The main advantage

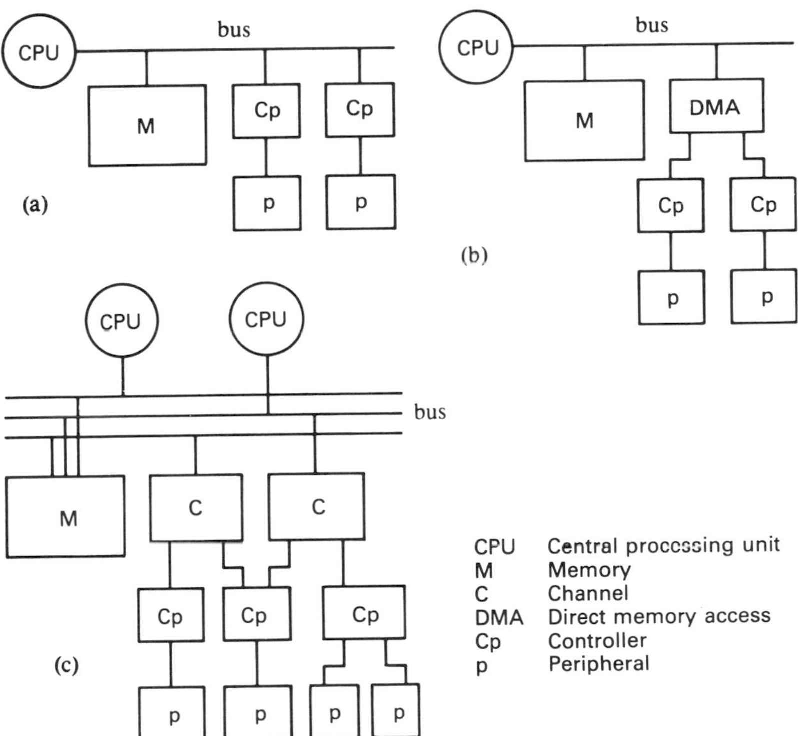

Fig. 2.5. Organization of input/output

of separating controller and peripheral is to connect several peripherals of the same type to a single controller; in this case, only one peripheral at a time can transfer information. It is generally possible, however, to carry out operations at the same time on other peripherals, as long as no information transfer is involved (moving a disk reading arm, rewinding a magnetic tape). How functions are shared between the controller and the peripheral depends on the type of the peripheral; generally, logical functions (sequencing and synchronization of operations, transmission of end or event signals) are left to the controller, and physical functions (transfer as such) are left to the peripheral. The distinction between controllers and peripherals does not generally appear in input-output programming.

3. A **peripheral** is a device capable of transferring information from or to an external medium. A controller-peripheral combination is defined by an interface including a whole set of functions (input-output, control and event signals) and a communication medium to transfer information.

A channel can control a single high throughput peripheral such as a disk, or be multiplexed between several peripherals with lower throughput. Simultaneous access by several processes (central units or channels) to main memory may give rise to conflicts. In cases of attempted simultaneous access, conflict is regulated by the hardware access mechanism, which imposes an access order according to a preestablished order of priorities. Channels have higher priorities than the central processing unit as they must react rapidly to external events. If a channel transfers information at maximum throughput, it may entirely use the central memory access capacity during transfer, thereby preventing programs on the central processing unit making progress; this phenomenon is called *cycle stealing*. The distribution of consecutive address locations between the central memory banks (interleaving) reduces the probability of simultaneous access to a single bank.

2.4.1.2 Peripheral addressing

Various units are named, at each level, using an address making it possible to distinguish between:

- Channels linked to memory
- Controllers attached to each channel
- Peripherals attached to each controller

At each level, this address is simply an sequence number. A peripheral is named by a composite address.

<channel number, controller number, peripheral number>

A controller may be linked to several channels and the peripheral to several controllers, which are necessarily of the same type. A peripheral is therefore linked to memory by several access mechanisms (only one of which will be in service at a given moment), and can be named by several addresses (fig. 2.6).

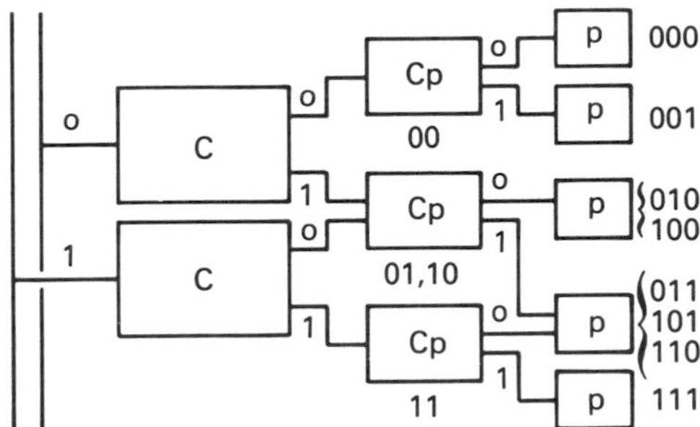

Fig. 2.6. Addressing input/output devices

This arrangement makes it possible to improve system performance and availability. The existence of multiple access routes to a peripheral reduces the risk of unavailability as a result of overloading or failure in a channel or a controller.

In certain computers (e.g. DEC) peripheral addressing directly uses reserved memory locations, which are associated with the status word or the data register of a specified controller. Access to a status word or to a data register takes place by means of ordinary memory access instructions. This approach simplifies naming of peripherals and programming of input output.

2.4.2 Peripheral driver modes

The program which controls the elementary operation of a peripheral is called a **driver**. The driver directly manages the interface for the peripheral controller, handles interrupts issued by it, and detects and handles cases of error. It is generally invisible to system users, who access input-output functions using relatively high level services implemented by supervisor calls. We shall consider the main forms of organization of peripheral driver, and elementary input-output primitives. More elaborate functions (input-output streams) using these primitives are described in chapters 6 and 7.

2.4.2.1 Synchronous input-output

In synchronous I/O, there is no parallelism between information handling and information transfer. The processor is busy throughout the transfer operation.

The approach below does not apply to a particular machine, but is representative of the organization of synchronous I/O in many computers.

1. Specification of the mechanism

The basic operation is the transfer of an elementary item of information of fixed size between a memory location and a peripheral; the size of the item depends on the peripheral in question, and we shall assume that it is a byte. The state of the single-peripheral system is defined by a status word contained in a controller. This status word includes a series of indicators, only three of which need concern us here (these are booleans).

Indicator	Meaning
ready:	The peripheral is ready to operate: the detailed conditions that need to be met depend on the peripheral.
finished:	Transfer has been completed; the peripheral is ready to transfer a new character.
error:	An error has taken place during transfer; its nature is defined by a code which appears in the status word.

The controller is controlled by the CPU using three input-output instructions whose effect is as follows:

INPUT (mem_addr, periph_addr):
requests the transfer of an input character

OUTPUT (mem_addr, periph_addr):
requests the transfer of an output character

TEST (periph_addr):
copies the status word into a register
in order to read the indicators

We shall write *mem_addr* and *periph_addr* for the addresses respectively of the memory and peripheral locations; for instructions *INPUT* and *OUTPUT*, the latter address is supplemented where appropriate by a device address (e.g. track and sector on disk).

2. Driver program

Assume that we have to output a sequence of *n* characters contained within an array *T[0..n−1]*. The character *T[i]*, if *i>0*, may not be output before the end of transfer of *T[i−1]*. To meet this condition, we carry out an iterated test (busy wait) on indicator *finished*.

```
init:  finished:= false;
       TEST(periph_addr);
       if ¬ready then
            <error handling>
       endif;
            ...
for i: =0 to n−1 do
       OUTPUT (addr T[i], periph_addr);
loop:  TEST (periph_addr);
       if error then
            <error handling>
       endif;
       if ¬finished then
            goto loop
       endif;
endfor
```

Synchronous I/O is used on the simplest microprocessors, or all cases where the processor cannot be valuably used during data transfer (recording of measurements, initial loading of a system).

2.4.2.2 Asynchronous input-output with interrupts

1. Specification of the mechanism

The mechanism described in 2.4.2.1 is extended as follows: setting indicator *finished* to true triggers an interrupt at a level associated with the peripheral in question. The choice of synchronous or interrupt mode is guided by whether the level is enabled or disabled.

2. Driver program

The end of transfer of character *T[i]* is signalled by an interrupt. If this is not the last character *(i<n−1)*, the following character may be sent. The process is started by the transfer of the first character. The transfer is requested by the main program using a supervisor call (*input* or *output SVC*), whose parameters are:

- The address of the peripheral
- The number of characters to transfer
- The source or destination address of the first character
- A boolean value *terminated*, whose setting to true marks the end of the transfer

```
main program                            interrupt handler
                                        (after output of T[i])
output SVC:
    terminated:=false
    i:=0;
    OUTPUT(addr T[0],periph_addr);
                                        <save context>;
                                        TEST (periph_addr);
    ....                                if error then
                                          <error handling>
                                        else
                                          if i<n-1 then
<parallel processing>                       i:=i+1;
                                            OUTPUT(addr T[i], periph_addr)
    ....                                  else
                                            terminated:=true
if terminated then                        endif
                                        endif;
    ....                                <restore context>
```

2.4.2.3 Programmed input-output by channel or DMA

A channel is a processor capable of executing a sequence of input-output operations, defined by a program in memory, on a peripheral linked to it. It includes a status word which contains, in particular, a program counter as well as indicators concerning the state of the operation under way. The program for a channel is made up of a series of **commands** each of which specifies an elementary input-output operation. The program must be prepared in advance by a central processor. The operating principle of a channel is as follows:

1. A channel can only be started by a central processor, using a special instruction *start_channel* (often written *SIO* for *start input-output*). This instruction initializes the status word of the channel, specifying in particular the address of the first command to be executed and the address of the source or the destination for the transfer. From then on, the channel and central processor work in parallel.

2. Once started, the channel executes its program. Execution can halt in three ways:

a. At the end of execution of the program

b. As a result of an error (hardware failure, program error)

c. On command from the central processing unit, which can halt execution of a channel program by means of a special *halt input-output* instruction (often written *HIO*)

The normal case is (a). The central processor is informed of the end of execution of the channel program by means of an interrupt. All necessary information on the execution of the input-output operation that has just been completed appears in the channel's status word, which the central processor may consult by means of a *test input-output* instruction (often written *TIO*). In case b), an interrupt is also issued, except of course if the failure concerns the interrupt device. In the same way, the status word of the channel will contain all necessary information on the cause of halting. Finally, the *halt input-output* instruction (case c) is only generally used for an emergency halt after detection of an abnormal state of affairs by the central processor.

3. At any moment, the central processor can use the *test input-output* instruction to read the status of a channel which is executing its program. This operation does not disturb the execution of the program. The state obtained is that of the most recent observable point.

As a channel is a processor specializing in input-output, the structure of its program reflects that specialization. A command essentially specifies:

- The nature of the operation to carry out (read, write, move a disk head, etc.)
- Where appropriate, the address of the beginning of the source or destination memory zone for the transfer
- Where appropriate, the number of characters to transfer

A specific command allows the channel to execute a (conditional) branch within its program. This makes it possible to program iterations. For example, the program for a channel managing input on terminals is an endless loop over a command which transfers the next character typed at the keyboard to a buffer.

Example: The IBM 370's channels. The channel controllers include the information listed above (specification of the transfer) and also contain three further indicators:

- A 'command chaining' bit: if this bit is set to 1, the next command will be executed after the end of the current command; otherwise, execution stops there.
- A 'data chaining' bit: if this bit is set to 1, the channel will, at the end of its current command, execute a command with the same operation code applying to

the same peripheral, but using the memory zone specified in the next command. This makes it possible to execute a transfer from or to a set of non-contiguous zones in memory.

- An interrupt request bit: if this bit is set to 1, an interrupt will be issued when the channel begins the execution of this command. This makes it easier to debug programs and to collect statistics.

A channel is started by an *SIO* instruction which specifies the address of the peripheral. It is necessary beforehand to place the memory address of the first command to execute and the protection key used in the course of transfer, in a reserved word in memory.

The description above is only intended to present the essential aspects of the operations of a channel. Three reasons in particular make the description of a real input-output system more complex.

- Multiplexing of channels and controllers, as generally occurs, makes it necessary to be able to determine as early as possible that a channel or controller has become available, in order to use the hardware efficiently; specific interrupts and indicators make this determination possible
- The need to take account of the characteristics of very varied peripherals, which complicates the set of commands used
- The detection and handling of errors, the concern of a large part of input-output supervisor programs

For specific studies of these questions, readers should consult the user manuals for the machine they are using.

A DMA is a simplified form of channel: the ‘program’ for a DMA is made up of a single command specifying a memory address, a peripheral address, the number of bytes to transfer, the direction of the transfer and finally the end of transfer message (whether or not an interrupt should be sent). The program is not loaded into memory but in a register in the DMA which plays the role of a status word: this register may be consulted during transfer to monitor the number of bytes still remaining to transfer.

2.4.3 Input-output buffered in memory

2.4.3.1 Specification of the problem

The considerable difference in speed between the central processing unit and peripheral devices makes it essential to *buffer* input-output, i.e. to interpose a memory zone, or **buffer**, between the peripheral and user programs. The aim is to reduce the inactive time of the central processing unit, by uncoupling its operations from those of the peripheral. User programs transfer information from or to the buffer; it acts in parallel as a source or destination for exchanges with the peripheral. Uncoupling between the central processing unit and peripherals is all the more effective the greater the size of the buffer; in order to save space in main memory, large buffers are stored on disk, a technique which we shall consider in section 2.4.4.

Our model is described by the following specifications:

- Exchanges with peripherals take place by means of records of fixed size
- The buffer has a fixed size, equal to N records
- For a user program, exchanges with the buffer must simulate exchanges with the peripheral; consequently, the order of loading or withdrawing records must be preserved between the buffer and the peripheral, and no record must be lost
- Unnecessary waiting must be reduced to a minimum, both for the central processing unit and for the peripheral
- The capacity of the media is not limited: during read operations, the input device is continuously supplied; during writing, the output device must constantly accepts records
- Transfer must take place without errors

2.4.3.2 Principles of the algorithms

1. Reading

The user interface of the reading program is a procedure

read (record)

which returns as result the value of the record read. This procedure, implemented by a supervisor call, has the effect of collecting the next record from the buffer. Reading is, however, only possible if the buffer contains at least one record that has not yet been collected; otherwise, the calling activity moves to the waiting state. In either case, a continuous supply to the buffer is guaranteed by reading a record from an input peripheral, if a transfer is not already under way.

The end of the transfer of a record into the buffer triggers an interrupt. To keep the peripheral active, the interrupt handler must start the next transfer, if there is still space in the buffer. If the calling activity is awaiting the arrival of a record, it must be restarted.

This mode of operation is expressed by the program skeleton below.

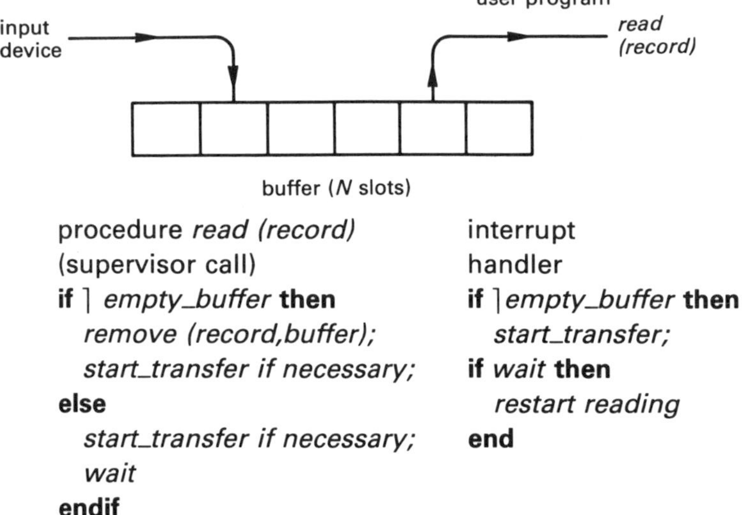

user program
input device
read (record)
buffer (N slots)
procedure read (record)
(supervisor call)
if ⌉ empty_buffer then
remove (record,buffer);
start_transfer if necessary;
else
start_transfer if necessary;
wait
endif
interrupt
handler
if ⌉empty_buffer then
start_transfer;
if wait then
restart reading
end

In this program, ‘if necessary’ means ‘if a transfer is not already under way’. Note that the system is initialized by reading the first record, which causes the following records to be transfered until the buffer is full.

2. Writing

The pattern for writing can be deduced immediately from the pattern for reading if we replace:

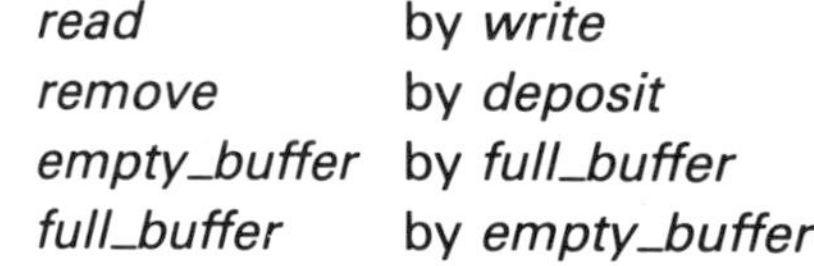

read by write
remove by deposit
empty_buffer by full_buffer
full_buffer by empty_buffer

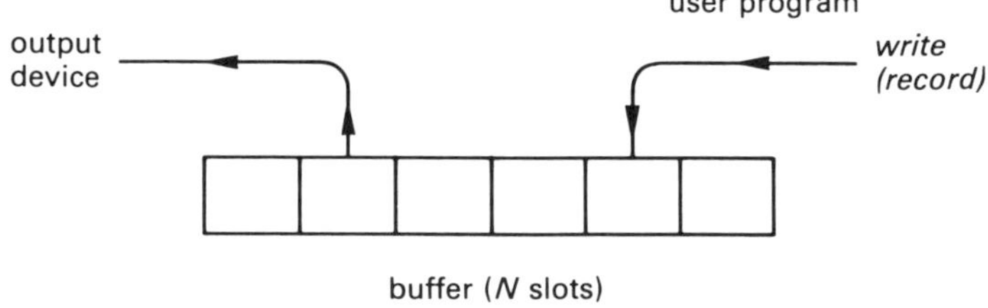

```
procedure write (record)            interrupt
(supervisor call)                   handler
if ⌉full_buffer then                if ⌉empty_buffer then
   deposit (record,buffer);            start_transfer;
   start_transfer if necessary      if wait then
else                                   restart writing
   start_transfer if necessary;     endif
   wait
endif
```

3. Programs

The programs are a direct description of the patterns above. The buffer is managed as a circular queue with two pointers: *head* for the next record to collect, *tail* to the slot where the next record is to read. The function *succ* returns a pointer to the successor of a slot; a simple implementation, in the case of a sequential buffer containing N slots of size L would be:

$$succ(ptr) = (ptr+L) \textbf{ mod } (L.N)$$

We assume that the activity requesting reading is the only one using the processor; to make it wait we therefore only have to set the processor into the waiting state. This solution is not practicable in cases of multiple activities (another activity would have to be restarted), but we consider it here in order to reduce the complexity of the example by isolating specific communication problems.

Note finally that transfer is controlled by a channel or a DMA, whose program we shall not give. This program is in general prepared beforehand: only parameter values change from one execution to another. The procedures *start_read* and *start_print* are responsible for preparing the program and starting transfers.

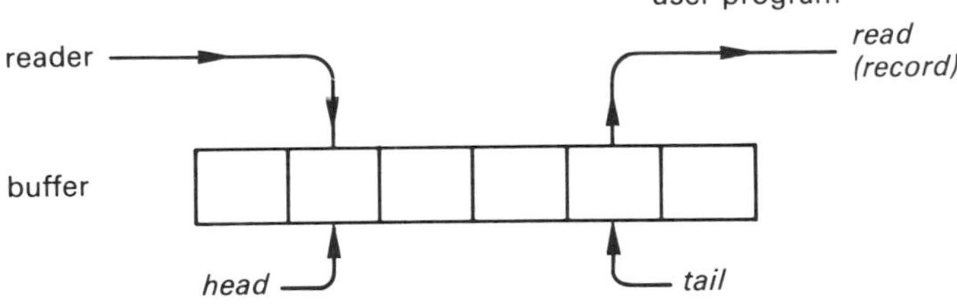

Variables		Initial values
L	:size of a slot (record)	constant
Nread	:number of locations in the buffer	constant
nempty	:number of empty locations	*Nread*
read_busy	:read busy indicator	*false*
head,tail	:head and tail pointers	0,0
next()	:pointer to next location	—

read(record)

```
save(svc_zone);
start:
if nempty < Nread then
  record:=buffer[head];
  head:=next(head);
  nempty:=nempty+1;
  if ¬read_busy then
    read_busy:=true;
    start_read(tail)
  endif
else
  if ¬ read_busy then
    read_busy:=true;
    start_read(tail)
  endif;
  waitpsw:=<wait,user,
    unmasked,addr start>;
  read_wait:=true;
  load_psw(waitpsw)
endif;
restore (svc_zone)
load_psw(old_svc)
```

handle_reader_it

```
save(it_zone);
tail:=next(tail);
nempty=nempty-1;
if nempty>0 then
  start_read (tail)
else
  read_busy:=false
endif;
if read_wait then
  old_it.act:=active;
  read_wait:=false
endif;
restore (it_zone);
load_psw(old_it)
```

start_read(tail)

```
construct channel.prog:
  <direction=read
  addr.memory=addr buffer[tail]
  byte_count=L>
SIO
  <prog=channel.prog
   periph=reader>
```

The way the above programs execute leads to a crucial remark. It is important to note that execution of the interrupt handler is triggered by the end of the physical transfer of a record, an activity which takes place in parallel to the execution of the program for the primitive *read (record)* on the processor. It is therefore possible that the interrupt will occur at *any (interruptible) point* in the execution of this primitive; this means interleaving the execution of the handler *between any two instructions* of the program *read(record)*. The consequences may be catastrophic, as can be seen in the following example: Consider the second instruction

```
if ]read_busy then
  read_busy:=true;
  start_read (tail)
endif
```

in the program *read_write*. It can be broken down as follows into elementary instructions:

```
(1)  load  R,read_busy
(2)  brz   R,sequence     --branch if true
(3)   ....
sequence: ....
           <wait>
```

Assume that the interrupt arrives between the execution of the instructions labelled (1) and (2). The value read in *R* by (1) is *true*; the interrupt handler will set *read_busy* to *false*. After interrupt handling, instruction (2) is executed with *R* set to *true* and the calling activity moves into the waiting state, where it will remain indefinitely as the peripheral has not been restarted. Other cases of inconsistency can be highlighted (see exercises) with other assumptions concerning the arrival of the interrupt.

The conclusion of this analysis is that consistency of common variables (such as *busy_read, nempty,* etc.) cannot be maintained if the end of input-output interrupt is allowed to come at any time. The supervisor call which implements the *read(record)* sequence must be executed with the *input-output interrupt masked*.

The constraint we have just examined is known as **mutual exclusion**; it is a consequence of the execution of asynchronous activities. It will be studied systematically in chapters 4 and 5.

The programs for an output peripheral (printer) can be written in an analogous way to those for reading. The comments concerning interrupt masks remain valid. We shall give the program with no further comment.

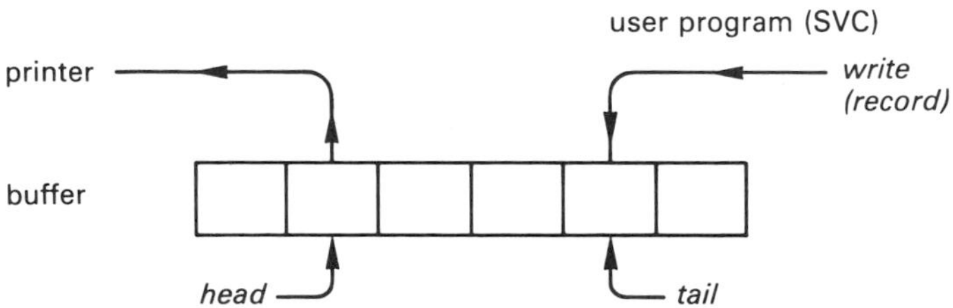

Variables		Initial values
L	:size of a location (record)	constant
Nprint	:number of locations in the buffer	constant
nempty	:number of empty locations	*Nprint*
prt_busy	:printer busy indicator	*false*
head,tail	:head and tail pointers	0,0
next ()	:pointer to next location	—

write(record)

```
save (svc_zone);
start:
if nempty>0 then
  buffer (tail):=record;
  tail:=next(tail);
  nempty:=nempty-1;
  if ¬prt_busy then
    prt_busy:=true
    start_print(head)
  endif
else
  if ¬prt_busy then
    prt_busy:=true;
    start_print(head)
  endif;
  waitpsw:=<wait,user,
unmasked,addr start>;
  write_wait:=true;
  load_psw (waitpsw)
endif;
restore (svc_zone);
load_psw(old_svc)
```

handle_printer_it

```
save(it_zone);
head:=next(head);
nempty:=nempty+1;
if nempty<Nprint then
  start_print(head)
else
  prt_busy:=false
endif;
if write_wait then
  old_it.active:=active;
  write_wait:=false
endif;
restore(it_zone);
load_psw(old_it)
```

start_print(head)

```
construct channel.prog:
  <direction=out
   memory.addr=addr buffer [head]
    byte_count=L>
SIO
  <prog=channel.prog
   periph=printer>
```

2.4.4 Input-output buffered on disk

System performance levels can be improved by handling all slow input-output by means of disk buffers. If these buffers are big enough, as is made possible by the space available on disk, they allow transfers from or to slow peripherals to be anticipated by read and write operations on disk. The disk buffer is filled or emptied at the same time as programs are executed on the central processor, and everything takes place, from the point of view of a program using slow peripherals, as though the peripherals had a throughput close to that of the disk. This mode of operation, shown in fig. 2.7 for the case of a printer, is called spooling (from spool, **Simultaneous Peripheral Operations On-Line**).

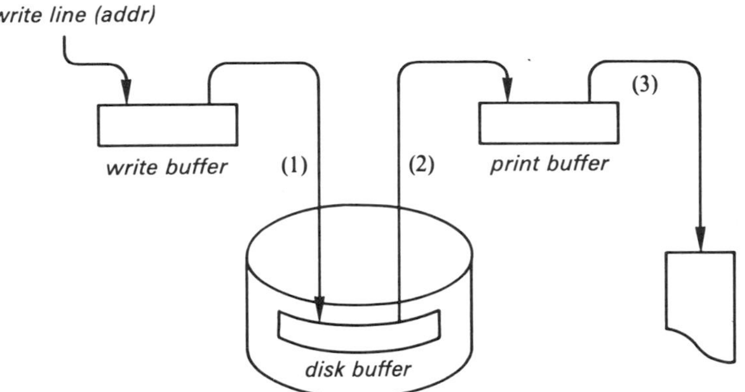

Fig. 2.7. Organization of an output stream buffered on disk (spooler)

We have to write a program for the primitive *write_line* and the handler program for input-output interrupt. The latter program must handle three cases, corresponding to the ends of transfer operations marked 1, 2 and 3 on fig. 2.7.

```
save(zone);
case cause of
   1: handle_write_disk_it      -- end of writing of a line image to disk
   2: handle_read_disk_it       -- end of reading a line image from disk
   3: handle_print_it           -- end of printing of a line
else: handle other causes of interrupts
endcase;
restore(zone);
load_psw(old_it)
```

We introduce busy indicators for the various transfers:

```
busy(print)            :printer
busy(disk_read)        :disk being read
busy(disk_write        :disk being written
```

These indicators are updated when transfer starts and when interrupts are acknowledged.

handle print_it

```
if ¬busy(disk_read) and
        ¬ empty(disk_buffer) then
    prepare disk read
endif;
if ¬empty(print_buffer) then
    start printing line
endif
```

handle_read_disk_it

```
if ¬empty(write_buffer) and
        ¬full (disk_buffer) then
    prepare disk write
endif;
if ¬full (print_buffer) and
        ¬empty(disk_read) then
    prepare disk read
endif;
if waiting then
        restart (write_line)
endif
```

handle write_disk_it

```
if ¬busy(print) then
start printing line
endif;
if ¬full (print_buffer) and
¬empty (disk_buffer) then
  prepare disk read
endif;
if ¬empty (disk write) and
¬busy (disk_read) then
  prepare disk_write
endif
```

write_line(addr) —SVC

```
test: if ¬ full(write_buffer) then
          copy (addr, write_buffer);
          if ¬busy (disk_write) and
            ¬ full (disk_buffer) then
            prepare disk write
          endif;
      else
          if ¬busy (disk write) and
            ¬ full (disk_buffer)then
            prepare disk_write
          endif;
          wait; goto test
      endif
```

The disk exchange control instructions (*prepare read* and *prepare write*) should be interpreted as follows: construct a transfer request and include it in a request queue; if the disk is free, start execution of the first request (and update the indicators). This mode of management is made necessary by the fact that several requests may be waiting simultaneously.

Interrupt handling can be simply explained as follows. An interrupt marks the end of a transfer to or a buffer *buf*. It is therefore necessary to:

a. Start the next transfer, if possible

b. If an activity is waiting because *buf*, its source buffer, was full, restart it again

c. If an activity is waiting because *buf*, its destination buffer, was empty, restart it

The possibility conditions in *a*) are that the source buffer is not empty and that the destination buffer is not full (if one of these buffers is replaced by a peripheral, the latter must be ready, as the interrupt has been received). In the case of supervisor calls (the *write_line* primitive), the mechanism for making the calling activity wait is not specified.

2.4.5 Bootstrap and initial load

In order to begin working on a bare machine, one must load the operating system program, which we assume is available on an external medium, into memory, and execute a branch to the first instruction in the program. This assumes that a read program at least is present in memory, and this will have to have been loaded first... On the first computers, a short program (a few instructions), input by hand into a fixed address in memory, through the keyboard, allowed loading of a more sophisticated loader capable of reading a complete version of the system. This process was called **bootstrapping**.

On modern machines, the initial short program is permanently resident in read only memory. Its execution is triggered by means of a reset switch, or sometimes automatically when the computer is powered up. This program reads, from a specified peripheral, a program whose first instructions, loaded into memory, and immediately executed, allow it to read the rest. A program given this form is called **self-loading**; its initial part (whose function is to read the rest) is called the *bootstrap*. When the system has been loaded once from the external medium, a copy of the bootstrap remains in secondary memory in order to be able to load a fresh version of the system in case of accidental destruction of the contents of main memory.

2.5 Bibliographic notes

A detailed study of run-time program management (stack organization) appears in [Aho 77, chapter 10] and [Wulf 81, chapters 4 and 16].

The best source for a detailed study of the operation of interrupts, traps and supervisor calls is the reference manual for a processor. They sometimes also contain examples of simple programs using these mechanisms.

A description of input-output devices (channels, DMA, controllers, peripherals) appears in texts on computer architecture; see for example [Baer 80], and it is also worth consulting reference manuals. A detailed study of input-output controller interfaces, oriented towards microcomputers, appears in [Stone 82], which also contains examples of peripheral driver programs.

Exercises

Exercise 2.1

Write an outline program for input-output with interrupts, making the following extensions to the outline given in section 2.4.2.2:

a. If a transfer error is detected, try to repeat the operation up to a maximum number *nmax* of attempts, before cancelling the input-output operation;

b. If the transfer does not take place within a specified maximum time *tmax*, cancel the input-output operation.

In both cases, call a specified procedure for handling the error.

Exercise 2.2

A computer is used to collect measurements. Periodically (with period *T*) it carries out a measurement cycle, as follows:

- Collection of measurements from the sensors (duration: *tmeas*)
- Processing of measurements:(duration: *tcalc*)
- Recording of results to disk:(duration: *trec*)

The three operations above must be executed in sequence for each cycle. A clock is available which issues an interrupt as the counter passes through zero. The task is to write system programs (main program, interrupt handler) in each of the following three cases. If appropriate, state the condition making processing possible given the duration of a different operation:

a. The sensors and disk controller are controlled by the CPU. Successive measurements cycles must be executed in sequence, and background processing takes place at other times.

b. Assume that

$$tmeas+tcalc < T < tmeas+tcalc+trec$$

Recording in cycle *i* must be carried out in parallel with collection for cycle *i+1*. We assume that the disk is controlled by a DMA.

c. Assume that

$$tmeas < T < tmeas+tcalc$$

Collection and recording for successive cycles has to be carried out in parallel. Assume that sensors are controlled by a DMA independent of that for the disk.

Exercise 2.3

A mouse is a device used to point at a location on a screen. The mouse is moved by hand in a horizontal plane and its movements are reproduced to within a scaling factor by those of a cursor displayed on the screen. Assume that an instruction *read_position (x,y)* makes it possible at any moment to read the position of the mouse, defined by its Cartesian coordinates x and y. An instruction *init_mouse* allows the current position of the mouse to be defined as the origin of these co-ordinates.

The aim of this exercise is to write a program making it possible to follow the movement of the mouse.

a. Assuming that the maximum speed of movement of the mouse is 10 cm/s, at what frequency must the coordinates be measured if it is intended to show the position of the cursor to within a pixel on a 30 × 30 cm screen, made up of 1024 × 1024 pixels (a pixel is the elementary displayable point on the screen)? Assume that the scaling factor is 1.

b. The mouse is managed by a periodically activated program, with a period T selected according to the result of *a*). Write the tracking program assuming that the following two procedures are available:

- *Display_cursor (X,Y)*, which displays the position of the cursor, centered at point X,Y, on the screen
- *Move_cursor (DX,DY)* which moves the displayed cursor through a vector with components (DX,DY)

A clock issuing an interrupt as the counter goes through zero is available.

Exercise 2.4

In the program for buffered input (section 2.4.3.2), assume that the instruction

```
nempty:=nempty+1
```

can be broken down into a sequence of elementary instructions (there is no increment instruction in memory). Show that allowing the arrival of an input-output interrupt at any point within this sequence can lead to inconsistencies.

Exercise 2.5

Draw up the outline of a program for an input spooler on the basis of the printer spooler described in section 2.4.4.

Exercise 2.6

Introduce the buffer management procedures and the peripheral activity indicators, as in section 2.4.3.2., to develop printer spooler programs as described in section 2.4.4. Carry out the same exercise for the input spooler described in the preceding exercise.

Exercise 2.7

Assume that printer spooler described in section 2.4.4 is used by the users of an operating system to print their files.

a. Why is it not possible to make the primitive *write (record)* directly available to users?

b. Using the primitive *write(record)* build up a program for a primitive *print_file* which could be made available to users.

c. Modify the programs to allow a user:

- To be told when file printing has been completed by the spooler
- To cancel printing of a file before it is executed

Exercise 2.8

On a computer, the microprogrammed bootstrap reads the contents of the first record of a specified disk into memory, and loads the status word contained in the first location of this record. Suggest an outline for the programmed bootstrap which appears in this record. **Hint:** The bootstrap must use a location array describing the organization on disk of the information to be loaded. The first program to be activated at the end of a bootstrap is a rudimentary absolute loader using this location information.

Exercise 2.9

Consult the bootstrap specifications for a microcomputer, and write a bootstrap for that machine.

Chapter 3
Organization of a simple operating system

This chapter has two aims:

1. To introduce some principles of software system structuring: hierarchical decomposition, levels of abstraction, objects and interfaces. The value of these concepts transcends the strict framework of system software; nevertheless, these questions take on a particular importance for operating systems because of their complexity, often considerable size and the interaction between software and hardware which characterizes them.
2. To apply these notions to the description of the structure and operation of a very simple operating system, making it possible to specify its main components and its internal interfaces.

3.1 Hierarchical decomposition and abstract machines

3.1.1 Top-down design and layered structure

A major factor making program design difficult is the distance separating the language in which problems are formulated and the language in which the algorithms to solve them are expressed. The term *language* in this chapter is used in the following general sense: a language defines objects (and mechanisms for their creation), actions (or primitives) that manipulate these objects and rules for combining actions. The concept of an object is defined in section 3.1.2.

We may also note that any language defines, at least conceptually, a *machine* capable of interpreting it: the instruction set for this machine is made up of the language primitives, its memory makes it possible to represent the objects defined by this language, and its execution mechanism is defined by the interpretation rules for its language. Such a machine is said to be *abstract* as it is not generally physically implemented.

Top-down design is an application of the Cartesian approach which decomposes a problem into a sequence of more elementary sub-problems that are easier to solve. With this in mind, we start by attempting to define a machine $\mathbf{M_0}$ such that the initial problem becomes easy to solve using objects and primitives implemented by the machine. The problem is then reduced to the implementation of machine $\mathbf{M_0}$ on the machine $\mathbf{M}$ which is actually available; to do this, we define a machine $\mathbf{M_1}$, and so on until we reach a machine $\mathbf{M_n}$ that is easily implementable on machine $\mathbf{M}$.

Apart from the simplification at each level to which just reducing the size of the problem leads, the power of this method is a consequence of the **abstraction** process which reduces a problem to its essential aspects, embodied in the specification of a machine; aspects regarded as secondary are left aside in this phase, and are only taken into account when the specified machine is being implemented. The specification of a machine, for its users, is reduced to that of its **interface** i.e. to the objects and operations provided by the machine; this concept is discussed in more detail in section 3.1.3.

If the implementation of a machine $\mathbf{M_i}$ uses an interface provided by machine $\mathbf{M_j}$, we say that $\mathbf{M_i}$ **uses** $\mathbf{M_j}$, or that $\mathbf{M_i}$ **depends on** $\mathbf{M_j}$. In fact, $\mathbf{M_i}$ depends only on the interface of $\mathbf{M_j}$ and not on the details of its internal structure. The relation between machines defined in this way is said to be a dependence relation. The structure of a system may then be written in the form of a graph whose nodes represent the machines defined by decomposition and the arcs represent the dependence relations. The structure resulting from the application of the top-down design method can therefore be shown in pattern (a) of fig. 3.1.

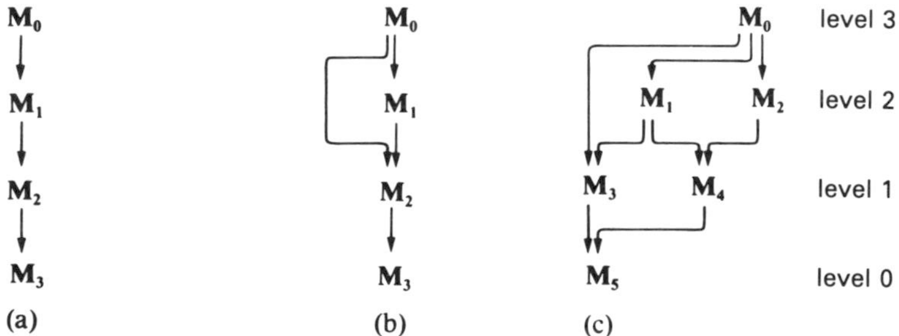

Fig. 3.1. Hierarchical decomposition patterns

This pattern may be generalized: if we accept that a machine can use primitives provided by any machine of a lower level, we obtain pattern (b); more generally, if the only constraint imposed on the dependence graph is that it must be acyclic, we obtain a scheme as in (c) where the machines are classified in layers, or levels of abstraction: a machine of level $i (i>0)$ only uses machines of level lower than i; the machine at level 0, or the base level, uses no other machine.

In practice, the top-down design method is never used in a pure way: the process involves iterations, and the definition of successive machines takes account of the designer's experience and of the existence of already implemented machines. Moreover, for a problem of some complexity, it is practically impossible to determine in advance the detailed specifications of interfaces: the elaboration of these specifications is based on the results of tests on partial implementations.

However it is reached, a hierarchical structure in terms of levels has several advantages, which derive from the **independence** introduced by abstraction:

- Independence for design: this is the aspect to which we have already drawn attention. The behavior of a machine for its user is entirely described by the specifications of its interface.
- Independence for modification: modifications to the implementation of a machine do not propagate to those that use it, so long as the specifications of the interface remain unchanged.
- Independence for debugging: once its interface has been specified, a machine **M** may be debugged independently of those which use it; conversely, once the interface for **M** has been correctly implemented, the machines that use **M** can be debugged independently of **M**.

3.1.2 Concept of objects

Hierarchical decomposition into abstract machines, discussed in section 3.1.1 does not cover all aspects of system structuring. In particular, it does not apply well to:

- Situations where elements must be created and destroyed dynamically
- The description of groups of elements with common properties

To make it easier to take these aspects into account, we introduce a new structuring tool, the concept of an **object**. This term does not currently cover a universally accepted concept: objects are characterized by a set of properties and mechanisms, some of which have been implemented in particular languages or systems, without a general and uniform model emerging. The concept of an object nevertheless provides a framework within which various important concepts for computer systems can be expressed with ease: naming, linking, types and protections.

An object is defined by the following attributes:

1. A **name** making it possible to specify an object and distinguish it from other objects

2. A **state** which is defined at any moment and may change through time

3. A set of operations, or **access functions**, making it possible in particular

- To create or destroy objects
- To read or modify the state of an object
- To combine objects with each other

The concept of a **class** of objects allows us to bring together objects with common properties: it is therefore an abstraction tool. Each class is associated with a set of access functions applicable to all objects in the class; each object in the class has a specific name and state. Each object belongs to a class; when an object is created, its name and its initial state are specified; the operations associated with its class are immediately applicable to it.

It can be useful to define subsets, within a class of objects, by common properties over and above those defined for the class. This is provided for by the concept of a sub-class. We can define a class *S* as a subclass of a given class *C*. Objects belonging to *S* have the properties associated with class *C* (the *super-class* of *C*), to which are added other specific properties of *C*; we say that sub-classes inherit the properties of their super-class.

The process of definition of sub-classes may be applied recursively. This makes it possible to build up a tree structured hierarchy of classes using the relation *is a sub-class of*.

In the design of operating systems, the concept of a class of objects is used to implement an abstraction for a particular physical object (or resource), with two aims:

- Making its internal operations invisible, by a redefinition of its interface
- Sharing it between any number of users, by a dynamic creation mechanism

The following is a list of the most common objects, showing the physical resource of which they are an abstraction:

• Files (see chapter 3,6 and 7)	secondary memory
• Streams (see chapter 6)	peripheral devices
• Processes (see chapters 4 and 5)	processing
• Virtual memory (see chapters 9 and 10)	physical memory
• Windows (see Chapter 11)	display

The creation and destruction of objects makes it possible to vary their number dynamically. Once it has been created, an object is accessible by means of the access functions specified for its class. Programs for these functions are generally shared between all objects in the class, but each object has its own data representing its state.

The general problems of access to objects (linking, representation, protection) are examined in chapter 6.

3.1.3 Interfaces and specifications

We shall here give a few ideas on the form of interfaces and the techniques used to specify them. We shall limit ourselves for the moment to interfaces whose activation mechanism is a procedure call; interfaces based on messages are mentioned in chapter 4.

An interface is associated with an abstract machine (section 3.1.1.) or a class of objects (section 3.1.2). It provides three types of information, which are the only means of access to the machine or the object:

- Data types and structures
- Procedures
- A set of rules for using data and procedures

The rules provide a set of operating instructions for data structures and procedures. They generally express restrictions on their use, and may take various forms:

- Data access restrictions (e.g. read only)
- Restrictions on the order of execution of procedure
- Constraints affecting simultaneous execution of procedures or simultaneous access to data

The problem of expressing interface specifications has not yet been given a satisfactory general solution. An aspect of specification that may be expressed formally and therefore be capable of automatic checking is the specification of the types of variables and procedure parameters. Two classes of technques are used to specify the effect of a procedure call:

- Statement of pre and post conditions
- Equivalence to another way of expressing the procedure algorithm

The most common form of expression still remains natural language.

When it comes to expressing constraints on use, there is again no universal solution. In many cases, it is possible to represent the state of a machine quite simply using a finite state automaton, with changes of state resulting from successive calls to procedures in the interface. Some ideas used in specification for the case of simultaneous activities will be given in chapter 4.

Let us now consider how possible errors can be taken into account in the specification of interfaces. Two general methods are used.

1. Consultation of an error code

Each procedure contains an additional parameter (error code). The parameter is modified by the procedure, and its final value is an indication on how the operation ran: errors can therefore be detected by consulting this variable.

2. Association with a handling procedure

A specific handling procedure is associated with every possible cause of error. If an error takes place, an appropriate mechanism automatically calls the corresponding procedure.

The first method is similar to the use of a condition code; the second is similar to the use of traps (see chapter 2), or to analogous mechanisms integrated into certain languages: *on-condition* in PL/1, *exceptions* in Ada.

Although it requires the use of an additional mechanism, the second method is preferable, for two reasons:

- Security: in case of error, the handling procedure is automatically called; in the condition code method, if the test for this code is omitted, an error may be propagated.
- Clarity: the association of a procedure with every cause of error clearly separates handling for cases regarded as *normal* from that of exceptional situations.

The definition of 'normal' and 'exceptional' situations and the characterization of possible causes of error are part of the task of specification, and fall within the designer's responsibility.

3.2 Organization of a single user system

We shall illustrate the design approach that uses a hierarchy of abstract machines by means of an example of an operating system, reduced to its simplest form to make the discussion easier. This is a minimal system, intended to manage a personal microcomputer, used by a single user (see section 1.2.1.). An example of such a system is CP/M([1]) for which a version exists for most common microcomputers. The system described here is based to a considerable extent on it, at least as far as its overall structure and main interfaces are concerned.

3.2.1 Specifications and general organization

3.2.1.1 System functions and command language

The computer managed by the system includes a processor, a main memory, and the following peripherals: a terminal (screen and keyboard), one or two disk drives and a printer. Peripherals are driven by the processor (the possibility of managing peripherals by means of a DMA will be considered in exercise 3.14).

The system must allow:

- Storage of information in files on disk
- Transfer of information between files and peripherals
- Writing, debugging, storage and execution of programs

It is intended to structure the operating system in such a way that it can be adapted easily to different machine configurations, and in particular to different types of secondary memory and peripheral devices.

([1]) CP/M is a registered trademark of Digital Research.

The user interface provided by the system is defined by a command language specified as follows:

<command> ::= <command name> <parameter list>
<parameter list> ::= empty/<parameter list> <parameter>
<parameter> ::= <filename>

Commands are input at the keyboard and immediately executed.

A **file** is a named collection of information, handled by means of access functions. Files are stored in secondary memory. Programs and user data are contained in files.

A certain number of basic commands are predefined by the system. Moreover, any executable program created by the user in a file can be executed as a command. We therefore have:

<command name>::=<predefined command name>/
<name of executable file>

By way of example, let us give a sequence of commands corresponding to the creation and debugging of a program in assembly language.

1. edit source — editing source program

Modify the contents of a file *source* containing the text of the program (or create it if it does not exist) using internal commands defined by an interactive editor provided by the system, whose operations will not be specified in detail here.

2. assemble source object — assembly

Assemble the program contained in *source* and store the object code in file *object*.

3. object data result — execution

Execute the program contained in the file *object* reading data in the file *data* and returning the results in file *result*.

4. debug — interactive debugging

After detecting an error, examine the state of variables; modify that state;

halt or restart execution of the current program. These actions are controlled by internal system commands for assistance to debugging, which are not specified here.

Sequence 1. to 4. above may be repeated until a satisfactory result is obtained.

3.2.1.2 Decomposition of the system; internal interfaces

A first version of the operating system could be implemented directly using the interface defined by the physical machine. We shall now show how this monolithic system can be broken down progressively into logically consistent subsets.

1. Management of files and streams

The first stage would be to isolate the subset of the system responsible for file management. To do so, we have to specify the structure of files and their access functions.

We assume that a file is organized as a series of records of fixed size. Reading and writing are sequential: for each file *f* a read/write pointer *ptr(f)* is defined, along with a boolean variable *eof(f)* and an access mode (read only or read and write). Access functions are defined as follows: The opening of a file allows it to be declared usable and to initialize its indicator.

```
open(f):
  if empty(f) then
    eof(f):=true
  else
    ptr(f):= <pointer to first record>
    eof(f):= false
  endif
```

The primitive *change_mode* makes it possible to determine the access mode to the file (this primitive is often included in the opening process). Access to records takes place by means of two primitives *read_next* and *write_next*

```
read_next(f,dest):      --dest = destination buffer
  if eof(f) then
    <error>               --reading beyond end
  else
    dest:=<record named by ptr(f)>
    advance(f)
  endif
```

The function *advance(f)* has the effect of making *ptr(f)* point to the following record in the file. If *ptr(f)* points to the final record, it remains unchanged, and *eof(f)* is set to true.

```
write_next(f,source):      --source = source buffer
  if mode(f) = read only then
    <error>
  else
    if end(f) then
      <add a location to the end of a file for a record>
      advance(f)
    endif;
    <record named by ptr(f)>:=source;
    advance(f)
  endif
```

Note that reading and writing take place sequentially starting from the current position of the pointer *ptr(f)* and both update the pointer.

close(f)

File *f*, assumed to be open, is now closed: it can no longer be read or written.

create(f)

A file called *f* is created, and is intially empty and closed.

delete(f)

File *f* is deleted; it can no longer be named, and the information it contains is lost.

More complete specifications of file access primitives are given in chapter 7.

The operating system may now be broken down into two layers (or *machines*): the file management system defined above (machine **FMS**), built on the physical machine **PHM**, and the command language interpreter (machine **CLI**), which uses the functions provided by the interface of **FMS**.

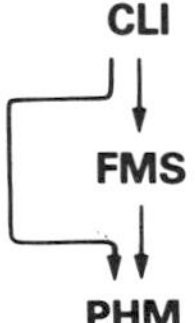

Note that machine **CLI** also uses the physical machine **PHM** directly for reading commands from the keyboard, for screen management and for printing files. If a strict ordering of levels is required, it is necessary to include input-output management in **FMS**. We shall therefore specify the functions to be carried out.

The concept of a file is an abstract implementation of exchanges with secondary memory. We shall introduce an equivalent level of abstraction for specifying exchanges with other peripherals. With this in mind, we shall define two 'logical peripherals' whose interface we specify as follows:

a. The *logical terminal*, made up of a keyboard and a screen, providing two functions:

read_line (buffer)

loads the contents of a line entered at the keyboard into a buffer in memory; elementary editing functions (deletion of a character, of a line, etc.) are provided; the characters input are displayed on the screen.

display_line (buffer)

provides a screen display of the contents of a line placed in a memory buffer.

b. The *logical printer* provides the function:

print_line (buffer)

which prints the contents of a line placed in a buffer in memory.

For the three functions above, the first byte of the buffer specifies the number of characters in the source or destination line for the transfer.

The definition of logical peripherals has two advantages:

- It provides more elaborate functions, that are closer to the user's needs, than those of physical input-output devices.
- It allows a physical peripheral to be replaced by another while maintaining the same user interface.

To allow such substitution, we shall specify a function

assign (logical.periph, physical.periph)

which modifies the association, initially defined by default, between logical and physical peripherals. Compatibility between functions must be respected (the logical printer must be associated with an output device, etc.).

The concept of a logical peripheral (also called an input-output **stream**) will be reconsidered and generalized in section 6.2 where it will be extended to files.

2. Implementation of input-output

The implementation of machine **FMS**, which manages files and streams, may itself be simplified if input-output primitives are available in a less rudimentary form than those directly provided by the physical machine. We therefore define a new machine called **PIO** (primitive input-output) which provides the following interface:

a. Exchanges with the disk. The disk is organized in tracks and sectors; the sector is the transfer unit; an address on disk takes the form:

(*drive nr, track nr, sector nr*)

The interface is made up of three functions:

select_drive (drive_nr)	: specifies the current medium; further transfers will take place with the disk loaded on that drive
read_sector (track,sect,dest)	: transfers the sector from disk to memory
write_sector (track,sect,orig)	: transfers a sector in memory to disk
track,sect	: track number, sector number
orig,dest	: memory buffers (with the same size as a sector)

b. Exchanges with other peripherals. The transfer unit here is a character. Three functions are defined:

read_char(c)	: reads a character from keyboard (result *c*)
display_char(c)	: displays the character on screen (origin *c*)
print_char(c)	: sends a character to the printer (origin *c*)

To make them easy to use by **FMS**, these operations are defined for logical peripherals. Access to associated physical peripherals is implemented by simple indirection via a mapping table (see section 3.2.2.2).

Note: We assume that special characters are used to call functions specific to each of these peripherals (form feed, cursor movements); the interface above therefore allows them to be implemented.

The implementation of the file management system can now be broken down into two simpler problems:

- To implement machine **FMS**, which provides the interface described in

1), using functions provided by the interface of machine **PIO**, described in 2)

- To implement machine **PIO** itself using the physical machine

The structure of the system may now be represented as shown in fig. 3.2.

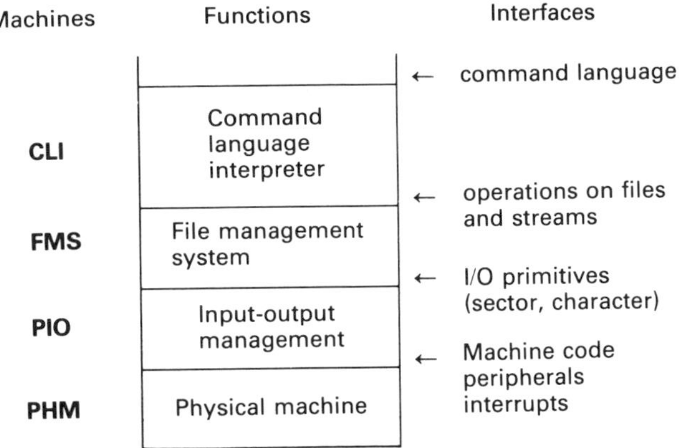

Fig. 3.2. General structure of the system

This decomposition of the system shows the main advantage of structuring in levels: modification, however deep it may be, of the internal organization of machine **PIO** or **FMS** leads to no modification in levels above them if the corresponding interface is unmodified. On the other hand, this remark emphasizes the importance of defining an interface specification correctly: the interface of **PIO**, for example, must make it simple to implement the machines using it, while remaining easy to implement itself. This overall design concept can only be an iterative process, which also draws on the designer's experience. As the process advances, the main interfaces will be progressively elaborated and become more stable. The cost of modification to an interface increases with the number of components which use it; it is therefore generally higher for the lower level interfaces of the system.

The external interface of the system, the interface for **CLI**, is defined by the command language. Internal interfaces (those for **PIO** and **FMS**) are implemented by supervisor calls.

3.2.2 Primitive input-output

The peripheral drivers are based on the synchronous approach described in section 2.4.2.1 We shall start by describing management of a disk unit, then input-output in character mode.

3.2.2.1 Input-output on disk

The description that follows will be based, in order to simplify our discussion, on a particular format of disks (8 inch floppy disk, single side, single density). The principles on which a system may be parameterized for various formats will be discussed in section 3.2.3.2.

A disk is organized in 77 tracks each consisting of 26 sectors; the size of a sector is 128 bytes. The sector is the unit of information transfer.

Exchanges with the disk are buffered, in order to accelerate sequential transfer, which is the most common mode. It makes most sense, in particular, to read a whole track at a time, as track searching time only occurs once for all the sectors. Consequently, *n* buffers of track size (26 128-byte sectors) are constantly reserved for this purpose. The number *n*, of the order of a few units, is set at system generation.

Note: Sectors regarded as 'consecutive' on a track by the system are not in fact physically contiguous on the disk, but separated by a fixed interval (generally six sectors). This arrangement allows time to carry out management operations (transfer validity checks) between access operations to two consecutive sectors, and therefore makes it possible to reduce the total transfer time for a series of such sectors. Sector numbers used in the system are therefore 'logical' numbers. Mapping between logical and physical sector numbers takes place for each transfer operation (see programs below), and the disk controller only recognizes physical numbers.

Assume that we have to read a sector whose number is *sect* on track *track*. If one of the buffers contains track *track*, reading takes place, without access to the disk, from the corresponding sector of the buffer. Otherwise, the contents of track *track* has first to be loaded into one of the buffers from the disk. We deal with the question of choosing a buffer later.

The write operation is a little more complex. To save transfers, a buffer is copied to the disk as late as possible. As long as it remains in memory, it reflects the current state of the sectors of the track and successive access operations to the same sector lead to no access to disk. Let us assume that we have to write to sector *sect* of track *track*:

- If track *track* is present in a buffer, the corresponding sector is modified and the operation ends, except in cases of *immediate writing* (see note below).
- If track *track* is not present, it must first be read into a buffer, unless the track is being written for the first time. This case occurs, in particular, on a first write to a newly created file, or if a file is being extended. In

this case, one only needs to allocate a buffer without reading taking place beforehand.

Note: Immediate writing. The write operation may specify that the sector to be modified should be *immediately* copied to disk. This is the case, for example, of sectors containing file descriptors (see section 3.1.3.2). In this way, we can reduce the probability of the contents of a disk becoming incoherent (invalid descriptor), in case of system breakdown occuring between modifications of the descriptor and writing of the buffer to disk.

Except in cases of immediate writing, a buffer is only copied to disk in two cases:

- If it is reallocated in order to load a new track in memory, according to the reallocation algorithm which is described below
- During flushing caused by closure of a file or a request for dismounting volume (see section 3.1.3.3)

The buffer reallocation algorithm is based on the property of locality of references (see section 9.2): the probability of access to information is all the greater if that information has been recently used. Buffers are therefore ordered by chronological order of the most recent references. When a buffer is needed, a choice is made in the following order of decreasing preference:

1. A free buffer (one that has not yet been used)
2. A buffer that is full but which has not been modified since it was loaded
3. Whichever of the remaining buffers has been refered to least recently (i.e. its most recent reference is older than that of any other)

In cases 1) and 2), the buffer is immediately usable. In case 3), its contents must first be copied to the corresponding track of the disk.

We shall now examine the principles on which disk driving programs are based. We shall consider programs reduced to their bare essentials, and adopt the simplest possible solutions. Improvements are suggested in the exercises.

We shall deal with the case of a single buffer ($n=1$) with the size of one track. Two indicators are associated with this buffer:

current_track	: number of the track loaded in the buffer (*nil* if buffer empty)
modif	: true if the contents of the buffer have been modified since it was loaded

The controller interface provides the following functions:

SELECT_DRIVE(drive)	: chooses drive *drive* as current drive
FIND_TRACK(track)	: moves the read-write head to track *track*
READ_SECT(addr,sect)	: reads the contents of sector *sect* of the current track into 128 bytes starting at address *addr*
WRITE_SECT(addr,sect)	: writes the 128 bytes starting at address *addr* to sector *sect* of the current track
TEST	: allows consultation of indicators *ready*, *finished* or *error* in the controller status word.

Remember that the interface provided by **PIO** for disk management is made up of procedures *select_drive*, *read_sector* and *write_sector*.

In view of the comments we made previously, procedure *write_sector* includes a *mode* parameter, which may take the values *normal_write*, *immediate_write* and *first_write*. We shall not describe *select_drive*, which is directly implemented by a controller function.

read_sector (track,sect,dest)

```
if track <> current_track then
  if modif then
    transfer_track
      (current_track,buffer,write)
  endif;
transfer_track(track,buffer,read)
endif;
dest:=buffer[sect]
```

write_sector (track,sect,orig,mode)

```
if track <> current_track then
  if modif then
    transfer_track
      (current_track,buffer,write)
  endif;
  if mode=first_write
    and free(track) then
    current_track:=track
  else
    transfer_track(track,buffer,
    read)
  endif;
endif;
buffer[sect]:=orig;
if mode=immediate_write then
  transfer_sector (orig,sect,write)
else
  modif:=true
endif
```

In cases of a first write operation, it is assumed that the flag *free(track)*, indicates that the whole of track *track* has been allocated for the first time.

The procedures above use two procedures internal to **PIO**: *transfer_track* and *transfer_sector* which constitute the disk driver.

```
procedure transfer_track (track,buffer,direction);
      FIND_TRACK(track)                      -- head movement
 test:TEST
      if ⌉ finished then
         goto test
      endif;
      for sect:=0 to sectno−1 do           -- sectno = 26
        transfer_sector (buffer[sect],sect,direction)
      endfor;
      modif:=false;
      if direction=read then
         current_track:=track
      endif

procedure transfer_sector(addr,sect,direction);
      sect:=conv(sect);                      -- physical number of a sector
      ntries:=0;
again:case direction of
         read:READ_SECT(addr,sect);
         write:WRITE_SECT(addr,sect)
      endcase
 test:TEST;                                  -- test for correct transfer
      if error then
         ntries:=ntries+1;
         if ntries<maxn then
            goto again
         else
            cause:=fatal_error               -- failure after maxn attempts
            <error trap>
         endif
      endif;
      if ⌉finished then
         goto test                           -- busy wait
      endif;
```

Procedure *conv* implements the conversion between logical addresses and physical sector addresses. Note that physical addresses only appear in the *transfer_sector* procedure.

In cases of transfer errors, the operation is repeated; if the error still occurs after *maxn* attempts, the driver forces trapping, most simply handled by displaying an error message, cancelling execution of the command under way and awaiting the next command (see section 3.2.4).

3.2.2.2 Input-output in character mode

Input-output in character mode use the synchronous driver method described in section 2.4.2.1, which we shall consider below for the case of writing a single character. To allow reassignment of peripherals, we shall specify the address of the controller as a parameter for the driver.

```
procedure output_char (c,p);        -- send character c to controller p
          TEST(p);
          if ⌉ ready then
             <handle error>
          endif;
          OUTPUT(c,p);
    test: TEST(p);
          if error then
             <handle error>
          endif;
          if ⌉finished then
             goto test
          endif;
```

A similar procedure *input_char(c,p)* is defined for reading. To implement exchanges with logical peripherals, an association table with three entries is defined:

periph_tab [keyboard] = address of the controller associated with the logical keyboard
periph_tab [screen] = address of the controller associated with the logical screen
periph_tab [print] = address of the controller associated with the logical printer

Operations on logical peripherals are therefore implemented as follows:

display_char(c) => output_char (c,periph_tab[screen])
print_char(c) => output_char (c,periph_tab[print])
read_char(c) => input_char(c,periph_tab[keyboard])

Note that the procedure *read_char* implements 'raw' reading; in particular the character input is not displayed on the screen, and is not interpreted. The implementation of these functions and management of the association table will be considered in section 3.2.3.4.

Note: The character reading procedure, which has been defined above, does not make it possible to take account of the arrival of an unexpected character. It is therefore impossible:

- To interrupt execution of a program if it does not read characters from the keyboard; a program in a loop can only be halted by rerouting the system
- To type ahead, i.e. to input characters on the keyboard before they are read by a program

The use of interrupts for driving the terminal makes it possible to remove these restrictions (see exercise 3.7).

3.2.3 File management system

3.2.3.1 Logical organization

The file naming system uses a two-level approach: the name of a file has the form

<drive name>:<identifier>.<type>

The name of the drive identifies the physical location of the file, i.e. the disk unit used; most often, it is implicit. Within a disk, or 'volume', the naming sheme is 'flat'; the *type* identifier speifies the nature of the file (translatable program, absolute commands, data, etc.). Files are organized sequentially, as a series of fixed size records (128 characters). The system provides primitives for sequential access to records, specified in section 3.2.1.2. All access functions must be built up from these primitives.

3.2.3.2 Physical organization

The allocation unit, or **block**, is a set of 8 consecutive sectors. The allocation state of the disk is described by an occupation table containing one bit per block (making a total of 250 bits; in fact, there are a few less as the first two tracks of the disk are permanently reserved). Finding a free block involves finding the first zero bit in this table; its number is that of the required block.

Information concerning a file is held in a **descriptor** which contains the following data:

- The file name (*<identifier>.<type>*)
- The size of the file (number of records)
- The number of the next record to read or write
- The file mapping table

The mapping table includes 16 bytes, containing the numbers of successive blocks in which the file is implemented. This makes it possible to represent 128 sectors, or 16 Kbytes. Larger files, called multi-section files, may be built by linking several descriptors, each of them describing a set of 16 blocks called the file's **section**. The number of sections is limited to 16, or 256 Kbytes in all.

Tracks 0 and 1, reserved for the operating system, contain in particular the volume occupation table and a bootstrap program. Descriptors of all files on the disk are held in a reserved zone starting from track number 2. These descriptors taken together form the volume **directory**.

To make it easier to adapt the system to various types of disk, the characteristics of disks are held in a table, created at system generation, and described in section 3.2.3.4; this table is used by all programs that need to know the physical organization of disks.

3.2.3.3 File operations

Opening a file means loading its descriptor into a reserved zone in central memory. The address of the descriptor is passed as a parameter to all further operations carried out on the file.

When an open file is closed, the descriptor in memory is copied back to the disk, and its location is freed, as well as the zone occupied in memory by the file itself. If there are still modified records from the file in an input-output buffer, they will also be written to the disk in immediate mode.

The creation of a file involves allocating it a descriptor on the disk; the file starts empty, and its mapping table contains only zeros.

The deletion of a file has the effect of freeing all the blocks it occupied on disk, as well as the location occupied by its descriptor. The directory and the occupation table are updated.

We shall give the underlying principles for sequentially reading or writing a record. File creation, deletion, opening or closing programs will be left as exercises (3.9 to 3.11).

Assume a file of name *f* is open. We shall write *descr* for its descriptor in memory, which contains the following fields:

descr(f).ptr	*read/write pointer*
descr(f).end	*end of file marker (see section 3.2.1.2)*
descr(f).size	*number of records in the file*
descr(f).impl	*file implementation table*

For the sake of simplicity, we shall assume the size of a file is limited to a single section. Multi-section files are considered in exercise 3.8.

```
procedure advance(f);
  if descr(f).ptr=descr(f).size−1 then
    descr(f).end:=true
  else
    descr(f).ptr:=descr(f).ptr+1
  endif

const block_size=8;          --number of sectors in block
    block_max=16;            --maximum number of blocks in section
procedure seq_read(f,dest);
  if descr(f).end then
    <error>                  -- read beyond end
  else
    compute(f,track,sect);   -- compute address of track-sector
    read_sector (track,sect,dest)
    advance(f);
  endif

procedure seq_write (f,orig);
  if descr(f).end then       -- extension to file
    block:=descr(f).size div block_size;
    sect:=descr(f).size mod block_size;
  if sect=block_size−1 then  -- last block full
      add_block(f)
    endif;
    descr(f).size:=descr(f).size+1;
    descr(f).end:=false;
    advance(f);
    compute(f,track,sect);
    write_sector(track,sect,orig,first_write)
  else                       -- no extension
    compute(f,tnack,sect);
    write_sector(track,sect,orig,normal_write)
  endif;
  advance(f)
```

Procedure *compute* calculates the track number *track* and the sector number *sect* corresponding to the record named by pointer *descr(f).ptr*. Note that writing takes place in 'first writing' mode in newly allocated blocks. Blocks are added by the following procedure:

```
procedure add_block(f);
  if block<max_block then
    allocate_block(allocated_blocks);
    if allocated_blocks=nil then
      <error>                 -- no more free blocks
    else
      descr(f).impl[block]:=allocated_blocks
    endif
  else
    <error>                   -- maximum size reached
  endif
```

Errors in procedure *add_block* lead to trapping and failure of the procedure *seq_write*.

3.2.3.4 Logical input-output and stream management

Using the interface provided by **PIO**, we can now carry out operations on the terminal and printer logical peripherals. Output to the printer can be simply written:

```
procedure print_line (buffer);
  number:=buffer[0];
  for i := 1 to number do
    print_char(buffer[i])
  endfor
```

The procedure *display_line* can be obtained by replacing *print_char* by *display_char*. Remember that the first byte in the buffer gives the number of characters to output.

Procedure *read_line* includes editing functions. With this in mind, special characters carry out particular functions:

DEL_CHAR	: delete the last character entered
DEL_LINE	: delete an entire line
BREAK	: interrupt the command under way
CR	: carriage return; terminate entry of the line

On calling the procedure, the first byte in the buffer contains its capacity (maximum number of characters to input); on return from the procedure, it contains the number of characters actually entered. If the buffer size is exceeded, entry of characters is halted (the user is alerted by the failure of characters to be echoed on the screen) and an overflow indicator is set.

```
procedure read_line (buffer);
  nmax:=buffer[0];
  i:=1;read_char(c);
  while i<nmax and c <> CR do
    if  c ∈{control characters}then
      process_special_char(c)
    else                          -- ordinary character
      display_char(c);            -- echo the character entered
      buffer[i]:=c
      i:=i+1                      -- next location
    endif;
    read_char(c)                  -- next character
  endwhile
  overflow:= c <> CR;             -- buffer overflow
  buffer[0]:=i−1;                 -- character counter


procedure process_special_char(c);
  case c of
    DEL_CHAR;
      if i>l then
        i:=i−1;
        display_char(BS)          -- backspace 1 char.
      endif;
    DEL_LINE:
      i:=1;
      display_char(CR);           -- return to start of line
    BREAK:
      display_line(message)       -- halt execution of command
      initialize_command;         -- return to CLI
    CR:
      i:=i+1;
      display_char(CR);           -- carriage return
      display_char(LF);           -- linefeed
  endcase
```

Note: Using interrupts to drive the terminal makes it possible to handle special characters within the interrupt handler (see comment in section 3.2.2.2). The procedure *read_line* is then reduced to collecting the contents of a buffer associated with the keyboard, when a line has been introduced (see exercise 3.7).

Finally, the function *assign* provides an entry in the table between logical and physical peripherals. It must check first that operating modes are compatible. To do so, it uses a table of physical peripherals, set up on system generation, which contains in particular, for each I/O device:

- The physical address of the controller to which it is linked
- Its operating mode (read, write)
- The transfer unit (character, block)

For disks, this table also contains records allowing complete parameterization of the operation of drivers and the file management system:

- Size of a sector and numbers of sector per block
- Number of tracks and number of sectors per track
- Number of tracks reserved for the system
- Maximum size of the directory

This table also contains the addresses reserved in the memory for information used by **FMS** and **PIO**:

- Read buffer for consulting the directory
- Disk occupation table
- Mapping table for logical and physical sectors

3.2.4 Command language interpreter

3.2.4.1 General approach

The general approach of the command language interpreter is that of an endless loop:

```
initialize_system
loop
   initialize_command
   read command
   analyse command
   if command correct then
      interpret command:
         prepare execution environment
         start execution
   else
      error report
   endif
endloop
```

The command is read into a memory buffer from the logical terminal using procedure *read_line* provided by the **FMS** interface. Analysis of the command determines its different fields. The first is the name of the command; the others are parameters transmitted to the program which handles interpretation. If the name is that of a system command whose program is resident in memory, interpretation can begin at once. Otherwise the file containing the command must first be loaded into memory. If it is not a standard system command, it may an executable program prepared by the user in a file. If it can find no such file, the interpreter displays an error message and awaits the following command.

The *initialize_system* sequence corresponds to initial loading, which may be triggered by a reset switch, or by a supervisor call reserved for internal system use in case of non-recoverable errors (see section 3.2.4.2).

The *initialize_command* sequence puts the system into a stable state: all modified buffers are flushed to disk, all files are closed; the interpreter displays a prompt, and awaits a command.

3.2.4.2 Execution environment

The interpreter's first task, before launching the execution of a command, is to prepare its environment, i.e. all the objects that would be used and the information making it possible to access them.

In the case of execution of a program submitted by the user, this environment includes (fig. 3.3):

1. Segments containing the program to be executed and data
2. The execution stack

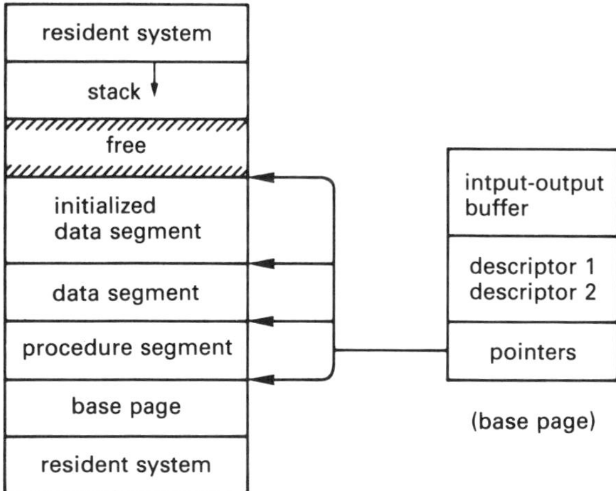

Fig. 3.3. Execution environment

3. A work zone of fixed size, called the base page which in particular contains:

- Pointers towards zones containing program segments and data and towards the free zone
- Descriptors of files specified in the commands
- A buffer intended for exchanges between files

We shall assume that only two segments (initialized and non-initialized) are associated with a program.

3.2.4.3 Loading a program

The loading operation has the effect of preparing the environment described above. It is executed immediately after the command has been analyzed. We shall describe the principle on which it is based in cases where the *<command name>* is that of a file containing an executable program. The header of such a file describes its contents: the size and position within the file of code and data segments, start of execution address, loading addresses of the segments for an absolute program, relocation information for a translatable program. Loading breaks down into the following steps:

1. Open file *<command name>* and read the file header to an internal buffer.
2. Determine whether the memory space available will allow loading.
3. Create the base page in the location reserved for it.
4. Load the program and data segments into the zones indicated in the header; if relocation has to take place, add the necessary displacement to the relocatable addresses; update information describing available memory.
5. Initialize the execution stack and push a return address to the command language interpreter onto the top of the stack.
6. Update pointers in the base page; store them in the 'command queue' buffer in this page.
7. Open the files (if there are any) whose names are parameters for the command and place their descriptors in the base page.
8. Execute a jump to the entry point of the program segment.

Note that these operations are executed in user mode and that a normal return from the executed program to the command language interpreter uses a procedure return. Such a return may also be implemented by a supervisor call, or follow on from trapping caused by an error.

To allow a user program to load another, the program loading procedure described above is available to users in the form of a supervisor call, alongside a procedure which returns the size and limits of the available memory space. Users can therefore write sub-systems operating as command language interpreters.

3.2.4.4 Handling execution errors

The detection of an error in the course of execution leads to assignment of an error code or a trap procedure, depending on whether or not the error occurred during execution of the primitive implemented by a supervisor call. Two cases have to be distinguished, depending on the seriousness of the error:

- Error in a user program, or in a non-critical part of a system program, such as the command language interpreter. Example: arithmetic overflow, or insufficient space to load a program.
- Error during a critical operation, i.e. one that may endanger data integrity. Example: non-recoverable error in a disk transfer operation.

The fundamental principle of error handling is to return, in all cases, to a stable system state, where execution can be restarted correctly, with as little loss of information as possible. Several stable states may be defined, and classified according to the extent to which they minimize information loss:

1. State proceding execution of the incorrect instruction
2. Interpreter awaiting command
3. Initial state of the system

A return to state 1) or 2) corresponds to handling of a trap in a user program. As described in section 2.3.1.3, trap handling can be left to a standard system procedure, or be carried out by a handler provided by the user. A return to state 2), sometimes called a 'warm start' is implemented by the *initialize_command* sequence; the work carried out by the last command is generally lost, but permanent data (files) are preserved.

A return to state 3), sometimes called a 'cold start', is a consequence of a serious error, leading to alteration to internal system tables or to disk files. It is implemented by the *initialize_system* sequence. Much information may be lost (the disk may be left in an incoherent state); there are, however, programs making it possible to reconstruct all or part of the contents of a disk after such an error, using redundant information (see section 7.5).

3.3 Sharing a machine: virtual machines

The example we have just been considering leaves out of account aspects associated with the sharing of a physical machine between several users. We shall now move on to a first consideration of the concepts involved, which will then be examined in more detail in the following chapters.

Consider a physical machine to be shared between several users. For each of these users we define a **virtual machine**, whose interface is identical to that of the shared machine. A virtual machine has no real existence, but its behavior is simulated, for its user, by means of an operating system program executing on the physical machine. The usual mode of sharing is **multiplexing,** which involves allocating the physical machine to users during successive time slices, according to the principle illustrated in section 2.3.2.3 for time-shared job management.

The identity between the interfaces of virtual machines and that of the physical machine can only be maintained to a first approximation. There are two comments to make here:

1. Sharing by multiplexing leads to degraded performance on virtual machines, and the degradation is all the greater the more virtual machines there are.

2. Making all the resources of the physical machine available to users poses difficult problems for protection in cases of resources which can affect system integrity, as is the case, for example, of privileged instructions. This is where the interface of a virtual machine is most commonly a subset of the interface of the shared physical machine, excluding privileged instructions and direct access to peripherals or to certain zones in physical memory. Certain systems, however, do implement complete virtual machines (see exercise 3.17).

Note that a virtual machine is a particular form of an abstract machine, characterized by the *sharing* of an underlying common machine between several virtual machines.

We shall illustrate this concept of a virtual machine by constructing a multi-user system offering the same interface as the single-user system developed in section 3.2. Each user therefore has access to a **CLI** machine identical to that specified. To allow communication between users, the file system is now shared.

Each user has a terminal assigned only to him or herself, and which presents the same interface as the logical terminal described in section 3.2. The logical printer, on the other hand, is shared and is managed together with the files.

The operating system provides each user with a virtual machine consisting of a virtual processor, restricted to user mode for the protection reasons indicated above, and a virtual memory.

We shall use the term **USR** for the virtual machine described above, and **KERNEL** and **MEM** for those system layers which implement the allocation of the processor and of physical memory respectively. The **KERNEL** layer (or machine) directly uses the physical machine. The peripheral management layer (the **PIO** machine) has the same interface as in section 3.2; it is now implemented using the nucleus. The allocation of secondary memory for storing files is left to a machine **SMM**, used by **FMS**. The general organization of the system is shown in fig. 3.4.

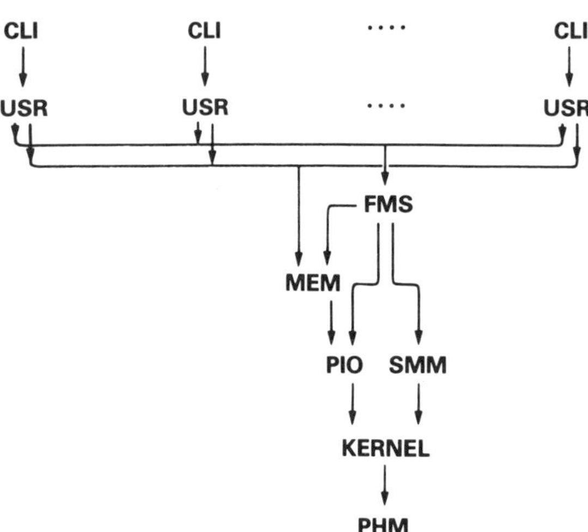

Fig. 3.4. Structure of a multiuser system

This version completes our decomposition of the system. The operation of the execution and communication mechanisms provided by the physical machine (interface **PHM**) was described in chapter 2. The detailed operations of the other components of the system will be studied in the following chapters. Chapter 4 considers the functions provided by a kernel for the management of parallel activities and the underlying principle for the implementation of a **PIO** machine using such a kernel. The specification and implementation of a particular kernel will be considered in chapter 5. The implementation of **FMS** and **SMM** is considered in chapter 7; the principles underlying the implementation of virtual memory (machine **MEM**) are examined in chapter 9, and illustrated with a particular implementation in chapter 10.

3.4 Bibliographic notes

The principle of hierarchical structuring of software systems was introduced, notably, in [Zurcher 68, Dijkstra 69]; [Saxena 75] is an illustration of the method for a model operating system. The application of the object concept to the structuring of operating systems was described in [Jones 78b]. The principles of modular decomposition are discussed in [Parnas 72b]; the design of interfaces is described in [Parnas 72a, Britton 81]. The languages including the concepts of module and interface, and adapted to programming systems are Mesa [Mitchell 79], Modula-2 [Wirth 82] and Ada [Ichbiah 79, Dod, 83, Le Verrand 85, Habermann 83].

Examples of operating systems with a layer structure are THE [Dijkstra 68, McKeag 76], Venus [Liskov 72], Thoth [Cheriton 79], Pilot [Redell 80, CP/M [Kildall 81], Tunis [Holt 83].

The implementation principles for a virtual machine are described in [Parmelee 72].

Exercises

Exercise 3.1

Write the function *conv(sect)* which returns the physical sector number corresponding to the logical sector number *sect*. Use the numerical values given above for the disk (26 sectors per track, with a gap of 6 between consecutive logical sectors). **Hint:** Use an array indexed by *sect*.

Exercise 3.2

Adapt the programs for primitive disk access functions (*read_sector* and *write-sector*):

a. To the case of *n* buffers of the size of a track ($n>1$)

b. To the case of *n* buffers of the size of a block (this simplifies handling of the *first write* mode)

Exercise 3.3

Write the trap handler for a *fatal error* in the disk driver.

Exercise 3.4

Assume that the disk controller has a command *READ_SECT_NUM(sect)* which returns, in *sect*, the physical number of the first sector to pass under the read-write head after receipt of the command. Using this command, rewrite procedure *transfer_track* so as to reduce the mean waiting time to the time taken for a sector to go past (instead of half a disk rotation).

Exercise 3.5

Using the record access functions *read_seq* and *write_seq*:

a. Specify and write the sequential access functions *read_char* and *write_char* which treat the file as though it were a sequential character file. The end of the character file (which is not necessarily the end of a record) is marked by a control character *END_OF_FILE*.

b. Specify and write the sequential access functions *read_line(f,dest)* and *print_line(f,source)* where a line is a series of characters ending with the *CR* character. The file ends with *END_OF_FILE*. A maximum size is specified for lines.

c. Using the procedure *print_line*, write a program which reads a file of lines, specified as in b), and prints it introducing a control character *FORM_FEED* every *n* lines.

Exercise 3.6

We shall enhance our file access interface with three functions allowing direct access to records:

move_ptr(f,pos)	: assigns value *pos* to pointer *ptr(f)*
read_direct(f,dest)	: reads the record named by *ptr(f)* into *dest*
write_direct(f,source)	: writes from *source* to record *ptr(f)*

The read and write functions above do not modify *ptr(f)*.

a. Specify handling for the case where *move_ptr* attempts to place *ptr(f)* beyond the end of the file.

b. Write the programs for the three direct access functions using the interface provided by **PIO**.

c. Program the sequential access functions using direct access functions.

Exercise 3.7

Re-write the *read_char* program using the input-output interrupt. The aim is:

a. To allow typing ahead, up to a specified maximum number of characters

b. To implement the editing functions specified in section 3.2.3.4

c. To react immediately to the *BREAK* character

Exercise 3.8

Modify the programs for the file access functions to take account of multi-section files. Define the extra fields that have to be included in the descriptor.

Exercise 3.9

Write the programs for functions *open(f)* and *close(f)*. Assume that file descriptors are stored sequentially in a reserved zone on the disk (the directory), whose origin and size are specified, with four descriptors per sector. Assume that a procedure *find_descriptor(f,track,sect,offset,p)* is available, which looks through the disk for the descriptor of the file named *f*. On return from the procedure, *track,sect* and *offset* specify a track number, a sector number and a position within this sector (from 0 to 3). If *p= true*, the descriptor is present in the location above; furthermore, a copy of it has been loaded into the fixed buffer *pdescr* in memory. If *p= false*, the descriptor has not been found; the triplet *(track,sect,offset)* specifies a location where it could be stored (if *offset* = *−1*, the directory is full).

Exercise 3.10

Write the program for procedure *find_descriptor* specified in the preceding exercise, using functions provided by interface *PIO*:

a. Using sequential search

b. Using a hashing function on the name, with handling of collisions by quadratic increments

Exercise 3.11

Write the program of functions *create(f)* and *delete(f)*. Assume the procedure *find_descriptor* specified in exercise 9 is available, as well as two procedures:

allocate_block (b) : request the allocation of a block; on return, *b*= its number, or *nil* if the disk is full;
free_block (b,c) : frees a block numbered *b*; on return, *c* = −1 if *b* was already free).

Exercise 3.12

Write outline programs in assembly language for procedures *allocate_block* and *free_block* as specified in the preceding exercise, assuming that a *TEST_BIT* instruction is available which operates on a bit string of the size of one memory word (n bits) and returns the number of the first 0 bit (or n if they are all set to 1).

Exercise 3.13

Write the program of procedure *intialize_command* (see section 3.2.4). Remember that this procedure must put the system into a state where it is waiting for the next command: empty buffers, files closed, free memory descriptor updated and prompt displayed on screen.

Exercise 3.14

The system described in 3.2 is now implemented on a computer whose disk is managed by a **DMA**. It is intended to modify the system in order to allow printing of the contents of a file simultaneously with processing of a command, consequently implementing a simple form of spooler. To do so, we add a command to the command language as follows:

print <filename>

which initiates printing; a new command can be immediately executed, while printing is taking place. The end of printing is indicated by a message to the terminal, which is only displayed after the end of execution of the current command, and before the prompt is displayed for the next command.

Modify the system to allow this kind of operation. Note that modifications cannot be allowed to a file that is being printed. **Hints:** Reserve a fixed buffer in memory for printing; use interrupts to drive the printer.

Exercise 3.15

This exercise is concerned with the implementation of a simple job sequencing monitor, analogous to those which existed in the fifties.

The computer includes a processor, a main memory, a terminal for the operator, a card reader and a printer. A job is made up of a deck of cards with the following structure:

- One card **JOB <job name> <max_time> <max_lines>*
- *The sequence of cards containing the source text of the program*
- *A *DATA* card

- The sequence of cards containing data
- An **END* card

Programs are written in only one language. They are compiled into absolute binary and immediately executed. The operating system, including the compiler, is entirely resident in memory.

Control cards are characterized by an asterisk (*) in the first column (cards contain up to 80 characters). The parameters appearing on a **JOB* card specify:

- The name used to identify the job, which will be printed at the head of the output listing
- A maximum use time for the central processing unit
- A maximum number of lines to print

A batch of jobs is made up of a series of jobs, terminated by an additional **END* card (the batch therefore ends with two consecutive **END* cards). The operator prepares the job batch and launches its execution. The operator communicates with the system through a terminal, using three commands:

START	: launch the execution of a batch of jobs, prepared and loaded into the card reader
STOP	: interrupt execution immediately (emergency stop)
TERM	: interrupt execution after the end of the current job

The system displays the contents of **JOB* cards on the operator's terminal as they are being read.

Peripheral driving is the responsibility of the processor. Each peripheral sends an interrupt at the end of transfer of a unit (a card, a line or a character depending on the device); a code identifies the transmitting peripheral. A clock is available, with an interrupt issued as it reaches zero. The processor has a supervisor mode and a user mode. The memory zone used by the system is protected; any attempt to access it by a program in user mode causes a trap.

The system provides users with three supervisor calls:

SVC *read*	: read a card (to read data)
SVC *write*	: print a line (to output results)
SVC *end*	: end of execution, return to monitor

These SVC instructions are not directly written by the user, but inserted by the compiler in the object program where necessary. The system provides elementary accounting functions: at the end of each job, it prints the total CPU time used, the number of cards read, and the number of lines printed.

Decompose this operating system in a hierarchical way, along the lines indicated in section 3.2. Write programs for the different parts (do not go into detail with the compiler, but define its interface to the rest of the system). Define handlers for interrupts, traps and supervisor calls (note that reading and writing programs provided to users are also accessible to the system, but by means of a procedure call). Ensure that an error in a user program cannot disrupt the system or threaten its integrity.

Exercise 3.16

Return once more to the batch processing system described in the previous exercise, with the same command language, and assume now that the computer is equipped with a disk driven by a channel, and that the system (which is still monoprogrammed) has input-output managed by a spooler. More precisely:

- Successive jobs making up a batch (programs and data) are read on a card reader and loaded into an input buffer on disk (as long as there is space in the buffer)
- A job is ready to be executed once all the cards making it up have been stored on disk. The program is loaded in its entirety in a contigous zone of memory (if insufficient space is available, execution is interrupted and the system moves on to the next job)
- Images of successive lines printed by the jobs are stored in an output buffer on disk

Assume that the input and output buffers on disk are of fixed size. Break the system down into its constituents and write the programs for the different parts (taking account of the remarks made in the previous exercise).

Exercise 3.17

The aim of this exercise is to examine a few problems posed by the implementation of virtual machines with *all* the capacities of the underlying physical machine, including privileged instructions and peripheral management. A virtual machine therefore differs from a physical machine only in its quantitative characteristics (memory size, disk size, number of peripherals and processor speed). We shall write **PHM** for the physical machine, and **VM** for a virtual machine; we shall use the term **supervisor** for the operating system operating on **PHM**, with the aim of implementing the **VMs**. We shall assume that a **VM** includes a terminal, a disk and a printer. There are as many physical terminals as there are virtual machines, but there is only one disk and printer associated with **PHM**.

a. Assume that the principle underlying the representation of a **VM** on **PHM** is in general terms as follows: the **VM** terminal is represented by the physical terminal; the main memory of **VM** is represented by a fixed zone of memory in **PHM**; the disk and printer of **VM** are represented, respectively, by two fixed zones of the disk of **PHM**. Printing a line on a **VM** is therefore represented by transfering the contents of a buffer from a central memory zone to the disk zone representing the printer (the contents of zones representing printers are listed later, on the physical printer, via the supervisor spool).

- Explain why it was decided to organize the system in this way, in particular as far as the printer is concerned.
- Explain why **VM** programs are necessarily executed in user mode for **PHM**.

b. To simulate the execution of privileged instructions on **VM**, we adopt the following approach: since **VM** is in user mode, the attempt to execute a privileged instruction leads to a trap. We then enter a supervisor procedure whose function is to interpret the privileged instruction executed on **VM**, using the representation on **PHM** of **VM** resources.

- Apart from the memory and disk zones, what information is necessary to the supervisor to represent the state of a **VM**? (think of the state of the processor, of couplers, of interrupts, etc.).
- Explain, with the data structures chosen, how the supervisor interprets an elementary input-output program on **VM** (print a line) with interrupt–driven I/O. Consider the same question for channel–driven.

Chapter 4
Management of parallel activities

One of the main characteristics of operating systems is the existence of simultaneous activities that are more or less closely coupled. This chapter considers the concepts and tools allowing such activities to be described and coordinated. Two introductory examples will allow us to identify the main problems.

4.1 Introductory examples

4.1.1 Buffered management of input-output

Let us return to the question of implementing output to a printer with management of buffers on disk, described in chapter 2. Our analysis of this mode of operations (fig. 4.1) highlights four activities which can take place simultaneously.([1])

1. The primitive *write_line* WL (central processing unit)
2. Writing to disk WD (channel 1)
3. Reading from disk RD (channel 2)
4. Physical printing PP (channel 3)

The term 'activity' is commonly understood as follows: a phenomenon that changes through time, whose progress can be monitored step by step (by a succession of printed lines, of bytes transferred or of increments of a program counter).

These four activities are to a considerable extent autonomous, as they execute on different processors with different programs. They are not, however, independent since they access common objects: two memory buffers, *mb1* and *mb2*, and one disk buffer, *db*. Two forms of interaction can be observed:

1. Possibility conditions for certain actions

Records cannot be removed from a buffer before they have been placed in it. Moreover, the capacity of buffers is limited; if a buffer is completely full of

([1]) In fact, reading and writing to disk are executed on a single channel, which can introduce restrictions on simultaneity of execution. Here we shall ignore these restrictions: this way of dealing with the question will be justified later.

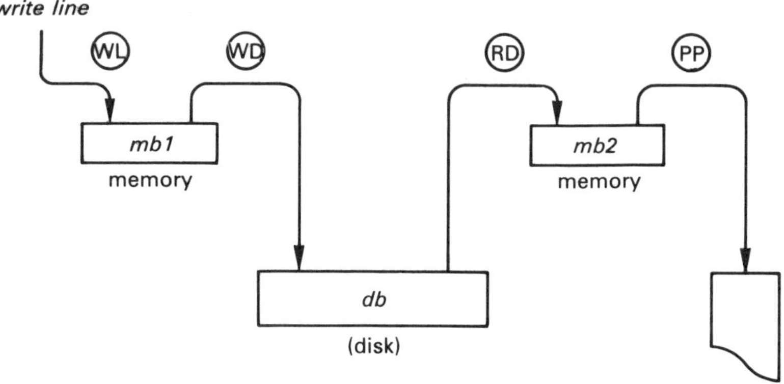

Fig. 4.1. Buffering a printer on disk

records that have not yet been removed, no further record can be placed in it without loss of information. Placing records in a buffer or removing them are therefore actions subject to the possibility conditions listed below.

Activity	Action	Condition
WL	write to *mb1*	*mb1* not full
WD	read from *mb1*	*mb1* not empty
WD	write to *db*	*db* not full
RD	read from *db*	*db* not empty
RD	write to *mb2*	*mb2* not full
PP	read from *mb2*	*mb2* not empty

The execution of these activities modifies the conditions: e.g. printing a line by PP makes the condition '*mb2* not full' true.

An activity that cannot execute an action because the associated condition is false must 'wait', i.e. the execution of the action is delayed until the condition becomes true. We discussed the implementation of this suspension and activation mechanism by means of interrupts in chapter 2.

2. Validity conditions for shared information

If, looking at the question in more detail, we consider access to buffers, we find that there is another form of interaction due to the possibility of simultaneous access by two activities to the same memory locations. For example, if WD reads the contents of a record in *mb1* that WL is modifying, the result of this read operation is likely to be inconsistent if no precautions are taken. Here again, the problem can be resolved by making one of the conflicting activities 'wait' until the other has completed access.

To summarize the conclusions of this first attempt at analysis we can say:

1. The work of a 'printer spooler' is implemented by four simultaneous activities, acting with a considerable degree of autonomy, which cooperate in its implementation.

2. Correct execution of the task imposes logical constraints on the progression of these activities. These constraints may lead to a delay in the execution of one activity while it waits for an event caused by another activity.

4.1.2. Industrial process control

Let us return to the example in chapter 1, where a computer is responsible for controlling a chemical reactor. Let us now consider two identical reactors, R_1 and R_2, operating in parallel. We shall examine two possible approaches to their control:

1. Assigning a separate computer to the control of each reactor
2. Using a single computer responsible for controlling the whole

The two solutions are shown in fig. 4.2.

Solution 1 is in no way different from the description given in chapter 1. As far as solution 2 is concerned, we have first of all to express the possibility condition for its implementation. Let P_1, P_2, D_1, D_2 be the procedure and data segments respectively necessary for controlling the two reactors R_1 and R_2. Assume that main memory can contain all these segments. Programs P_1 and P_2 are executed alternately by the processor. Using the same kind of reasoning as in chapter 1, we can see that the relation $2t<T$ must now be true (remember that T is the sampling period for measurements, while t is the

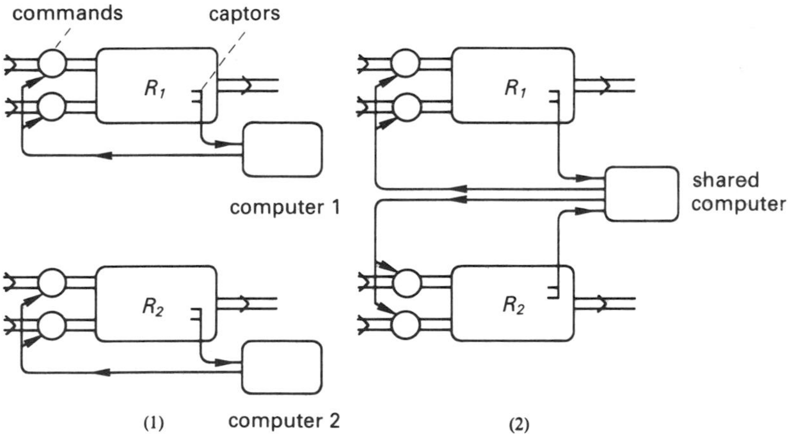

Fig. 4.2. Control of two chemical reactors

length of time taken for the processing associated with a set of measurements). This being the case, the two reactors in solutions 1 and 2 seem to behave identically, to an external observer. It should, however, be noted that solution 2 imposes a stricter constraint on computer performance (memory space and processor speed).

Let us now consider the ways in which solution 2 could be implemented.

1. Sharing the processor

Between two successive executions of P_1, the processor is used for P_2, and its internal state (contents of registers, of the processor status word and of the program counter) is modified. To allow resumption of P_1, this information must be saved at the end of each execution sequence and restored at the beginning of the next sequence. The same is obviously true for the execution of P_2.

2. Sharing the program

As the text of P_1 and P_2 is identical, a possible approach would be to hold only a single copy of it, called P, to save memory space. Let us examine the conditions necessary for this sharing of the program:

- The text of the program must not be modified by its execution; it is generally accepted that all programs must have this property, if only for the sake of keeping them comprehensible, even without taking account of possible sharing.
- When program P is executing for reactor R_i (i=1 or 2), it must access the data segment D_i; this selective data addressing must therefore be implemented by a mechanism which does not modify the text of the program.

Let us consider two possible solutions to this addressing problem:

a. Absolute naming. The program names its data using absolute memory addresses. In this case, the only solution is to transfer physically the data segments D_i into locations named by these addresses. This solution is very constraining since it requires copying of the two segments D_1 and D_2 each time the processor switches between the two activities.

b. Indirect naming. The program names its data by way of a base register which contains the implementation address of either segment D_1 or of segment D_2, as appropriate. Only the base register has to be reloaded each time switching takes place, just like the internal registers and the program counter.

Note that solution b., unlike solution a., lends itself perfectly to *simultaneous* execution of program P by several processors sharing a common memory and each with its own set of registers.

A program that can be used in a single copy in this way for several, possibly concurrent, independent activities which may be simultaneous, is called **reentrant**. This mode of utilization therefore implies:

- That the text of the program is *invariant* during its execution
- That data specific to each activity are *uniformly addressed* by the program

Moreover, if the various activities are sharing a single processor, its state information (in particular information concerning data addressing) must be saved each time switching takes place.

To summarize the conclusions of our study of this second example, we can say:

1. Two logically independent activities have been highlighted: control of reactors R_1 and R_2. These activities may be implemented on two separate machines in which case there are no links between them.

2. Economic constraints may lead to these activities sharing common resources: hardware and programs. For sharing to proceed correctly, constraints must be applied to the execution of activities (alternating use of the processor) and on the way shared objects are used (saving the execution context and making programs reentrant).

By way of conclusion on both examples, two concepts can be stressed:

- The existence of evolving **activities** which may execute concurrently
- The existence of **relations** between these activities: cooperation for the execution of common tasks, competition for the use of shared resources

These relations are imposed by how 'correct operations' are specified. They may be expressed in execution constraints leading to one activity being temporarily delayed.

The rest of this chapter sets out to provide a more formal basis to these concepts, introducing the ideas of processes and synchronization, and describing how they can be implemented in a computer system.

4.2 Concept of a sequential process

The concept of a process will first of all be introduced in a concrete way for the case of a computer with a single processor and memory addressable by the processor. It will then be extended to the abstract definition of a process independently of its physical medium, making it possible to introduce the concept of synchronization.

4.2.1 Single process: context

The concept of a process provides a model to represent the activity resulting from the execution of a program on a machine. The state of the machine is defined by the state of the processor (contents of the addressable registers and internal registers) and the state of the memory (contents of locations). This state is modified by the execution of instructions by the processor. Each execution of an instruction constitutes an **action**: an action has the effect of taking the machine, within a finite time, from an initial state to a final state. This effect is described in the specifications for the instructions.

We shall consider the execution of an instruction as indivisible, or **atomic**, i.e. we shall not define or observe the state of the machine during the execution of an instruction. The timescale used to monitor the state of the machine is therefore a parameter *t* which takes a series of discrete increasing values corresponding to the beginning and ends of instructions.([1]) These instants are called **observation points**, and the corresponding machine states are called **observable points**. Speaking loosely, we can use the same term for the observation points. These make it possible to associate a date (the current value of *t*) with a given state of the machine; such a dated state defines an **event**. Events make it possible to monitor modifications in the machine's state. The beginning and end of an action *a* are events whose dates are written *start(a)* and *end(a)*; we always have *start(a)*<*end(a)*.

The execution of a program can therefore be expressed as a sequence of actions $a_1, a_2, \ldots a_i, \ldots$, with $end(a_i < start(a_{i+1})$.([2]) Such a series forms what is called a **sequential process** (or simply **a process**).

A process may therefore be described by the succession of events $start(a_1)$, $end(a_1)$, $start(a_2)$,... This sequence of dated states of the machine is called the **time trace** (or history) of the process. We can also define a process as a sequence of activities, in the sense defined by section 2.1.

We use the term **context** of a process for all the information that the actions and the process may consult or modify. Returning to the model of sequential execution introduced in section 4.2.1, the context of a process resulting from the execution of a program includes:

1. The processor context (status word and registers)

2. A memory context, or workspace (procedure segments, data, execution stack)

3. A set of attributes associated with the process, and specifying different properties

a. *Name*. The name of a process, by which it is identified, is generally an

([1]) To be rigorous we ought to add *interruptible points* which certain long duration instructions include; this means considering the execution of such an instruction as a series of several actions.

([2]) To simplify our discussion, we shall consider the end of an action and the start of the next action as two distinct events, with different dates, even though the corresponding states are identical.

internal number assigned to it on creation and allowing access to the representation of its context (see section 4.5.2).

b. *Priority*. The priority of processes makes it possible to schedule them for processor allocation (see sections 5.2 and 5.3). If all processes have the same priority, allocation takes place in 'first come, first served' order.

c. *Rights*. The rights of a process specify the operations it is allowed to carry out, with the aim of protecting information (see section 6.1.4).

The time trace of a process is defined by the sequence of states of its context (processor and memory) observed after the execution of each instruction. In fact, by definition, the state of the rest of the machine is not modified by the execution of a process. This is the usual concept of a trace used for program debugging.

4.2.2 Relations between processes

We shall now consider the execution of a set of processes and their mutual interaction. The concepts introduced in section 4.2.1 can be extended as follows to a set of processes:

- The time trace of the processes as a whole is the sequence of events made up of the start and ends of actions resulting from the execution of their programs.
- The contexts of the different processes may have common parts. Two processes whose contexts are disjoint are said to be independent; they cannot interact. That part of the context of a process which belongs to no other context is called its private context.

Example: Consider two processes sharing a reentrant procedure. The executable segment which contains this procedure belongs to their common context. The data segment and the stack for each process belongs to their private contexts.

4.2.2.1 Concurrent processes

Consider two distinct programs *P* and *Q*, each with a procedure segment and a data segment in memory. We shall call the processes resulting from the execution of the two programs *p* and *q* respectively. The execution of the pair *(p,q)* can take place in various ways, characterized by the particular form of its time trace. These traces are shown in fig. 4.3.

The different patterns can be characterized as follows:

- Pattern 1: one process is executed in its entirety, and then the other, e.g. *p* first
- Pattern 2: a series of instructions from *p* is executed in alternation with a series of instructions from *q*, until both processes are complete
- Pattern 3: the execution of *p* and *q* is simultaneous; this requires two separate processors

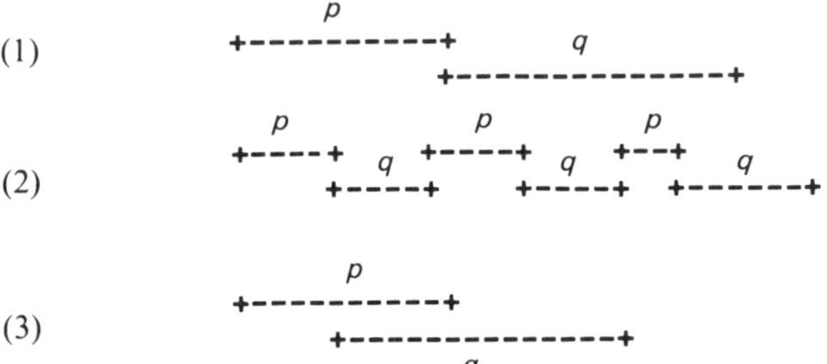

Fig. 4.3. Execution of a set of processes

To compare these modes of execution, a useful concept is that of an **observation level**. We can consider a series of actions in a process as a single action, i.e. observe the development of a process taking a larger execution unit than the instruction. For example, if we redefine the elementary action as the execution of a procedure, the trace of the process will include only states at each procedure call or return. The most detailed level of observation (that of machine instructions) is called the base level.

Let us start by adopting a level of observation where, by convention, the complete execution of each of the programs *P* and *Q* represents a single action. The definitions which follow are based on this level.

a. The type 1 pattern is that of **sequential** execution of *p* and *q*; it is characterized by the condition

end(q)<start(p) **or** *end(p)<start(q)*

b. The type 2 and type 3 patterns are **parallel** execution modes; they are characterized by

end(p)>start(q) **and** *end(q)>start(p)*

Let us now return to our base level. We can now distinguish between patterns 2 and 3. In fact, in pattern 2, because there is only one processor, only one action can be under way at a given moment, in contrast to pattern 3. We say there is **real parallelism** in pattern 3 and **pseudo-parallelism** in pattern 2. Real parallelism requires two separate processors.

Two important comments need to be made:

1. Distinctions between these different execution modes depend on the level of observation chosen. For example, at the base level, the distinction between patterns 1 and 2 disappears: they are both sequential.

Example: The users of a time-sharing operating system on a monoprocessor have the impression that their programs are executing in parallel, as their level of observation is that of commands made up of many instructions. On the other hand, at the base level, these instructions are atomic and are executed sequentially by the processor. The example of the chemical reactors in section 4.1.2 is similar.

2. The choice of base level itself depends on the level of detail of phenomena we intend to regard as elementary. If we want to study the execution of 'pipelined' instructions on a microprogrammed processor, we would choose as base level that of micro-instructions, and we would include the microprogram memory and internal registers as part of the context considered.

Let us now examine the concrete implementation, at base level, of an execution mode such as 2. At each reallocation of the processor, the context of the process under execution must be saved, allowing later resumption of its execution. If there is sufficient memory to contain all segments permanently, we only need to save the processor context. If, at any given time, main memory can only contain the procedure and data segments of a single process, these segments must also be saved to disk. This explains the operational definition, that is often used, of the context of a process as all the information that has to be saved to allow later resumption of the process if its execution is interrupted. We shall meet this definition of a context again when we consider the implementation of a process management kernel in chapter 5.

4.2.2.2 Competition between processes; virtual resources

The situation described in patterns 1 and 2 is not based on any logical link between p and q, but only on the fact that there is just one processor. It may be characterized as follows: consider a set of processes whose contexts have an object in common, such that at any given instant only one process may use that object. We then say that this object is a **critical resource** for the processes, or that the processes operate under **mutual exclusion**, or that they are in **competition**, for the use of the resource. In the situation described, the processor is a critical resource for processes p and q.

It is clear that mutual exclusion to a resource leads to 'serialization' of the execution of competing processes, for any actions that require this resource (in the present case, all the actions). Patterns 1 and 2 differ only in the level of detail at which this serialization takes place.

Correct operation of a set of processes contributing to a common task also implies logical relations of **cooperation** between them, as illustrated in section 4.1.1. It is useful to be able to separate cooperation from competition for physical resources, in order to simplify our understanding and implementation of the two types of relation. To do so, we use the concept of a **virtual resource** introduced in section 3.3 with respect to machines: each critical physical resource is associated with as many imaginary (or virtual) copies of the resource as there are processes in competition for its use. We then have to deal with two clearly separate problems:

1. Implementing the cooperative relations between processes each of which (conceptually) has the physical resources which it needs and whose parallelism in execution is not restrained by competition for resources.

2. Dealing with the problem of competition for physical resources by appropriate serialization of the execution of the processes in question. We also use the concept of **allocation** of physical resources.

The introduction of virtual resources has a very important consequence that we can illustrate using the example of the processes *p* and *q* defined in section 4.2.2.1. Let us provide each of these processes with a virtual processor. Everything then takes place, conceptually, as though the processes were executing in parallel, following a pattern that can be called logical or virtual, analogous to pattern 3 in fig. 4.3. However, we have to note that this logical pattern is merely a condensed notation for all the possible real patterns which are of necessity or form 1 or 2 as there is only one processor. All that is conserved when we move from a real pattern to a virtual pattern, for a given process, is the order of events (starts and ends of actions) and not the absolute value of the interval of time separating them. In the absence of other information, there is nothing to be said *a priori* on the order of events associated with two different processes: it is precisely the object of synchronization to introduce such constraints if they are required for cooperation. The timescale used to monitor events in the logical pattern is called **logical time**; its relations with real time are illustrated in fig. 4.4.

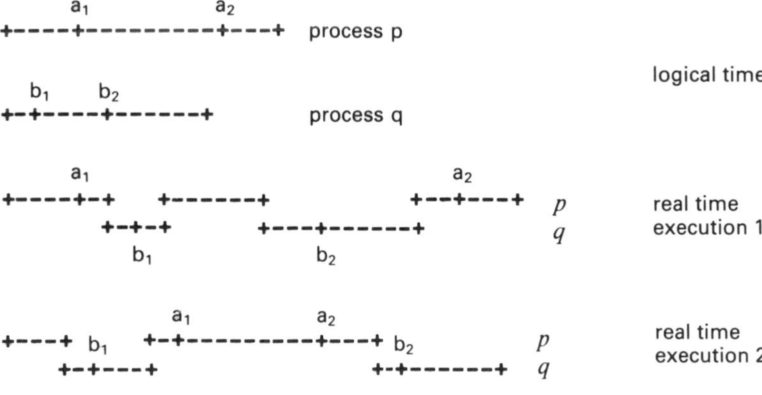

In all cases a_1 precedes a_2, b_1 precedes b_2

Fig. 4.4. Logical time and real time

In what follows, we shall only consider logical cooperative relations between processes provided with all the virtual resources they need. The time trace of these processes is therefore described in logical time. A consequence is that *we must avoid making any a priori assumptions concerning the relative speeds* of the processes in question: this is a consequence of the considerable simplification introduced by the concept of a virtual resource, allowing us to ignore allocation mechanisms. There is only one exception to this rule: this will be the study of so-called **real-time** synchronization, where physical time is involved as a measure of duration and not simply as a means of relative ordering of events.

The problem of concretizing virtual resources, i.e. of allocating physical resources, will be considered separately, in chapters 5 and 8 for processor allocation, and in chapters 9 and 10 for memory allocation.

4.2.2.3 Mutual exclusion

The introduction of virtual resources allows us to leave it to the allocation mechanisms to sort out the problem of mutual exclusion for access to corresponding physical resources. This problem may also be posed in another form as the following example shows.

Example: Two processes *p* and *q* both have to update a common variable *n* (e.g. *n* is the state of a bank account to which both *p* and *q* are depositing a sum). The corresponding actions may be written, in the programs for *p* and *q:*

```
process p              process q
Ap:n:=n+np             Aq:n:=n+nq
```

Let us break these actions down into instructions, writing *Rq* and *Rp* for registers local to *p* and *q* respectively:

```
process p              process q
(1) load Rp,n          (1') load Rq,n
(2) add Rp,np          (2') add Rq,nq
(3) sto Rp,n           (3') sto Rq,n
```

If these actions are executed in the order 1,1′2,2′,3,3′, their overall effect is that of executing *n:=n+nq* and not *n:=n+np+nq:* one of the updating procedures has been lost and the final value of *n* is incoherent. To avoid this incoherence, actions *Ap* and *Aq* must be executed under mutual exclusion; we also say that they constitute **critical sections** for *p* and *q*. We must have the condition

end(Ap)<start(Aq) **or** *end(Aq)<start(Ap)*

This serialization condition, which has the effect of making *Ap* and *Aq* atomic, is therefore identical to the condition we discussed in section 4.2.2.2 for access to a critical physical resource.

Mutual exclusion extends the indivisibility property of actions at base level to sequences of actions. The possibility of executing indivisible actions is at the base of mechanisms that implement synchronization. This is why we shall assume from the outset, in our study of these mechanisms, that we are able to implement mutual exclusion. We show in section 5.1 how this is actually done.

4.3 Synchronization between processes

4.3.1 Expression and implementation of precedence constraints

Two examples will help us formulate the logical constraints imposed by cooperation.

Example 1: Process *p* transmits information to process *q* by writing to a segment *a* consulted by *q* (we assume that transmission takes place only once). We must have:

end(write(a))<start(read(a))

This relation expresses the constraint that reading of *a* by *q* may not begin before the end of writing of *a* by *p*.

Example 2: Rendez-vous. Consider *N* processes $p_1 \ldots p_N$. We define, in the program for each process, a so-called rendezvous point which the process may not go past until *all* the other processes have reached their own rendezvous point.

If the program for p_i takes the form:

<start$_i$>;
<rendezvous>
<rest_of$_i$>

then the synchronization constraints may be expressed as follows:

$$\forall\ ij \in [1..N]:\ end(start_j) < start(rest\_of_i)$$

We can therefore express synchronization constraints in the following two equivalent forms:

1. We can impose an order of precedence, in logical time, on certain points in the time trace of the processes

2. We can impose a condition that has to be met before certain processes can be allowed past particular points in their time trace.

Such special points are called **synchronization points**.

Expression 2) shows that the synchronization constraints may be satisfied by making the process 'wait' to execute an action, until a certain condition is satisfied. This concept of waiting cannot be expressed using the tools introduced so far; this is why we introduce a new state for a process, in which the process is said to be **waiting** or **blocked**, as opposed to the states implicitly considered so far, where the process is said to be **active**. A process entering the suspended state, from an observable point *t*, stops advancing at that point and ceases executing its actions. When the process reenters the active state, it resumes execution, and its private context returns to the state it had at point *t* (the non-private part of its context may have been modified by the execution of other processes). We use the term **blocking** for the transition active → blocked and **activation** or **wake-up** for the reverse transition. The way in which blocking and activation are implemented will be discussed in section 4.3.4.

Note: We have already met the concept of a blocked state when we dealt with the allocation of a processor in cases of alternate execution (pattern 2). At a given instant, the process which is not executing on the processor is in fact in a blocked state, as defined above. Generally accepted terminology sometimes distinguishes between blocking due to competition for physical resources (or 'technological' blocking) and blocking resulting from logical synchronization constraints (or 'intrinsic' blocking). In practice, and for reasons of economy, the two concepts are often identified. An intrinsically blocked process cannot use the physical resources available to it when it was active; these resources can therefore be taken from it in favor of another process that is active. Identification of the concepts does not, however, invalidate our distinction between logical synchronization and resource allocation. It is expressed in the concrete way in which mechanisms for logical synchronization are implemented (see section 5.2).

We shall now use the concept of blocking to specify synchronization between processes. This specification takes place in two stages:

1. Defining the synchronization points for each process
2. Association of a *passing condition* with each synchronization point, expressed in terms of the system's state variables

Let us illustrate this form of specification for the two preceding examples. We shall write *sp* for a synchronization point, and *permit (sp)* for the associated passing condition. If the condition is true, the process concerned is authorized to execute the instruction labelled *sp*.

Example 1: **var** *f:boolean* **init** *false*

```
process p                    process q
write(a);                    <start_q>;
f:=true;                     sp:read(a)
<rest_of_p>
                          permit(sp):f=true
```

We have introduced a state variable f to express the condition: 'the process p has completed action *write(a)*'.

Example 2: **var** *n: integer* **init** *0;*

```
process p_i
<start_i>;
n:=n+1
sp_i:<rest_of_i>

permit(sp_i):n=N (i=1,...N)
```

The state variable n here is the number of processes that have arrived at the rendezvous point.

4.3.2 Problems of implementing synchronization

We shall now attempt to implement synchronization specified by passing conditions. To do so, we have to define a suspension mechanism. For this purpose we introduce the concept of a stored event. A stored event e is a variable which can take two values: *happened* and *not_happened*; a stored event initially takes the value *not_happened*. Two operations are possible on stored events; both are indivisible

```
e:= <value>        -- assignment of an immediate value
wait(e)
```

The operation *wait(e)*, executed by process *p*, means the following:

```
if e=not-happened then
  state(p): = blocked        -- p is made to wait for e
endif
```

When a stored event takes the value *happened*, all processes waiting for e, if there are any, move to the active state.

Note: This concept of a stored event is analogous to that used in language PL/1.

Let us now attempt to implement synchronization in our two examples using this mechanism.

Example 1: **var** *e:stored_event;*

```
process p                  process q

write(a);                  <start_q>;
e←happened                 wait(e);
<rest_of_p>                read(a)
```

An analysis of this system, (which includes no state variable other than the stored variable *e*) can be carried out by enumerating all the possible time traces. It shows that synchronization takes place correctly since operations on stored events are indivisible.

Example 2:
```
var e: stored_event
    n: integer init 0;
    process p_i
    <start_i>;
    (A) n:=n+1;
    (B) if n<N then
          wait(e)
        else
            e:=happened
        endif;
        <rest_of_i>
```

More detailed analysis, similar to what was done for the example in section 4.2.2.3, shows that this program is incorrect. Actions (A) and (B) may be broken down as follows, writing R_i for a register local to process p_i:

```
(1) load  Ri,n
(2) ai     Ri,1          -- immediate addition
(3) ci     Ri,N          -- immediate comparison
(4) br (≥)label          -- branch if Ri≥N
   <wait(e)>
   ...
label:...
```

Consider a situation where all the processes are waiting at their rendezvous point, apart from two of them, p_j and p_k. If p_j and p_k execute with a time trace (1*j*, 1*k*, 2*j*,...), then each will find the final value of *n* equal to $N-1$ and will be blocked. All the processes will therefore be indefinitely blocked.

The analysis above shows that synchronization conditions cannot be correctly expressed using waiting operations alone. The consultation or modification of state variables involved in these conditions must also take place under *mutual exclusion*. It is this observation that leads us to introduce a synchronization mechanism which automatically provides for this kind of operations.

4.3.3 A synchronization mechanism: monitors

4.3.3.1 Definition

A **monitor** is made up of a set of state variables and a set of procedures using those variables. Certain of these procedures, called external procedures, are accessible to users of the monitor; the names of these procedures are called entry points to the monitor. Processes using the monitor for synchronization do not have direct access to state variables. They can only use the monitor by calling its external procedures; these contain operations making it possible to block or activate processes in a way that is compatible with the specification of the problem. The blocking and activation conditions are expressed as functions of state variables, and the execution mechanism in the monitor ensures that these variables are handled under mutual exclusion. Finally, a monitor contains an initialization program, executed once and only once when the monitor is created.

Blocking and activation of processes are expressed, in the monitor procedures, by means of conditions. A **condition** is declared as a variable, but has no *value*: a condition *c* can only be handled by three operations, or primitives, whose effects we can describe as follows (writing *p* for the process executing them).

```
c.wait   : suspends process p, and makes it wait for c
c.empty1: a function with a boolean result (true if no process is
          waiting for c, false otherwise)
c.signal: if ⌉c.empty then
          <activate one of the processes waiting for c>
          endif
```

The processes waiting for condtion *c* are held in a queue associated with *c*. A condition can be regarded as providing a means of naming such a queue of processes.

A process activated by *c.signal* resumes execution at the instruction immediately following the *c.wait* primitive which blocked it. The need to ensure mutual exclusion for access to state variables imposes a further constraint on the activation mechanism: when a process *p* activates a process *q* by a *signal* operation, *p* and *q* may not be simultaneously active. It is therefore a requirement that *p* be blocked, until *q* itself blocks or leaves the monitor. To avoid indefinite blocking of *p*, it is a requirement that transfer of control from *p* to *q* is uninterruptible, and it is guaranteed that a process temporarily blocked by the execution of *c.signal* is activated before a new process may execute a monitor procedure.

Section 4.4.6 gives a critical analysis of this mechanism and proposes other means of implementing primitive *signal*.

Note: The problem of mutual exclusion associated with the primitive *signal* does not arise if the primitive is the *last* operation executed in a monitor procedure. This case frequently appears in practice; certain implementations and monitors (e.g. Concurrent Pascal) even make it an obligatory rule.

4.3.3.2 *Examples of use*

The application of monitors and the notation used to represent them are illustrated by the two examples we have already met. More complex examples are given in section 4.4.

Example 1:

```
sync: monitor
        var done:boolean;
            finished:condition;
      procedure end_write;
        begin
        done:=true;
        finished.signal
        end

      procedure start_read;
        if ]done then
          finished.wait
        endif

      begin          -- initialization
        done:=false
        end
      end sync
```

The monitor is used as follows:

```
process p              process q

write(a)               <startq>
sync.end_write         sync.start_read
<rest_of_p>            read(a)
```

Example 2: rendez-vous: **monitor;**

```
var n         :integer;
  all_there:condition;

procedure arrive;
  begin
  n:=n+1;
  if n<N then
    all_there.wait            -- not all arrived
  endif;
  all_there.signal            -- the last one is there
  end;

  begin                       -- initialization
  n:=0
  end
end rendez_vous
```

The program for process p_i can be written:

```
process p_i

  <start_i>
  rendez_vous.arrive;
  <rest_of_i>
```

It is important to see how synchronization operates: the process arriving last at the rendez-vous executes *all_there.signal* and activates one and only one of the waiting processes. The latter, in turn, executes *all_there.signal* activation the next, and so on. This hardly intuitive way of operating expresses an inherent difficult in the semantics of the primitive *signal* (see section 4.4.6).

4.4 Implementation of synchronization

4.4.1 Typical problems

Experience shows that logical synchronization problems met in practice may, in most cases, be reduced to combinations of a small number of elementary situations for which a general solution is known. Sections 4.4.2 to 4.4.5 will consider these typical problems, using monitors as a fundamental tool. The typical problems considered are the following:

- Access by a set of processes to a common shared resource
- Communication between processes; application to the client-server relation
- Management of peripherals and buffered input-output
- Real-time synchronization

Criticisms of the monitor mechanism, and a few proposed variants, will be examined in section 4.4.6.

4.4.2 Management of a shared resource

Let us consider a resource (hardware or software) shared between several processes. The use of this resource is subject to a number of rules intended to preserve specified properties, or **integrity constraints**. These constraints are specific to each resource: we have already met some examples. One way of guaranteeing that the rules for using a resource are respected is to adopt the following approach:

- The way of using the resource includes mandatory application of access procedures associated with the resource; any attempt to use it in a way which is not compatible with this approach is automatically detected
- Access procedures are held in a monitor (or several monitors), programmed so as to respect integrity constraints

The simplest case is that of a resource whose only integrity constraint is that it should be used under mutual exclusion. Simply bringing together its access procedures in a single monitor will ensure that this constraint is respected.

We shall now consider two other commonly encountered examples.

4.4.2.1 Allocation of pooled resources

Consider a resource existing in a fixed number N of copies, or units. A process can, on request, acquire a number n of these units, use them, and then free them. Between acquisition and liberation, a unit is said to be **allocated** to the process using it. All units are equivalent from the point of view of the user processes; such resources are said to be pooled. Examples of pooled resources are buffers in main memory or on disk, magnetic tape units, etc.

We shall adopt the following rules:

- A unit can only be allocated to one process at a time
- A unit can only be allocated to a requesting process if it is free (allocated to no process)
- A freeing operation always applies to the last resources acquired by the process executing it

- An allocation request leads to blocking if it fails (insufficient number of free units)

Note that other rules might be imagined (see chapter 8): non-blocking allocation requisition, fractional liberation, etc.

We define two procedures, *request* and *free*, held in one monitor. The use of a resource is governed as follows.

```
ps:resource.request(n);   -- request for n units
                          -- wait in case of failure
<use the units acquired>
resource.free(n);         -- freeing of units acquired
```

The synchronization condition can be written as follows for any process:

$$permit(ps):n \leqslant nfree$$

where *nfree* is the current number of free units.

In writing these programs, we shall leave aside problems of identification and naming of a particular unit, and consider the expression of synchronization alone.

A first form of the monitor *resource* can be obtained by translating the synchronization condition directly:

```
resource: monitor
  var nfree:integer;
      available:condition;

procedure request(n);
  begin
  while n<nfree do
    available.wait;                    --chain activation
    available.signal
  endwhile;
  nfree:=nfree-n
  end

procedure free(n)
  begin
  nfree:=nfree+n;
  available.signal
  end;

  begin                                --initialization
  nfree:=N
  end
end resource
```

We have made no assumptions concerning the order in which processes are queued for condition *available*. Consequently, we have to provide for *all* processes being activated whenever a resource is freed, in order to serve all those that may be. This solution is cumbersome and may be expensive if there are many processes. It is then preferable for the request queue management to be programmed explicitly, which means we have to provide a distinct condition per process.

To write the programs, we shall assume that a discrete type *process* has been defined; the variables of this type name processes.

```
resource: monitor;
  type element: struct
                  size:integer;
                  proc:process
                  end;
  var nfree : integer;
      available : array [process] of condition;

  <declaration of queue q and its access
procedures: add, remove and first>

procedure request(n);
  var e:element;
  begin
  if n>nfree then
    e.size:=n;
    e.proc:=p;                  -- p is the calling process
    add(e,q);                   -- in order of increasing size
    available[p].wait
  endif;
  nfree:=nfree-n
  end;

procedure free(n)
  var e:element;
  begin
  nfree:=nfree+n;
  while first(q).size≤nfree do
    remove(e,q);                -- element removed = first(q)
    available[e.proc].signal -- e.proc = activated process
  endwhile;
  end;

  begin                         -- initialization
  nfree:=N;
  q:= <empty>
  end
end resource
```

This solution is far more flexible and general than the first, as it makes a clearer separation between the expression of synchronization (resulting from the structure of the monitor) and the allocation policy (defined by the queue management procedures: *add* and *remove*).

4.4.2.2 *The readers and writers model*

Let us now consider a file handled by two different classes of processes: readers, which consult the file without modifying its contents, and writers which can modify its contents. The number of readers using file access procedures at any moment is *nread* and the number of writers is *nwrite*. Maintaining the consistency of the files leads to imposing the following constraints:

(nwrite=0) **and** *(nread⩾0)* -- file being read
or *(nwrite=1)* **and** *(nread=0)* -- file being written

Let *file* be a monitor responsible for implementing these constraints. We shall impose the following form of access to the file.

reader process	writer process
file.start_read;	*file.start_write;*
<access to read>	*<access to write>*
file.end_read;	*file.end_write;*

The procedures *start_read,...end_write* have to implement the constraints expressed above. We shall start by translating these constraints in terms of passing conditions; to do so, we have to define priority rules between readers and writers.

By way of example, let us assume that readers are given priority (no write operation is allowed if readers are waiting). We define the following state variables:

wrt = write operation underway (boolean)
nr = number of readers waiting or active

The passing conditions can then be expressed as follows:

permit(read):⌉*wrt*	(no write operation underway)
permit(write):⌉*wrt* **and** *nr=0*	(no read or write operation under way, no readers waiting)

The monitor below directly expresses these conditions

file: **monitor;**

```
var wrt            :boolean;
    nr             :integer;
    c_wrt,c_read: condition;

procedure start_read;
  begin
  nr:=nr+1;
  if wrt then
    c_read.wait;
    c_read.signal                  -- chain activation of readers
  endif
  end

procedure end_read;
  begin
  nr:=nr-1;
  if nr=0 then                     -- the last reader has finished
    c_wrt.signal
  endif
  end;

procedure start_write;
  begin
  if wrt or nr>0 then              -- writing or reading under way
    c_wrt.wait
  endif;
  wrt:=true
  end;

procedure end_write;
  begin
  wrt:=false;
  if nr>0 then                     -- priority to waiting readers
    c_read.signal
  else
    c_wrt.signal
  endif
  end;

  begin                            -- initialization
  wrt:=false;
  nr:=0
  end
end file
```

Other priority rules may be defined and programmed (see exercises).

4.4.3 Interprocess communication

Communication between processes may be implemented by access to a set of common variables. This means of communication is unstructured and may be inefficient as it requires mutual exclusion to these variables. It is therefore only used in special cases, such as inside a synchronization kernel (see section 5.3), where overall mutual exclusion is restricted to brief and well protected sequences. In general cases, other communication tools are used. We shall start by considering the basic approach to the communication of messages between processes, the producer and consumer model, whose implementation we shall describe using monitors, in section 4.4.3.1. Another approach, described in section 4.4.3.2, is to consider communication operations as primitive synchronization mechanisms. Finally, in section 4.4.3.3 we shall present a common application of communication: the client-server model.

4.4.3.1 The producer and consumer model

A common approach to communication is that where one process (the producer) sends messages to another process (the consumer) using a fixed-size buffer in common memory. Messages are of fixed size, and the buffer may contain N messages.

Communication is specified as follows:

- A given message can be collected only once, after it has been deposited
- Messages must not be lost; if the buffer contains N uncollected messages, no further message can be deposited
- An 'impossible' operation (deposit of a message in a full buffer or collection of a message from an empty buffer) blocks the process which attempts to execute it

The passing conditions may be expressed as follows, writing N for the number of messages contained in the buffer and not yet collected:

```
permit(deposit):n<N          -- buffer not full
permit(collection):n<0       -- buffer not empty
```

Respect of these constraints is ensured by a monitor *buffer* used as follows:

```
producer process                              consumer process
  ...                                           ...
produce(transmitted_message);                 buffer.collect(received_message);
buffer.deposit(transmitted_messsage);         consume(received_message);
  ...                                           ...
```

The monitor *buffer* can be written as follows, if we directly transcribe the passing conditions:

```
buffer: monitor;
var n:0..N;
    not_full,not_empty:condition;

  <declaration of procedures add and remove>

procedure deposit(m:message);
  begin
  if n=N then
    not_full.wait
  endif;
  n:=n+1;
  add(m);
  not_empty.signal
  end;

procedure collect(var m:message)
  begin
  if n=0 then
    not_empty.wait
  endif;
  remove(m);
  n:=n-1;
  not_full.signal
  end;

  begin                                  -- initialization
  n:=0
  end
end buffer
```

Procedures *add* and *remove* define the policy adopted for managing the buffer and for the internal representation of messages. A frequent approach represents messages as the successive elements of an array managed as a circular queue. Messages are therefore collected in the same order as they are deposited. The buffer management procedures may be written:

```
type message:<description of the message format>;
  ptr:0..N-1;

var queue:array [ptr] of message;
  head,tail:ptr;

procedure add(m:message);
  begin
  queue[tail]:=m;
  tail:=tail+1 mod N
  end;

procedure remove (var m:message);
  begin
  m:=queue[head];
  head:=head+1 mod N
  end;

<complete initialization with the operations:
  head:=0; tail:=0;>
```

This approach can be extended to multiple producers and consumers. The monitor procedures ensure that producers and consumers respectively access messages under mutual exclusion. Nevertheless, in the case of multiple consumers, this approach does not allow us to send a message to a particular consumer: it is only possible to guarantee that a message will be collected by one and only one consumer, without being able to specify which.

4.4.3.2 Communication primitives

Exchanging messages between processes, as well as being a means of transmitting information, may also be used to order events in distinct processes, since the transmission of a message always precedes its reception. We can therefore consider the possibility of defining message exchange procedures as though they were primitive mechanisms, and use them for process synchronization.

The basic primitives in message communication are:

send (message,destination)
receive(message,source)

The specification of these primitives must define:

- The nature and form of messages exchanged
- The naming of transmitting and receiving processes
- The method of synchronization used for these processes
- Error handling

We shall consider these four aspects in turn.

1. Nature of messages

Depending on the level of expression at which the communication mechanism has been defined, messages may be specified by a type, analogous to that of a language object, or by their physical size. That size may be fixed or variable. It is often preferable to use fixed size messages, which are easier to implement, and to transmit variable size messages by reference, passing the physical address or the identifier of the information to transmit.

2. Addressing modes

Processes which exchange messages may specify each other using their own names (direct naming) or the name of an intermediate object or **mailbox** (indirect naming). These names are used as *source* and *destination* parameters. The second approach makes it easier to modify dynamically both the interconnections between processes and the actual composition of the set of communicating processes.

In the case of direct naming, the *source* parameter of primitive *receive* may be interpreted in two ways:

- Either as a parameter: the receiver specifies explicitly that it is awaiting a message from a particular source (selective reception)
- Or as a result: the receiver receives a message addressed to it and also the identity of the transmitter

In the case of indirect naming, the association of processes with the mailbox may be static or dynamic. In the second case, two primitives, *connect* and *disconnect* respectively, allow the association of a process with a mailbox (as receiver) to be made, and to be broken. In certain systems, only one receiver may be associated with a particular mailbox; mailboxes with this restriction are often called **ports**. A process, on the other hand, may be associated with several different ports. If the association between a receiving process and a port is static, a port name will specify the receiving process without ambiguity, as in direct naming.

3. Synchronization modes

Various synchronization modes may be specified for communication primitives. The reception operation generally suspends the receiver if there is no message. Certain systems provide a primitive which tests whether a mailbox is empty, to avoid blocking. As far as transmission is concerned, two synchronization modes are used:

- The producer-consumer approach, where the mailbox is implemented by a buffer. Transmission is non-blocking, except if the buffer is full. The use of variable size buffers, with dynamic allocation of slots, reduces the probability of a transmitter being blocked.
- The **rendezvous** approach, where the transmitter is blocked until the receiver collects its message. This approach may be regarded as a limiting case of the previous one, where the buffer size is 0.

Finally, if a process is associated for reception with several ports, it is possible to define a synchronization mode, called **multiple wait**, where the arrival of a message at any of the ports activates the receiver.

4. Error handling

The aim of error handling is to avoid indefinite blocking of processes, which may occur in various circumstances:

- Transmission of a message to a destination (process or port) which does not exist. In this case, the primitive will not block the sender; the error is handled by returning an error message or by a trap.
- Deletion of a process from which others are expecting a message or a reply: the waiting processes are activated and receive an error message.

The situation above is not always detectable. Consequently, a common technique is to set an upper limit to the waiting time for a message, and to activate the waiting process at the end of that time (see section 4.4.5).

We shall illustrate the implementation of communication mechanisms using a few representative examples.

Example 1: The Thoth system [Cheriton 79]. Communication in the Thoth system uses direct naming and synchronization by rendezvous. Messages are of fixed size. Four primitives are used:

```
id:=send(message,iddest)
```

which sends *message* to process *iddest*; the transmitter is suspended until it receives a reply, which is sent back in *message*. The primitive returns the identity of the process which sent back the reply (or *nil* if the destination process does not exist).

id:=receive(message,idorig)

This receives a message; the originating process may or may not be specified. The value returned is the identity of the transmitter.

reply(message,iddest)

Sends back a reply to the specified destination (which must wait for it); it does not cause suspension; no effect if no process is waiting for the reply.

forward(message,idorig,iddest)

This operation, which will not cause suspension, is used by a process after receiving a message sent by *idorig*, to forward the message (which may be modified) to *iddest,* which must then reply to *idorig*.

Example 2: The Unix system [Ritchie 74]. Communication between processes in the Unix system uses buffers called 'pipes' managed on the producer-consumer model. The messages transmitted are characters. A pipe links up a transmitter and a receiver, and a connection is established dynamically. This mechanism is described in greater detail in section 6.2.3.1.

Example 3: The rendezvous mechanism in Ada [Ichbiah 79, DoD 83]. The Ada language allows for the definition of processes (called tasks). The syntactic form for communication between tasks is a procedure call, but the transmission of parameters and results operates along the lines of the transmission of messages with rendez-vous. Receipt may be conditional (a call is only accepted if a specific condition is satisfied) and there may be multiple waiting (nothing is specified about how to select calls to accept if several calls are eligible, and the selection must therefore be regarded as random).

Let us illustrate this mechanism by means of the body of a cyclical task which manages a buffer on the producer-consumer model (*n* is a local variable counting the number of messages, *N* is the size of the buffer).

```
select
  when n<N=> accept deposit(in:message);
    buffer[tail]:=message;
    tail:=tail+1 mod N;
    n:=n+1
or
  when n>0=> accept remove(out:message);
    message:=buffer[head];
    head:=head+1 mod N;
    n:=n-1
end select
```

If both conditions (or guards) are true, the task may accept and handle calls from both procedures *deposit* and *remove*, indifferently, and in an unspecified order. Note that the buffer is associated with an active entity (the task that manages it) and not with a passive entity like a monitor.

4.4.3.3 Application: client-server relations

A common application of communication between processes is provided by the client-server relation. A **server** process is required to provide a service (execution of a predefined program) to **client** services. The following approach can be used:

```
server process                    client process

loop                              server_port.send(request)
   server_port.receive(request)
   <execution of service >        ...
   [client_port.send(result)]     ...
endloop                           [client_port.receive(result)]
```

(sequences between square brackets are optional)

The server process is associated with a port where clients specify their requirements, by sending a request to it; the server is blocked as long as there are no waiting requests for service.

The service required may involve sending results to the client. In this case, the client's request to the server must include the name of a port at which it will be blocked until the result is sent there.

It is possible, without modifying the above approach, to provide for several equivalent server processes, any one of which may satisfy a service request. These servers are then associated for reception to the same mailbox.

The model described in section 4.4.2.1 (allocation of pooled resources) and the client-server model above are representative of two main means of obtaining a service by processes in an operating system: procedure calls through a monitor, or activation of a cyclical server process, by message sending. The choice of one of these two models is generally determined by considerations of efficiency (the server approach is preferred if there is real parallelism between the clients and the server), or of uniformity of structure.

4.4.4 Input-output management

We shall now show how management of input-output may be built into the monitor mechanism. We shall start by describing the management of a single peripheral, then, as an application example, the principle of buffered management of input-output.

4.4.4.1 Management of a peripheral

Each peripheral is associated with a monitor whose external procedures allow execution of input-output operations on this peripheral. The monitor has the following general form (we assume that the system uses a monoprocessor).

```
periph: monitor;
var ...,end_transfer: array [...] of condition
    <declaration of state variables of the peripheral>
...

procedure transfer(i,<parameters>);

  begin
  <mask interrupts>;
  if state <> ready then
    <handle error(periph.not ready)>
  endif;
  start_transfer(i,<parameters>);
  end_transfer[i].wait;        -- interrupt unmasked
  if state <> ok then          -- while waiting
    <handle error(transfer incident)>
  endif;
  <unmask interrupts>
  end;
...
  begin
  <initialization>
  end
end periph
```

The procedure *start_transfer* prepares the program for the appropriate exchange operation (construction of the program for the channel or the DMA, taking the exchange parameters into account) and launches its execution (instruction **SIO**). The calling process then waits until transfer is complete, which it knows thanks to the appropriate condition *end_transfer*.

The arrival of an interrupt marking the end of the exchange of type *i* automatically causes the execution of the following sequence:

```
if end_transfer[i].empty then
  <handle error (unexpected interrupt)>
else
  end_transfer[i].signal
endif
```

For a process executing an input-output operation by calling an exchange procedure in this monitor, the exchange seems to be synchronous: on return from the procedure, information has been correctly transferred (or an error has been detected and printed out). Nevertheless, the suspension mechanism avoids busy waiting and the processor can be used during the transfer by another process.

4.4.4.2 Printer spooler

We can now write the program for the printer spooler described in section 4.1. We need three buffers, two in central memory *mb1* and *mb2*, of respective sizes *N1* and *N2*, and another on disk, *db*, of size *Ndisk*. To simplify our analysis, we shall assume that transfers take place in blocks of fixed size equal to that of a line. The buffers are managed by monitors which all have the same structure whose role is:

- To guarantee mutual exclusion on buffer operations
- To provide for synchronization on 'buffer full' and 'buffer empty' conditions

These monitors, called *buffer1, buffer2* and *bufferdisk*, have the same structure as that described in section 4.4.3, with *N* replaced respectively by *N1, N2* and *Ndisk*. If we define *mb1, mb2* and *db* as arrays of records of size one line, and *head* and *tail* as pointers local to each monitor, the procedures for depositing and collecting records can be written as follows:

```
<in buffer1>

procedure add(ln:line);
  mb1[tail]:=ln;
  tail:=tail+1 mod N1

procedure remove(var ln:line);
  ln:=mb1[head];
  head:=head+1 mod N
```

```
<in buffer2>

procedure add(ln:line);
  mb2[tail]:=ln;
  tail:=tail+1 mod N2

procedure remove(var ln:line);
  ln:=mb2[head];
  head:=head+1 mod N2
```

In the monitor *disk_buffer,* deposit and collection are input-output operations using the disk management monitor:

```
procedure add(ln:line);
  disk.write(ln,db[tail]]);
  tail:=tail+1 mod Ndisk

procedure remove (var ln:line);
  disk.write(ln,db[head]);
  head:=head+1 mod Ndisk
```

The input-output program is implemented by the cooperation of four processes whose programs are sketched out below (three operating system processes and the user process). To simplify our discussion, we have omitted error handling sequences and we have assumed that the system operates continuously, with no limit on the number of lines that can be printed. Programs use the three buffer management monitors, *buffer1, buffer2* and *disk_buffer* and two peripheral management monitors, *ptr* and *disk* constructed on the lines of *(periph)* described in section 4.4.5.1.

```
 process              process                  process
print_lines          write_disk               read_disk

loop                 loop                     loop
  buffer2.collect(ln);  buffer1.collect(ln);    disk_buffer.collect(ln);
  lptr.write(ln)        disk_buffer.deposit(ln) buffer2.deposit(ln)
endloop              endloop                  endloop
```

Printing a line is requested by the procedure:

```
procedure write_line(ln:line);
  buffer1.deposit(ln)
```

Note that the programs above are much simpler than those used by interrupts. The modular structure introduced by monitors allows complete separation between buffer and peripheral management. Modifications to the size of a buffer only modify the monitor which manages that buffer; replacing a peripheral by another only requires rewriting of the monitor managing that peripheral.

4.4.5 Real-time synchronization

Real-time synchronization involves time not only as a way of ordering events but as a measure of absolute duration. This kind of synchronization is used in so-called 'real time' applications involving interaction with external devices (e.g. control of industrial processes). It should be remembered that absolute synchronization is based on the use of a **clock**, implemented by a quartz oscillator emitting pulses at regular intervals. These pulses may be used:

- To trigger an interrupt at each pulse
- To decrement the contents of a counter register automatically; when the contents reach 0, an interrupt is triggered

In what follows, we shall use the second mode of operation. The time unit is the period of the clock.

The main practical problems associated with absolute sychronization may be resolved if we have a primitive

suspend(t)

whose effect is to suspend the calling process during a physical time equal to *t* units of time. Our discussion below will examine how this primitive may be implemented using a clock.

Note: The problem would be easy to solve if each process had its own dedicated clock: we would only need to load the value *t* in the counter and await the interrupt when the counter reaches zero. Implementing primitive *suspend* using a single common clock means implementing a virtual clock for each process.

To solve the problem, we consider:

- An **absolute time** which at any instant measures the time since an initial instant
- A **sequencing set**, i.e. a list of processes to activate in the order of their absolute activation times

Any process calling the primitive *suspend(t)* joins the sequencing set at a position corresponding to its absolute activation time, before it is suspended.

We shall write *base_t* for the absolute time at which the clock was last 'wound up', i.e. the last time the counter was set; let the last value to which it was set be *wait_t*. The absolute exact time is therefore given at any instant by

exact_t=base_t+wait_t−counter

as *wait_t−counter* is the time since the last time the counter was set. When the clock is interrupted (when the counter goes through 0), the time since the last setting is equal to *wait_t*; we can then update *base_t*:

```
base_t:=base_t+wait_t
```

The variable *base_t*, once it has been initialized, is correctly maintained on condition that the scheduler is never empty; this condition is generally guaranteed by introducing a process called the *watchdog* whose program is:

```
process watchdog
  loop
    suspend(max_t)
  endloop
```

where *max_t* is a 'great' interval of time. The watchdog therefore generally remains at the end of the sequencing set.

The mechanisms we have been describing are implemented in a monitor called *clock*, which has two entry points: procedure *suspend* (called by *clock.suspend(t))* and procedure *handle_it*, which implements handling of the clock interrupt (passage of the counter through 0). The scheduler is implemented by a queue containing process descriptors. A descriptor is made up of the identity of a process and its absolute activation time; the queue is organized in increasing order of activation times.

We shall assume that the clock interrupt activates a process whose only action is to call the procedure *clock.handle_it*.

```
clock: monitor;
type desc: struct
             i:process;
             Wakeup_time  :integer
             end;
var counter,wait_t;
    base_t,exact_t:integer;
    activate:array [process] of condition;
<declaration of the queue and its access procedures>
<enter,remove,first,empty>
```

```
procedure suspend (duration:integer);
  var  proc:desc;
  begin
  exact_t:=base_t+wait_t-counter;
  proc.Wakeup_time:=exact_t+duration;-- absolute activation time
  proc.i:=p;                          -- p= calling process
  enter(proc,queue)                   -- in Wakeup_time order
  if proc=first(queue) then
    wait_t:=counter:=duration;
    base_t:=exact_t
  endif;
  activate[p].wait
  end;

procedure handle_it;                  -- handles the interrupt
                                      -- counter at zero
  var proc:desc;
      delta_t:=integer;
  begin
  remove(proc,queue);                 -- first in the queue
  base_t:=base_t+wait_t;
  if empty(queue) then
    delta_t:=max_t
  else
    delta_t:=first(queue).Wakeup_time-base_t
  endif;
  wait_t:=counter:=delta_t;            -- → next activation
  activate[proc.i].signal
  end;

  begin                               -- initialization
  base_t:=<initial time>;
  counter:=wait_t:=max_t;
  enter(watchdog,queue)
  end
end clock
```

Note: The method used above (maintenance of a sequencing set and absolute time) is also used to implement **discrete simulation** programs. Such programs implement a model in which the various processes executed in a pseudo-parallel way represent activities that are really parallel. The time used is a simulated time, i.e. a variable representing the passage of physical time, which respects the proportionality between intervals of simulated time and the corresponding intervals of physical time.

4.4.6 Criticisms and variants of monitors

The major criticism of the monitor mechanism concerns the semantics of the primitive *signal*. The role of this primitive is to restart a process blocked at a synchronization point, as soon as the passing condition for this point becomes true. The mode of operation specified aims to ensure that the condition cannot be modified between the execution of *signal* and the restart of the process.

This mode of operation has the disadvantage of requiring that the passing condition appears in two points in the program (before the wait and before the restart) and it provides no simple way of handling the case where several processes are awaiting the same condition. Moreover, a restart signal for which no process is waiting is lost. Consequently, several variants of monitors have been proposed, to overcome these limitations. We shall consider two of them.

1. In a suggestion advanced by [Kessels 77], the primitive *wait* takes the form:

wait (C)

where *C* is a boolean expression (the explicit form of the waiting condition) using global monitor variables. This primitive causes the process to wait while *C* has the value false. Conditions appearing in the *wait* primitives are re-evaluated automatically each time a process leaves the monitor or moves into the waiting state. If one of the conditions then becomes true, one of the processes waiting for this condition is restarted. The primitive *signal* no longer exists.

Use of this construction can be illustrated by the producer and consumer program. The monitor procedures presented in section 4.4.3.1 are modified as follows:

```
procedure
deposit (var m:message)
  begin
  wait (n<N);
  n:=n+1
  add (m)
  end
```

```
procedure
collect (var m:message);
  begin
  wait(n>0);
  n:=n-1;
  remove(m)
  end
```

Passing conditions are therefore given explicitly. The general applicability of this construction is limited by considerations of efficiency, which make it impossible to include local variables of processes or procedure parameters in the waiting condition.

2. In the implementation of monitors in language Mesa [Lampson 80], verification of the passing condition is the responsibility of the restarted process, which repeatedly tests the condition. Operation *signal* has the status of a hint and can therefore be triggered by a condition less demanding than the pasing condition. This implementation is described in detail in section 5.3.

Another extension allows explicit specification of the order in which processes awaiting a condition may be restarted, to handle cases such as that described in section 4.4.2 (resource allocator). To make this possible, an integer parameter *priority* is specified in the primitive *c.wait*; processes in *c.queue* are arranged in increasing order of *priority* (the lower the value of this parameter, the higher the priority).

With this extension we can rewrite procedure *request* in monitor *resource* from section 4.4.2.1 as follows:

```
procedure request(n)
  begin
  while nfree<n do
    avail.wait(n)                -- in order of size
  endwhile;
  nfree:=nfree-n;
  avail.signal
  end
```

A process will therefore only restart the next if it has itself been served.

4.5 Dynamic management of processes

In the simplest system, the number of processes is fixed and they are created once and for all on system initialization. In other systems, in particular interactive systems, processes are managed dynamically. So, for example, in Multics, a new process is created whenever a user logs in, and in Unix whenever a command is executed. Process creation or deletion primitives may be reserved for the use of the operating system, or they may be made available to users. The creation of a process is expressed by the allocation and initialization of its context, for which the elements were described in section 4.2.1. The deletion of a process leads to the freeing of all the resources that had been allocated to it.

The first primitives proposed for dynamic management of processes were *fork* and *join*. Historically, these operations were introduced to handle the parallel execution of programs on a multi-processor, before the concept of a process had been clearly defined. We shall describe one of the many variants of these primitives.

Let P be a procedure. The command

```
id:=fork(P)
```

executed by a process p (the father) creates a new process q (the son) executed in parallel with p. The primitive *fork* returns the identity of q as its result (or *nil* if creation was impossible). The initial context of q is a copy of that of p. The son process ends with a primitive, called *exit* or *quit*, which causes it to disappear.

After the creation of a process q by *fork*, the primitive *join (q)* allows the father process to set a rendezvous point with the son. The execution of *join (q)* suspends the father until q has executed *exit*. There are several variants of *join*, in particular to allow a multiple rendezvous (see exercise).

Example: In the Unix system, primitive *fork* (without parameters) creates a process whose workspace is a copy of its creator's, including the program counter. The two processes can only be distinguished by the value returned by the primitive (0 for the son; the identity of the son or *nil* for the father). A primitive *wait* allows the father to wait for the end of execution of one of its sons (but without being able to choose which, if there are several). A process completes its execution with primitive *exit*. Primitive *exec(P)* allows a process to change context, by calling a specified procedure P.

The following illustrates the use of primitives *fork* and *exec*:

```
...
id:=fork();
if id=0 then                  -- I am the son
  exec (P)                    -- the son's program
else                          -- I am the father
  if id=-1 then               -- nil: creation impossible
    <handle error>
  else
    <the father's program>
  endif
endif
```

Primitive *wait* is used as follows:

```
id:=wait(code)                -- blocked until the end of a son
    ...                       -- id = number of the terminated son
                              -- code = cause of termination
```

Primitives *fork* and *join* have the same advantages and problems as **go to** in sequential programming. They make it possible to create a set of processes obeying random precedence constraints (fig. 4.5*a*). On the other hand, it is difficult to control the progress of a set of processes using these primitives.

Consequently, more restricted constructions such as **parbegin-parend** tend to be prefered:

```
parbegin
P1;
P2;
...
Pn
parend
```

Executed by process p, **parbegin** creates n son processes of p, called $p_1, p_2, \ldots p_n$, which inherit the context of p and execute respectively procedures *P1, P2,...Pn*. Process p is bloacked until all the p_i have completed execution. Its execution resumes at instruction **parend** (fig. 4.5*b*).

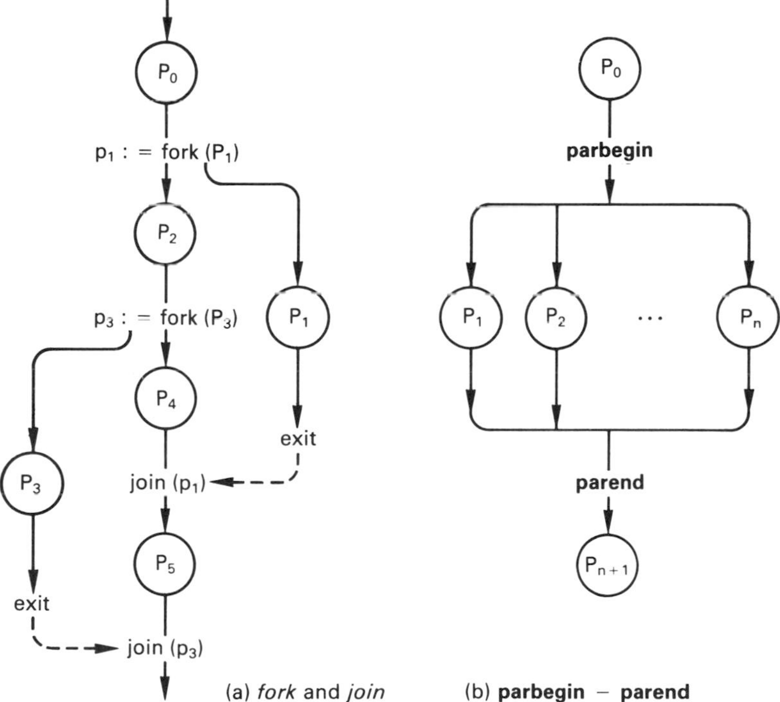

Fig. 4.5. Process creation primitives

Another solution is to use the primitive *fork* alone (without *join*). As with **parbegin-parend**, the relation of filiation organizes the processes into a tree structure. The hierarchical relation between the process and its descendants is used to control execution: a process has more extensive rights than its sons; it may suspend their execution or delete them, in particular in cases of error.

A process can only be deleted by its father. All the resources allocated to it are then freed. Its name may no longer be used as its context is no longer defined. Since the execution of a process is controlled by its father, the deletion of a process (or its self-destruction by *exit*) must lead to the deletion of its descendants.

The way in which process management primitives are implemented is discussed in section 5.3.

4.6 Bibliographic notes

The concept of sequential processes and synchronization were introduced in [Dijkstra 65a]; a formal presentation is given in [Horning 73]. These concepts are now discussed in all texts on operating systems: see in particular [Brinch Hansen 73, chapter 3; Shaw 74, chapters 3 and 7; Crocus 75, chapter 2; Habermann 76, chapters 3 and 4; Peterson 83, chapters 9 and 10]. Several monographs have also been written on this subject ([André 83, Ben-Ari 82, Holt 78]). [Andrews 83] gives an overview of synchronization mechanisms.

Conditional critical regions were the first mechanism proposed for overcoming the defects of semaphores ([Hoare 72, Brinch Hansen 72a]). Monitors were introduced in [Brinch Hansen 72b and 73, Hoare 74]; a discussion of an analogous mechanism, called 'secretaries', appeared in [Dijkstra 71]. The primitive *signal* is discussed in [Howard 76a]; its replacement by the automatic evaluation of the condition was proposed in [Kessels 77]. An experiment in the use of monitors with implementation of an operating system is reported in [Lampson 80]; see also [Keedy 79]. Modern systems using monitors are described in [Brinch Hansen 77, Holt 83].

The initial formulation of the readers and writers problem is given in [Courtois 71]; see also [Brinch Hansen 72a]. The producer and consumer problem was introduced in [Dijkstra 65a]; see also [Dijkstra 72]. Primitives for communication between processes by message transmission are described in [Brinch Hansen 70]; see also [Baskett 77, Cheriton 79]. The model for communication by means of rendez-vous (CSP) is described in [Hoare 78]. Other references on communication by messages are given in section 5.4.

The primitives *fork* and *join* appeared in [Conway 63, Dennis 66]. The **parbegin-parend** construction is introduced in [Dijkstra 65a].

The specification of synchronization is an open problem; various avenues of approach have been explored, and an overview appears in [André 81, Andrews 83]. Research articles giving a fair idea of the field are [Campbell 74, Owicki 76, Robert 77, Misra 81]. Synchronization using monitors has been incorporated into several programming languages: Concurrent Pascal [Brinch Hansen 75], Mesa [Mitchell 79], Modula-2 [Wirth 82], Concurrent Euclid [Holt 83]. Synchronization by means of rendezvous is used in the Ada language [Ichbiah 79, DoD 83, Le Verrand 85].

Exercises

Exercise 4.1

Show how the execution of programs are coroutines (see section 2.1) may be expressed in terms of processes. Specify the context and the synchronization mode for these processes.

Exercise 4.2

In the readers and writers program presented in section 4.4.2.2, readers may occupy the resource permanently, causing writers to be suspended indefinitely.

1. Propose a solution giving priority to writers, where access to the resource is forbidden to new readers if a writer is waiting.

2. The solution above runs the risk of making readers wait indefinitely. Specify an operating mode treating readers and writers fairly, and write the program for the corresponding monitor.

Exercise 4.3 [Dijkstra 65a]

A barber's shop is organized as shown in the diagram below:

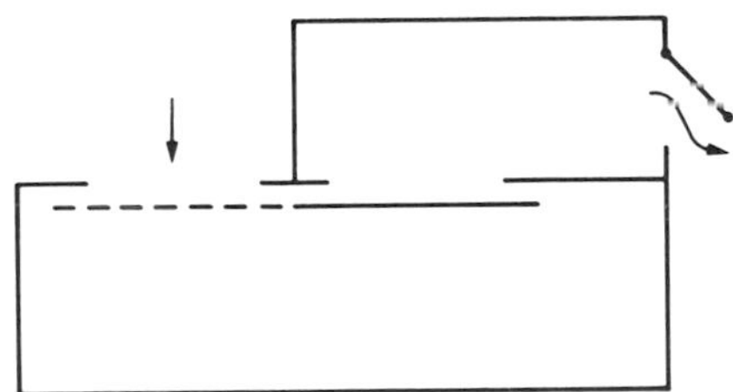

The entrance door and the communicating door between the waiting room and the barber's salon will let one client in at a time. A sliding door is arranged in such a way that one of the openings is always closed. When the barber has finished shaving a client, he lets the next come in; if the waiting room is empty, he sits in it and falls asleep. If a customer finds the barber asleep, he wakes him up; otherwise he waits his turn in the waiting room.

Representing the barber and the clients by processes, program the operation of the system using a monitor.

Exercise 4.4 [Brinch Hansen 73]
A railway line linking two towns A and B includes a single track section.

We represent the trains by processes, as shown below:

```
trains A→B

  ...
single_track.entry_west
  <using single track>
single_track.exit_east
  ...
```

```
trains B→A

  ...
single_track.entry_east
  <using single track>
single_track.exit_west
  ...
```

The role of the *single_track* monitor is to guarantee that all trains using the single track at any given moment are travelling in the same direction.

1. Write the program for monitor *single_track* assuming that there is no limit on the number of trains on the single track.
2. Same question, with a fixed limit of N on the number of trains present on the single track.
3. Examine, in the two cases above, what risk there is of starvation and how it can be avoided.

Hint: Compare this problem with that of readers and writers.

Exercise 4.5 [Dijkstra 71]
Five philosophers are sitting in a circle around a table laid out as shown:

Each of them, represented by a process p_i $(i=0..4)$ behaves as shown in the following program:

```
loop
  think      -- requires no resource
  eat        -- requires two forks
endloop
```

Philosophers can only use the two forks on either side of their plate. The duration of the *thinking* and *eating* phases are random but finite.

1. Show that a solution where forks are allocated one by one can lead to deadlock in the system (permanent blocking of at least two processes).

2. Write a monitor *forks* implementing the allocation of forks without deadlock. A call to the procedure *eat* is replaced in the program process p_i by the sequence:

```
forks.collect(i)
eat
forks.deposit(i)
```

A call to procedure *collect* suspends the calling process as long as at least one of the forks adjacent to its plate is being used by its neighbours. A call to procedure *deposit* frees these two forks.

3. Examine the risk of starvation (indefinite blocking of a single process) and propose means of avoiding it.

Exercise 4.6

Use a monitor to specify and implement two primitives *send* and *receive* which provide for communication between two processes by way of a buffer whose capacity is one message, with synchronization by rendezvous.

Exercise 4.7

The program below represents two processes operating as producer and consumer and synchronized by busy waiting.

```
producer

loop
produce(message);
test_p:   if n=N then
          goto test_p
          endif;
          n:=n+1;
          add(message);
  endloop
```

```
consumer

loop
test_c:   if n=0 then
          goto test_c
          endif;
          n:=n-1;
          remove(message);
          consume(message)
  endloop
```

Procedures *add* and *remove* are those given in section 4.4.3.1.

Discuss the validity of these programs, and make any necessary modifications to them, assuming in turn that:

1. The consultation, incrementation and decrementation operations for a memory variable are indivisible

2. Only loading and storage of a register, its incrementation and its decrementation are indivisible; incrementation and decrementation of a variable on the other hand, require that it be loaded into a register.

Exercise 4.8

The program below represents two processes operating as producer and consumer and synchronized by busy waiting.

```
producer

loop
     produce(message);
test_p: if NP-NC≥N then
        goto test_p
     endif;
     add(message);
     NP:=NP+1
endloop
```

```
consumer

loop
test_c: NC-NP≥0 then
          goto test_c
     endif;
     remove(message);
     consume(message);
     NC:=NC+1
endloop
```

Discuss the validity of this program, under the same assumptions as those of exercise 4.7. What is the interpretation of *NP* and *NC*? How should they be initialized?

Exercise 4.9 [Dijkstra 72, Hoare 74]

A system includes *n* pairs of processes communicating in pairs on the producer-consumer model. Buffers are of variable size and are managed dynamically. When a producer needs a slot to deposit a message, it requests one from a slot store, fills it and chains it to the end of the buffer. When a consumer collects a message from a slot, it returns that location to the store. The store initially contains *N* slots, each of which is identified by an address *addr[0..N−1]*. Write the management monitor for the store on the following assumptions:

1. All pairs of processes are handled in the same way.
2. The priority of a pair of processes is higher the fewer slots it has acquired (this policy is intended to maintain fairness if different pairs of processes are operating at very different speeds).

Procedures necessary for the management of buffers should be specified as though they were queues of slots.

Exercise 4.10

Use monitors to program the measurement collection problem in exercise 2.2.

Exercise 4.11

Modify the monitor for managing a peripheral by associating a watchdog timer with it, so that error handling is triggered if transfer is not complete within the timeout period.

Exercise 4.12

It is intended to use the output spool described in section 4.4.4 to implement a file printing server. Clients communicate with the server using the command *print(f)*, where *f* is a file name. Assume that the server has the information necessary to read the sequence of lines making up file *f*.

1. Write the program for the printer server.
2. Modify the program to allow a client:

- To cancel a printing request, before it has taken place
- To be alerted when printing of a file is finished, by means of a message deposited in a specified mailbox

3. Modify the spooler and server programs to allow the management of several printers operating in parallel.

Exercise 4.13

We are attempting to set up a monoprogrammed job sequencing monitor, along the lines described in exercise 3.15. Jobs are read sequentially from a card reader, and results are listed to a printer.

The system is made up of three processes: *reading*, which manages the reader, *execution*, which sees to the handling of a job, and *printing*, which manages the printer. Process *execution* takes the form:

```
loop
   <read (card)>
   <handle (card)>
endloop
```

where the program *<handle (card)>* may contain calls to *<print (line)>*.

1. Assume first of all that all input-output operations are buffered in central memory. Use monitors to implement cooperation between the three processes.

2. Modify the programs in 1) to be able to handle cases of error in the course of execution (it is assumed that process *read* knows how to detect the first card in the job).

3. Modify the preceding programs to include management of the operator console (with the same specifications as in exercise 3.15).

4. Modify the preceding programs to include management of the input and output spooler (see preceding exercise).

Exercise 4.14

A server's clients are divided into two classes, called 1 and 2. Requests from clients in class 1 have priority over the others: the server will only handle a class 2 request if no requests from class 1 are waiting. Requests within a class are handled on a first come first served basis. A field in the request makes it possible to identify the class of the requesting process.

1. Program synchronization between clients and the server using monitors. **Hint**: Use a queue per class of requests, and a distributing process to feed these queues from the requests received.

2. This approach runs a risk of starvation. Modify the specifications and implementation to eliminate this risk, while preserving privileged handling of class 1 requests.

Exercise 4.15 [Brinch Hansen 72a, 72b; Hoare 72b]

A **conditional critical region** is a synchronization construct which may take two forms (a and b below). C is a condition (a boolean expression); S is a simple or composite instruction; C and S use a variable v declared beforehand by:

var *v*: **shared** *t*

where t is a type (which may be a record type, making it possible to declare a set of variables).

form a): **region** *v* **when** *C* **do** *S*
form b): **region** *v* **do** *S* **await** *C*

Let p be the process executing the critical region. In case *a)*, p evaluates C in a critical section; if C is true, it executes S and leaves the critical section; if C is false, it is blocked outside the critical section. In case *b)*, the test for C and the possible blocking of a process follow the execution of S. In both cases, a blocked process is reactivated while another process leaves the critical region associated with variable v; it then reevaluates condition C.

Using conditional critical regions, program:

- The resource allocator
- The reader-writer model
- The producer-consumer model
- The philosopher problem (exercise 4.5)

Exercise 4.16

Using monitors with Kessels' conditions (section 4.3.1.3), solve the following problems:

- The resource allocator
- The reader-writer model
- The producer-consumer model
- The philosopher problem (exercise 4.5)

Compare this construction with the use of monitors.

Exercise 4.17

Using the Thoth system message communication primitives (section 4.4.4.2) program:

- The resource allocator
- The reader-writer model
- The client-server model

Exercise 4.18 [Reed 79]

An **event counter** is a synchronization mechanism made up of an integer variable E on which two operations are defined:

advance (E)	$E:=E+1$
wait (E,v)	blocks the calling process while $E<v$

These primitives have the following properties, whatever the number of processes executing them:

- The effect of executing n operations *advance(E)* is $E{:}=E+n$.
- Let f be the event 'passing execution of primitive *wait(E,i)*'; let a_i be the i-th operation *advance(E)*. Then a_i precedes f.

Note that it is not specified that the primitives must be executed under mutual exclusion.

A **sequencer** is a synchronization mechanism made up of an integer variable t accessible by a primitive *ticket*, executed in a critical section. A call to *ticket(t)* returns an integer value equal to the number of calls to *ticket(t)* which preceded the current call.

Using event counters and sequencers, program:

- The resource allocator model (first come, first served)
- The producer-consumer model, with multiple producers
- The client-server model

Exercise 4.19

Suggest a specification for a primitive *join* allowing rendez-vous between several processes. **Hint:** Use a counter, initialized by *fork*, decremented by *join*; specify the rules of access to this counter.

Chapter 5

Implementation of synchronization mechanisms

This chapter is concerned with the implementation of the process and synchronization concepts within an operating system. The mechanisms used are based on the implementation of mutual exclusion, which is studied in section 5.1. The guiding principles for the representation and management of processes (context representation, processor allocation) are discussed in section 5.2, and illustrated in section 5.3 by an outline example of the implementation of a synchronization kernel.

5.1 Implementation of mutual exclusion

The mechanisms to implement mutual exclusion on a program sequence are based on a single principle: the use of a mutual exclusion mechanism already available at a lower level. Variables common to the competing processes are always used, and the consistency of these variables must itself be guaranteed. At the basic level (that of the hardware), there are two elementary mechanisms: mutual exclusion for access to a memory location, and interrupt masking. These two mechanisms are sufficient in principle for all requirements. Efficiency considerations lead to implementation in hardware or firmware of more elaborate devices such as the *Test and Set* instruction or semaphores.

5.1.1 Specification of the problem

Let us start by defining the mutual exclusion problem.

Let $(p_1,...p_n)$ be a set of processes that we assume to be cyclical; the program of each includes a critical section. Mutual exclusion is guaranteed by two program sequences (prologue and epilogue) which enclose the critical section of each process. We shall assume that any process entering a critical section leaves it at the end of a finite time; the validity of this assumption is discussed in section 5.1.3.4.

The solution must have the following properties:

a. Mutual exclusion: at any instant, at most one process is executing the critical section of its program

b. Unnecessary blocking: if no process is in its critical section, no process may be blocked by the mutual exclusion mechanism

c. Fault tolerance: the solution must remain valid in cases of faults in one or several processes outside their critical section

d. No starvation: a process which has requested authorization to enter its critical section must not wait indefinitely (assuming that all processes have the same priority)

e. Symmetry: the prologue and epilogue must be identical for all processes, and independent of their number

Given the specifications, we attempt to build up a solution of the form:

```
<initialization>              -- common to all processes

<program for the process pi>:
  loop
    <prologue>                -- entry to critical section
    <critical section>
    <epilogue>                -- exit from critical section
    <remainder of program>
  endloop
```

We have to write the *initialization, prologue* and *epilogue* sequences.

5.1.2 Mutual exclusion by busy waiting

Before describing the implementation of mutual exclusion by elementary process blocking and reactivation operations, we shall consider a mechanism allowing simulation of the effect of these operations, while maintaining processes in the active state. A process in **busy waiting** simulates blocking by carrying out repeated tests of a passing condition, which may be updated by other processes.

5.1.2.1 Dekker's algorithm

Let us first consider the case of two processes p_0 and p_1. The first approach is to represent the waiting condition by a shared variable c (where c is a complementary condition to the passing condition); we therefore have

$$c = \text{'a process is in its critical section'}.$$

We can therefore try the following program:

```
initialization:     c:=false;
prologue:           test: if c then
                             goto test
                       else
                             c:=true
                       endif;
epilogue:           c:=false;
```

More detailed analysis, along the lines carried out in section 4.2.2.3, shows that this program will not resolve the problem posed, unless additional assumptions are made. Let us break down the critical section prologue sequence into instructions:

```
process p0                              process p1
(1) test0: load R0       c        (1') test1: load R1      c
(2)        br (R0=0)     test0    (2')        br (R1=0)    test1
(3)        stz           c        (3')        stz          c
```

where *true* is represented by 0, and *false* by 1, **br** is a conditional branch and **stz** sets a memory location to 0. If the order of execution is 1, 1′, 2, 3, 2′, 3′, it is clear that mutual exclusion fails. The problem is that process p_1 can consult c between the moment at which p_0 has itself consulted c (finding it false) and the moment where p_0 has set c to true. In other words, we would have to make the sequences of actions (1,2,3) and (1′,2′,3′) indivisible. This is the principle underlying the special instruction *Test and Set* (see section 5.1.2.2).

One solution (Dekker's algorithm) can, however, be built up without using any other mutual exclusion mechanism than the indivisibility of access, for reading or updating, to a memory location. We shall give a variant of the algorithm for two processes; it can be extended to any number of processes (see exercise).

The program uses three variables common to the two processes:

```
var c:array[0..1] of boolean;
  turn: 0..1;

initialization: c[0]:=c[1]:=false;
                turn:=0;

prologue:       -- for process i
                -- we assume j=1−i (the other process)
  c[i]:=true;
  turn:=j;
test: if c[j] and turn=j then
        goto test
      endif;

epilogue:       -- for process i
  c[i]:=false;
```

This solution, the proof of whose validity is left as an exercise, is primarily of theoretical interest. In practice, special instructions are used (see section 5.1.2.2) which perform the test and modification sequence in an indivisible way.

Busy waiting can also be used as an elementary synchronization mechanism for problems other than those of mutual exclusion.

Example: Let us return to the problem in example 1 of section 4.3.2 (communication between two processes through a common segment). Let us once more use boolean variable *c* for the waiting condition:

c = 'process *p* has finished writing to segment *a*'

Initially, *c* = *false*. The programs can be written:

```
process p              process q
  ...                    ...
write (a);             test: if ]c then
c:=true                          goto  test
                            endif;
                            read (a)
```

Enumeration will show that the solution is correct for this case: whatever the order in which the two processes execute their actions, reactivation of *q* is, at most, delayed by one busy wait cycle. This property remains true even if we assume that several processes $q_1,...q_k$ are waiting for p to finish writing.

The only mutual exclusion mechanism necessary in this case is that for access to a memory location.

The property which ensures the validity of the above approach is that the modification of variable c is caried out by a *single* process. Note that this approach is the same as that met in chapter 2 for management of input-output on the CDC 6600: each pair of processes communicates by means of a pair of indicators, each of which is updated by one process and consulted by another. Except in this case, provision has to be made to execute test and modification instructions under mutual exclusion.

5.1.2.2 Busy waiting in a multiprocessor environment: Test and Set

To allow for busy waiting in the case where several processes must update and consult common variables, certain machines have an instruction which implements consultation and updating of the contents of a memory location in an *indivisible* way. This instruction, often called *Test and Set* (**tas**), is used for multiprocessors; in monoprocessors, mutual exclusion can be simply provided by interrupt masking.

Let m be the address of the memory location considered, or **lock**, and let R be a register. By convention, if the lock is set to 0, the critical section is free, if it set to 1, it is occupied. The effect of *Test and Set* is as follows (we write *Mp[m]* for the memory location of address m):

```
tas R,m: <prevent access to Mp[m]>
                R:=Mp[m]
                Mp[m]:=1
         <free access to Mp[m]>
```

We can now program mutual exclusion by busy waiting using the following sequence:

```
initialization: stz           m    --Mp[m]:=0
prologue:       tas           R,m
                br (R<>0)     $-1  -- iterative test
epilogue:       stz           m
```

The use of **tas** is used only for mutual exclusion affecting brief sequences such as supervisor call programs in an operating system. Examples are given in section 5.3.

Let us summarize the characteristics of busy waiting:

1. Busy waiting is not an economic solution for pseudo-parallel processes as it wastes processor time. It is acceptable for a multi-processor for brief sequences, or where the processor used by the waiting process is not reusable by another activity.

2. Care must be taken in the consultation and modification of shared variables. Apart from particular cases such as that in the example in section 5.1.2.1, critical sections must be used. Special instructions *(Test and Set)* make this possible. All solutions are based, in the final anlysis, on the elementary mutual exclusion provided by access to a memory location.

5.1.3 An elementary mutual exclusion tool: semaphores

5.1.3.1 Definition

Historically, semaphores were introduced as a general, low-level synchronization mechanism, and their use was not limited to mutual exclusion. This presentation concentrates on high-level mechanisms. We therefore use monitors as the main synchronization device, and restrict semaphores to their more "structured" use for mutual exclusion. The use of semaphores for general synchronization is examined in exercises 5.4 to 5.9.

A **semaphore** *s* is formed by the association of a counter with integer values, written *s.c*, and a queue, written *s.f*. On creation of a semaphore, the counter receives an initial value *s0* ($s0 \geq 0$), and the queue *s.f* is empty. A semaphore is used to block processes while waiting for the condition for their reactivation to be fulfilled; blocked processes are placed in *s.f*. A semaphore *s* can only be handled by two operations, called primitives, *P(s)* and *V(s)*: the value of the counter and the state of the queue are inaccessible, even for reading. Writing *p* for the process process executing *P(s)* or *V(s)*, and *q* for a process belonging to *s.f*, the algorithm for these primitives can be written:

```
P(s):                          V(s):
s.c:=s.c-1;                    s.c:=s.c+1;
if  s.c<0 then                 if  s.c≤0 then
   state (p):=suspended;          remove (q,s.f);
   add (p,s.f)                    state (q):=active
endif                          endif
```

These operations are executed under **mutual exclusion**.

Implementation of semaphores and the primitives *P* and *V* is described in section 5.3. The operations *add* and *remove* allow respectively the insertion of a process into a queue and the removal of a process from a queue. We make no assumption here on the policy adopted for managing these queues: the synchronization algorithms must be independent of it. The policy actually adopted, associated with the allocation of the processor, is discussed in Chapter 5, as well as the details of the blocking and activation operations.

Note 1: The operation of a semaphore can compare to that of a turnstile using tokens. Each token deposited allows one opening of the turnstile, letting one and only one person through. Several tokens may be deposited beforehand. Operation *P* corresponds to an attempt to pass through the turnstile, which may lead to the requestor having to wait. Operation *V* corresponds to a token being deposited; if people are waiting, a single one of them can go through the turnstile.

Note 2: The execution of primitive *P* may block a process; it can then only be activated by another process executing *V* on the same semaphore. The execution of *V* is never blocking.

5.1.3.2 Properties

The main properties of synchronization semaphores can be deduced from certain *invariant* relations: these relations, initially true, remain true after the execution of any number of operations *P* and *V*.

1. For a semaphore *s*, we shall write:

- *np(s)* for the total number of times operation *P(s)* has been executed
- *nv(s)* for the total number of times operation *V(s)* has been executed

We obtain a relation:

$$(1)\ s.c = s0 - np(s) + nv(s)$$

It is because *s.c* initially has the value *s0*, and each operation *P* reduces this value by 1, while every operation *V* increases it by 1. As these operations are executed under mutual exclusion, no updating can be lost.

2. Let *nblock(s)* be the number of processes blocked in queue *s.f*. We obtain the relation:

$$(2)\ nblock(s) = \textbf{if } s.c \geq 0 \textbf{ then } 0 \textbf{ else } -s.c \textbf{ endif},$$

which can also be written

$$\text{'2'}\ nblock(s) = max\ (0, -s.c)$$

Relation (2) is true initially. The table below, which traces the effect of operation*P* and *V* on the value of *nblock*, shows that these operations leave the relation invariant.

	$s.c<0$	$s.c.=0$	$s.c>0$
Effect of P(s)	+1	+1	--
Effect of *V(s)*	−1	--	--

Note: The absolute value of counter *s.c* can therefore be interpreted as follows:

- If $s.c \geqslant 0$ it is the number of processes which could execute *P(s)* without suspending (if no *V(s)* operation is executed in the meantime).
- If $s.c>0$ it is the number of processes suspended in queue *s.f.*

3. Relation (2) may be written in another form which will be useful later. Let *nt(s)* be the number of 'transitions' through primitive *P(s)* by the processes: it is the total of the number of executions of *P(s)* without blocking and the number of reactivations carried out by *V(s)*. We therefore have:

$$nblock(s) = np(s) - nt(s)$$

Substituting this value into relation (2'), we obtain:

$$-nt(s) = max(-np(s), -s.c-np(s)),$$

or again

$$nt(s) = min(np(s), s.c.+np(s))$$

Using the value of *s.c* drawn from (1), we finally obtain:

$$(3)\ nt(s)=min(np(s), s0+nv(s))$$

This relation can be interpreted intuitively with the analogy of the automatic turnstile: the number of people going through the turnstile is equal to the smaller of two numbers — the total number of tokens deposited (including the initial stock) and the number of people who have attempted to go through.

5.1.3.3 Mutual exclusion using semaphores

The programs below resolve the problem of mutual exclusion for *n* processes. It cannot, however, be guaranteed that there will be no starvation, in the absence of any assumption on how the queue is managed (see section 5.1.3.4).

initialization : **semaphore** *mutex* **init** *1*
prologue : *P(mutex)*
epilogue : *V(mutex)*

Let us show that this solution conforms to the specifications in section 5.1.1. We have to establish properties a, b and c.

Let *nc* be the number of processes in their critical section at a given instant. We have:

$$(4)\quad nc = nt(mutex) - nv(mutex)$$

The properties required can be established by applying relation (3) from section 5.1.2.2 to semaphore *mutex*, which gives us:

$$(5)\quad nt(mutex) = \min(np(mutex), 1 + nv(mutex))$$

a. Mutual exclusion

We have, by (5):

$$nt(mutex) \leqslant 1 + nv(mutex)$$

From which we can deduce, given (4), that $nc \leqslant 1$: mutual exclusion is guaranteed.

b. Absence of blocking

Let us assume that no process is in its critical section. We therefore have $nc = 0$, or

$nt(mutex)=nv(mutex)$,
or again
$nt(mutex)<1+nv(mutex)$
From which we can deduce, given (5):
$nt(mutex)=np(mutex)$,
or again
$nblock(mutex) = 0$

Property b is therefore established, as well as property c, since we have made no assumptions concerning the state of the processes outside their critical section.

Note: If we give semaphore *mutex* the initial value $k > 1$, the reasoning in *a)* above shows that $nc \leqslant k$. The maximum number of processes in their critical section is therefore limited to k.

5.1.3.4 Difficulties in mutual exclusion by semaphores

The solution given above does not eliminate all problems posed by mutual exclusion. Let us consider the main difficulties met in practice.

1. Nested critical sections deadlock

Consider two processes p and q whose programs include two separate critical sections, corresponding, for example, to the use of two separate resources.

```
        process p                process q
          ...                      ...
(1)     P(mutex1)        (1')    P(mutex2)
          ...                      ...
(2)     P(mutex2)        (2')    P(mutex1)
          ...                      ...
        V(mutex2)                V(mutex1)
          ...                      ...
        V(mutex1)                V(mutex2)
```

If the time trace of the execution of p and q begins by (1, 1', 2, 2'), a situation will be reached where both processes are indefinitely blocked, as neither can be awakened by the other. This situation is called **deadlock**.

It can be shown that deadlock cannot occur if the different critical sections are nested *in the same order* for all processes where they appear. A more thorough study of deadlock appears in Chapter 8 for the question of resource allocation.

2. Indefinite waiting in a critical section

The validity of a solution proposed is based on the fact that all processes leave their critical section at the end of a finite time. We have seen in 1) that this assumption may be invalidated by the nesting of critical sections. Other causes of waiting may occur. For example, the blocking or failure of a process in its critical section, or its execution of an infinite loop, may paralyze all other processes in competition with it. In cases of a global critical section (i.e. one affecting all users) implemented in an operating system, the following solutions may be used:

- Any process executing a global critical section receives a special status, throughout its execution, assigning special rights to it: high priority, protection against deletion, etc.
- A watchdog timer (see section 4.4.5) is set as the process enters its critical section; if the process has not left within a predefined time, the operating system forces it to exit and therefore frees the critical section. This solution is not free of risk, as global data handled in a critical section may become inconsistent. One must therefore be able to restore data to an earlier state regarded as valid, which implies periodic saving.

3. Starvation

The mutual exclusion algorithm guarantees that one and only process enters its critical section if several candidates apply when the critical section is free. Nevertheless, a particular process may be indefinitely delayed: this is the phenomenon known as **starvation**, which we shall encounter again when we consider resource allocation. Processes attempting to enter the critical section wait in queue *mutex*. Their order of activation (by operation *V(mutex)*) depends on the way the queue is managed, an issue on which we have made no assumptions.

In the very frequent case where semaphore queues are managed on a 'first come, first served' basis, without priority, there is no risk of starvation. Any process will become the first in a queue after a finite time, on the assumption at any rate that the critical section lasts a finite time.

5.2 Functional structure of the synchronization kernel

The concept of processes and the operations associated with them are not generally included in the basic instruction set of machines. They have to be implemented by a set of programs or microprograms which together form the process management **kernel**. In a description of an operating system in terms of a hierarchy of abstract machines (see chapter 3), the kernel (as its name implies) is the lowest level layer, implemented directly on the bare physical machine. The abstract machine implemented by the combination (physical machine, kernel) may be seen as a 'process machine' which, as well as the basic instruction set, also has primitives making it possible to create, delete and synchronize processes. Like any abstract machine, the machine implemented in this way hides certain features of the underlying physical machine. For example:

- The concept of a process, equivalent to that of a virtual processor, makes the way physical processors are allocated invisible to the user of the kernel. At levels higher than that of the kernel, the number of these processors only influences the system performance level and not its logical structure.
- The synchronization primitives implemented by the kernel hide the physical mechanisms for context switching, such as interrupts.

The structure of a synchronization kernel depends both on the specifications of the physical machine (interrupt management, structure of the status word, single or multi-processor, etc.) and the specifications of the abstract machine to be implemented, in particular the synchronization mechanism adopted. It is nonetheless possible to distinguish certain common characteristics in this structure, which we shall describe before we go on to examine a particular implementation.

5.2.1 Process states and queues

So far, we have treated processes as only having two possible states: active and blocked. Once we take account of the allocation of a physical processor we have to break down the active state into two new states. An active process is called **active** in the narrow sense of the word if it is actually executing on a physical processor; it is said to be **ready** if it cannot execute, because no processor is available. This distinction is based only on the availability of a processor and not on a logical condition. Figure 5.1 shows the states of a process and transitions between these states.

Transitions 3 and 4 (blocking and activation) are *intrinsic* transitions resulting from synchronization between processes. *Technological* transitions 1 and 2 are associated with the allocation of physical processors to processes. In particular, transition 2 takes place when the allocation algorithm removes the processor from a process which still needs it; this operation is called **preemption** of the processor.

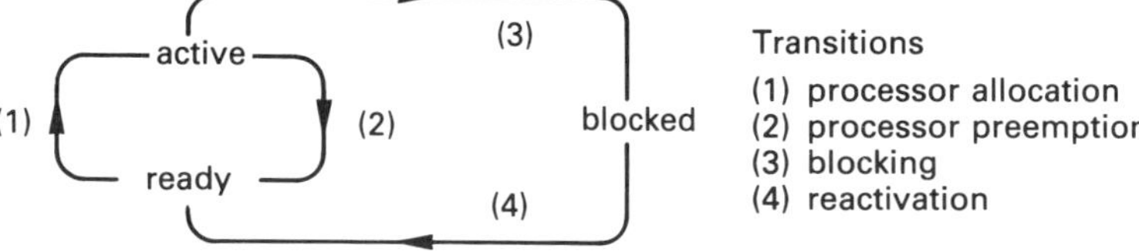

Fig. 5.1. Process states

Process management is based on queues. Consequently, a process queue is associated with each different cause of blocking (semaphore, condition in a monitor, etc.) to hold the blocked processes. In the same way, ready processes are maintained in a queue, whose management makes it possible to implement a method of allocating physical processors. If we assume that the next process to be selected is always the first of those ready, the allocation method is defined:

- By the algorithm governing entry into the queue of ready processes
- By the algorithm that determines the preemption of physical processors

The set of programs implementing these algorithms is called a **scheduler**. A study of processor allocation algorithms appears in chapter 8.

The program implementing selection as such (choice of the processor, context management, etc.) is called a **dispatcher**. The general model for process queues is shown in fig. 5.2. Movement of processes between queues corresponds to state changes.

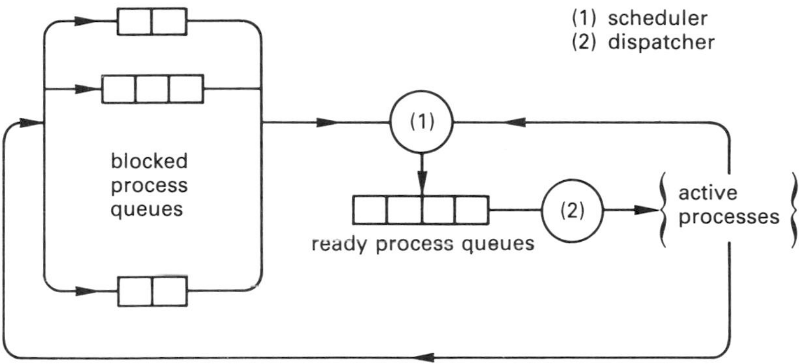

Fig. 5.2. Process queues managed by a kernel

5.2.2 Context management and models of primitives

1. Contents of the context

The allocation of a physical processor makes it necessary to keep a copy, for each process, of the context describing the state of the processor for that process. To do so, each process is associated with a collection of information resident in memory and called the **state vector** or **context block**, and which includes:

- Information on the state of the processor, necessary for its reallocation (contents of the status word, of registers)
- The values of the process attributes (priority, access rights)

- Parameters to the workspace for the process (procedure and data segments, execution stack)
- Management information (states, chaining links)

A more detailed description of the context block for a process is given in section 5.3.

2. Organization of the kernel

The execution of kernel programs is triggered in two ways (fig. 5.3):

- By a call to a process management primitive (creation, deletion, synchronization, etc.; these primitives are implemented in the form of supervisor call)
- By an interrupt: the interrupt handling programs are part of the kernel, since these interrupts are translated as synchronization operations and are invisible to the upper layers

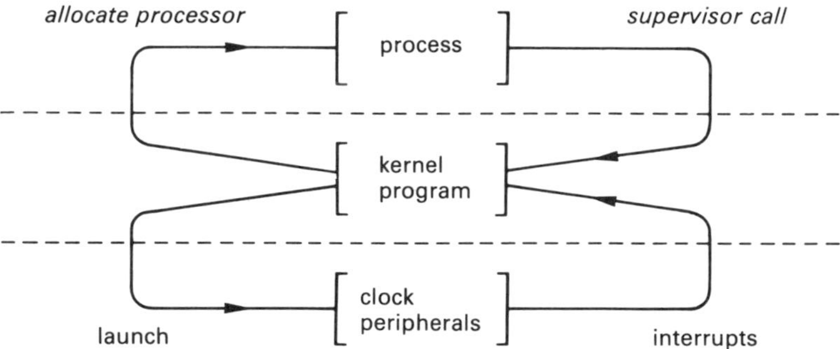

Fig. 5.3. Communication with a synchronization kernel

In all cases, the mechanism allowing entry to the kernel includes automatic saving of the status word and, possibly, of registers, for the processor executing the supervisor call or handling the interrupt. Depending on how the machine is organized, this information is saved in a fixed location (associated with the interrupt level or the supervisor call) or on a stack (particularly in the case of multiprocessors). The parts of the context saved in this way are those for the process active on the processor in question, at the moment the interrupt or the supervisor call was issued.

Programs for primitives and interrupt handlers manipulate context blocks and process queues; to maintain the coherence of the information, these programs must be executed *under mutual exclusion*. The execution of a kernel program ends in all cases with a reallocation of the processor or process, i.e. with a call to the dispatcher. As the queue of ready processes may have been modified by the execution of a primitive, the new active processors may be different from the last active process on the interrupted processor.

The program for a kernel primitive follows the general model below:

```
prologue;               -- saving the context and
                        -- entrance to the critical section
check;                  -- checks rights and parameters
  <program body>        -- handles the process queues
allocate_processor;     -- dispatch a program
                        -- exit from the critical section
```

The *prologue* sequence, which is common to all these operations, implements saving of the context of the process executing the operation, as well as its entrance into the critical section. The *check* sequence is used to check that the process calling the primitive has the right to do so, as well as the validity of the parameters transmitted. Kernel primitives handle common information whose consistency must be maintained: it is therefore important to make sure that operations are only executed correctly. The detail of the checks carried out depends on the primitives. The *allocate_processor* sequence is the dispatcher program. It implements the reallocation of the processor and exit from the critical section.

Note: On exit from a primitive, it may occur that the processor is reallocated, without the slightest doubt, to the calling process. In this case, time can be saved by using a very simplified version of *allocate_processor* which restores the context of the calling process saved by the *prologue* sequence. The detailed nature of this local optimization depends on the structure of the machine, and in particular on the way context is saved in a supervisor call.

Note that the difference between single and multi-processor systems appears essentially in the implementation of mutual exclusion and processor allocation (the *prologue* and *allocate_processor* sequences).

The handling of interrupts by the kernel must be an integral part of the synchronization mechanisms adopted. Two basic approaches may be considered:

1. Associate a handling process with an interrupt. This process (and it alone) can wait for a given interrupt, using a special instruction.

2. Associate an activation operation (*signal* for a condition, *V* for a semaphore, etc.) with an interrupt.

The problems of interrupt masking and priority are generally handled by assigning standard priorities to processes.

5.3 Implementation of a synchronization kernel

We shall now consider the implementation scheme adopted for a particular synchronization kernel. This description is given by way of illustration, and many other choices would have been possible, both for the interface and for the implementation details (see exercises).

5.3.1 General organization

5.3.1.1 Interfaces

a. Process management

Processes may be created and deleted dynamically, and are organized hierarchically by a filiation relationship (see section 4.5). A process is created using the primitive:

create (p,initial context, attributes)

The attributes of a process include its priority (expressed by an integer) and its (rights to execute certain operations). The initial context specifies the initial state of the processes status word and registers, and the workspace associated with the process (stack, private data). The process is created in the ready state. Its number *p* is returned as a result (value *nil* if its creation is impossible). A function *myself* allows a process to find out its own number.

The three primitives that follow apply to an existing process *p* and can only be executed by its father. In addition, procedure *kill* can be applied by a process to itself (self-deletion).

kill (p)

Deletes process *p*, and all its descendants.

suspend (p)

Interrupts the execution of process *p* and places it in a special queue. The execution of *p* can only be restarted by using *restart*.

restart (p)

Restarts execution of process *p* which had previously been interrupted. Primitives *suspend* and *restart* are introduced for security reasons, and particularly to allow debugging of a process under the control of its father.

Use of primitives *create, kill, suspend* and *restart* are subject to possession of a right, which appears in attribute *Rights* in a process.

b. Synchronization

Processes are synchronized using monitors. Interrupt management is an integral part of the monitor mechanism: an interrupt is associated with a condition. The specification of monitor primitives, which is slightly different from that given in section 4.3, is examined in detail in section 5.3.2. Monitors are declared in the programs of processes; a monitor is created on compilation of a program where it is declared and it is usable thereafter according to the slope rules defined by the language used (which is not specified here).

5.3.1.2 Data structures and algorithms

On its creation, a process receives a fixed number which will name it and allow it to access its context block. This is made up of the following fields:

Loc	:save zone for the processor status word
Reg	:save zone for the general registers of the processor
State	:state value (ready, blocked, ...)
Prio	:process priority
Rights	:process rights
Son, etc.	:chaining links in the process hierarchy
Succ, etc.	:chaining links in queues

Process management uses queues, ordered in decreasing priority, and managed by a set of access procedures, specified below (*p* names a process, *q* a queue).

add (p,q)

Adds *p* to *q*, with a rank corresponding to its priority (and in order of arrival for processes of the same priority).

first (q)

Returns the number of the process at the head of queue *q* (or a special value *nil* if *q* is empty); does not modify *q*.

remove (p,q)

Removes the first process from queue *q*, and returns its number in *p* (does nothing and returns *nil* if *q* is empty).

extract (p,q)

Extracts from queue *q* the process with number *p* specified, whatever its rank; returns value *nil* in *p* if the process was not in the queue.

empty (q)

Returns the boolean value *true* if queue *q* is empty, and *false* otherwise.

Figure 5.4 shows the organization of a queue of processes.

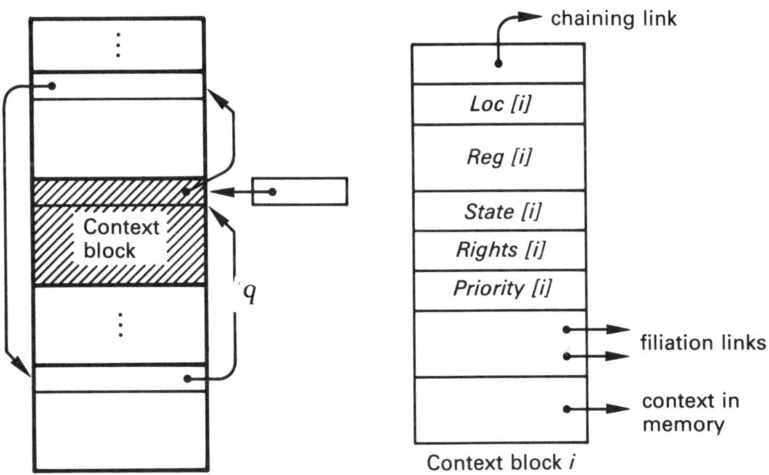

Fig. 5.4. Organization of a process queue

5.3.2 Implementation of monitors

Many implementations of monitors have been proposed (see the bibliography in section 5.4). The implementation described here is drawn from language Mesa [Lampson 80], whose validity has been demonstrated be extensive experience of its use. Compared to the traditional concept of a monitor (section 4.3.3), it has the following differences:

1. *The semantics of the primitive* signal. The initial specification of *c.signal* makes it clear that one of the processes waiting for condition *c* (if there are any) is immediately activated, which implies that the process executing *signal* must be temporarily suspended. In the present specifica-

tion, the process activated is simply made ready and must reenter the monitor; it therefore finds itself in competition again with other processes awaiting entry, and is not certain of being immediately activated. The condition triggering its activation may therefore be modified before the activated process restarts its exectution in the monitor. With this new interpretation, we therefore have to change the form of the suspension operation. A construction of the form:

```
if ⌉ <OK to proceed> then
   c.wait
endif
```

becomes:

```
while ⌉ <OK to proceed> do
   c.wait
endwhile
```

Although it introduces a risk of starvation, this construction has several practical advantages. It avoids a context switch, at the cost of an additional evaluation of the condition. It makes it possible, above all, to define useful extensions easily (multiple activation, or watchdog timers) as specified below. Finally, note that proving the monitor's validity is simplified, as the transition condition *<OK to proceed>* is evaluated on reactivation: the process which executes *signal* has only to satisfy a weaker condition than the transition condition.

2. *Multiple reactivation.* The problem with multiple reactivation can easily be resolved by introduction of a new primitive *c.broadcast* whose effect can be expressed as follows:

```
while ⌉ c.empty do
   c.signal
endwhile
```

Given that all reactivated processes test the condition again and submit a new request for access to the monitor, this primitive will indeed have the effect expected of it.

3. *Watchdog timers.* For security reasons, and in particular to avoid deadlocks, it may be useful to associate a watchdog timer with a monitor condition. The timer period is the maximum time for which a process can be blocked in the queue associated with the condition. At the end of the

timeout interval, specified handling is executed. This handling may simply be reactivation of the process (which again tests the transition condition) or it may be its transfer to a special stack (see section 5.3.2.3).

Let *M.c.timeout* be the timeout interval associated with a conditon *c* in monitor *M*. We assume that a clock *absTime* giving the absolute time is available. The following instruction must be added to the program for primitive *c.signal*:

```
wakeupTime[p]:=absTime+M.c.timeout
```

where *wakeupTime[p]* is a new field in the context block for process *p*. A 'watchdog' process reactivated at regular intervals scans all contexts and carries out the specified handling for all processes for which *wakeupTime[p]>absTime*.

5.3.2.1 Basic algorithms

The program of a monitor must provide two functions:

- Mutual exclusion to the monitor procedures
- Suspension under reactivation associated with primitives *wait* and *signal*

Any monitor *M* is therefore associated with the following data structures:

- A mutual exclusion lock *M.lock*, which can take values *free* and *occupied*, and a queue *M.queue* associated with this lock. Initially, *M.lock=free* and *M.queue=<empty>*.
- Each condition *c* in *M* is associated with a queue *M.c.queue,* as well as with a timeout interval *M.c.timeout* and, for the conditions associated with an interrupt, a boolean indicator *M.c.it_occurred*.

The queue of ready processes is written *ready_q*.

We shall give the programs for the four sequences *enter, exit, c.wait* and *c.signal* for a monitor *M* (the sequences *enter* and *exit* are inserted by the compiler and enclose the execution of any external monitor procedure). Let us first define the lock management procedures:

```
request_lock (M,p):

    if M.lock=occupied then
        add (p,M.queue);
        State [p]:= blocked
    else
        M.lock:=occupied;
        add(p,ready_q);
        State [p]:=ready
    endif
```

```
free_lock (M):

    if empty(M.queue) then
        M.lock:=free
    else
        remove(q,M.queue);
        add(q,ready_q);
        State [q]:=ready
    endif
```

The four sequences can be written as follows, using these procedures:

enter(M):

```
prologue;
p:=<calling process>;
request_lock(M,p);
allocate_processor;
```

exit(M):

```
prologue;
p:=<calling process>;
free_lock (M);
add(p,ready_q);
allocate_processor;
```

c.wait:

```
prologue;
p:=<calling process>;
add (p,M.c.queue);
State [p]:=blocked;
free_lock (m);
allocate_processor;
```

c.signal:

```
prologue;
p:=<calling process>;
if ]empty(M.c.queue) then
   remove (q,M.c.queue);
   request_lock (m,p);
   request_lock (m,q);
   free_lock (M)
else
   add (p,ready_q)
endif;
allocate_processor;
```

Remember that the *prologue* sequence ensures that the context is saved on entry to the critical section, and the sequence of *allocate_processor* ensures that the processor is allocated on exit from the critical section. Their program is given in section 5.3.4.

Note that, in primitive *signal*, the calling process *p* and the activated process *q* are added (by *request_lock*) to the queue waiting for entry to the monitor. The activated process at the end of the primitive is the first in this queue (which may be the third process). We have not attempted to reduce the number of transfers between queues in order to obtain optimal implementation

5.3.2.2 Interrupt handling

To assure consistency between synchronization mechanisms, each interrupt is associated with:

- A condition in a monitor
- A cyclical process which implements interrupt handling; in the rest state, this process is waiting for the condition

A condition can only be associated with a single interrupt level. The occurrence of an interrupt causes the execution of *signal* on the associated condition. The relative priority of interrupts is expressed by that of their handling processes.

As it stands, this mechanism is not infallible. Mutual exclusion to monitor procedures, guaranteed by the lock, cannot apply to interrupts.([1]) An interrupt may thus occur while the handling process is still busy, and it is therefore lost. To avoid this phenomenon, we use a boolean indicator (the "wake-up waiting switch") to store the occurrence of an interrupt. Programs are written:

```
<handling process>

      loop
test: if ]M.c.it_occurred then
        c.wait;    --avoid losing an interrupt
        goto test
      endif;
      <interrupt handler>
      endloop

<occurrence of the interrupt associated with M.c>

      M.c.it_occurred:=true;
      c.signal
```

5.3.2.3 Error handling

The underlying principle of error handling is to block the process which caused the error and to send a message to the father process which would be able to take the necessary steps (correction of the error and restart, or deletion of the failed process). To do so, a special queue *error_q* is used (depending on the way the system is organized, a single queue may be used, or a queue per user, per subsystem, etc.).

We assume that an error in the course of execution of a process leads to a trap, whose handler can be written

```
prologue;
p:=<calling process>;
add (p,error_q);
<specific handling>;
State [p]:=suspended;
allocate_processor;
```

([1]) Except if interrupt masking is being used to implement locking. This solution (used in particular in Modula-2) is only applicable to monoprocessors and may not be acceptable if there are constraints on the time taken to react to an interrupt.

We have defined a new state ('suspended') which applies to a process whose activity has been interrupted by an event regarded as abnormal (execution error or action taken by primitive *suspend*; see section 5.3.3).

We shall not go into detail here on <*specific handling*>, which must have been specified by the father process at the moment the process was created. This program includes notably recording of diagnostic information (identity of the failing process, nature of the error), which must be transmitted to the father process by a mode to be specified according to the urgency (updating of an indicator, reactivation, etc.).

5.3.3 Implementation of operations and processes

5.3.3.1 Creation and deletion

The main problem posed by dynamic management of processes is the allocation of context and process names. Two main methods are used:

- A fixed number of locations is reserved to context blocks; locations not used are marked by a special value *(nil)* in their *State* field; each block is named by a fixed number, which is that used to name the associated process.
- Locations reserved to context blocks are allocated dynamically in memory; process numbers are also allocated dynamically, and a mapping table associates the memory address of the context block of each process with its number.

In all cases, we assume a procedure *allocate_context(p)* is available to implement the allocation of the context (context block and workspace); it returns as a result the number *p* of the process (*nil* if creation impossible, e.g. because of lack of memory space). Methods for the allocation of workspace are not specified in detail here (see chapter 9). The number of the process created is itself returned as the result of the primitive below:

```
create (p,initial context):

    prologue;
    check;                    -- checking of rights
    allocate_context (p);
    if p <> nil then
      initialize_context(i);
      add (p,ready_q)
    endif;
    add(calling process,ready_q);
    allocate_processor;  -- p is returned as result
```

The initial context is specified by the creating process: it must define the initial value of registers and of the status word of the created process, the initial state of its workspace and, finally, attributes such as priority and rights. Certain fields in the status word are predefined and may not be modified (mode, interrupt masking, etc.). For elements associated with protection (access rights), the created process may not have rights greater than the creator process; otherwise, protection would easily be overridden (see section 6.1.4).

The deletion of a process must lead to freeing of the resources that were allocated to it. Amongst these resources, only the name and context are directly managed by the kernel; other resources, such as files, are acquired by specific mechanisms.

The deletion of a process in a critical section may lead to deadlock. Critical sections directly controlled by the kernel are those of monitors. A process can be associated with the number of locks it owns (it may be involved in several nested calls) and its deletion may be deferred until that number becomes nil. Another solution is to examine the state of each lock periodically and to free it if the process owning it has been deleted.

The principle underlying the primitive *kill* is given by the program layout below:

```
kill (p):

    prologue;
    check;          -- checks on rights
    free_context (p);
    add (calling.process, ready_q);
    allocate_processor;
```

The procedure *free_context* must ensure that resources occupied by the deleted process and its descendants are free:

```
free_context(p):

    list:=<list of sons of p>;
    free_context_block(p);
    free_memory(p);
    for q∈ list do
            free_context(q)
    endfor;
```

5.3.3.2 Suspension and resumption

The primitive *suspend* allows a process to control the activity of a son process, by forcing its execution to be interrupted. A common use of this facility is the suspension of a process in an infinite loop. The process interrupted in this way is transferred to a special queue, which may be the *error_q* queue used for traps.

The effect of the primitive *suspend* may in fact be assimilated to that of a trap and its program is analogous to a trap handler.

The suspension of a process poses a similar problem to that of its deletion if the process is in a critical section in a monitor.

```
suspend (p):

    prologue;
    check;
    <handle critical section>;
    q:=<queue containing p>;
    extract(p,q);
    add(p,error_q);
    State [p]:=suspended;
    add (calling process,ready_q);
    allocate_processor;
```

The primitive *resume* allows a process to reactivate a suspended sum, possibly after modification of its context.

```
resume (p):

    prologue;
    check;
    remove (p,error_q);
    State [p]:=ready;
    add (calling process,ready_q);
    add (p, ready_q)
    allocate_processor;
```

5.3.4 Mutual exclusion and processor allocation

5.3.4.1 Implementation for a monoprocessor

For a single processor, mutual exclusion is simply implemented by interrupt masking. For this purpose, an interrupt mask must be set up in the status words specifying programs associated with primitives or with interrupt handling. If *active_proc* is a global variable which contains the number of the active process, and *saveloc* the location where the processor status word was saved at the moment the supervisor call or interrupt was issued, the prologue can be written:

```
prologue:
  <interrupt masking>        -- mask in a status word
  Loc [active_proc]:=saveloc;
  save_registers (Reg[active_proc]);
```

The dispatcher program, which implements exit from the critical section as well, allocates the processor to the first process in the queue of ready processes. To simplify the handling of this queue, it is convenient to introduce a further process of low priority, which always stays at the end of the queue and is never suspended. This process, which is therefore never activated unless it is the only one ready, executes a background job of low urgency or a simple waiting loop. This guarantees that the queue of ready processes is never empty.

The dispatcher program is as follows:

```
allocate_processor:
  remove (activeproc, ready_q);
  load_registers (Reg[active_proc]);
  load_psw (Loc[active_proc]);
```

Figure 5.5 illustrates the operation of the kernel, showing the overall effect of a processor reallocation after suspension of the active process.

5.3.4.2 Multiprocessor implementation

The description below is based on [Holt 83].

Let us start by specifying the hardware organization of a system. Processors, of which there are n, are identical and access a common memory. Each processor is named by a number (from 0 to $n-1$) and knows its own number. Two instructions are specific to multiprocessor operations:

Test and Set (R,m):	provides for mutual exclusion (see 5.1.1.2).
Interrupt (k):	causes an interrupt on processor *k*

An interrupt or a supervisor call causes the status word and registers of the processor in question to be stored on a memory stack specific to that processor.

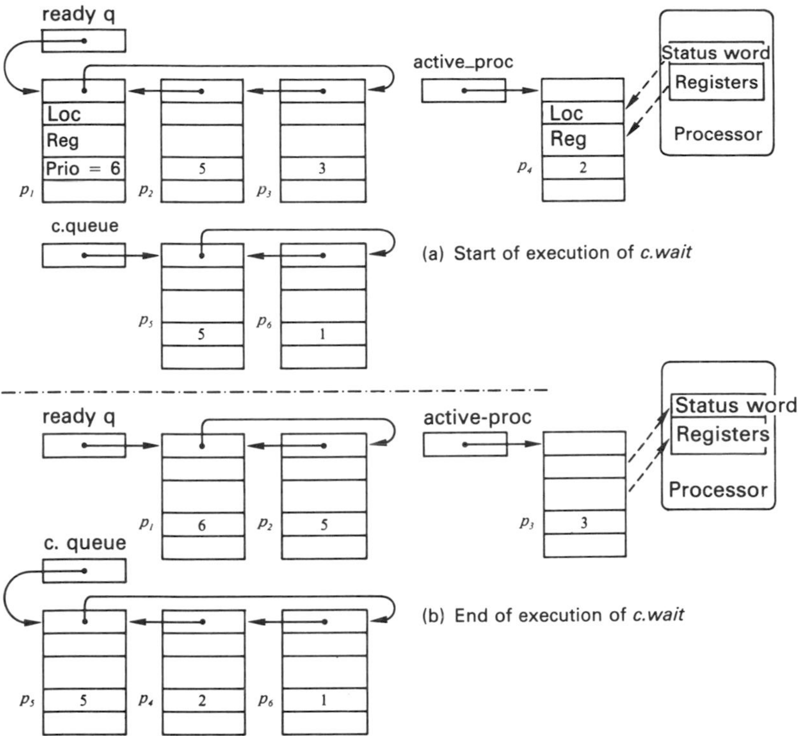

Fig. 5.5. Processor allocation

Any kernel primitive may execute on any one of the processors. As far as interrupts are concerned, we distinguish between those intended for a specific processor (processor clock, *Interrupt* instruction) and those which are general (e.g. input-output) which can be handled on any processor. In this case, we interrupt the processor executing the process with lowest priority. The number of that process is held in a reserved memory location *kmin*, and we assume that a hardware device directs general interrupts towards the processor of number *kmin*. We use the same choice criterion for processor reallocation.

We add a further *n* processes of low priority to the queue of ready processes, to ensure that it is never empty. The number of the active process on processor *k* is written *active_proc[k]*.

Mutual exclusion to kernel primitives uses a lock, consulted and updated by the *test and set* instruction.

```
prologue:                -- processor k

   <mask interrupts>;
   Loc[active_proc[k]]:=top(loc_stack);
   Reg[active_proc[k]]:=top(reg_stack)
test: Test And Set(R,lock);
   if R<>0 then
      goto test          -- busy wait
   endif
```

The dispatcher must ensure that the *n* active processes are at any moment those with highest priority from amongst the eligible processes. As execution of the current primitive might have modified the queue of ready processes, the priority of the first ready process is compared with that of the active processor on the processor *kmin*. If it is greater, the processor is preempted using the instruction *Interrupt.*

```
allocate_processor:                      -- on processor k

   remove(active_proc[k],ready_q);
   pr1:=Prio[first(ready_q)];
   pr2:=Prio[active_proc[kmin]];
   if Prio[active_proc[k]]<pr2 then      -- updating of kmin
      kmin:=k
   endif;
   lock:=0;                              -- end of critical section
   if pr1>pr2 then
      Interrupt(kmin)                    -- preemption
   endif;
   load_registers(Reg[active_proc[k]]);
   load_psw(Loc[active_proc[k]]);        -- interrupts unmasked
```

The preemption interrupt handler (for instruction *Interrupt*) simply has to reallocate the interrupted processor:

```
<handling of preemption interrupt and processing k>
   prologue;
   add(active_proc[k], ready_q);
   allocate_processor;
```

5.4 Bibliographic notes

The problem of mutual exclusion is formulated in [Dijkstra 65a], which presents Dekker's solution for two processes. The simpler version presented here is due to [Peterson 81]. The mutual exclusion algorithm is generalized to *n* processes in [Dijkstra 65b]. Other solutions are given in [Knuth 66, Eisenberg 72, Lamport 74]. The monograph [Raynal 84] is entirely dedicated to this problem.

The use of semaphores and primitives *P* and *V* for mutual exclusion and synchronization is discussed in [Dijkstra 65a and 71]. The semaphone invariant was introduced in [Habermann 72]. The implementation of semaphores and the management of interrupts in a synchronization kernel are described in [Wirth 69]; see also [Shaw 74, chapter 7]. The use of semaphores for programming operating systems is illustrated in [Dijkstra 68, Bétourné 71, Lauesen 75].

The first descriptions of the organization of a synchronization kernel appeared in [Saltzer 66, Lampson 68]. A simple kernel implementing communication by messages (the RC4000 system) is described in [Brinch Hansen 70 and 73]. Other examples of message kernels are Demos [Baskett 77], Thoth [Cheriton 79], Accent [Rashid 81], Chorus [Banino 80, Zimmermann 84]. Kernels implementing monitors are described in [Brinch Hansen 77, Lampson 80, Wirth 82, Holt 83]; these kernels are integrated into programming languages (Concurrent Pascal, Mesa, Modula-2, Concurrent Euclid respectively). The implementation of monitors is also studied in [Howard 76a, Lister 76, Schmid 76].

Exercises

Exercise 5.1

A multiprocessor has an instruction

XRM *Reg, addr*

whose effect is to exchange the contents of register *Reg* in the process executing the instruction and the contents of the memory location with address *addr*, blocking access to that location for as long as the operation lasts. Show that this instruction may be used instead of *Test And Set* to implement mutual exclusion by busy waiting.

Exercise 5.2 [Peterson 81]

Show that the algorithm described in section 5.1.2.1 implements mutual exclusion as specified.

Exercise 5.3 [Dijkstra 65b]

Generalize to the case of *n* processes the mutual exclusion algorithm by busy waiting from section 5.1.2.1.

Exercise 5.4

A semaphore *s* is said to be a **private** semaphore associated with a process *p* if only process *p* may execute the operation *P(s)*, while other processes can only execute *V(s)*. The initial value of *s.c* is set to 0.

The basic scheme for the use of a private semaphore is that of the client-server, with process *p* playing the role of the server:

```
process p (server)            process q (client)

loop                          ...
  P(s)                        V(s) -- request for service
  <execution of service>      ...
endloop
```

1. Show that this scheme is valid whatever the number of clients.
2. Show that this scheme may be extended to any number of identical and equivalent servers (in the sense that the service required may be provided by any one of them).
3. Show how the client and server can communicate (to transmit parameters and any results there may be)
   - Using global variables shared by all processes
   - Using messages

Hint: Access to global variables must take place in a critical section; take care to avoid indefinite blocking of the server in this critical section.

Exercise 5.5

Using the private semaphore model introduced in exercise 5.4, deal with the producer and consumer problems. **Hint:** Deal first with the case of an infinite buffer. Then construct a symmetrical solution for a buffer of finite size, treating the consumer as a 'producer of empty buffers'.

Exercise 5.6

Using the private semaphore model (exercise 5.4), show how the execution of coroutines may be represented by means of processes.

Exercise 5.7

Using processes synchronized by private semaphores (exercise 5.4), represent the operation of input-output on the CDC 6600 (see section 2.2).

Exercise 5.8

Use private semaphores (exercise 5.4) to deal with the synchronization problems posed in chapter 4:

- The barber problem (exercise 4.3)
- The dining philosophers problem (exercise 4.5)
- The multiple producers and consumers problem (exercise 4.9)

Exercise 5.9

To supplement the primitives in Thoth (section 4.4.2) we add the primitive

wait_interrupt (level)

which suspends the calling process until an interrupt arrives on the specified level.

1. What restrictions should be applied to the use of this primitive, and how should they be implemented?
2. What constraints does this primitive impose on process priority?
3. Using primitives specified in this way, program the measurement problem from exercise 2.2.

Exercise 5.10

Using semaphores, give an outline implementation of a synchronization kernel implementing communication by messages using primitives from the Thoth system (see section 4.4.4.2), including the *wait_interrupt* primitive from the previous exercise.

Exercise 5.11

Produce another implementation of the kernel specified in the preceding exercise using queues directly.

Exercise 5.12

A set of communication primitives by means of messages can be specified as follows:

create (port)

which creates a new port, to which the calling process and it alone can connect as receiver;

connect (port)

which associates the calling process, as receiver, with the specified port;

disconnect (port)

dissociates the calling process from the specified port (no message must be waiting at the port);

send (message, port)

sends the message to the specified part; non-blocking, unless the buffer is full;

receive (message, port)

receives a message from the specified port (the process must be associated with it); blocking if there are no messages.

Once a process has been created, it is initially associated with a port whose name can be determined from that of the process.

1. Show on what basis a kernel can be built up to implement these primitives, using queues directly. Specify and handle error cases.

2. Specify and program a primitive allowing multiple waiting by a process for several ports.

Exercise 5.13

Write the program for procedures *allocate_context* and *free_context* as specified in section 5.3.3, on the following two assumptions:

1. The process context blocks are held in a table containing a fixed number of entries.

2. The context blocks are allocated dynamically to a memory zone managed as a heap.

Exercise 5.14

Write programs for operations *fork, join* and *exit* defined in section 4.5, using procedures for the management of queues and contexts described in sections 5.3.1.2 and 5.3.3.

Exercise 5.15

Assume that a synchronization kernel implements monitors along the lines described in section 5.3.2. We want to build up the process management system above this kernel, using monitors. For this purpose, we assume that a single primitive process that cannot be deleted is created with the system itself. All other processes are its descendants. The process management operations *(create, kill, suspend, resume)* are implemented by the external procedures (entry points) of a monitor, *process_management*. Write the program for this monitor (assuming that queue and context management procedures are accessible within the monitor).

Exercise 5.16

Write the program for process queue handling procedures specified in section 5.3.1.2, with the following two forms of organization: singly-linked lists and doubly-linked lists with a pointer to the last element. Given the operations carried out, discuss the advantages of each of these two forms of organizations as a function of the mean number of processes in the queues.

Exercise 5.17

Construct the data and program structures needed to implement semaphores and primitives P and V using the queue management procedures specified in section 5.3.1.2. How can interrupt management be integrated with a kernel implementing these semaphores? Take as an application example the driving of a peripheral, with or without a watchdog timer.

Exercise 5.18

Show how the resource allocator program given in section 4.4.1 may be simplified using the primitive *broadcast* described in section 5.3.2. Note the program for this primitive using the procedures and data structures described in section 5.3.1.2.

Exercise 5.19 [Hoare 74]

The aim of this exercise is to provide an implementation of monitors, as specified in section 4.3.3, assuming that semaphores are available.

1. We start by limiting our considerations to the case where the primitive *signal* can only appear at the end of an external procedure of the monitor. Show that it is enough to use a mutual exclusion semaphore for use of the monitor and a semaphore per condition. Write the program for the entry and exit sequences for the monitor and those for the primitives *wait* and *signal*.

2. Now consider the general case where the primitive *signal* may appear anywhere in the body of a monitor procedure. Rewrite in this case the programs for question 1. **Hint:** Use an additional semaphore making it possible to suspend processes which have executed the primitive *signal*; these processes must be reactivated as soon as possible and have priority over those which are awaiting entry to the monitor.

Exercise 5.20

Write the programs implementing monitors with Kessels' conditions (section 4.3.1.3)

1. Using semaphores
2. Using queues directly (see section 5.3.1.2)

Exercise 5.21 [Schmid 76]

1. Write the programs implementing conditional critical regions (exercise 4.15):
   a. Using semaphores
   b. Using queues directly

2. Can the programs be made more efficient if a condition is only reevaluated if a variable in it has been modified? **Hint:** Specify and implement dependence relations between expressions with respect to the bodies of regions; these relations may be determined statically by a compiler.

3. Apply the result of 2) above to implement monitors efficiently letters with Kessels' conditions (section 4.3.1.3).

Exercise 5.22

Modify the programs implementing monitors to include waiting with priority (section 4.4.6).

Exercise 5.23

Suggest an implementation of monitors in a monoprocessor, using interrupt masking to ensure mutual exclusion to monitor data. Discuss the advantages and disadvantages of this approach to the one described.

Exercise 5.24

Suggest an implementation of event counters and sequencers (exercise 4.18):

- Using semaphores
- Using queues directly

Exercise 5.25

Suggest an implementation of the rendezvous mechanism in the Ada language (section 4.4.4.2):

1. Using semaphores
2. Using monitors
3. Using queues directly (see section 5.3.1.2)

Exercise 5.26

In the critical section entry sequence of a multiprocessor, can one interchange busy waiting using *Test And Set* and interrupt masking?

Exercise 5.27

In a multiprocessor system, it may be possible to dedicate a particular processor exclusively to the execution of kernel programs. Compare this solution with that of pooled processors.

Chapter 6

Naming, storing, and binding objects

This chapter is concerned with the underlying principles of information management in an operating system. The concept of an object, introduced in chapter 3, provides the guiding thread through this study. We shall start, in section 6.1, by identifying a number of fundamental concepts which will allow us to understand more clearly the various mechanisms of information management within a system: names, access paths, links and object protection. We shall apply these concepts to a study of two major fields: naming and binding of files (section 6.2) and linking of programs and data (section 6.3). Finally, in section 6.4 we shall present the basic hardware and software mechanisms making object management easier (segments and capabilities) with examples of their implementation in systems.

6.1 Underlying principles of information management

The concepts of a name, of a value, of a type, of naming and of representation appear in computer science in many different guises. The elaboration of a general model for these concepts is still an open problem. Here we shall merely present a simplified model, derived from a study of programming languages, which allows us to account for the most common situations.

6.1.1 General definitions

A computer system program describes a system as a set of objects (in the sense used in section 3.1.2); the objects, and the operations associated with them, are those specified by the language used. To implement a system described in this way on a computer installation, we have to define a concrete **representation** for each object, in the form of a set of data in memory, of peripheral devices, etc. Implementation of a system is then expressed by actions modifying the state of these representations.

This representation process uses two basic approaches. In the **compilation** approach, abstract objects specified by the program are replaced, during a preliminary translation phase, by their representations. These are executable objects directly interpreted by a hardware device. In the **interpretation** approach, on the other hand, a software system (the interpreter) is fed directly with the program; it assigns (statically or dynamically) a representation to each object, and implements the mapping between the abstract object and the representation in the course of each access operation. Interpretation is generally less efficient than compilation, as the mapping has to be set up during each access operation, but it lends itself better, for this very reason, to dynamic management of objects (replacement of an object by another, changes in object representations). In practice, it is common to combine the two approaches in a way that takes account of the specific constraints in particulare circumstances.

The system program uses **names** to identify the objects that make it up. The name of an object is an item of information with two functions: on the one hand, it identifies the object named, i.e. it distinguishes it from other objects; on the other hand, it provides an 'access channel' to the object, i.e. it undergoes interpretation allowing actions to be carried out on the object. This interpretation is defined by the semantics of the language used. Examples of names are identifiers naming variables and procedures in a programming language or files in a command language.

When a system is implemented on a computer installation, the objects making it up are concretized by their representations; each representation is defined by an item of information allowing physical processes to access them, using interpretation rules. These items of information are also names; nevertheless, as they are physical locations, we tend to use the term **addresses** in this case. These may be addresses of memory locations, or also addresses of processes or peripherals on a bus, track or sector numbers on a disk, etc. In section 6.1.2, we shall study the structure of representations and the interpretation of names.

We shall use the general term **binding** for the establishment of a correspondence between a system program and its concrete representation. Binding is expressed, in the final analysis, by the establishment of a mapping between identifiers and addresses. That mapping is often set up in successive stages: we move from the identifier to the address through a series of relations called the **access path**. Binding will be studied in section 6.1.3 and many examples given of it in sections 6.2 and 6.3.

6.1.2 Interpretation of names

6.1.2.1 Composition of the access path

We shall now analyze in greater detail the nature of relations which make up an access path. Let us remember that the aim is to move from an identifier (say *X*) which names an object to a concrete representation (say *R*) of this object, in order to carry out an access function which consults or modifies the state of that representation. Assuming that the object considered is a variable that can be represented in a single memory location, we can start by distinguishing between two extreme situations corresponding to the two methods of execution described above:

1. 'Pure' interpretation: the identifier X is passed as argument to a procedure which determines the location of R, executes the expected action and if appropriate returns the results requested.

2. 'Pure' compilation: in the course of a separate translation stage, all occurrences of identifier X in an initial program (or 'source' program) are replaced by the (absolute) address of the representation R. We assume that the language is capable of being translated in this way and, in particular, that it involves no dynamic management of variables at run time. The resulting program (or 'object' program) is then executed; the absolute address is interpreted by the physical processor to access R.

Let us for the moment leave aside considerations associated with types, i.e. with the specification and representation of permitted access functions, and only consider problems of physically locating objects. In the interpretation approach, location is determined at access time, by the executing of a procedure which computes an address from an identifier.([1]) In the compilation approach, there is substitution beforehand of new information (the address) for the identifier; the correspondence between identifiers and addresses is determined in the compilation stage. In both cases, a relation between the address and the representation is implemented, through interpretation, by the physical processor. These relations are shown in fig. 6.1.

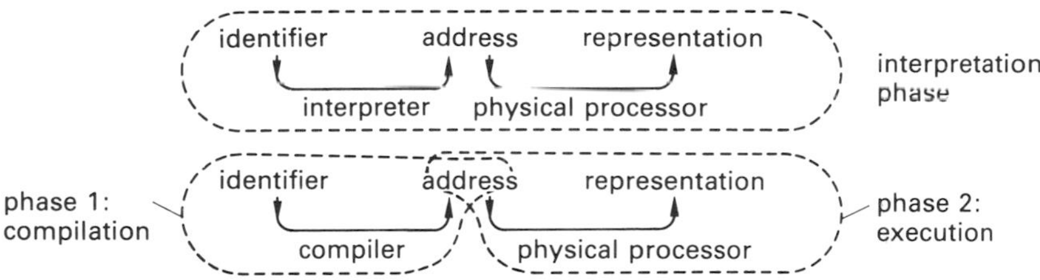

Fig. 6.1. Examples of access paths

In practice, we most often meet an intermediate situation in which both approaches are applied at different stages. For example, in a language which includes dynamic management during execution, the addresses of certain objects (arrays with variable dimensions, variables local to procedures, etc.) can only be determined at run time and the method used is therefore partly

([1]) This representation is determined in the course of execution of the procedure, whether or not it is returned as the result of that procedure.

based on interpretation. In what follows, we shall meet many other examples of mixed methods of this kind.

The two types of relations we have just been considering establish a correspondence between an object and a name: they are, by definition, **naming** relations. The target object of a naming relation may itself be reinterpreted as a name: the access path is therefore a combination of any number of naming relations. An object which plays the role of a relay in an access path is also called a **reference**. Examples of references are pointers in the Pascal language, or descriptors, a construct which we shall meet in many examples.

The combination of several naming relations is a naming relation. This leads to two consequences (see fig. 6.2):

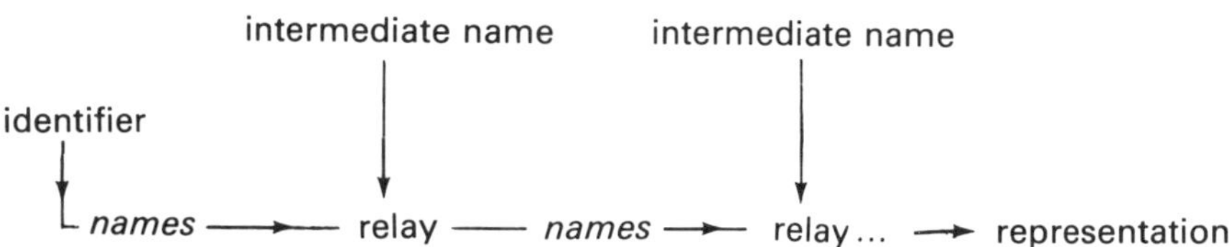

Fig. 6.2. Access path

1. The starting name of an access path names not only the final term of the path (the representation) but all intermediate terms (references).

2. Once an access path has been established, the representation can be accessed from the name of any of the intermediate references.

In sections 6.2 and 6.3 we shall examine many practical applications of this mechanism.

Note 1: The various relations that make up an access path are implemented at different moments. For example, the relation *names* between the identifier X and the reference towards R is only implemented during the compilation stage, in the symbol table managed by the compiler. If this relation is to be used during the execution phase (to assist debugging), the symbol table must be stored. We shall consider this point again in section 6.1.3.

Note 2: A specific terminology is sometimes used to distinguish the various naming relations: a relation established by the execution of a procedure is called *delivering*; the relation between a reference and the object it names is called *referencing*; the relation between an address and the object represented in the memory location corresponding to it is called *containing*.

6.1.2.2 Representation structures; descriptors

The simple approach we have just described only applies to elementary objects, such as integers, real numbers or characters, whose representation occupies only one memory location and for which access functions are directly represented by instructions on a physical machine. We have to add to the mechanism to take account of two aspects:

1. The existence of **composite objects**, whose internal structure may be complex and whose size can vary during the lifetime of the object

2. The need to implement complex access functions to composite objects

To be absolutely rigorous, the representation of an object would have to include all the information allowing it to be found and used. In practice, it is convenient to separate the representation into two physically distinct parts:

1. A collection of items of information of a fixed and generally small size called a **descriptor** of the object, which contains:
   - Information describing the composition of the objects and the physical location of its parts (number, nature and size of components, pointers, etc.)
   - Information on the way an object may be used: type, protection, lifetime, names or addresses of access procedures, etc.

2. Representation as such (i.e. the 'value') of the object; note that a descriptor is a reference, in the sense defined in section 6.1.2.1

Note 1: Tagged machines. On certain machines (e.g. Burroughs B6700), the value of an object and any supplementary information on its use are represented in a single location. The supplementary information, called a **tag**, is interpreted by machine instructions. For example, an arithmetic operation one of whose operands is in memory, takes place in fixed or floating point depending on whether the tag specifies an integer or a real operand. The concept of a tag is therefore similar to that of a descriptor.

Note 2: Information defining access functions to an object are in fact distributed between the text of procedures carrying out this access and the object descriptor. The way information is distributed depends on the characteristics of the physical machine available and the qualities required of the system: efficiency in execution, ease of modification, etc. For example, judicious use of all information associated with the type of an object makes it possible to check the validity of its use during compilation or linking. At the other extreme, execution by interpretation alone, which is more costly, makes it possible to do without the concept of a type, leaving checking to the execution stage.

The use of a descriptor for access to an object makes it obligatory to use an access program which interprets the descriptor (unless the machine used has *ad hoc* instructions; see note 1 above, and section 6.4).

The use of descriptors has the following advantages:

1. If an object described is passed as a parameter to a procedure, it is only necessary to transmit the descriptor, or its address: it is much simpler to

manage information whose size is fixed and known in advance than information of variable size.

2. The descriptor is an obligatory 'transition point' for access to the object referenced and can therefore be used to implement access checking, measurements, etc.

3. The descriptor allows for indirect access to the object referenced, allowing dynamic modifications to the access path (substitution of one object for another) or relocation of the object in memory without recompiling the source program.

4. The sharing of objects between several users with different rights or access procedures may be implemented by setting up as many descriptors as there are users; these descriptors reference the same objects and therefore contain the same information about physical location.

Example: An array is generally referenced by a descriptor, containing the starting address of its position in memory, the number of locations occupied by an element, the number of dimensions and, for each dimension, the extreme values of the indices. This information makes it possible to compute the address of any element in the array; it also makes it possible to check that the indices entered are within the permitted ranges.

The concept of a descriptor is heavily used in file management systems (see section 6.2 and chapter 7). Another application is for implementing segmented addressing mechanisms. Segmentation is an elementary tool to assist software structuring. A **segment** is a composite object, of variable size, whose memory representation occupies a series of consecutive locations; it allows objects with logical links between them to be grouped together. Segmentation allows a user to organize programs and data as a set of segments, without worrying about how they are physically located. For example, each procedure in a composite program may occupy a distinct segment. In machines with segmented addressing, each segment is referenced by a descriptor; the names of these descriptors is directly interpreted by the processor. The concept of a segment and its extensions are examined in section 6.4.

6.1.2.3 Scope and lifetime; context

We could envisage a situation where a set of objects in a system is immutable and uniformly accessible at any moment by all processes, and in the same way as memory as a whole is fixed and accessible to a physical processor (in the absence of any protection device). This is not usually the case: the set of objects accessible to a process changes through time, for the following reasons:

1. *Decomposition of applications*. The methods used to structure a complex application start by defining components (modules, procedures, etc.). Each of these components is associated with a distinct set of accessible objects.

2. *Dynamic management*. The set of objects accessible to a process can change in composition because of the nature of the application itself: objects may be created or deleted during execution.

3. *Protection*. A si[illegible]cess from reaching an object it is forbidden t[illegible]h between the process and the objects for as[illegible]avoids having to make costly checks during [illegible]

4. *Efficiency*. If we [illegible]mong others, searching is all the more efficie[illegible]ects is. If, furthermore, storing of objects use[illegible]rarchy, it is desirable to determine as accura[illegible] the number of objects that are potentially [illegible]g the faster memory.

We must therefor[illegible] of dynamic changes, on the one hand in the [illegible]s paths to objects from a process. A numbe[illegible] for this purpose.

We use the term [illegible]rs. A **context** associated with a dictionary is [illegible] objects named by identifiers in the diction[illegible]n access path from one of the identifiers). T[illegible] is the state of the set of objects making u[illegible]

Simply providi[illegible]define a context: we have also to specify th[illegible]o be applied to the identifiers making it up. We use the te[illegible] for the combination of a dictionary and the information (programs, data, interpretation rules) necessary to use the dictionary. Such information can take different forms depending on the language used (command or programming language).

In a program, the **scope** of an identifier is the program region where the identifier is valid, i.e. can be used as the origin of an access path. In other words, a process may use this identifier to name an object while it is executing that particular part of the program.

We use the term **lifetime** of an object for the time during which it exists (i.e. the period separating its creation from its deletion). This concept also applies to an access path.

When a process executes a program, the set of objects to which it can gain access is defined at any moment by applying the interpretation rules specified by the current environment to the identifiers valid at that moment: here we are back at the concept of a process execution context introduced in chapter 4.

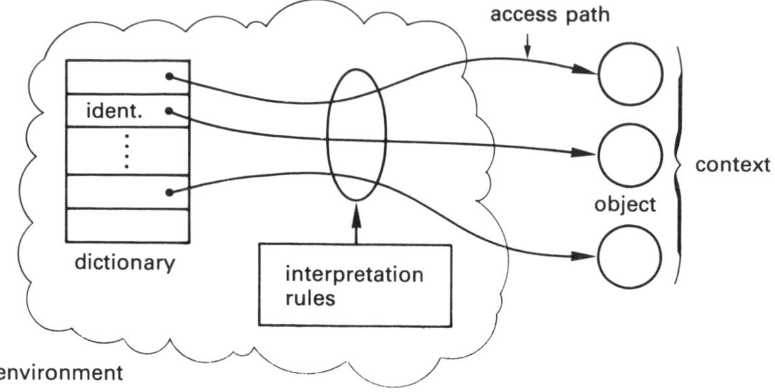

Fig. 6.3. Execution context of a process

Example: Consider a process (assumed to be unique) associated with a user of an interactive system. In the environment defined by the command language interpreter, the dictionary includes the names of files accessible to the user. When the user orders the execution of a procedure, the environment changes: the dictionary includes identifiers defined within the procedure by the scope rules of the language and interpreted according to the rules specific to that language. Depending on how the operating system was specified, file identifiers may still be usable or not (with their own interpretation rules).

Note that though the execution stage of a process (the 'values' of the objects in its context) may be modified at each instruction, the composition of the context itself (the identity of the objects that make it up) changes less frequently. Let us consider the main events which may modify the composition of a process context.

1. A change of environment, implying a change in the composition of a dictionary, and possibly the application of interpretation rules: procedure calls, on entry to a new block (in a block structured language), a change of the current directory (in a command language), etc.

2. Explicit modification of the access path from an identifier in the dictionary: association of a file or peripheral with an input-output stream.

3. Explicit creation or deletion of an object named by an identifier in the dictionary: creation or deletion of a file, allocation or disposal of a dynamically managed variable.

An examination of these different cases highlights the differences between the lifetime of an object, of an identifier naming that object and of an access path leading to that object. Different situations are possible: an identifier may be linked in turn to several different objects; conversely, an object may be named in turn (or simultaneously) by several different identifiers; finally, an object may become inaccessible (no path leads to it). In general, for security reasons, the lifetime of an object must be at least equal to that of the access path leading to it. The existence of inaccessible objects leads to problems of recovering the memory space they occupy: 'garbage collection' techniques make it possible.

Example: By way of example, we shall indicate the various classes of objects accessible to a process executing a procedure, assumed to be expressed in a high-level language. These classes differ in their lifetime, the duration of their binding and the way their objects are shared.

1. *Objects internal to the procedure:* these are instructions which make up the text of a procedure. They are named by labels used in branching instructions. Their lifetime is that of the procedure.

2. *Local objets:* these are variables declared within a procedure. These objects are created each time the procedure is called and deleted on return from the procedure. In cases of recursive calls, a new copy of each local object is created on each call, and its identifier names the latest copy created (the others remain inaccessible until a return to the corresponding level takes place).

3. *Remanent and global objects:* these are objects which preexist a call to a procedure and supply a return from it; their lifetime is either that of the processes (remanent objects) or that of an enclosing procedure (global objects).

4. *External objects:* these are objects constructed and maintained independently of a procedure and the process considered (other procedures, files, etc.). Their lifetime is independent of that of the procedure and of the process; they may be created or deleted dynamically during its execution.

5. *Parameters:* formal parameters are identifiers used within a procedure and bound, at the earliest, when the procedure is called. Objects to which they are bound are called actual parameters; they are provided by the calling procedure or are external objects. Binding between formal and actual parameters may take different forms depending on the rules defined by the programming language: call by name, by value, or by reference. These forms differ by moment at which the binding is established and by how long it lasts. Parameters are unbound on return from the procedure.

When several processes share a procedure, each of them has its own copy of local, remanent and global objects. External objects exist in a single copy, as does the (invariant) text of the procedure.

6.1.3 Linkage

Binding is the process of building the access path. That process covers a wide range of situations. We shall analyze it from the point of view of several criteria: the nature of the naming relation established, the moment the link is made and the length of time the link lasts; we shall also discuss the main techniques used.

6.1.3.1 Characteristics of a link

A link between two objects in a program may be established at different moments of its lifetime in the system:

1. When the program is written. This is the case of a program written directly in binary code, where each object is named by the absolute address of its location. Such a program is immediately executable, but modifications are difficult to make and entail a high risk of error. In practice, the only objects bound during program writing are universal identifiers naming constants.

2. During a translation stage (assembly or compilation). The link is definitively made if the identifiers are replaced by absolute addresses. The disadvantage is that the program can no longer be moved in memory without being recompiled (if there is no address relocation mechanism). In addition, the binding established during translation is generally only partial:([1]) identifiers will be be replaced not by an absolute addresses, but by addresses relative to the program origin (displacements). Absolute addresses are determined during the final stage below.

3. During the loading and link editing stage. The loading stage is used to replace relative addresses by absolute addresses, by determining the point of origin of programs in memory. The link editing stage establishes links for external references (remember that these are identifiers naming objects constructed or stored independently of the program being processed). Loading and link editing may be combined into a single operation or carried out separately. The algorithms implemented are described in section 6.3.

An operation analogous to link editing is binding of input-output streams with files or peripherals. In the same way as link editing, this operation, described in section 6.2.3.2 may be implemented before execution or in the course of execution.

4. During execution; the binding is then said to be **dynamic**. Binding may be delayed until the execution stage for several reasons.

- The necessary information may not be known before, in particular if the objects named are created dynamically and are therefore unknown at compile time.
- The access path itself may be modified in the course of execution: this is the case if an identifier is reused to name several objects in turn (e.g. an input-output stream used with several different files).
- The interpretation mechanism itself imposes a dynamic binding: this is

([1]) Except in job sequencing systems called 'compile and go' where programs are translated and executed immediately; these systems are used for short programs intended to be used only once.

the case, for example, of local variables in a recursive procedure, whose addresses can only be determined in the course of execution.

Dynamic binding generally involves completing an access path which has already been partially established.

The table below summarizes the characteristics of binding according to the moment when it is established.

Binding	Conditions	Characteristics
Early		
	Information known in advance execution conditions determined once and for all	Efficiency on execution Access path not modifiable
Late		
	Information partially known	Need to store linkage information
	Variable execution conditions	Increased execution time Adaptable programs

If the main criterion is the ease of use of a system and its adaptability to different execution conditions (which is often the case in interactive work), it is a good idea to *delay binding time*. The main motivation for early binding is efficiency on execution.

6.1.3.2 Binding techniques

The construction of an access path uses two basic techniques: substitution and chaining, whose operation we shall illustrate by means of an example (fig. 6.4). Let X be an identifier, R be the representation of the object it names and a the address of R. Binding by substitution involves replacing all occurrences of X by a. Binding by chaining involves replacing all the occurrences of X by the name r of a relay object, which is provided with the address a. This process can easily be generalized to a path made up of any number of relations; the two techniques can be combined into a single binding operation.

Two characteristics distinguish the techniques from each other:

- Duration of the link. An access path established by substitution is not modifiable without restarting the linkage process. On the other hand, it is easy to modify a chained binding: we simply need to provide the relay with a new object name.

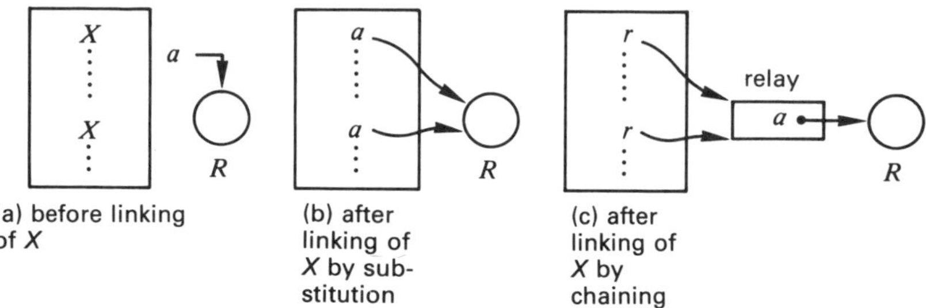

Fig. 6.4. Linking by substitution and linking by chaining

- Efficiency on execution. Traversing a path involves additional indirection which increases access time to the objects named.

When implementing a link, account has to be taken of the characteristics of the machine which is to interpret the access paths established; in particular, it is important to make the best possible use of address computation mechanisms allowing access to memory locations and therefore to object representations. Two such mechanisms are indexing and indirect addressing. They are commonly used as follows:

- Indexing makes it possible to name a series of contiguous (or regularly spaced) locations using names formed from consecutive integers. A set of objects stored in such a series of locations and named in this way is called a **region of objects**.
- Indirection is a natural way of implementing access by chaining. Combining indexing and indirection (in that order) allows consecutive integers to be used to name a series of objects whose names are stored in a series of contiguous locations. Such a set of relays is called a **linkage region**.

The use of these techniques is illustrated by numerous examples in sections 6.2 and 6.3. The use of other addressing mechanisms such as base registers and segmentation is discussed in section 6.4.

6.1.4 Protection

6.1.4.1 Introduction

The term **protection** is used for all the methods and tools intended to specify the rules for using objects and to guarantee that the rules are obeyed. Protection is generally provided by a combination of hardware and software mechanisms.

There are close links between the naming of objects and their protection.

Here three aspects have to be borne in mind:

1. A simple way of preventing the process from ever gaining access to an object is to eliminate any access path to this object, i.e. to remove it from the context of the process.

2. If the operations allowed on an object are specified by its belonging to a class or a type, it is possible to check before execution (i.e. at the compilation or link editing stage) that the object is being used in a way that conforms to the rules specified.

3. If checking has to take place at run time, the obligation to go through an access procedure makes implementation easier and reduces the risk of error. The procedure may be implemented in software (an obligatory interpretation stage) or in hardware (obligatory transition through a device interpreted by the machine, such as a capability (see section 6.4.3)).

We shall start by considering a simple model which makes it possible to introduce the main concepts needed for a study of protection. Mechanisms allowing the implementation of protection in a computer system are described in section 6.4.

6.1.4.2 Domains and access rights

Among the objects making up a computer system, we use the word 'active' for all those which act on other objects by modifying their state. Operating rules may be expressed by specifying the **access rights** of each of these active objects, i.e. the set of operations it may execute on other objects.

We need a more precise definition of the concept of an 'active object', i.e. one which defines the entities with which rights are associated. We could decide to associate rights directly with processes; such a decision, however, makes it difficult to find a simple expression for:

1. The possibility that a process's rights may change dynamically

2. The fact that in similar circumstances several processes may have the same set of rights

To take account of these two aspects we introduce the concept of a protection **domain**. This is a particular case of the concept of an environment; a domain defines:

- A set of accessible objects, or context
- For each of these objects, a set of permitted operations (rights)
- A mechanism providing for access to objects in a way that respects the restrictions above

A process always executes in a specifically defined domain; its context is that associated with the domain and it has the specified rights over the objects in that context. A special operation (domain call) allows processes to change domain. A domain is itself an object on which the call operation may be executed; other operations are defined below.

Example: Consider a set of processes executing on a procesor. Two domains (supervisor and user) may be defined depending on the mode of execution specified by the status word. In supervisor mode, the process may execute all the instructions in the processor; in user mode, it can only execute non-privileged instructions. A process can change domain by executing special instructions; if it is in supervisor mode, it only needs to load a status word specifying user mode; if it is in user mode, it can only move into supervisor mode following a trap or a supervisor call leading to a mode change. Note that, in this case, it can only execute the program associated with the trap or the supervisor call and not just any program. It is this restriction which ensures that the protection mechanism operates properly.

Protection domains may be defined in several ways; the following are a few possible choices:

- A domain for the operating system, and one for each user
- A domain for each subsystem implementing a particular function
- A domain for each environment (defined, for example, by an ordered pair such as (procedure, current file directory))

The choice may depend on the functions required and above all on the mechanisms available (see section 6.4).

Let us assume, for the time being, that the number of objects is fixed. Protection rules may be represented in the form of a two-dimensional array called an **access matrix**. This array has a row per domain D_i and a column per object A_j (Note that as domains are a particular form of object, they also appear in the columns). Entry *(i,j)* contains the rights a process executing in domain D_i has on object O_j (see fig. 6.5).

The notation *nil* means that O_j does not appear in the context for domain D_i and cannot therefore be named by a process executing in that domain. The notation <> is used for an empty access list. In either case, O_j is inaccessible in D_i; the difference becomes clear if we want to give D_i rights over

	file1	file2	periph	D_1	D_2	D_3
D_1	<read, write, exec.>	<read, write>	<allocate, preempt>	<>	<call>	<change rights>
D_2	<read>	<read, exec.>	<request release>	<call>	<>	<call>
D_3	<exec.>	nil	<>	nil	<call>	<>

Fig. 6.5. Example of a rights matrix

O_j: in the first case, we first have to introduce O_j into the context for D_i, i.e. to bind it; in the second case, we only need to extend an already existing list.

In practice, the access matrix is very sparse, i.e. there are many entries *(i,j)* containing *nil* or $<>$. The access matrix is not therefore represented as such. Two representation techniques are used:

1. Representation by columns: access lists

An **access list** associated with an object is a list $(D_i, <d_i>)$ where D_i names a domain containing the object and $<d_i>$ is the set of rights the domain has on the object. For example, if a domain is associated with each user in a time-sharing system, the access list for a file contains a list of operations each of the users is allowed to carry out on that file.

A common method to reduce the size of the representation of an access list is to specify default rights for all domains over an object. For example, it might be specified that read-only access to all files is allowed, by default, for all users. The access list then only has to contain the ordered pairs $D_i<d_i>)$ for rights differing from the default option.

2. Representation by rows: list of rights and capabilities

The **list of rights** associated with a domain is a list $(O_j, <d_j>)$ where O_j names an object appearing in the context of a domain and $<d_j>$ is the set of that domain's rights on O_j. A process executing in the domain in question acquires that list of rights; each time it accesses an object, the access mechanism checks that the operation under way is legitimate, i.e. that it appears in $<d_i>$. To maintain a good level of efficiency, the mechanism should be hard-wired. The most primitive form is the supervisor-user bit in the status word of the processor. A more sophisticated form is a **capability** (see section 6.4.3) which brings together an object address and the status rights allowed on it in a single data structure, interpreted at each access operation. The list of rights in a domain then becomes a list of capabilities.

A domain change is a major operation, which allows a process to modify its environment and its rights over objects. Such a change often takes the form of a procedure call, when the process has to return to its initial domain. To ensure that protection rules are respected, precautions have to be taken every time rights are extended. This can happen either during a procedure call or on a return. To monitor the change operation, we impose the requirement that both calls to and returns from a domain can only take place by executing specified procedures (call or return **gates**) whose (protected) program ensures that the specified rules are respected. The domain protection mechanism prevents changes in domain except through gates.

Example: In the case of domains defined by supervisor and user modes, the call gates, in user mode, are defined by traps and supervisor calls implementing primitives in the operating system interface. Programs for these primitives, which are protected, check that transmitted parameters are valid. As rights in supervisor mode are always more extensive than in user mode, a return gate is unnecessary if primitives are entirely executed in supervisor mode; a gate becomes necessary if the primitives have to call a user mode procedure, as there will be an extension in rights on return.

Sections 6.4.2 and 6.4.3 give a more detailed study of protection mechanisms as well as examples of their use in operating systems.

6.1.4.3 Protection problems

We shall now briefly present a few of the problems associated with the implementation of protection mechanisms in operating systems.

1. Hierarchical protection

In this simple situation, the aim is to protect a subsystem *A* against errors or abuse occurring in a subsystem *B*, which uses services from *A*, but has no other rights over *A*. *A* accesses all information in *B* without restriction. *A* might, for example, be an operating system and *B* a user program. The problem is solved by hierarchical mechanisms such as supervisor/user modes, with obligatory use of a supervisor call to communicate between *B* and *A*. The protection ring model (see section 6.4.2.5) is a generalization of this principle.

2. Mutually suspicious subsystems

We say that two interacting subsystems are mutually suspicious if each specifies that certain information must be protected against errors or abuse from the other. This situation cannot be handled by a hierarchical protection mechanism.

3. Allocation and revocation of access rights

The problem posed here is that of dynamic modification of access rights. The aim, in particular, is to be able to extend or restrict the rights of a domain. If transmission may be transitive (the extension of rights in a domain allows it in turn to pass on those rights), it may be difficult to determine at any time what rights are associated with the use of a given object. There is then a problem if we decide to restrict or to revoke those rights for all or some of the domains which may access the object. A possible solution is to require all access operations to go through a single point (a descriptor). But this method does not make it possible to handle cases of selective revocation, for which it may be necessary to maintain reverse links between an object and the domains accessing it.

6.2 Application 1: naming and binding of files and input-output devices

The concept of a file was introduced in chapters 1 and 3, as an information storage unit for a user. A study of the organization of files and the implementation of their access functions is given in chapter 7; in this chapter, we shall simply examine modes for file naming, binding with programs using them and their relations with input-output operations. We do not need to understand the internal organization of a file for this study: all we are concerned with is naming it as a single whole, in a command language or in a program.

6.2.1 File access paths

A file is a composite object: it therefore has a descriptor, which in particular contains the information necessary to locate it physically and to implement access functions to it. For the operating system, giving the name of a file descriptor (physical address or index in a descriptor table) allows access to the file. This descriptor name, generally unknown to users and reserved for the operating system's use, is called the file's **internal name**. A file's descriptor and internal name are unique. The content of a file descriptor is discussed in detail in section 7.4.

Users name files by means of identifiers known as symbolic names (the variety of names used is a matter of convenience; see section 6.2.3). Such symbolic names are generally defined in an environment common to several users, or to the whole system. The data structures making it possible to build the access path to a file using one of its symbolic names are called **directories**. The structure of directories and the interpretation of symbolic names are described in section 6.2.2.

Apart from internal and symbolic names, a third type of name is often defined, called the temporary or **local** name. A local name is defined in an environment specific to the user, and which only exists temporarily (e.g. for as long as a program is executing). There are three advantages in using such names:

- Efficiency: local names are defined in a smaller environment than symbolic names and their interpretation is therefore quicker (directories are only searched when the local name is declared and not each time a file is accessed).

- Ease of use and adaptability of programs: the same local name can be reused to name different files at different times, making it possible to reuse a program with different files without having to modify its text.
- Selective access: the interpretation of local names makes it possible to implement selective access to a file for individual users (different access functions or access rights).

Links to local names are established by chaining: a local name specifies a relay called the local descriptor which itself has direct or indirect accesses to the unique descriptor of the file.

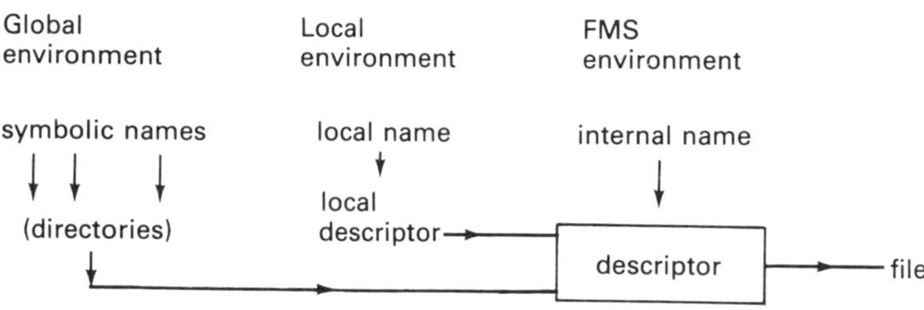

Fig. 6.6. Access paths to a file

6.2.2 Symbolic naming of files; directories

In this section we shall consider the way a user can name files by means of identifiers, or symbolic names, and the data structures, or directories, making it possible to find a file descriptor starting from its symbolic name. To simplify our discussion, we shall assume that descriptors are directly contained in the directory; in fact, it is common for a directory to contain part of the descriptor, accompanied by an internal name allowing the rest to be found.

6.2.2.1 Introduction

A directory defines an environment, in the sense used in section 6.1.2, i.e. a set of identifiers, or dictionary, and rules for the interpretation of these identifiers.

The simplest form of organization can be illustrated by a table which associates the descriptor of the file with the identifier that names it. This table is managed by one of the usual techniques (sequential organization, hash-coding, etc.). Such a form of organization is described in section 3.3. It handles all names at the same level, which has the following disadvantages:

- In a single user system, it is useful to be able to classify files under various headings.

- In a multi-user system, possible conflicts due to different users using the same name for different files impose a restriction on the user's freedom of choice of names.
- In all cases, a search for a file with a particular name scans all the names, while information on the nature of the file or on where it belongs could accelerate the search by restricting the field of enquiry.

For all these reasons, a single-level form of organization (fig. 6.7a) is only used in very small single-user systems. Instead, a hierarchical organization is generally preferred, where files and directories are organized into a tree structure. This structure is reflected in that of the identifiers. The depth of the tree structure may be limited: e.g. a two-level structure (fig. 6.7b) makes it possible to define a directory for each user of the system, with the directories themselves belonging to a general directory.

The general model of hierarchical organization, which we shall describe now, was introduced by the Multics system; a number of systems drew their inspiration from it.

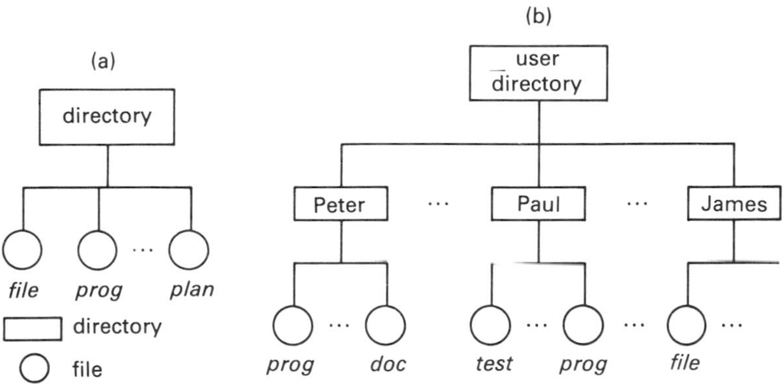

Fig. 6.7. One or two level file organization

6.2.2.2 Tree-structured organization

A tree-structured organization is defined as follows:

- Each directory is associated with a set (which may be empty) of other directories and files; these objects are said to be included in the directory; they are named by an identifier called a **simple name**. The relation between a directory and another included in the first is called filiation; it allows the definition of a **son** (the included directory) and a **father**.
- There is one and only one directory called the **root** which has no father. Any other directory has one and only one father.

The filiation relation defines a tree structure of directories whose origin is the root directory. The term ancestor is used for a directory which can be reached from another by means of a series of father relations, while the term descendant is used for a directory that can be reached from another by a series of son relations.

Starting from a given directory, there is a single path through the tree structure to each descendant. This property is used for naming: the name of a directory is made up of a concatenation of the successive simple names for its ancestors, from the starting directory; the name of a file is a concatenation of the enclosing directory and its simple name. In identifiers constructed along these lines (called qualified or composite names), a special symbol ('>' in Multics, '/' in Unix) is used to separate successive simple names.

It is then possible to associate an environment with each directory; the dictionary of this environment is the set of names, whether simple or qualified, built up as described above; the context is the combination of the directory considered, its descendants, and all files included in these directories. The environment and names associated with the root directory are called **universal**.

For example, in the Multics system, the symbol '>' is used as a separator to build up qualified names; used alone, it names, by convention and in any

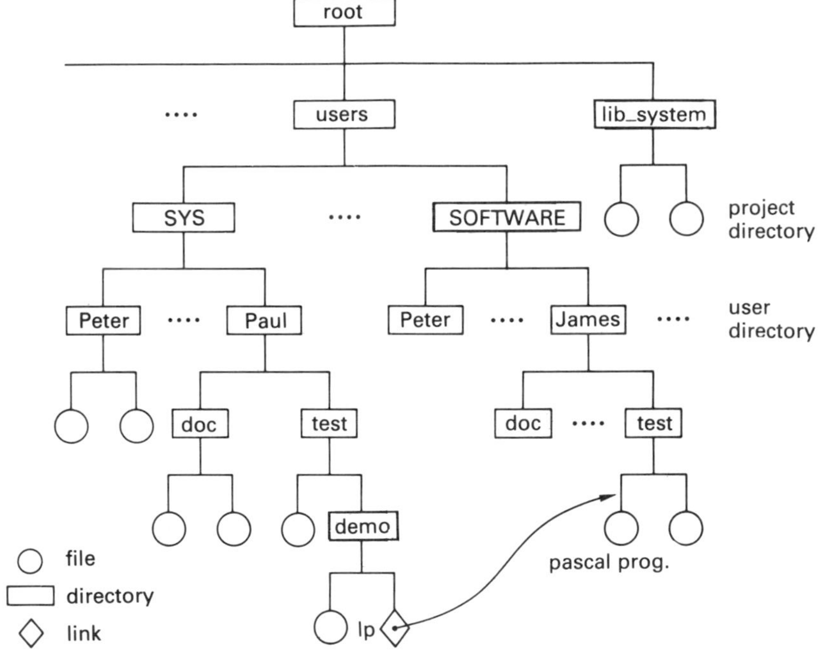

Fig. 6.8. Tree-structured organization of a file management system

environment, the root directory. A working directory is associated at any moment with any interactive user. By convention, the user environment is formed from the union of the environment defined by the current directory and the universal environment. The user can therefore use a universal name (beginning with '>') for any object; a simple name can be used for objects included in the working directory; a qualified name can be used for objects included in the descendants of this directory.

This mode of naming makes it possible to name any file; however, the universal name may be too long for objects at a great depth within the hierarchy. To allow a simpler form of naming of objects which are not descendants of the working directory, two extensions are defined in the construction of names:

1. Naming the father. By convention, a special symbol ('<' in Multics, '..' in Unix) can be used in any directory other than the root to name that directory's father. It can be used repeatedly ('<<' names the grandfather, etc.). This allows a simple way of naming objects included in 'brother' or 'cousin' directories of the working directory.

2. Creation of links. A **link** is the association between a simple name (link name) and another name (target name). The creation of a link in a directory introduces the simple name (link name), which must be kept distinct from other simple names appearing in the directory. This operation is linkage by chaining: when the link name is interpreted, in the environment of the directory where it was created, it is replaced by the target name.

Example: In the example shown in figure 6.8 (based on Multics), the root includes several directories holding information necessary for system management (tables, libraries, etc.), as well as the general user directory. The organization of the user directory is based on a breakdown into 'projects'. Each user associated with a project has a directory which is given the user's name, and can organize information by creating links and descendants of the directory. For example, the file with universal name

>users>SOFTWARE>James>test>prog.pascal.

may also be named in other ways, depending on the directory which defines the current environment:

working directory	name
>users>SOFTWARE>James	*test>prog.pascal*
>users>SOFTWARE>Peter	*<James>test>prog.pascal*
>users>SYS>Paul	*<<SOFTWARE>James>test>prog.pascal*
>users>SYS>Paul	*test>demo>lp (example of a link)*

Note too that the user called Peter is involved in two projects and has a separate directory for each.

The possibility of creating links means that the naming system does not have a pure tree structure, and this can lead to difficult problems because of the multiplicity of access paths to an object. Various solutions are possible, which we shall illustrate by means of two examples.

Example 1: Links in Multics. In the Multics sytem, a link may name a file, a directory, or another link. The links have a lower status than other names. The target name is only interpreted when the link is used and not when it is created: it is possible to create a link with a target name designating no object. In the same way, the deletion of an object has no effect on the links which had that object as target; on the other hand, objects cannot be deleted by naming links pointing towards them. Finally, the problem of creating loops (links pointing indirectly towards themselves) is avoided, during interpretation, by setting a limit to the number of links which may form an access path.

Example 2: Links in Unix. In the Unix system, links can only be created to files and not to directories. The target name is interpreted during creation and must name an existing file. From the moment the link has been created, its status is identical to that of any other file name. Links may be eliminated, but deletion of the final link towards a file leads to deletion of the file. "Soft" links can also be defined; they are analogous to those in Multics.

6.2.2.3 Extensions and additions

Various operations on names and environments make file naming easier.

1. Interpretation of names

File names may undergo interpretation before use for object access. By way of example, here are two commonly used operations:

a. Suffixes. The file identifier structure can be used to provide information on their contents, and particularly on their types. For example, if

<file id.> ::=<simple.id>[(.<suffix>)]
<suffix> ::=<simple.id>
<simple.id>::=<identifier containing no '.'>

then a suffix or suffixes can specify the file type. The suffix *pascal* might identify a Pascal source file, the suffix *bin* is used for a relocatable binary file, the suffix *run* for an executable file, etc. Apart from the advantages for classification, these conventions make it easier to provide automatic handling of files, and in particular type checking before use.

b. Matching. Matching file names makes it possible to find files whose name contains a particular pattern of characters. If we agree that the character '*' may be replaced by any simple identifier, the notation *.*pascal* names any Pascal source file (in the current environment); the notation *dir>f** names all files (without a suffix) appearing in directory *dir* and whose name begins with *f*, etc. This makes it possible, for example, to specify that a class of files should be handled in a particular way.

2. Search rules

The concept of the current environment can also be extended by defining a sequence of environments (e.g. $E_1, E_2, \ldots E_n$) to be searched in turn if the file being looked for is not in the current environment. A user can specify, for example, that if a file is not in his or her particular directory, it should be searched for in the project's directory, then in the system directory, etc. This makes it easier, in particular, to provide tools common to several users. We say that the sequence $(E_1, \ldots E_n)$ defines a search rule.

3. Multiple naming

Finally, a file may be given several different names in a single environment, e.g. to create abreviations or to allow search rules to be applied. It is also possible to add or delete names (on condition that at least one name is maintained at all times). Such multiple naming is different from the creation of links: in particular, when a file is deleted, all identifiers naming it are deleted from the enclosing directory, while any links pointing to it are unaffected.

6.2.3 File binding and input-output

6.2.3.1 Input-output streams

A program exchanges information with the outside world by means of input-output operations allowing communication with a file or a peripheral. When a program is being written, it is not always possible to know which file or peripheral will be used for input-output; we often want to be able to use different file or peripherals each time the program is run. For this reason, it is useful to be able to delay the binding between a program and the files or peripherals it uses. We therefore introduce the concept of an **input-output stream**, a simple form of which we have already met (logical peripherals) in section 3.3.

An input-output stream is an object which has all the characteristics of an input-output device (name and access operations), but which has no real existence. To be used for information transfer, a stream must first be linked, by means of an operation called **assignment**, to a file or a peripheral. Information transfer described by operations on the stream then takes place on the file or peripheral associated with the stream. A stream may be reassigned each time the program is executed, but the text of a program, which only refers to the stream name, remains the same.

The implementation of the stream assignment uses a linkage technique based on chaining. Each stream is associated with a descriptor. The assignment operation consists of providing that descriptor with a pointer towards the file or peripheral descriptor to be associated with the stream. When input-output is executed on the stream, indirection allows the corresponding device to be reached (fig. 6.9).

The diagram in fig. 6.9 assumes that the stream descriptor points towards the procedure and the buffer zone used for input-output. The corresponding link may be implemented, depending on the system, either during assignment of the stream or during a subsequent opening stage (see chapter 7).

As for linkage editing, the assignment of streams used by a program will be carried out in two stages:

- Before execution of the program, by means of a command language instruction
- During execution, by means of a system primitive implemented by a supervisor call

Operating systems offer users a series of predefined streams that are initially associated, by default, with particular peripherals. For example, in an interactive system may define a standard input stream and a standard output stream; when a user lags in, these streams are associated, by default, with the keyboard and screen. They may be temporarily reassigned to files; in cases of error, the default assignment is automatically reestablished to allow the user to intervene.

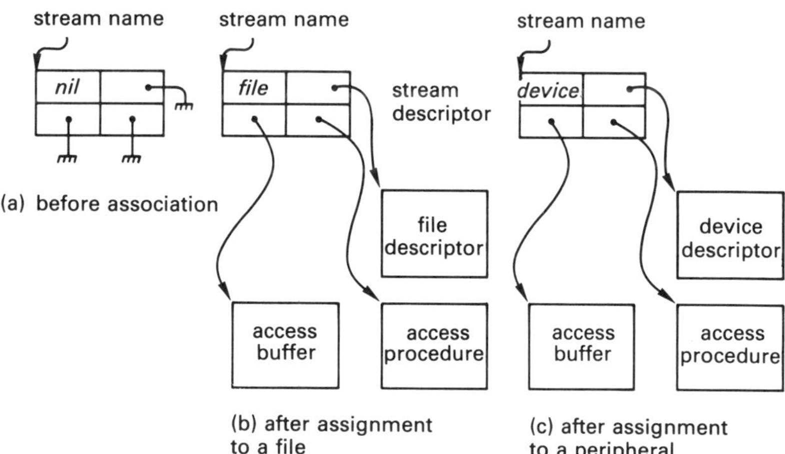

Fig. 6.9. Assignment of an input/output stream

Systems also commonly provide the possibility of creating new streams, which are added to those which have been predefined. Like stream assignment, stream creation may be requested by a command or a supervisor call.

Example: Streams in the Unix system. In the Unix system, files and peripherals are named in a uniform way. Two types of names are used: symbolic names, which are identifiers built up in a hierarchical way, and local names, which are integers. Symbolic names are interpreted in an environment global to all processes, and local names in the environment specific to each process. The creation and interpretation of local names are described in section 7.6.

Local names are also used to name **streams**. By convention, local names 0, 1 and 2 respectively name the standard input stream, the standard output stream and the stream on which error messages are transmitted. Every command is executed by a process created for this purpose, and which uses these three streams. Initially, the default associations for streams 0 and 1 are with the user's own keyboard and screen.

The system provides the following operations on streams:

1. Reassignment of streams. If *input_stream* and *output_stream* respectively name an input and an output stream, and *file_id* is a file identifier, the commands

command input_stream<file_id

and

command output_stream>file_id

respectively reassign *input_stream* and *output_stream* to *file_id* before executing *command*. If *input_stream* or *output_stream* is not specified, it takes the default value, respectively 0 or 1, corresponding to the standard streams. Consequently, the command:

a <source >dest

causes the execution of command *a* after having reassociated the input and output standard streams to files *source* and *dest* respectively.

2. Creation of pipes. A **pipe** (as they are called in Unix) is a buffer allowing two processes to communicate on the producer-consumer pattern. It includes an input stream (deposit) and an output stream (collection). A pipe can be created in two ways:

a. Implicitly, in the command language. A command of the form

a | b

where *a* and *b* are elementary commands has the following effect:

i. Creation of two processes, i.e. *proc_a* and *proc_b*, respectively responsible for executing *a* and *b*

ii. Creation of a pipe

iii. Reassignment of the standard output stream for *proc_a* to the pipe input stream, and the standard input stream for *proc_b* to the pipe output stream

From then on the processes operate as a producer-consumer pair. Several pipes can be created using a sequence *(a|b|c...)*; this allows chaining of a sequence of commands as a 'pipeline'. This construction may be combined with reassignment of streams (e.g.: *<source|b|c...>dest*).

b. Explicitly, by means of a supervisor call. A supervisor call allows a pipe to be created and local names to be obtained for its input and output streams; these names may then be associated with files. The local names are known to the calling process and its descendants.

6.2.3.2 Management of removable volumes

A **volume** is a removable information storage device. To access this information, the volume must be installed on an appropriate I/O device. The use of volumes allows:

- Extension (with no limit other than the volume's storage capacity) of the capacity of an installation
- File transfers between different installations

Examples of removable volumes are magnetic tapes (on spools or cassettes), floppy disks, disk packs, disk cartridges.

Security and ease of use require that a removable volume meets the following conditions:

1. That it contains all information making it possible to identify and physically locate the files it contains
2. That it can be installed on any device compatible with its nature

We talk about **mounting** a volume for the operation of physically installing the volume on a device and including its files in the current environment of the system. This is a binding operation which includes a physical aspect (allocation of a device, determination of physical addresses) and a logical aspect (extension of the current environment).

Mounting is requested by the command

mount <name of logical volume> <device type>

the *<name of logical volume>* is the identifier chosen to name the files in the volume, by means of a predetermined convention (e.g. *<logical volume>:<name of file>*). The *<device type>* information is optional if it can be deduced from the name of the volume or if the system only knows one type of device; conversely, the user may specify a given device if he knows it is available. The command is interpreted in two stages as follows:

1. Allocation of the device. If appropriate, the system looks for a device on which the volume can be installed. To do so it maintains an occupation table for the various devices which can receive fixed volumes: tape streamers, disk readers, etc. The system indicates the address of the device allocated (or displays a message showing that no device is available).

2. Physical installation. The operator physically installs the volume on the device. At the end of this operation, the system updates the occupation table.

3. Binding. The system now sets up its links.

a. Logical binding. An address on the volume, fixed once and for all by convention, contains the directory of all the files on it. This directory is read and included in the current environment, by means of a volume descriptor named by the name of the volume selected and pointing towards the volume directory.

b. Physical binding. The logical volume descriptor is provided with the physical address of the device.

The binding is now complete. The **FMS** can now determine the physical address of any file in the volume by means of the ordered pair:

<physical address of device> <address of file on volume>

Figure 6.10 summarizes these various operations.

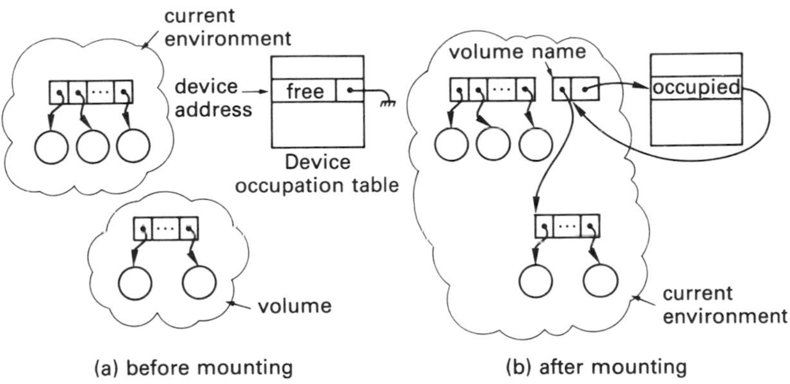

Fig. 6.10. Installation of a removable volume of files

The dismounting operation breaks the link to files on the dismounted volume, deleting the volume descriptor, and freeing the physical device it occupied.

Section 7.6 contains an example of a mounting operation.

6.3 Application 2: Linking of programs and data

6.3.1 Stages in a program's life cycle

In section 6.1.3.1. we presented the various moments at which a link could be established between the instructions and data making up a program.

Here we shall consider the most common approaches, before showing how they can be implemented. This discussion is intended above all to illustrate an application of the concept of binding and not to give a detailed description of the technical aspects of the operations of a loader or a linkage editor, for which readers should consult the bibliography (section 6.5).

1. Interpreted program

data
source program *interpreted program* *results*

2. Compiled program

a. Single program

source program translator relocatable object program
loader
absolute object program
data machine
results

A comparison of these two patterns highlights an important difference between interpretation and compilation: in an interpreted program, the effect of a modification to the source program is felt immediately; in a compiled program, the whole cycle has to be restarted; the use of composite programs merely increases that difference.

b. Composite programs

Forming a single program from a series of programs created independently takes place using relocatable object programs connected by means of external references. This operation may be combined with loading. The format of relocatable object modules consequently defines a common convention to which all translators must conform; it is also in this form that shared programs are stored in libraries.

relocatable object program
relocatable object program loader/link editor absolute object program
relocatable object program

6.3.2 Operation of a loader

The function of a **loader** is to give a relocatable object program (or module) an absolute form. This operation consists of replacing all addresses relative to the origin of the module by absolute addresses. For this purpose, a preliminary task is carried out during the translation phase: the records making up the object module are assigned a lag indicating whether or not they contain a relocatable address, and the position of this address within the record (if it is not specified once and for all). Relocatable addresses may appear:

- Either in the address part of instructions
- Or as data, in 'address expressions' intended to be used as indirection relays or to be loaded in base registers

The loader operates by substitution: any relative address *a* is replaced by an absolute address $a+orig$ where *orig* is the absolute address at which the module is loaded. On a machine with base registers, we shall see that this task is considerably simplified; this is because relocation is implemented on execution by computation of the address, on condition that base registers are correctly loaded.

If the loaded program has to be executed immediately, a further function of the loader is to determine the absolute address where module execution must start. This address is sometimes determined by convention (e.g. the first location of the module). More generally, the module may include several entry points, named by identifiers; it then contains an entry point table, built up by the translator, which associates a relative address with each of those identifiers. These addresses are converted into absolute addresses; the address of the entry point is determined from the identifier by searching through the table.

To illustrate this mode of operation, we shall now give a possible format for a relocatable object module and the program corresponding to the relocation loader.

```
header              <module_id,size,...>
module body
...

                    <addr,n,r,code>
                    ...
entry point table
...
                    <identifier, relative address>
                    ...
```

A record in the module body takes the form

<addr,n,r,code>

with:

addr:	relative address of <*code*> in the module
n	:size of <*code*> in bytes
r	:1 or 0 (relocatable code or not)
code	:*n* bytes of the program

The loader algorithm is as follows:

```
Call parameters: identity of module (file name)
               : load_addr (absolute loading address)
               : start_id (entry point identifier)
read (header);
<check that size allows loading>
loop
  read record;    -- <addr,n,r,code>
  if r=1 then
    relocate(code)
  endif;
  abs_addr:=addr+load_addr;
  <store code starting from abs_addr>
until body of module finished;
read (entry point table);
find(start_id,exec_addr);
if full then
  <exit error>    -- or select default address
else              -- default
  exec_addr:=exec_addr+load_addr
endif;
<jump to address exec_addr>
```

The procedure *relocate(code)* modifies <*code*> by relocating the relative addresses it contains: each of these addresses is incremented by *load_addr*. The position of these addresses within the record must therefore be known (generally, each record contains a single instruction in which the address occupies a fixed position).

The use of base registers simplifies the loader's task: relocation then takes place automatically, before execution, by loading the program absolute address into a base register. The use of several base registers makes it possible to relocate several program sections independently (e.g. procedures in one place and data in another). The only information the loader must relocate is then the address expressions used to load base registers.

6.3.3 Operation of a linking loader

We shall now describe the operating principle for a linking loader, which combines the functions of a linkage editor and a loader. The linkage editor receives on input a set of relocatable object modules and builds them into a single absolute object module. For each object module, it must therefore:

1. Determine its loading address
2. Carry out modification of relocatable data
3. Set up external reference links

6.3.3.1 Linking by substitution

In linkage editing by substitution, every reference to an external object in a module is replaced by the absolute address of that object.

By definition (see section 3.1.1) a module *A* **uses** a module *B* if the program of *A* refers to objects contained in *B*. The graph of the relation *uses* may contain cycles loops, so the linkage editor uses a two pass algorithm. The first pass assigns locations to modules and therefore determines the absolute address of all external objects; the second pass resolves references to these objects.

The format of object modules discussed in section 6.3.2 is supplemented by a table of external references which contains the identifiers of all external objects used by the module; an external reference in the program is replaced by a reference to the corresponding entry in the table. Collecting information together in this way makes it possible to keep a single copy of each external identifier and avoids the need to scatter identifiers throughout the body of a module.

In order to write the linking loader algorithm, we first define a possible format for relocatable modules.

header	*<module_id,size,...>*
table	...
of external	*<external identifier>*
references	...
module	...
body	*<addr,n,r,code>*
(program)	...
table	...
of external	*<identifier,relative address>*
definitions	...

A record from the module body now has the following meaning

addr	:relative address of *<code>*	
n	:size of *<code> in bytes*	
code	:program (or data) sequence	
r	:address relocation indicator	
	0	:absolute information
	1	:relocatable information (internal)
	<0	:external information ref. no − *r* in table of external references

Communication between the two passes is provided by a global table of external identifiers, built during the first pass, and which for each external object contains the ordered pair

(identifier, absolute address)

We shall now specify two access procedures to this table:

add(id,val) add the pair
(id,val) to the table

find(id,val) search for a pair whose identifier is *id*
if *fail*: not found *val* has no meaning
if ¬ *fail*:returns the associated value *val*

Note: The global table of external references plays a similar role to that of a symbol in an assembler. The techniques used in assembler used in assemblers (e.g. backward chaining) an be transposed to linkage editor).

The input parameters to the linking loader are:

- The starting address for the executable module *(load_addr)*
- The names of files containing the modules to bind
- The libraries to be searched when unresolved references are met

The program for pass 1 can be written:

```
init_addr:=load_addr                    --address as start of module
repeat                                  --iteration on the modules
  read(header);                         --(module_id,size)
  <process_header>;
  repeat                                --iteration on external references
    read(ref_id);
    <process_external_ref>
  until reference table exhaused;
  read(module body);                    --no processing
  repeat                                --iteration on external definitions
    read(def_id,def_addr);
    <process_external_def>
  until def table exhausted;
until no more modules to process;
<end_pass1>
```

While building up the table of external references, the value *val=0* associated with an identifier means, by convention, that it has been met in at least one reference, but not yet in a definition. This is therefore a (provisionally) unresolved reference.

Here are the various procedures:

```
<process_header>:

find(module_id,val);              --name of module
if fail or val=0 then             --new ref.
  add(module_id,init_addr)
else
  error('double definition')
endif;
base:=init_addr;                  --start of current module;
init_addr:=init_addr+size;        --start of following module
<check if size allows loading>

<process_external_def>;

find(def_id,val);
if fail or val=0 then
  add(def_id,base+def_addr)       -- absolute address of external def
else
  error('double definition')
endif

<process_external_ref>:

find(ref_id,val);
if fail then
  add(ref_id,val)                 --no action if ref_id
endif                             --already entered

<end_pass1>:

for all (ref_id,val) such that val=0 do--unresolved ref
  <search through the specified library for the module containing
  ref_id and determine its location address (this module will be loaded
  into memory with the program)>
  <calculate val and add (ref_id,val)>
```

On completion of pass 1, the global table of external references will have been built. Except in cases of error, every identifier in that table will be associated with an absolute location address.

The aim of the second pass is to carry out relocation of addresses and loading into memory, using information held in the table of extenal references.

```
<pass2>:

repeat                                  --iteration on modules
  read(header);
  find(module_id,val);
  base:=val;
  read(external ref.table);
  repeat                                --iteration on ref. table
    <process_record>
  until body of module exhausted
until no more modules to process;
<end_pass2>:
```

The procedures in phase 2 are:

```
<process_record>:

loc_addr:=addr+base;
if r=1 then                               --relocatable internal ref
  <relocate_rec(base)>
else
  if r<0 then                             --external ref
    ref_id:=<entry no – r in external ref. table>;
    find(ref_id,val);
    relocate_rec(val)
  endif
endif;                                    --nothing to do if r=0
<load rec starting at loc_addr>

<end_pass2>:

find(entry_id,val);
if fail or val=0 then
  error('unknown exec. address')          --or default choice
else
  exec_addr:=val
endif;
<print contents of external ref table>--'location map'
<branch to address exec_addr>
```

Printing the contents of the external reference table, in the form of a **location map**, makes it possible in particular to identify errors (double definition, unsatisfied reference) and makes debugging easier by showing the location of data in memory. The location map is a series of lines in the form:

<external.id> <absolute address> <error diagnosis if present>

6.3.3.2 Linkage by chaining

1. Transfer vector

The transfer vector technique is relatively little used as such for compiled programs. We shall nonetheless examine its operating principles, since:

- It can be used for interpreted programs, or programs combining interpreted and compiled modules.
- It makes it possible to introduce in primitive form the concept of a linkage segment, which we shall consider in more detail in what follows.

Each module contains a table called the **transfer vector**, which contains an entry for each external reference. In the body of the module, any reference to an external object is replaced by an *indirect* reference to the corresponding entry in the transfer vector. The first pass of the linking loader takes place as in section 6.3.3.1; the second pass involves filling the entries in the transfer vector for the various modules with the corresponding addresses for external objects. On execution, access to an external object is therefore implemented by indirection via a word in the transfer vector. This method is expensive on space (transfer vectors have to be stored) and in time (indirect references). It works well when it comes to replacing a module in a program that has already been linked; this is why it is useful for interpreted programs, or system debugging.

2. Base registers

We include the use of base registers under the heading of linkage by chaining since a base register used to address a program section can be regarded as acting as a relay for that section.

As in the case of a loader, addressing by base registers simplifies the task of the linking loader. Two ways of using these registers have to be distinguished:

1. Base registers freely accessible to users: in this case, conventions have to be defined to allow, for example, for the use of specified base registers to address a subprogram, a data zone, a parameter block, etc. These conven-

tions are implemented by translators, or directly by users if they are programming in assembly language.

2.Base registers managed by the operating system and inaccessible to users: in this case, the system associates a base register with each independent component (program or data zone) and sees to the reallocation of these registers if there are not enough of them.

In both cases, the linking loader's task is to compute address expressions to be loaded into base registers.

In the second case, it must also insert register loading instructions into object modules (generally in the form of supervisor calls).

6.4 Mechanisms for object management

6.4.1 Segmentation

The use of base registers we have just been describing allows independent relocation in memory of the procedures and data making up a program. The mechanism is, however, subject to constraints:

- For the user, the need to conform to naming conventions for the use of base registers
- For the operating system, the need to manage allocation of base registers if there are not enough of them

These constraints would be removed if the user could name 'elements of information' with a freely chosen name and if the system had a memory loading and linkage mechanism for these elements. Segmentation is an attempt to provide a means to meet these requirements.

A **segment** is a set of data regarded as an independently named logical unit; its representation occupies a set of contiguous locations. A segment can be of variable size. Within a segment, information is named by a **displacement**, which is an address relative to the start of the segment. A data item can therefore be named by an ordered pair (segment name, displacement) which is called its **segmented address** (fig. 6.11).

It is important to note that segments are mutually independent both from the physical and the logical point of view. Physically, a segment may be located at any address, on condition that it occupies contiguous locations. Logically, the various segments managed by a system are independent and have to be considered as a series of distinct linear addressing spaces. Even if segment names are often represented by consecutive integers, there is no necessary contiguity between the final location of segment i and the first location in segment $i+1$. The use of a negative displacement or a displacement greater than the size of the segment is an addressing error.

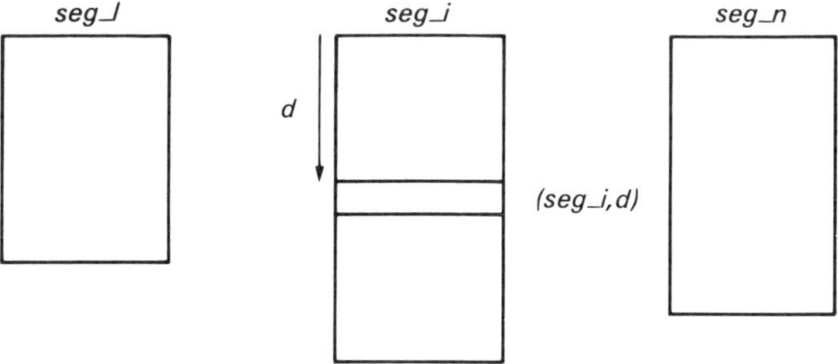

Fig. 6.11. Segmented addessing

Segments are used:

- As units for breaking a program down logically, in order, for example, to represent the various associated procedures, modules or data items (arrays, structures)
- As units for *sharing* between various users
- As *protection* units (a natural consequence of sharing): the segment is the entity with which access rights are associated

The implementation of segmented addressing on a machine uses the general principle shown in fig. 6.12.

A descriptor is associated with each segment; it contains at least the starting address of the segment, its length and its access rights. A table of segments contains all the descriptors; a segment is named by the index of its descriptor in that table. Implementations differ according to the way they organize the table of descriptors. Three forms of organization are possible:

1. Global table. A single table covers all descriptors; the unique name of a segment is the index of its descriptor in this table. The descriptor contains

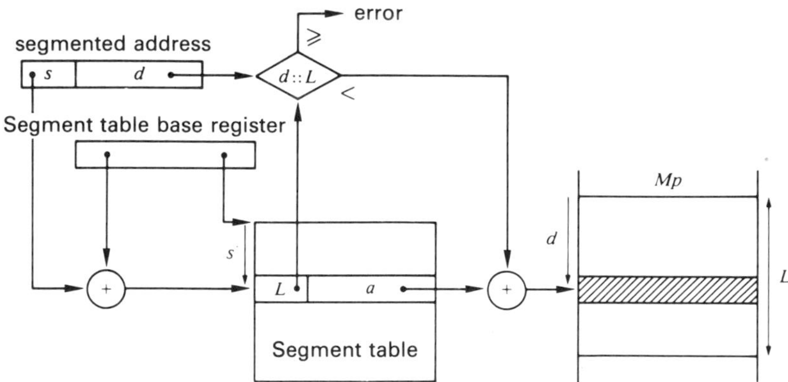

Fig. 6.12. Implementation of segmented addressing

an access list defining the rights of all users of the segment. This method allows segment sharing but constrains all users of the segment to use the same name for a shared segment.

2. Multiple tables. There is a separate table for each environment; in a particular environment, the segment name (if it is accessible in that environment) is the index of its descriptor in the local table. A segment accessible to several environments therefore has several descriptors, and several distinct names.

3. Mixed organization. Each segment has a central descriptor containing its physical location characteristics (size, address). It also has a local descriptor in each environment in which it is accessible; that descriptor contains information specific to the environment (notably access rights); it points towards the central descriptor. A segment therefore has a distinct name in each environment but its physical characteristics are held together in a single place, the central descriptor.

Figure 6.13 shows these different forms of organization.

We shall illustrate the use of segments with the example of the Multics system, which makes use of a general and powerful mechanism implemented in hardware and integrated into the system.

6.4.2 Example: segmentation, linking, protection in the Multics system

The Multics system was first designed and implemented at MIT between 1965 and 1970, on hardware specially developed for the project, the GE 645. A version is available on Honeywell 68 hardware (Bull 68-DPS). It is a shared time system providing a large community of users with permanent access to a set of common services and the possibility of sharing and exchanging information.

We give a simplified description here; for a more detailed discussion, please see the bibliography (section 6.5).

6.4.2.1 General principles

In the Multics system, all information is organized into segments, and the machine directly interprets segmented addresses. A process is associated with each user present, as well as with certain system activities such as background jobs, input-output, user login, etc. All segments may potentially be shared by any number of processes; all procedures may be called recursively. Each process can name segments independently of other processes: the sharing of segments takes place without sharing names. A selective protection mechanism allows definition both of access rights specific to each user for every segment, and of classes of processes with a set of rights in

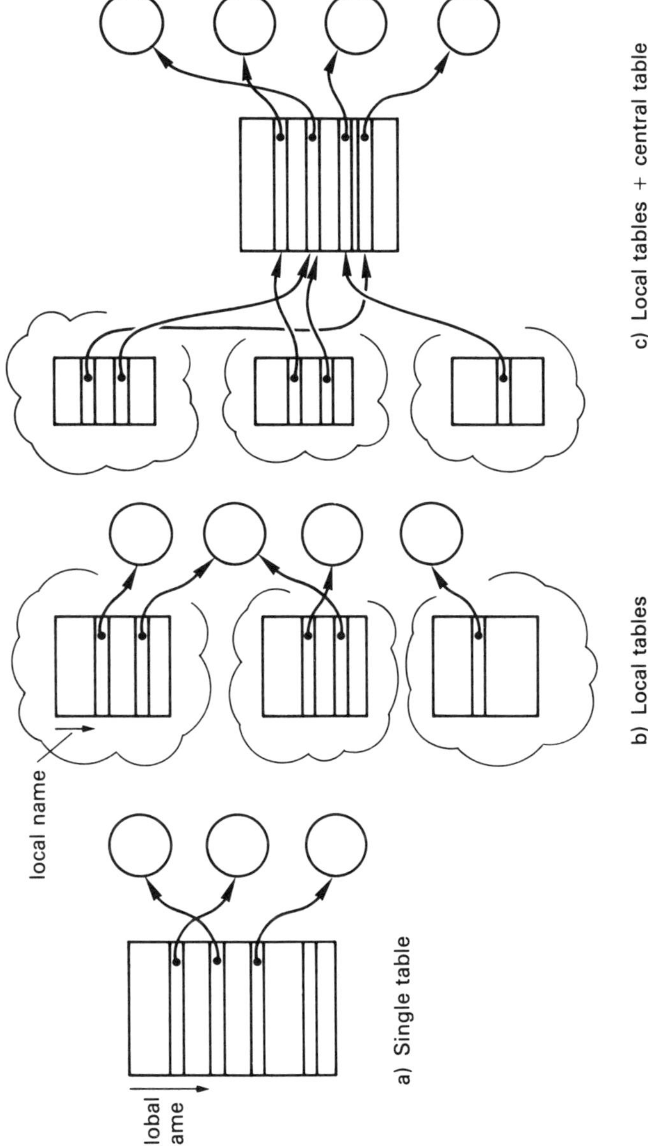

Fig. 6.13. Organizations of segment tables

common. Finally, segments are directly used not only as addressing units, but also as information storage and symbolic naming units: the concept of a segment is identified with that of a file. Input-output uses streams, which can be associated either with a segment or with a peripheral device.

In this description, we shall leave entirely aside problems of allocating memory to segments. We shall simply assume that a segment descriptor contains the information making it possible to locate the segment in physical memory. Some ideas on the mechanisms used are given in chapter 9.

6.4.2.2 Addressing and object access mechanisms

1. Segment naming

Let us start by defining the environment of a process. At the symbolic level, in the system's command language, an object is named by an ordered pair (segment identifier, internal identifier). Segments are organized into a tree-structured directory, and their symbolic naming has already been discussed in section 6.2.2.3. The environment of a process is therefore defined, at the symbolic level, by its working directory and its search rules.

Descriptors of segments accessible to a process are held in a special segment called the process *descriptor block*. In instructions interpreted by the processor, every segment is named by a number, which is the displacement of a descriptor within the descriptor block of the process currently executing. The descriptor block itself is named by a base register called *DescrBase*. This register is automatically used by the addressing mechanism, and updated each time a process is activated.

The link between the symbolic level and the instruction interpretation level is implemented, for each process, by a table called the Known Segments Table (KST) for the process. Each entry in this table gives the symbolic name and the number of each segment present in the control block. The constitution and use of this table are described in section 6.4.2.4.

A segment shared by several processes in general has a separate number in each process descriptor block. Physical location information appearing in each descriptor is identical (fig. 6.14).

2. Access to objects

In what follows, we shall consider the execution of a procedure *P* by a process *p*. We shall use the term **procedure-segment** for the (invariant) segment resulting from the compilation of the source text of *P*. This segment exists in a single copy; it is shared by all processes executing *P*. Its contents are described in detail in section 6.4.2.4.

If a process *p* executes a procedure *P*, it may access a set of objects making

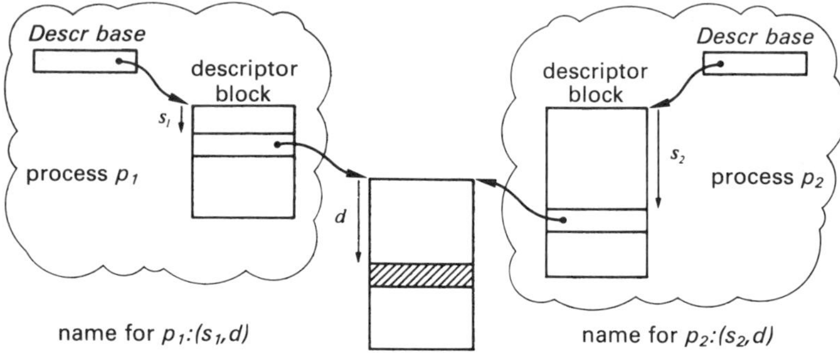

Fig. 6.14. Naming a segment in Multics

up the execution context of *P* for *p*. These objects are listed in section 6.1.2.3 and classified as internal objects, local objects, private objects, external objects and parameters. We shall see here how process *p* names them.

The instructions interpreted by the processor are split into two classes depending on whether or not the location address belongs to the current procedure segment. We shall write

procseg :the number of the current procedure segment
BR :a base register number; such a register contains a segmented address *(s,d)*
disp :a displacement

The table below gives, for each of these two types of instruction, the form of the address appearing in the instruction (the primitive address) and the segmented address of the object named.

Type	Primitive address	Actual segmented address	Nbr of bits in *disp*
0	*(***t0***,disp)*	*(procseg,disp)*	18
1	*(***t1***,BR,disp)*	*(s,disp+d)*	14

Type 1 instructions may, moreover, include indirect addressing, indicated by the prefix '*'.

When a process executes a procedure, its environment is defined by five base registers, whose functions are as follows:

- The descriptor block base register, *DescrBase*, which has already been mentioned
- The procedure base register, *ProcBase*
- The linkage segment base register, *LinkBase*
- The stack base register, *StackBase*
- The parameter base register, *ParamBase*

a. *Addressing the current procedure.* The register *ProcBase* acts as a program counter: it contains the segmented address *(procseg,d)* of the instruction currently being executed (*procseg* is the number of the current procedure segment and *d* is the displacement of the instruction within the segment). Any instruction of displacement *disp* in the current procedure may therefore be addressed by:

(t0,disp)

This mode of addressing is used for branching instructions within a procedure.

b. *Addressing external objects.* An external object cannot be directly named, within a procedure, by a segmented address: there is no reason why its segment number should be identical for all the processes that share the procedure. Consequently, a system of naming by chaining is used: the segmented addresses of external objects named by a procedure during the execution of a process are stored in a **linkage segment**, with one copy for each (process, procedure) pair. We shall write *L(p,P)* for the linkage segment of a procedure *P* for a process *p*. Every external object of *P* is indirectly named, in the executable code of *P*, by way of a relay in the linkage segment *L(p,P)*. For a given object, the displacement *disp* of that relay is made deliberately the same in all linkage segments for *P*; the naming of externals is therefore the same for all processes sharing *P*. The *LinkBase* register contains the segmented address of the first word in *L(p,P)* i.e. *(segl_P,0)*. The primitive address of an external object is (fig. 6.15):

***(t1,LinkBase,disp)**

which uses *(seglP)* as the segmented address of the relay.

Construction of the linkage segment is described in section 6.4.2.4.

c. *Private objects.* For the same reason as for externals, private objects must be named in a uniform way within the procedure, even though there is a copy per process. A special segment per process could be used, with naming by means of a particular base register; in fact, for economic reasons, private objects are held together in a reserved zone of the linkage segment. If a private object is stored in location *disp* of this segment, it can be named by the primitive address

(t1,LinkBase,disp)

which does indeed provide the segmented address *(segl_P,disp)*.

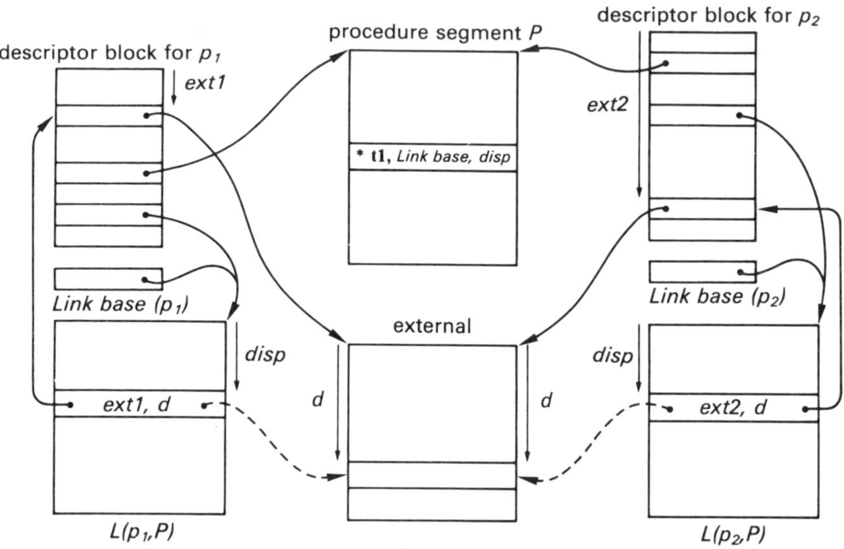

Fig. 6.15. Addressing principle for external objects

The creation and initialization of the private object zone in the linkage segment are described in section 6.4.2.4.

d. *Addressing of local objects and procedure parameters.* The sequential execution mode in a process was described in section 2.1. An execution stack is used to allocate local objects and to pass parameters. Such a stack exists for each process; it is contained in a particular segment. The register *StackBase* allows access to the segment; it contains the segmented address *(stackseg,d)* of the base of the environment region associated with the execution of the current procedure. Each local object is associated with a constant displacement *disp*, calculated during compilation, which defines its position in the current region of the environment. Such an object is named by the primitive address:

*(***t1***,StackBase,disp)*

which provides the segmented address *(stackseg,d+disp)*. Figure 6.16 shows the organization of the execution stack.

The stack contains a header, which includes several pointers. Two of them will be useful to use in what follows:

- A pointer to the top of the stack (segmented address of the first free location for the creation of a work space or a new region)
- A pointer towards the table of linkage segments, which indicates the number of the linkage sector for each procedure known to process *p*

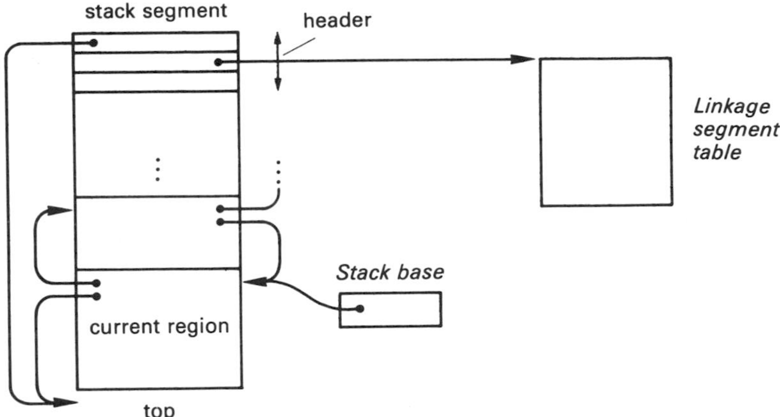

Fig. 6.16. Process execution stack

Parameters are passed by means of an array, built up by the calling procedure, containing their segmented addresses, calculated by the procedure using the addressing rules we have just been considering. This array is stored on the stack and could therefore be addressed, *a priori*, as a local object. In fact, the protection mechanism requires that, for each process, a distinct stack should be managed per 'protection ring' (see section 6.4.2.5); the stack for the calling procedure may therefore be different from the called stack, and inaccessible to the latter. This is why use is made of a special base register *ParamBase* which contains the segmented address of the array of parameter addresses. The *i*-th parameter therefore has the primitive address:

*(**t1**,*ParamBase*,*i*)

6.4.2.3 Environment switching: procedure calls and returns

Changes in the environment of a process take place through procedure calls and returns. The following functions have to be carried out.

During calls:

- Preparation of parameters
- Saving of the current environment
- Change of environment (modification of base registers)

On return

- Preparation of results
- Restoration of the calling environment

We shall consider the underlying principles for each of these operations in turn.

1. Procedure calls

Preparing parameters and saving the current environment are implemented by a sequence of instructions inserted into the compiler before the call instruction as such. The segmented addresses of the actual parameters are first calculated using the addressing rules defined by their type, and stored in an array on the stack; the segmented address of the origin of this array is loaded into *ParamBase*. The registers to save, apart from *StackBase* and *ProcBase*, are stored on the stack. The call instruction is then executed.

Let us write *P* for the calling procedure, and *Q* for the called procedure. We shall write *(procseg_q,entry_q)* for the segmented address of the first instruction in *Q* (we assume that a procedure segment may have several entry points; *entry_q* is the displacement of the entry point of *Q* within its segment). *Q* is named in the executable program *P* by the displacement *dispq* of a word in the linkage segment for *P*. Once the link between *P* and *Q* has been established, as we assume has clearly happened (see section 6.4.2.4), this word will contain the segmented address *(procseg_q,entry_q)*. The calling instruction to *Q* from *P* therefore takes the form:

*call_proc *(***t1***,LinkBase,disp_q)*

The effect of this instruction is as follows:

a. Load into *StackBase* the segmented address of the top of the stack for *Q* (the segment which contains the stack is determined by the protection mechanism — see section 6.4.2.5; if there is no change of ring, *StackBase* is not affected).

b. Push onto the stack for *Q* the values (before the call) of registers *ProcBase* and *StackBase*; these values will be used by *Q* during the return sequence to *P*.

c. Execute a jump to the first instruction in *Q*. *ProcBase* now contains *(procseg_q,entry_q)*.

The entry sequence to *Q* has the following effect:

a. Load *LinkBase* with the segmented address of the linkage segment for *Q*; this address is contained in the entry *procseg_q* in the table of linkage segments for procedures known to *p* (remember that this table is named by a pointer in the header of the stack segment).

b. Reserve, if necessary, the space for local data on the stack of *Q*. The size of this space is determined by the compiler.

Reservation of local objects involves updating the top of the stack by adding its displacement to the size of the local object zone (including the save words for *ProcBase* and *StackBase*), and the creation of forward and backward pointers in the region defined.

The environment change is complete: *ProcBase, StackBase, LinkBase* and *ParamBase* have their new values; *DescrBase* remains unchanged. The overall effect of the procedure call is shown in fig. 6.17.

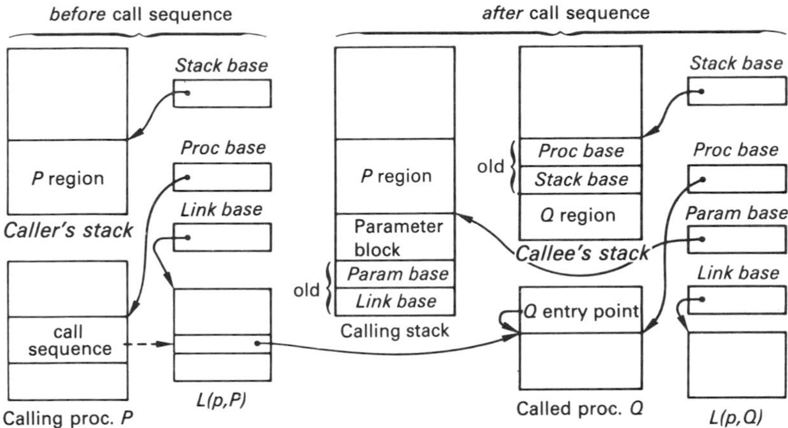

Fig. 6.17. Overall effect of a procedure call

2. Procedure return

The procedure return instruction has the following effect:

a. Freeing of the environment region created on the stack. This operation involves popping the segmented address of the base of a region (contained in *StackBase*) from the stack.

b. Restoration of *StackBase* and *ProcBase*, using the values stored at the top of the stack. This restores the procedure segment and stack for the calling procedure.

c. Execution of the restoration sequence (inserted by the compiler immediately after the call instruction). This sequence restores the registers stored in the calling procedure stack immediately before the call; if appropriate, it again makes use of *LinkBase* and *ParamBase*.

In this way, the environment from before the call is entirely reconstructed. Any results there may have been are obtained by modifying the objects passed as parameters.

6.4.2.4 Dynamic linkage

We shall now examine how identifiers are bound to segmented addresses. Remember that an object (a procedure or data item) is named symbolically in a program by an ordered pair *(segment identifier, internal identifier)*. This ordered pair allows unique identification of the object by means of the file management system. Linkage has the aim of replacing that ordered pair by a segmented address, the only kind the processor can interpret. In section 6.4.2.3, we considered the final part of this linkage process, which uses information contained in linkage segments. We shall now see how this information is built up from identifiers.

This description comes in two parts: the creation of the linkage segment when a procedure is executed for the first time by a process, and the substitution of addresses for symbolic information, i.e. dynamic linking.

1. Linkage between processes and procedures

A procedure segment, produced by a compiler, contains three parts:

1. The invariant code for the procedure
2. The table of external objects
3. The linkage segment model

This organization is shown in fig. 6.18 (for ease of representation, the three zones are shown as disjoint even though they belong to the same segment).

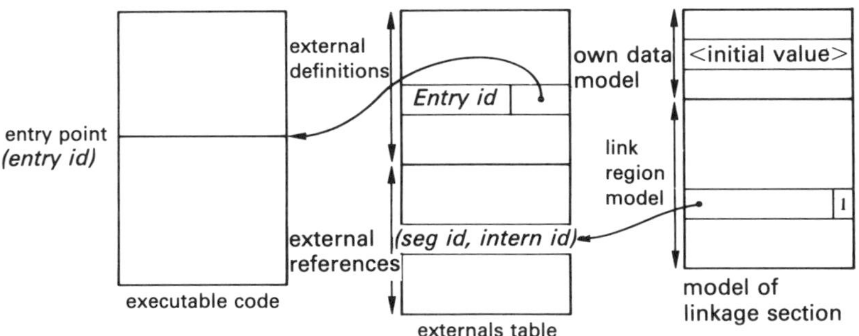

Fig. 6.18. Organization of a procedure segment

The table of external objects has two parts: definitions and external references. The external reference part is a table of identifiers *(seg.id,internal.id)* of external objects named by the procedure. For each entry point in the procedure, named by an internal identifier, the definition part is the displacement of the entry point within the executable code part.

The linkage segment model has two parts:

1. The model for the private object zone, holding the initial values of these private objects determined on compilation

2. The linkage region model, including the following information for each external reference:

- A pointer to the location in the external object table containing its identifier (this form of indirect naming of identifiers makes it possible to store them in a single copy in the external objects table)
- The trap indicator, a boolean value initially set to true, whose role will be explained below

When a procedure P is first called by a process p, the linkage segment $L(p,P)$ is created by copying the linkage segment model from P. An entry is allocated to it in the control block for p, which has the effect of defining a number *segl_P* for it, recorded in the linkage segment table for p. The linkage region in $L(p,P)$ still only contains pointers to identifiers; we shall now see how these references are resolved.

2. Dynamic linking

In the Multics system, external references are resolved when access is first made, and the link remains established for all further accesses. This mode of operations has three advantages compared to 'traditional' linkage editing, carried out statically before execution as described in section 6.3.

1. In a program made up of several modules, in order to take account of modifications to a module next time it is executed, only the module modified needs to be recompiled. This leads to a major saving in time in debugging, and provides a benefit usually only available in interpretation.

2. It is possible to link external objects which did not exist at the start of execution, in particular objects created or modified dynamically during execution.

3. Only external objects actually used are linked; no unnecessary link is established.

The cost of these benefits is the need to use more complex data structures and procedure calls (indirect access).

Let *(Q_SEG,Q_ENTRY)* be the symbolic identifier of an external procedure Q called by P. In $L(p,P)$, the displacement word *q_disp* associated with this reference contains a pointer to this identifier in the table of external objects for P, and a trap indicator initially set to true. In the code of P, a call to Q has the form:

```
call_proc *(t1,linkage_base,q_disp)
```

Execution of this instruction for the first time has the following effect:

1. The *q_disp* word in the linkage segment will be read; as the trap indicator is true, a trap takes place and the linkage editor is called; it receives as parameter the symbolic reference *(Q_SEG,Q_ENTRY)* from the external object table, and it executes steps 2 and 3 below.

2. The table of segments known to p (see section 6.4.2.2) is consulted. If the identifier *Q_SEG* appears in it, the number *q_segproc* is obtained; otherwise, a search is launched for the number through the directories using the search rules in force; an entry is assigned to it in the control block for P, yielding the number *q_segproc*; the ordered pair *(Q_SEG,q_segproc)* is added to the table of segments known to p.

3. The 'definitions' part of the external object table for segment *Q_SEG* will be explored to find *Q_ENTRY*; let *q_entry* be the corresponding displacement in *q_segproc*. The linkage segment *L(p,Q)* is now created, if it did not already exist,([1]) by copying the model in *q_segproc*. The entry *q_disp* in *L(p,P)* is provided with the segmented address *(q_segproc,q_entry)* and the trap indicator is set to false.

4. The trap ends and the call instruction is reexecuted; this time, all its references are resolved and access takes place as in section 6.4.2.3, by indirection via *L(p,P)*. Any further access will follow the same pattern.

Figure 6.19 shows the overall effects of dynamic linkage editing.

In case of failure in the search for *Q_SEG* or of *Q_ENTRY* in phase 2 or 3, program execution is interrupted with the error message (reference not satisfied).

Note 1: Dynamic linking in the case of a reference with a segment of external data follows a pattern which is similar but simpler, since there is no need to create a new linkage segment.

Note 2: In fact, for reasons of economy, the different linkage segments for procedures known to a process p are held together in a single segment, and make up the 'linkage sections' for that segment. The protection mechanism makes it necessary to manage such a segment per ring for each process. The table called a 'linkage segments table' above is therefore in fact a table of linkage sections, containing the segmented address of the linkage section for each procedure known to p; there is one such table per ring for each process. This mode of operation makes of modification to the underlying principle of the algorithms described.

Note 3: Traditional linkage editing, before execution, is also possible by means of an explicit call to the linkage editor. External objects must then, of course, be available. The overall effect of the operation is identical to that of dynamic linking; furthermore, the objects linked and their linkage sections (if there are any) are held in a single segment.

([1]) *L(p,Q)* could have been created, for example, during a call to p from another entry point of the same procedure segment *Q_SEG*. Its existence can be detected by consulting the linkage segment table for p.

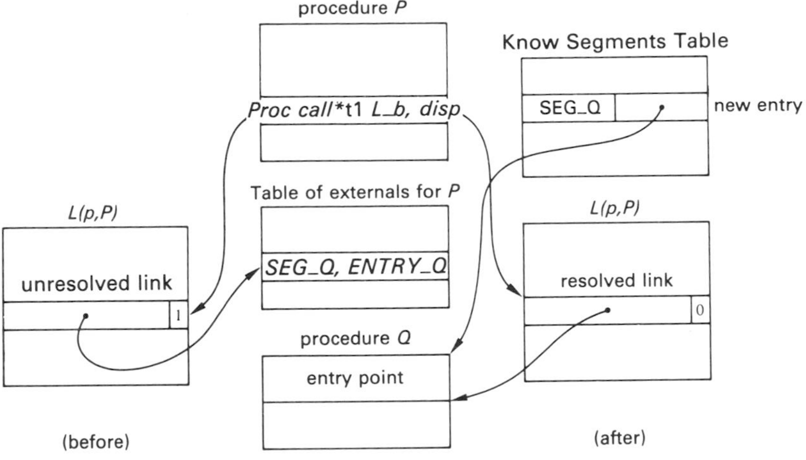

Fig. 6.19. Effect of dynamic linking

6.4.2.5 *Protection: the ring principle*

In the Multics system, protection is implemented using eight domains, called **protection rings**, named by their numbers 0, 1, ... 7; this sequence defines a hierarchy of domains, in order of decreasing status. At any instant, a process executes in a ring, called the current ring, whose number is part of the process context.

A process is always executed for a 'client' (a user or an internal system function such as an input-output operation). The rights of a client on a segment are a subset, which may be empty, of *(read, write, execute)*. Specific rights are associated with directories, but we shall not consider this aspect here. Each segment is associated with:

- An access list which specifies the rights of the clients to the segment; elements in this list take the form (*name of client, <list of rights>*); a client whose name does not appear in the access list has no rights over that segment.
- A list of brackets and (for a procedure segment) of entry gates, whose construction and use we shall consider next

Let *p* be a process, executing on behalf of a client called *c*; let *cr(p)* be the number of the current ring for *p*. Access by *p* to a segment *s* is controlled as follows:

1. A search is launched for the name *c* in the access list for *s*; if it appears in it, let <*l*> be its list of rights; if *c* does not appear in the access list, or if the nature of the access operation it is attempting to carry out is incompatible with <*l*>, *p* is trapped for violation of protection. To reduce the number of

checks, the access list is consulted only once, at the moment *s* is added to the table of known segments for *p*. The list of rights, brackets and gates, if there are any, is then copied into the descriptor for segment *s* which is created in the control description for *p*.

2. If the access mode is compatible with <*l*>, the number of the current ring *cr(p)* is compared with the access brackets for *s*, applying the rules specified above; if there is incompatibility, protection violation trapping again occurs.

There are four access brackets for a segment; they are defined by three ring numbers *nw, nr, nc* such that $nw \leqslant nr \leqslant nc$.([1])

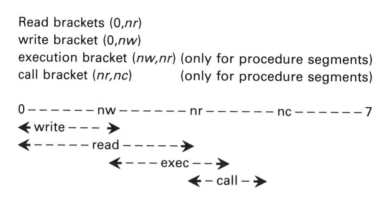

Read brackets (0,*nr*)
write bracket (0,*nw*)
execution bracket (*nw,nr*) (only for procedure segments)
call bracket (*nr,nc*) (only for procedure segments)

```
0 ------- nw ------- nr ------- nc ------- 7
<- write --- ->
<------ read ------->
              <--- exec -->
                         <- call ->
```

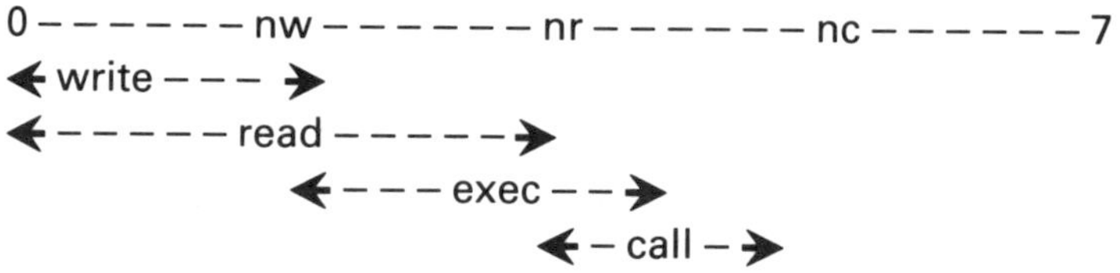

These brackets are used as follows.

1. For access other than a procedure call or return (read, write, execute an instruction): if *cr(p)* lies in the interval specified by the corresponding brackets, access is allowed and *cr(p)* is unchanged; otherwise, trapping takes place for violation of protection.

2. For a procedure call or return, the situation is more complex as there may be a change of ring. For procedure calls, three cases must be distinguished:

a. Call with an increase in status $(nr \leqslant cr(p) \leqslant nc)$. This call causes trapping, to allow a check to be made. If entry to the procedure takes place by one of the allowed points of entry, or **gates**, the call is executed and *cr(p)* receives the value *nr* (i.e., the process receives the minimum status necessary to execute the procedure); otherwise, protection is violated and the call is not executed. Return takes place without restrictions, and *cr(p)* returns to its initial value.

b. Call with no change in status $(nw \leqslant cr(p) \leqslant nr)$. This call is allowed

([1]) Any kind of overlapping between brackets would in principle be possible; the present choice was based on considerations of economy.

without any restriction other than the mandatory use of a gate; the current ring is unchanged; return takes place without restriction, and without changing ring.

c. Call with reduction of status $(cr(p)<nw)$. This call is allowed without restriction, and $cr(p)$ receives the value nw. Consequently, parameters passed by the calling procedure may be inaccessible to the called procedure, since rights are reduced; these parameters must be copied beforehand by the calling procedure into a segment accessible to the called procedure. In cases of calls with reduction in status, the process can no longer return to its original ring, unless the calling procedure has passed the name of a procedure called a return gate, whose execution allows checking of the increase in status caused by the return.

If $cr(p)>nc$, no access is allowed.

The execution of an instruction therefore gives rise to checking operations which may become very complex: if computation of the address includes indirections involving several segments, checking must take place for each of them. A hard-wired mechanism allows checking to be accelerated, and ensures that the protection system cannot be deliberately circumvented.

Example: Base registers contain not only a segmented address but also a ring number. The interpretation mechanism for instructions will not allow a process to load a ring number greater than or equal to that of its current ring into a base register. This ensures, for example, that a process cannot increase its power in any unauthorized way when it returns from a procedure by constructing, before it executes a call, a return address in a ring below its current ring.

6.4.3 Capability systems

The hierarchical organization defined by protection rings in Multics does not allow use to be made of the domain concept in all its generality. This is because any segment accessible to process executing in a ring i is also accessible to those executing in any ring $j<i$. This has two consequences:

- An error leading to unexpected access may propagate, without being detected, between a ring j and a ring $i>j$.
- It is impossible to implement mutually suspicious subsystems: if they are executed in the same ring, access checking is impossible; if they are executing in different rings, one has complete authority over the other.

One way of removing these restrictions might be to associate the concept of the domain with an ordered pair (procedure, ring). But this is impossible, as all procedures executing within the same ring for a given process share the same control block, and their contexts are not disjoint. Moreover, within a single ring, the gate mechanism may be circumvented by making direct use of a jump instruction, which is not subject to checking. These limitations restrict the use that can be made of rings. They also explain why more flexible mechanisms have been developed.

6.4.3.1 Underlying principles of capability systems

The idea which led to the development of capability systems was that of bringing together addressing and access control into a single mechanism. In such systems, access to an object is only possible through a generalized pointer which describes both the physical location of the object and the operations allowed on it. The distribution and modification of these pointers, called **capabilities**, clearly have to be the responsibility of a primitive protection mechanism, whether implemented in hardware or software.

Two general methods may be considered to implement such protection:

- Using a tag (see section 6.1.2.2) attached to any memory location or register and specifying the nature of its contents. Capabilities are identified by a particular tag and their use can therefore be monitored by the instruction interpretation mechanism.
- Keeping capabilities together in special segments, called capability lists, or **C-lists**. Protection is then enforced at the moment that access takes place to the segments.

For reasons of economy, it is the second method that has been tried most often.

The first experiments in the use of capabilities were implemented in software: CAL-TSS and Hydra. Specialized machine architectures were developed later: Plessey 250, CAP, IBM 38, Intel iAPX 432.

6.4.3.2 Example of a capability system: Plessey 250

The Plessey 250 was the first capability computer developed industrially. It was used for telecommunication applications. Although it was designed in 1971–72, the principles underlying its operations remain valid and recent projects such as the Intel iAPX 432 have drawn heavily on them.

1. Elementary objects and operations

a. Segments and capabilities. The Plessey 250 uses the principle of C-lists for the protection of capabilities. There are therefore two types of segments: ordinary segments, whose locations are interpreted as instructions or data, and C-lists, whose locations are interpreted as capabilities. In the rest of this discussion, the term 'segment' will be used for an ordinary segment and the term 'C-list' will be kept only for segments containing capabilities, while the term 'object' will cover both segments and C-lists.

Access to a segment or to a C-list is only possible through a capability, specifying the address of the object in memory and the access rights allowed. These rights vary depending on whether one is dealing with a segment or a C-list:

- For a segment: *Read, Write, Execute (R, W, X)*
- For a C-list: *ReadCapability, WriteCapability, DomainCall (RC, WC, DC)*

The rights appearing in a capability uniquely identify the object they name as a segment or as a C-list. There is only one exception to this rule: certain domains in the operating system handle capabilities containing both types of rights, and can therefore treat a single object as being *simultaneously* a segment and a C-list. This facility is used during object creation (see subsection 5a) and during execution stack management (see subsection 3a). Apart from these cases, the nature of the contents of a location is defined by the nature of the object, segment or C-list, where it appears.

The processor contains eight ordinary registers *R0...R7* and eight capability registers *C0,...C7*. An ordinary register can only take immediate values for the contents of a segment location; a capability register can only receive the contents of a C-list location.

The same object may be accessible through several capabilities, whose access rights may differ. The approach in fig. 6.20 is used to make such multiple access as efficient as possible.

A System Descriptor Table (SDT) contains a descriptor for each object present in main memory, containing the physical addresses of its base and limit. The capability of an object contains no physical address, but a pointer

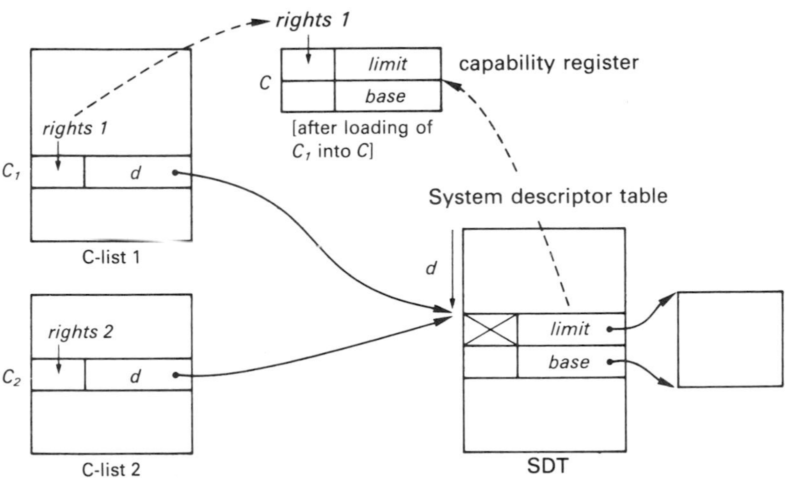

Fig. 6.20. Capabilities and descriptors in the Plessey 250

towards an entry in the SDT. Consequently, an object can be displaced in memory without having to update the various capabilities naming it. Once a capability has been loaded from a C-list into a capability register, the base and limit addresses contained in the descriptor are copied into the register from the SDT. This avoids indirection during later access to the register.

The SDT resides in memory and is named by an internal register inaccessible to users. Management of the SDT is studied in subsection 5a.

b. Addressing objects. In an instruction, locations are named by a primitive address with the form *(C,X,disp)*. *C* is a capability register, which names an object; *X* is an ordinary register, used as an index; the displacement of the location in the object is *disp+ (X)*.

When an instruction is interpreted, two checks are carried out:

- Compatibility of the operation code with the access rights contained in the capability register naming the object handled
- Comparison of the actual address computed with the base and limit addresses

Detection of incompatibility or out of bounds offset leads to trapping. Furthermore, operations on capabilities are protected: the only operation allowed is copying, between C-lists and capability registers, will possible restriction of rights.

2. *Domains*

Remember that a domain defines a set of objects accessible by a process, each of them associated with a set of access rights. In the Plessey 250, domains are implemented by C-lists which contain the capabilities of all the accessible objects; the access rights of each of these objects appear in its capability. The C-list is called the **capability block** for the domain.

A domain always includes procedure segments. It is by calling one of these procedures that a process 'enters' a domain and handles the objects it contains. Its context is then defined by the capability block for the domain. Amongst the accessible objects (i.e. objects named by a capability contained in the capability block) there may be other C-lists and, notably, the capability blocks of other domains which may be called from the current domain (see below, subsection 3b).

3. *Execution environment*

a. Execution stack. Four registers managed by the operating system and inaccessible to application programs define the current environment of a process (fig. 6.21).

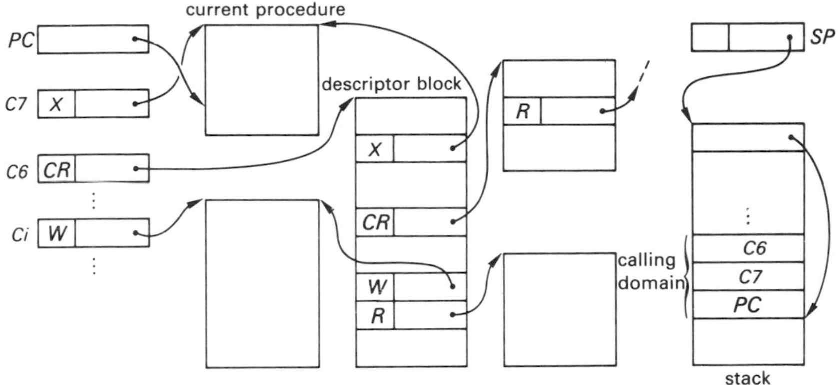

Fig. 6.21. Execution environment in the Plessey 250

- Register *C6* contains a capability naming the capability block of the current domain, with right *ReadCapability*.
- Register *C7* contains a capability which names the procedure segment currently being executed, with right *Execute*; note that this segment, which belongs to the current domain, is also named by a capability in the current capability block.
- A register *PC* (program counter) gives the displacement, within the current procedure segment, of the instruction being executed.
- A register *SR* (stack register) contains a capability which names a segment containing the execution stack for the process.

The set of objects addressable at any given moment is defined by the contents of the registers above and of the capability registers *C0* to *C5*, that are directly usable by the process. These registers may be loaded from any C-list for which the process has a capability with the right *ReadCapability*.

b. Domain calls and returns. A change of domain is implemented by instruction

call *C,disp*

where *C* is a capability register containing a capability for the capability block of the called domain, with *DomainCall* rights. The displacement, within that capability block, of the capability for the procedure segment used as entry point to the called domain, is *disp*. This capability must contain right *Execute*.

The effect of the call instruction is to change the current environment of the process, which becomes that defined by the called domain, and to maintain a link to the calling domain to allow a return:

- The current contents of registers *C6, C7* and *PC* are pushed onto the top of the execution stack.
- *C6* is loaded with the capability of the called domain; it is automatically assigned right *ReadCapability*.
- *CR7* is loaded with the capability of the called procedure segment and *PC* is set to 0 (the entry point of a procedure segment is by convention its first instruction).

None of the other registers is modified and they may be used, for example, to pass parameters.

The instruction **return** leads to the restoration of *C6, C7* and *PC* using the values saved on the top of the stack, and updating of the top of stack pointer.

The progress of a process can therefore be seen as a walk through a network of domains interconnected by capabilities with *DomainCall* rights (fig. 6.22).

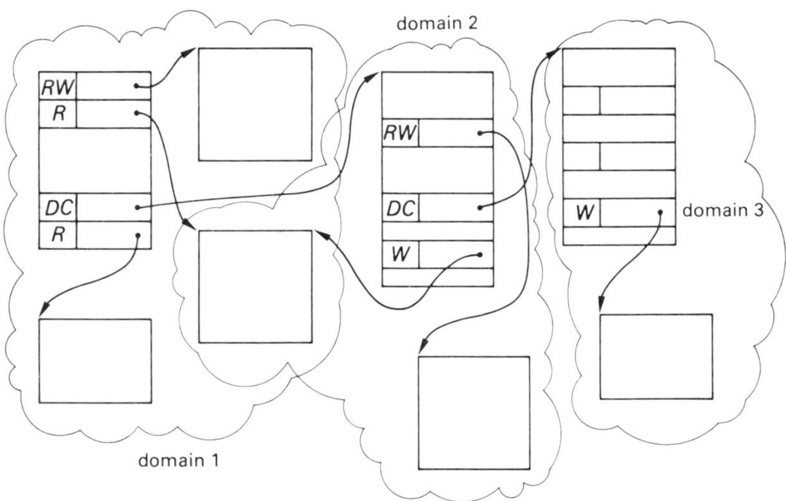

Fig. 6.22. Domain network in the Plessey 250

These domains may share objects. Note that the network is built up statically, before execution, by a linkage editor which constructs the C-lists by resolving the external references of a set of programs. There is no dynamic linking.

Note finally that segments containing process stacks are special objects, as they contain both capabilities and data. They can only be handled by operating system programs which execute in a protected domain.

4. *Use of domains: constructed objects*

The concept of a domain makes it possible to construct a complex object (a set of data uniquely accessible by a specified set of operations) from elementary objects which are segments and C-lists. The capability block of the domain contains the capabilities of data segments and of procedures representing the data and operations of the objects construcred, with the required access rights. If the capability block is made to include capabilities for capability blocks of objects that have already been construced, this procedure can be applied iteratively.

To illustrate this type of construction, we shall describe its use by that part of the operating system which is responsible for process management. As it is a constructed object, a process is represented by a collection of the following elementary objects:

- The stack segment of the process, which has already been mentioned
- One or several segments containing the current context of the process (state, priority, etc.)
- The procedure segments implementing the possible operations on the process (block, activate)

Capabilities for these objects are held in a C-list which makes up the capability block of the process object; any process which has a capability for this capability block, with call rights, may suspend or activate the process represented, but it cannot, for example, read or directly modify its context or its execution stack.

Processes are created dynamically by other processes. The creator process calls a particular domain of the operating system (see subsection 5b) which builds up the structure of the new process using parameters provided by the creating process, and assigns the latter a capability for the capability block of the created process, with call rights.

5. *Implementation of the operating system*

The operating system for the Plessey 250 is made up of a set of domains each of which carries out a particular function: management of memory, of processes, of files, etc. These domains are called by user processes as needed, and their protection, like that of all domains, is guaranteed by the general capability mechanism. We shall very briefly describe two of these domains.

a. Memory management.The domain responsible for memory management creates and destroys objects, and assign locations for them in main or secondary memory. It is the only domain within the system allowed to create capabilities. When an object is created, this domain allocates it space in main and secondary memory, creates a descriptor in the SDT and assigns the requesting process a capability for the object created.

An object can be deleted by an explicit command; its descriptor is invalidated in the SDT, but the corresponding entry cannot be freed as long as any capability in memory points towards it. An object can also be implicitly deleted, if it is named by no capability. The memory space it occupies can only be recovered by a garbage collector.

Each object has a reserved zone on disk, allocated when it is created. The address of this zone appears in the corresponding entry of the SDT, with a mark indicating whether the object is present in main memory. To maintain the consistency of the information on disk at any moment, every capability contained in a C-list stored on disk points to the disk address of the object named. This has two consequences:

- If a C-list is transferred to or from disk, all capabilities appearing in it must be modified.
- An object must have an entry in the SDT if it is named by a capability present in main memory, even if the object itself is not present.

An attempt to access an object not present in main memory leads to its being loaded from disk; memory zones are freed, if necessary, by flushing the least recently used objects back to the disk (see chapter 9).

b. Process management. Operations carried out by the process management domain are creation and deletion, which have already been mentioned, and the dispatcher function (processor allocation). The latter function is carried out by special instruction, *change_process*, whose parameter is a capability towards the stack segment of the process to select, with rights *R, W, RC* and *WC*. Apart from the stack as such, this segment contains a static zone for saving registers other than *C6, C7* and *PC*. The effect of *change_process* is as follows:

- It stores the registers of the selected process in the appropriate zones of its stack (*C6, C7* and *PC* on the top, the others in the static zone).
- It loads the registers of the process to select from the corresponding zones of its stack.

6. *Conclusion*

The concept of a domain implemented on the Plessey 250 provides for more flexible protection mechanisms than rings. In particular:

- It makes it possible to implement objects constructed by assembling existing objects, with strict limitations on the operations allowed.
- It makes it possible to implement mutually suspicious subsystems. Protection of the called domain is implemented by the gate mechanism

(obligatory entry points) and the constitution of the capability block for the domain, which defines access rights to all its objects. The calling object may also protect the object constructed, which it transmits as parameter, using the same mechanism.

The main limitations are due to the absence of a dynamic linkage mechanism, which makes it obligatory to build up the set of domains implementing an application beforehand. The possibility of transmitting a domain as parameter nonetheless allows a certain form of dynamic construction.

6.5 Bibliographic notes

The fundamental principles of access to objects in computer systems are discussed and illustrated in [Banino 78, Saltzer 78]. The historic reference on segmentation is [Dennis 65]. The development of addressing mechanisms, from base registers to capabilities, is discussed in [Fabry 74].

The concepts of a capability and of a domain appear in a primitive form in [Dennis 66]. The current protection model is discussed in [Lampson 69 and 71, Graham 72, Saltzer 75], as well as in [Peterson 83 (chapter 11)]. Various, generally unresolved, problems relating to protection are discussed in [Lampson 73, Redell 74].

Protection within the general organization of systems is described in [Denning 76, Linden 76]. An example of a system kernel in which considerable work has been done on protection is described in [Popek 79].

The hierarchical naming of files, introduced in Multics, is described in [Daley 65]. Input-output streams are discussed in [Feiertag 71]. Similar concepts for the Unix system are described in [Ritchie 74] and their use in [Bourne 83].

Loaders and linkage editors are studied in texts on basic software; see in particular [Graham 75 (chapter 4)]. A detailed description, based on the IBM 360–370 system, is given in [Presser 72].

A complete description of the highly original architecture adopted for Multics software and hardware is given in [Organick 72]. The principles underlying virtual memory are discussed in [Bensoussan 72]. A more up-to-date discussion of addressing mechanisms appears in [Banino 78]. The implementation of protection rings is described in [Schroeder 72]. [Saltzer 74] discusses all aspects of protection.

The Plessey 250 system is described in [Cosserat 74, England 74]; overviews include [Ferrié 78] and [Levy 84].

Capability systems are discussed in the monograph [Levy 84], which describes the main implementations. Apart from references on the Plessey 250, already quoted above, detailed case studies are available on CAL-TSS [Lampson 76], Hydra [Wulf 81], CAP [Wilkes 79] and Intel iAPX 432 [Kahn 81].

Exercises

Exercise 6.1

Examine the problems posed by the revocation of access rights to an object in a protection mechanism. Assume that the owner process is to be given the possibility of selectively granting or revoking access rights to an object. Examine separately the cases where the granting of rights is transitive (a process can pass on the rights it has received). **Hints:** Two possible mechanisms are indirection and the creation of backward links.

Exercise 6.2

During the mounting of a removable volume in the directory of a file system, what are the problems posed by:

- The possibility of creating links that do not go through the root of the volume
- The possibility of creating multi-volume files

Exercise 6.3

Describe the implementation of procedures for mounting or removing a volume, along the lines discussed in section 6.2.3.2, specifying the necessary data structures.

Exercise 6.4

If a file system directory is represented by a graph whose nodes are directories and files, and whose arcs are naming relations, the Multics file system (without taking account of links) can be represented by a tree, and the Unix system (where there is no difference between links and ordinary names) can be represented by a directed acyclic graph (with the subgraph containing directories alone remaining a tree structure).

Examine the advantages, disadvantages and implementation problems of more general structures.

Exercise 6.5

Propose a pattern making it possible to implement linkage editing in one phase along the lines of a restart chain used in one-pass assemblers.

Exercise 6.6

It is intended to implement a mechanism for the execution of modular programs on a machine with segmented addressing. A module includes a set of global variables and procedures which access these variables. The procedures of a module M may be called from another module, which **uses** M. Consider only the case of a single process.

A segment is identified by its descriptor's index in a general table of segments. Two segments are associated with a module, one containing the code of its procedure, the other its global variables. Two base registers BRP and BRD contain their segment numbers, for the module currently being executed. The ordinal counter PC contains the displacement of the current instruction within the procedure segment. A special segment acts as the execution stack; the parameters for procedures are passed by value through the stack.

We say that procedures in modules used by a module *M* are 'external' to *M*. They are named by means of a linkage segment, each of whose locations *n* contains the numbers of the procedure and data segments of the module *E* used by *M*. A base register BRL contains the number of the linkage segment for the current module. The procedure segment of a module *M* is organized as follows:

- The first location (displacement 0), contains the base address of the linkage segment for *M*.
- The *m* next locations contain the displacements of the entry points for the *m* procedures of the module.
- The rest of the segment contains the executable code of these procedures.

In the program for a module *M*, a call to the *k*-th procedure of the module described by the *n*-th location of the linkage segment of *M* is implemented by an instruction **call** *n,k*.

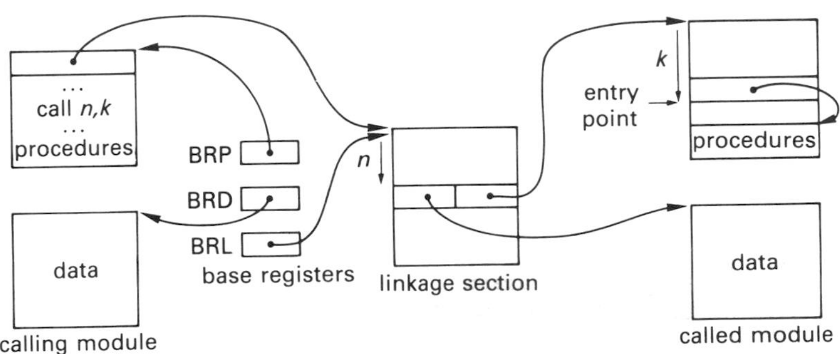

1. Does this approach make it possible to implement several modules each of which uses a set of common procedures and has a distinct set of global variables? What advantage does this possiblity give?
2. Describe in detail the sequence of operations to execute during a call to an external procedure for a module, and during a return from that procedure.
3. Does this pattern allow dynamic linking? Describe the data structures necessary and the principles underlying such an implementation.
4. Examine the possibility of implementing this approach within a capability architecture of the Plessey 250 type.

Note: This approach is based on the execution model for the Mesa language [Lampson 82].

Exercise 6.7

Examine a possible extension to the Plessey 250 addressing and execution pattern to allow dynamic linking.

Exercise 6.8

We want to represent 'constructed' objects (objects made up of several segments) of a certain class (see section 3.1). A class is characterized by a common object structure and by access procedures which are the only ones allowing these objects to be handled.

1. Show how such objects can be represented on the Plessey 250. Describe the elements common to objects in a single class.

2. Is it possible to define access procedures whose parameters are several objects of a single class?

3. Examine the possibility of allowing a constructed object to be shared between two processes. Specify the common elements and those that are specific to each process. Is it possible to forbid a particular process from carrying out certain operations on the object? Is it possible to forbid certain operations to all processes executing within a particular domain?

Exercise 6.9

Describe the data structures and the algorithm necessary for managing C-list transfers between main memory and disk on the Plessey 250.

Chapter 7
File management systems

Examples of the use and implementation of files have already been met. This chapter gives a detailed study of file management in operating systems: logical organization, representation of information, implementation of access functions, protection and security. These concepts are illustrated by the example of file management in the Unix system.

7.1 Introduction

7.1.1 Functions of a file management system

The term **file** is used for a collection of information held as a unit for storage and use in a computer system. The lifetime of files is usually longer than the execution of a program or a work session: their permanent medium is therefore secondary memory. A file is an object in the sense defined in section 3.1.3: it has a name which allows it to be identified and it is provided with access functions, i.e. with operations allowing consultation or modification of the information it contains. That part of an operating system which provides for the storage of files and implements access functions is called the **file management system** (abbreviated to FMS).

A user of the computer system organizes information into files according to personal requirements, applying a structure, or organization, we call **logical**. Access functions are expressed using this structure. The representation of information in files in secondary memory (location address, information coding) defines their **physical** organization. Representing the logical structure of files in terms of physical organization is the responsibility of the FMS.

A common principle in usual logical structures is to define a file as a collection of elementary items of information of the same nature, called **records**. A record may itself have a detailed structure (we then use the term **field** for its subdivisions). Examples of logical organization are given in section 7.2.

The main functions carried out by a file management system have already been considered in section 3.2. They cover:

- Creation of a file (definition of a name, possibly allocation of space)
- Deletion of a file (freeing the name and the space allocated to the file)
- Opening a file (declaration of intent to use it with specified access functions and rights)

- Close an open file (prevent any further access)
- Various consultation and modification functions: read, write, extend, etc. (the details of these functions depend on the logical organization defined for files)

These functions are the basic operations provided in any FMS. In addition, there are various functions whose detailed nature depends on the organization of the FMS: specification and consultation of access rights, consultation of various characteristics (creation date, modification date, etc.), operations on names (redefinition, etc.). Examples of such functions are given below.

The storage of files and the implementation of access functions mean that the FMS must provide for:

- The management of physical media in such a way as to mask the details of physical organization from the user
- File security and protection, i.e. guarantees of file integrity in cases of accidents or deliberate misuse, and the application of specified rules governing file usage (access rights, conditions of sharing)

The FMS plays a central role in an operating system, as it must manage most of the information belonging to users and to the system itself. The FMS is often closely linked with the input-output system: it is conceptually convenient to make no distinction between files and peripheral devices as sources or destinations of information transfers during the execution of a program (see section 6.2.4). In systems which have special addressing and information naming devices such as virtual memory or segmented memory, the FMS must also be able to use these mechanisms, with which it is sometimes identified (see sections 6.4, 6.9 and 6.10).

7.1.2 General organization of a file management system

The FMS implements the correspondence between logical organization and physical organization of files. Logical organization, the only form of organization known to users, is determined by considerations of ease and generality; physical organization, associated with the characteristics of the memory media used, is determined by considerations of space and of efficiency of access. These two forms of organization are generally different, and each is defined by specific data structures managed by the FMS.

It is therefore natural to give the FMS a hierarchical structure, including at least two levels corresponding to the two forms of organization above: any action defined at the logical level is interpreted by a set of actions at the physical level. Intermediate levels may be defined to aid design or to meet specific requirements (portability).

To separate the logical organization of a file from its physical organization, it is convenient to introduce an intermediate organization which plays the role of an interface. This intermediate organization is simply a segment, a sequence of adjacent locations named by consecutive integers called logical addresses, or displacements. This makes it possible to separate the two stages involved in establishing a correspondence between the logical and physical organization of a file (fig. 7.1):

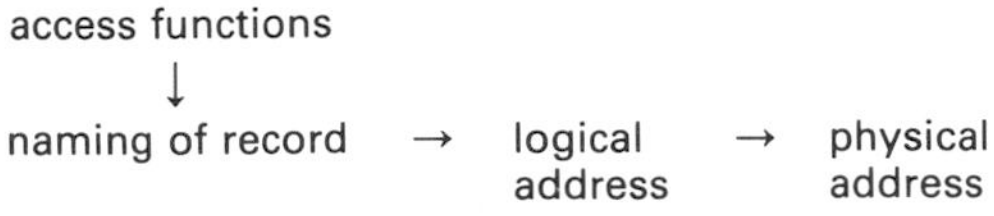

```
access functions
       ↓
naming of record   →   logical    →   physical
                       address        address
```

Fig. 7.1. Logical addressing in a file

- Translation into logical addresses of names specified by file access functions (names used for records, or fields within records)
- Translation of logical addresses into physical addresses

This pattern is given purely by way of illustration and is not necessarily implemented by the FMS; in particular, for reasons of efficiency, the intermediate stage is sometimes by-passed, with access functions directly translated into physical addresses. Note too that in a machine which allows for segmented addressing, the representation of files is reduced to the first stage: the physical location of segments is left to the operating system.

To complete the model above using the ideas presented in section 6.2 on file naming, the organization of the FMS can be built up along the lines shown in fig. 7.2.

This structure should not be regarded as a rigid framework providing a model of all possible forms of organization for an FMS, but as a guideline for defining the most common functions and data structures. The rest of this chapter gives a top-down presentation of a hierarchy defined in this way.

The main forms of logical organization for files are described in section 7.2. Sections 7.3 and 7.4 are concerned with physical organization and with the implementation of access functions. Security and protection problems are dealt with in section 7.5. Finally, an example of an FMS (Unix) is given in section 7.6.

7.2 Logical organization of files

7.2.1 Introduction

We shall now examine the main modes of logical organization of a file and their implementation. At this stage of our study, we shall merely translate

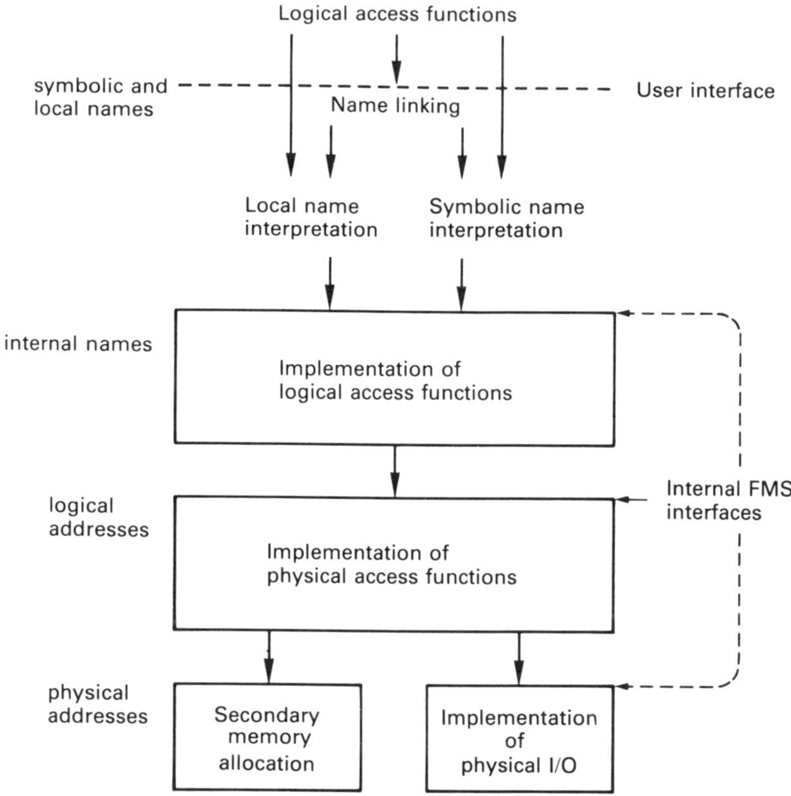

Fig. 7.2. Organization of a file management system

the location of records handled by access functions into logical addresses or displacements; the determination of their physical addresses will be examined in section 7.4.

To specify the logical organization of a file, we start by defining an abstract structure for the file. To do so, we shall use a simple model for the description of data, allowing us to specify records, to define the overall organization of a file and to express access functions. We shall then specify the concrete representation of information contained in the file.

A file is a collection of records. Each record is associated with a fixed number n of **attributes**, which is the same for all records. An attribute is defined by a name and by a range of values. The name identifies the attribute: different attributes have different names. The range of values specifies the possible values that the attribute can take.

The specification of a file organization in addition has to give the constraints which records must meet. These constraints may take various forms (order of records, restrictions on the values of attributes, relations between attributes, etc.). Record naming, in access functions, is based on their attributes, taking account of the constraints specified.

To illustrate these definitions, we give two examples which will be reused later.

Example 1: Sequential character files. Each record in the file has the following attributes:

(number,<integer>)
(content,<ASCII character>)

The constraint is that records in the file are ordered, with successive records taking consecutive integer numbers.

In the following representation, the attribute *number* is not explicitly represented, but defined by the order of the records. In the same way, attribute *content* is represented only by its value. Overall, the file is simply represented in the form of a sequence of characters.

The use of the attribute *number* makes it possible to specify various access functions. For example, considering consultation alone:

read(next) reads the character following the current position specified (that of the last read); it returns its value in *next*
read(i,c) reads the character whose number is *i*; it returns its value in *c*

In both cases, we have to specify the effect the function will have if the character is not present.

The first function is of the *sequential access* type (see section 7.2.2), and the second is of the *direct access* type (see section 7.2.3).

Example 2: Document file. Each record in the file, which is used for library management, has the following attributes:

(reference,<book identifier>)
(author,<character string>)
(publisher,<character string>)
(year,<integer>)
(subject,<character string>)

The constraint is that two different records must have different book identifiers as reference (in other words, a book is uniquely determined by its reference).

Let us consider the representation of this file. If we agree an order for the five attributes of a record, the names of these attributes (which are the same for all records) need not be explicitly given. Each record is represented by a sequence of five fields each of which has a fixed format determined by a field representation.

Direct access functions may be specified, naming a record by its *reference* attribute (that name is unique). To specify sequential access functions, we would first have to order the records using a further constraint (e.g. the definition of an order for references, authors, years, etc.).

Logical organization methods for files (representation of data, implementation of access functions) are a direct application of algorithms for data structures: tables, queues, lists, etc. which takes us beyond the scope of this book. We shall simply give a brief description of common forms of organization, leaving it to readers to refer to specialized literature (see the bibliography in section 7.7) for a more detailed study. The main aim of this description is to identify the constraints implied by each of these forms of organization for the physical location of files.

7.2.2 Sequential access

In sequential organization, records are given in specific order; they can be named by consecutive integers. These order numbers cannot, however, be used by access functions; only the 'successor' function is available. Sequential access is the natural mode for files physically located on a medium where access to locations is itself sequential, such as magnetic tapes.

A file *f* can be opened for reading or writing. Certain forms of organization allow writing to any record (as in the example in chapter 3). In the organization we are describing, writing always takes place at the end of the file, and opening for writing initializes the file to *<empty>*.

The opening of a file is carried out by the operation:

```
open(mode):

  if mode=read then
    f.rest:=<remaining articles in the file>
  else
    f:=<empty>
  endif;
  f.mode:=mode;
  advance
```

where *advance* is defined as follows:

```
if f.rest=<empty> then
  f.end:=true
else
  f.ptr:=<pointer to first(f.rest)>;
  f.rest:=f.rest−first(f.rest)
endif
```

The record read operation is written:

```
read(f,record):

    if →f.end then
      record:=<record named by f.ptr>;
      advance
    endif
```

Writing adds a record to the end of a file:

```
write(f,a):

  if mode=read then
    <error>
  else
    allocate new record;
    if fail then    --maximum size reached
      <error>       --or no more space
    else
      f.loc:=<pointer to location of new record>;
      <copy record into location named by f.loc>
    endif
  endif
```

These access functions use logical addresses. If the current record is not the last in the file, the logical address of its successor is given by

address(current record)+size(current record)

If records are of variable size, the size of the current record can be calculated from the contents of that record (generally, it is given explicitly).

7.2.3 Direct access

In organizations using direct access, the access functions are expressed as a function of attributes of records; these attributes are generally the values of the different fields. We use the word **key** for any field of a record whose value can be used to specify the record; depending on the organization adopted, one or more fields may be used as a key. Here are a few examples of common forms of organization.

7.2.3.1 *Single key*

In a file using a single key, every record has one key which identifies it without ambiguity; the rest of the record is the information that it actually contains. Different records therefore have different keys. We shall define a procedure *find (key,record)* which, for any value of the key, gives one of the following results:

- The logical address *record* of the (single) record whose key has that value (success)
- A warning that no such record exists (failure), using one of the mechanisms described in chapter 3 (exception or condition code); the value of *record* indicates where the record could be inserted (a special value if there is no more space)

The *find* procedure is used for a set of elementary direct access functions:

```
read      (key,info)
add       (key,info)
delete    (key,info)
modify    (key,info)
```

The functions *read, delete* and *modify* cause an error if the *find* procedure fails; conversely, the function *add* produces an error if procedure *find* succeeds.

Note: We can also define a function *write(key,info)* which would either *add* or *modify* a record depending on the result of procedure *find*. Opting for two distinct functions makes formulation more precise and more reliable (though it is more cumbersome in certain cases).

The ways of implementing procedure *find* are an important field in the study of data structures (see the bibliography in section 7.7). Here we shall simply sketch the main approaches used.

Two classes of methods are used: hash coding and indexes.

a. Hash coding

In hash coding, we attempt to implement the *find* procedure directly, by building a function *record=f(key)*. The function *f* is called the hash function.

We could start by considering the use of the identity function: e.g. in the case of a key taking integer values, this would mean taking the value of the key as address (or k times that value if a record occupies k locations). However, this is not generally a practicable method. Consider, for example, a file whose key contains nine digits; such a file would occupy 10^9 logical locations. If the mean size of the file was 10^5 records, the rate of usage of the file for valid records would only be 10^{-4}. If we want to avoid such a waste of space, we again come up against the problem of choosing a function that will establish a correspondence between logical and physical addresses. The use of the identity function is therefore limited to those rare cases where the range of values over which the key can vary is used with a high rate of occupation.

An ideal hash function carries out a permutation between keys and logical addresses, limited to the number of items in the file. To simplify matters let us assume that logical addresses are $0,\ldots n-1$, for a file containing n records. The hash function must have the following properties:

- For any record in the file, with key *k:*

$$0 \leq f(k) < n \qquad (1)$$

- For any pair of records:

$$f(k1) <> f(k2) \quad \text{if } k1 <> k2 \qquad (2)$$

In practice, property (2) is very difficult to meet: we have to accept that **collisions** are possible, i.e. that there may be keys which do not satisfy this property. The number of distinct values calculated by the hash function is then less than n. In cases of collision, a further stage is necessary to identify the record required, or to assign it a location in the case of insertion. The choice of a hash function so as to reduce the probability of collisions, and the choice of methods of handling collisions, must take account of the way in which the file is used:

- The probability of occurrence of different values of the key
- The relative frequency of the record search, insertion and deletion operations

Figure 7.3 shows the organization of a direct access file using hash coding.

If we manage to ensure that the number of collisions is low, the main advantage of hash coding is its rapidity: searching for an item requires only one disk access operation if no collision takes place. On the other hand, in the very frequent case where the set of keys is ordered, the hash function does not generally ensure that there is a simple relation between the order of keys and the order of logical addresses of the corresponding records. Consequently, sequential access on the order of the keys must be implemented by a sequence of direct accesses, with no simplification. Indexed access methods make it possible to overcome this disadvantage.

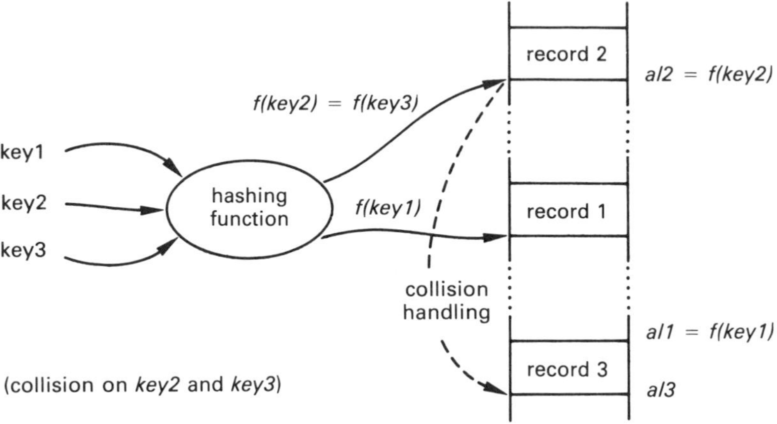

Fig. 7.3. Direct access by hash coding

b. Indexed files

Indexed access methods apply to cases where the set of keys is ordered. The relation between a key and a logical address is expressed by a table called an **index**, where the order of the keys is significant. The underlying approach to indexed organization is shown in fig. 7.4.

The approaches actually used in practice are more complex, to allow:

- Searches through the index to be speeded up
- Record insertion or deletion to be made easier

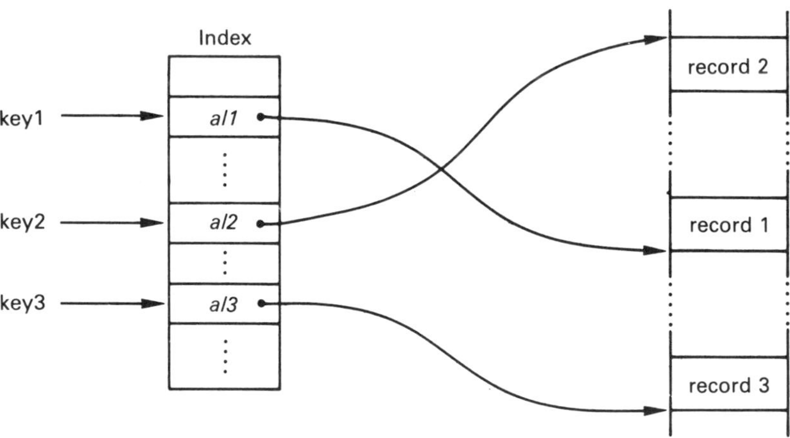

Fig. 7.4. Direct access by indexing

Let n be the number of records in the file. If the index is organized sequentially in key order, and searching for a key takes place by sequential scanning, the mean number of comparisons (and therefore of access operations to the index) is of the order of $n/2$. This number can be reduced to $log_2 n$ by adopting a tree-structured organization for the index ($log_2 n$ is the mean depth of a balanced binary tree with n nodes). If there are many insertions and deletions, the tree runs the risk of becoming unbalanced; in the least favourable case, its depth returns to order n. Consequently, use is made of a particular form of tree called B-trees, for which it can be guaranteed that search times actually remain of the order $log_2 n$ (see the bibliography in section 7.7).

If a file used in direct access must also be used for sequential access, it can be organized using a mixed method, called sequential indexed, with a multi-level index in which physical addresses are given directly. This approach is described in section 7.3.2.

7.2.3.2 *Multiple keys*

We shall now consider the case where several keys can be used for a record; there are in general several records for which a particular key has a given value. A key whose value determines a record in a unique way is called the primary key; this term can also be applied, by extension, to a combination of keys.

The basic technique used to manage a file with multiple keys is multi-list organization. A different index is used for each key. Each entry in the index associated with a given key, corresponding to a distinct value of that key, points to the head of a list containing all the records for which the key in question has that value. To implement the lists, each record therefore contains as many pointers as there are distinct keys. Figure 7.5 illustrates this organization using the example of our library management file.

Apart from the reference index, we have introduced an author index and a publisher index. Each entry in the author index is the head of a list containing all records whose *author* field has the same value. The pointers in these lists are logical addresses. It is therefore easy to find all the books written by a particular author, or published by a particular publisher. Combinations of these requests can be satisfied by taking the intersection of lists.

Note that we can condense the representation of the file by using circular lists including the corresponding entries in the indexes (with the list of works written by Paul, for example, ending with the entry *Paul* in the index of authors). This makes it possible to delete the *author* and *publisher* fields from the *info* part of the representations of records, since they can be found

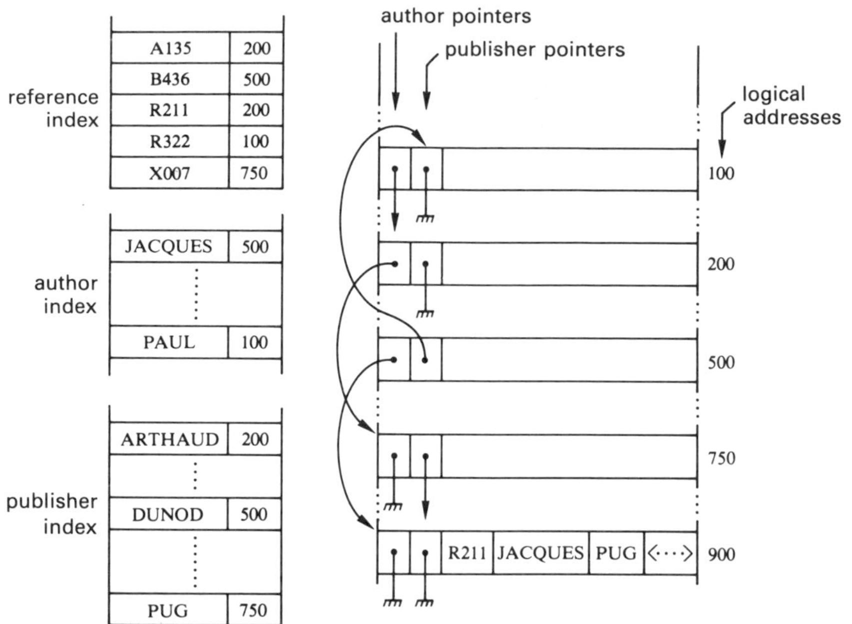

Fig. 7.5. Multilist organization for a file with a multiple keys

by scanning the corresponding lists. Taking this idea to its limit, we could create a distinct index for each field; the representation of our fields woud then only contain pointers, and all information would be in the indexes. A file represented in this way is said to be **inverted**. It makes it easy to answer queries concerning a combination of fields. It can, however, make it difficult to obtain all the information concerning a particular record. Consequently, inverted organization is generally combined with direct organization using a primary key. The secondary indexes then contain lists of values of the primary key. This form of organization is shown in fig. 7.6 for the example of the library management file.

We shall conclude our study of logical access functions by pointing out that it is common to construct complex access functions from elementary functions. For example, files in the Unix system are character files for which a set of direct access primitives is supplied (see section 7.6). More complex access functions have to be programmed using that set of primitives.

7.3 Physical orgainzation of files

In our hierarchical model, the problems of the physical organization of files can be formulated as follows: define the location in secondary memory of a set of files on the following assumptions:

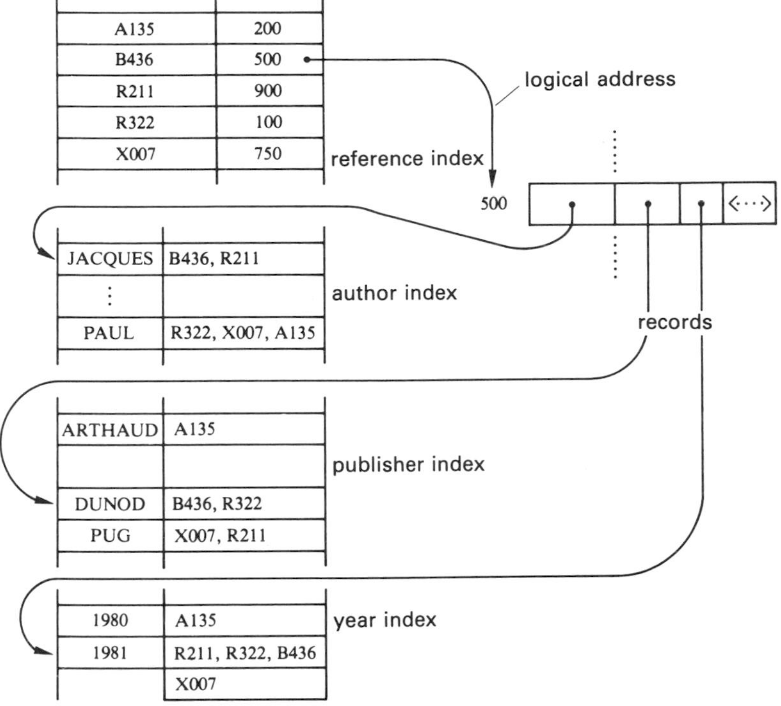

Fig. 7.6. Organization of an inverted file

- Each file is defined logically as a segment, i.e. as a collection of data occupying contiguous locations, referred to by logical addresses, or displacements.
- Except in particular cases (see section 7.3.1 on magnetic tapes), secondary memory is of the disk type, using fixed or moving heads. This memory is organized as a set of blocks of fixed size. The block addressing mode is described in section 7.3.3; all we need to know is that blocks are named by ordered physical addresses, with consecutive addresses naming contiguous blocks.

Note that, if the operating system implements segmented virtual memory, the physical location of segments and the implementation of elementary access functions (read, write, execute) are handled by the system. It is also possible to combine the file and segment concepts. The functions of the FMS are reduced to management of names and logical organization: this is what occurs, for example, in the Multics system. Readers are referred to chapter 9 for a study of the physical implementation of segmented memory.

In what follows, we shall consider the case in which the FMS directly manages the physical location of files. Two classes of methods can be distinguished according to whether or not contiguity in logical addressing is respected in physical locations.

7.3.1 Sequential storage

In sequential storage, each file occupies a set of consecutive blocks in secondary memory. This is the only mode of storage possible on magnetic tape: files are stored consecutively on the tape, each file being separated from the next by a special end of file character. The descriptor of a file is generally located at the head of the file, and sometimes repeated at the end of the file. Within a file, records are stored consecutively; if they vary in size, their size is given at the head of each record. The end of file character is automatically detected by the tape streamer controller. A 'end of file search' operation makes it possible to move rapidly from the start of one file to the next, e.g. to find a file with a particular name.

Sequential storage can also be used on disk. Its main advantage is that it is efficient both for sequential access (data items with successive logical addresses are located in adjacent blocks) and for direct access (the calculation of a physical address from a logical address is very simple and does not require a disk access). It does, however, have major disadvantages in cases where file creation, deletion and size modification are frequent:

- Fragmentation of secondary memory after a large number of file creation or deletion operations: free space is distributed over a large number of small zones that are difficult to use. Fragmentation can be overcome by periodic reorganization of files by 'compacting', but this operation is very long and costly.
- Difficulties in varying the size of a file: a file cannot be extended without copying it entirely into a larger zone, unless provision has been made for its extension, and the corresponding space has therefore been reserved for it. Shortening of files leads to further fragmentation.

Consequently, sequential storage is only used on disk in cases where the disadvantages above can be reduced:

- File sizes and numbers do not vary (e.g. files created once and for all and later used for consultation only)
- Very primitive systems on micro-computers, where simplicity of implementation is a major factor

Readers should refer to section 9.4.2 and to the bibliography in section 9.8 for a study of sequential storage techniques.

7.3.2 Non-contiguous storage

We shall now abandon the assumption that items are stored in contiguous locations. Blocks in secondary memory are now equivalent; in certain mixed methods, however, contiguity considerations may still be a factor.

As a first stage in our analysis, we shall introduce the information necessary for the implementation of access functions; the redundant information required for security will be described in section 7.5.

7.3.2.1 Linked blocks

Physical blocks containing consecutive logical locations are linked together; each block must therefore contain a pointer used for chaining. The descriptor contains a pointer towards the first and last block, and the number of blocks occupied (fig. 7.7).

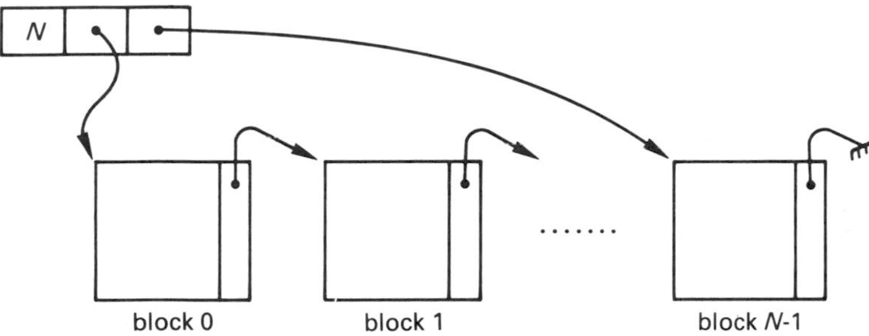

Fig. 7.7. Allocation of linked blocks

The last block in the file, which may not be entirely full, must include an indication of the number of locations it contains. A location therefore has to be reserved in each block for that information, or at least a bit to mark the last block. It is easy to extend the file by adding information to the end, since a pointer to the last block is available.

This mode of allocation is most suitable for sequential access. This is because a block can only be accessed by following the link structure; as each read of a pointer requires a disk access, direct access involves a high overhead. This form of organization performs badly for extensions to a file elsewhere than at the end: it would have to be possible to include partially filled blocks with the risk of wasting space, or allow for double linking, or some similar mechanism. It can therefore be simpler to reallocate all the blocks following the extension. The use of linked storage is limited to small systems, notably for the organization of files on diskettes.

7.3.2.2 Mapping tables

To allow efficient implementation of direct access methods, the access time to a block must be independent of its address. This is made possible by holding all the pointers in a single mapping table.

We shall consider several variants of these methods, which differ by the way the table is organized. The main problems are guaranteeing the uniformity of access time for large tables, and allowing insertion and deletion of blocks at any point in the file.

1. Single table

Figure 7.8a shows a form of organization with a single table. The size of the file is limited to the number of blocks whose descriptors can be held in a table (which is itself held in an integer number of blocks).

2. Linked table

The form of organization shown in fig. 7.8b, the location table is made up of a series of linked blocks. This avoids the size limitation, and it becomes possible to insert blocks in the middle of a file, as long as free locations are provided in the middle of the table. Reorganization due to insertion then only affects one block in the table. The size of the location table is however limited by the overheads involved in searching through the table. For large tables, the form of organization described below is more efficient.

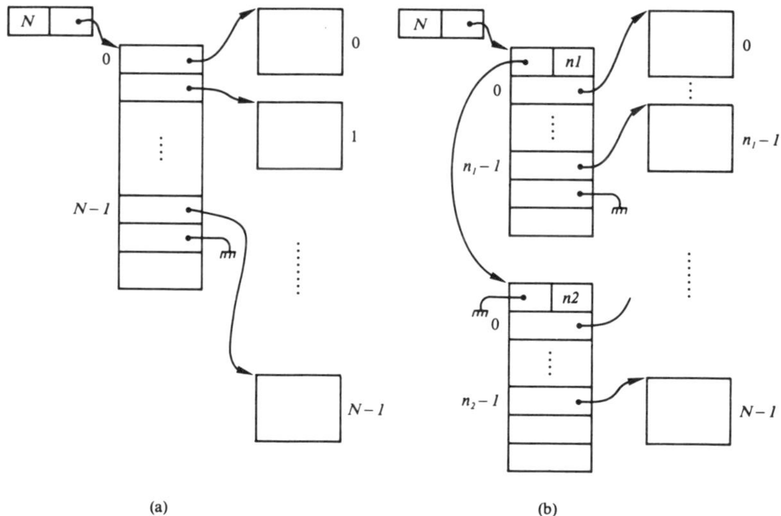

Fig. 7.8. One-level file mapping tables

3. Multi-level table

Figure 7.9 shows a form of organization where the mapping table for a file is organized in a tree. Usually, the tree is limited to two or three levels.

This form of organization allows rapid direct access to a block of given logical address; it allows insertions as long as the precautions described below are taken.

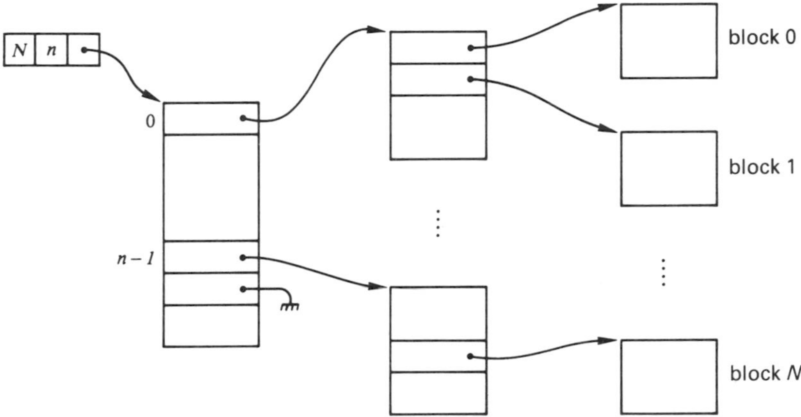

Fig. 7.9. Two-level file mapping table

4. Application: indexed sequential organization

By way of example, we shall consider a frequently used form of organization, that of indexed sequential files. This is an approach which does not clearly separate logical and physical organization: the index and the mapping table are held together in a single data structure.

This form of organization applies to files for which we want to allow both direct access (by means of keys) and sequential access (specified by an order on the keys). To simplify our discussion, we shall describe a system using a single key.

The underlying principle is to organize the index (ordered by the values of the key) as a multi-level mapping table, which gives physical addresses instead of logical addresses. Moreover, for the first storage operation at least, an attempt is made to place logically contiguous information into physically contiguous blocks, in order to allow efficient sequential access.

Figure 7.10 shows the underlying principle of indexed sequential organization for the file described in example 2 of section 7.2.1. The key used is the

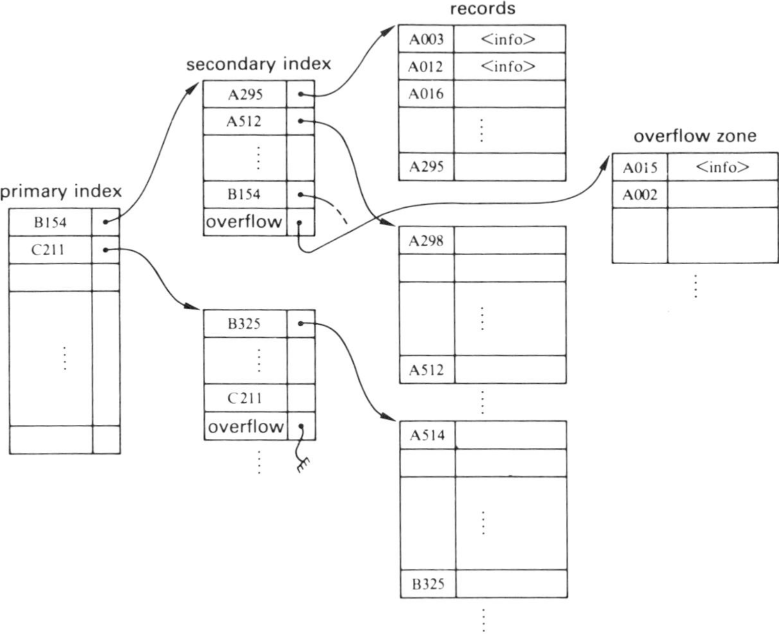

Fig. 7.10. Indexed sequential file

reference number. A two-level form of organization has been adopted. Entry i of the primary index (key *kp[i]*) points towards a secondary index which references items whose key k satisfies the condition

$$kp[i-1] < k \leqslant kp[i]$$

In the same way, each entry in the secondary index points to a zone where records are stored sequentially, with the same organization of keys. The latter zone is of a sufficiently small size to be read as a whole into memory during access to any record it contains. As the primary index is held in central memory when the file is openend, consultation of a record requires two disk accesses for the first read in a zone, and no further access for consultation of successive records in the zone. Sequential access is therefore fast, and direct access remains possible thanks to the index.

The main problem in indexed sequential access arises when it comes to inserting or deleting records. When the file is first built up, locations may be left free in each zone, which is then reorganized by compacting during modifications. If all the locations provided are full, overflow zones are used: such a zone is associated with each secondary index and records are stored in it in their order of insertion. Searching for a record then becomes a longer process; once the overflow zones are very full, it may be better to reorganize the file entirely, allocating new ordinary zones and, if necessary, creating new secondary indexes.

7.3.3 Allocation of secondary memory

The problem of allocating secondary memory is similar to that of allocating main memory; the specific constraints are:

- Allocation by blocks of fixed size
- The high cost of access
- The specific characteristics of each medium: organization into tracks, and fixed or mobile heads

The secondary memory allocator interface has two primitives:

request_zone(n,a)

data: n (integer), number of contiguous blocks requested
result: a (address), address of first block
exception: insufficient number of blocks

free_zone(n,a)

data: n (integer) number of contiguous blocks freed
a (address), address of first block
exception: certain blocks are already free

The case $n=1$ is frequently met and may justify the introduction of special primitives *(request_block,free_block)*.

The data structure used most often to describe the state of occupation of memory is a bit string, where the i-th bit shows the state (free or occupied) of block number i.

This occupation table may become large: for example, 12.5 Kbytes are needed to describe occupation on a 200 Mbyte disk allocated in 2 Kbyte blocks. To improve the efficiency of allocation algorithms, a multi-level table can be organized, using the levels into which secondary memory is iteself physically broken down.

Example: Moving-arm disks are organized into **cylinders** (a set of blocks accessible from a given position of the moving arm). Each cylinder includes the occupation table for the blocks it contains; furthermore, a cylinder usage table, loaded into main memory, shows the number of free blocks in each cylinder. Searching for a free zone can then take place without moving the arm, if the cylinder corresponding to the current position contains a sufficient number of free blocks; otherwise, a cylinder can be chosen amongst those which are closest to the current position of the arm.

For reasons of security (see section 7.5), the state of a block (free or occupied) is generally also shown in the block itself.

7.4 Implementation of elementary access functions

7.4.1 Organization of descriptors

A file descriptor must contain various types of information:

- Information on physical location
- Information concerning usage
- Information on protection and security

7.4.1.1 Physical location

Information on the physical location of a file has already been described in section 7.3. If information is held in units of fixed and small size (contiguous storage, linked blocks) it can be directly contained in the descriptor; otherwise, (linked mapping tables, or multi-level tables), the descriptor only contains a pointer to the mapping table, as well as overall information: size of the file, size of the mapping table, etc.

7.4.1.2 Information about usage

Information concerning the usage of a file can be classified as follows:

1. *State information*. Such information defines the current state of the file: open or closed, degree of sharing (number of users who have simultaneously opened the file), unavailability for reorganization, etc.

2. *Information on contents*. This information allows the contents of a file to be interpreted. We can in particular associate files with a type specifying the operations allowed. We distinguish, for example, between such types as 'ASCII text', 'relocatable binary', 'absolute binary', 'directory', etc. This makes it possible to check, in particular when the file is opened, that the usage to which it is being put is compatible with its type.

3. *Information on logical structure.* This includes information making it possible to move from the logical to the physical structure of the file. For example, in the case of records of fixed size, it is common to select a record size which is a multiple or a sub-multiple of the size of a physical block. The ratio between the block size and the record size, sometimes called the 'blocking factor' then appears in the descriptor.

4. *Information on past usage*. Such information may be statistical (number of times a file has been opened, number of accesses, mean time between accesses, mean degree of sharing); it gives a clearer idea of the operation of the system, to assist in improving it. For example, information on usage may assist automatic management of the secondary memory hierarchy: files unused for a long time may be transferred to archival memory to free space in rapid access memory (see section 9.6). Such information may also be used for security functions: recording the date of latest access and latest modification allows monitoring of the use made of the file.

Information concerning protection of security files is described in detail in section 7.5.

We shall now consider the implementation of elementary access functions (or primitives) as defined in section 7.1.

Like most functions in an operating system, these primitives may be called in two ways: by commands, or by supervisor calls. At the command language level, files are generally named by their symbolic name, which is interpreted in the current context. When a primitive is called by a supervisor call, during the execution of a program, files are generally named by a local name, which is that of a descriptor valid within the program being executed. The correspondence between symbolic names and local names is implemented by association commands. The interpretation of file names is common to all primitives.

For each primitive, we shall describe:

- Its interface specifications
- The principle underlying the algorithm which implements it
- Possible errors

7.4.2 Creation and deletion

7.4.2.1 Creation

1. Interface specifications

The parameters to provide are:

```
filename
type       (optional)
size       (optional
initial state     (optional)
```

Most often, the size and initial state parameters are not given and take a default value: size = 0, file closed, predefined access list.

2. *Operations*

- Create a descriptor for the file; this gives us an internal name.
- If the name provided is an external name, create an entry with this name in the current director.
- Allocate memory to the file; even if its size is initially nil, a file generally contains a header which occupies its first block.
- Initialize the descriptor with information concerning location, size and protection (initial access list or rights).
- If the descriptor is not directly contained in the directory, associate the entry created in the directory with the internal name of the file (address of the descriptor).

3. *Errors*

- Name supplied incorrect (incorrectly constructed or naming a file that already exists)
- Insufficient secondary memory space for the file

The file cannot be created and an error message is displayed.

7.4.2.2 *Deletion*

1. *Interface specifications*

The only parameter to provide is the filename. The effect of the operation is to prevent any further access to the file, by invalidating all its names, and to liberate all the resources it was using (table entries, memory).

2. *Operations*

- Free all the memory allocated to the file.
- Free the memory allocated to the descriptor, and make the internal name reusable (or invalidate it definitively).
- Delete the symbolic name of the file from the directory which includes it, and also, if appropriate, from the tables of local names.

This final operation may be difficult if there are several access pathways to a file. One of the following solutions can be adopted:

- If the multiple access pathways are links, nothing needs to be done as subsequent access by way of these links will lead to the internal name. The fact that the file no longer exists will then be detected (unless another file with the same name has been created in the meantime).
- If the multiple access pathways are names (which can happen in a directory using a structure other than a tree) use is made either of backward links (a costly method) or of a reference counter stored in the

descriptor, and which counts the number of access pathways available. A file can only be deleted if only one access pathway to it exists. This solution is used, for example, in the Unix system (see section 7.6).

7.4.3 Opening and closing

7.4.3.1 Opening

1. Interface specification

Parameters for the opening operation are:

filename
usage conditions:
  access mode (read, write, execute, etc.)
  access procedure (sequential, direct, synchronous, etc.)
  transfer parameters (buffers, etc.)

The opening operation is intended to put a file into a state where access is possible using the specified mode. This operation has two advantages for an FMS:

1. Protection the FMS can check:

- On opening, that the user is allowed to access the file under the specified conditions
- Each time the file is accessed, that the access conditions are compatible ith those specified when the file was opened
- In cases of sharing, that user access conditions are mutually compatible

2. Efficiency. The FMS can accelerate access to open files, loading their descriptors and mapping tables into memory as well as the text of their access procedures. The file itself may be transferred to a more rapid access medium; if it is on a removable volume that has not been mounted, a request for mounting will be issued.

The name provided as parameter may be an external or local name. It is often during file opening that a local name is assigned to a file. For as long as the file is open, the FMS must have rapid access to the information needed for its use: descriptor and use conditions valid for as long as the file is open. This information is held in a local descriptor, whose lifetime is as long as the file remains open; the local name is the name of this local descriptor.

2. Operations

The following operations are carried out on opening:

- Location of the file, and possibly transfer to a more rapid access medium; if necessary, a request to mount a fixed volume

- Checks on the user's right to open the file in the specified mode (by consultation of an access list)
- Creation of a local descriptor (if the file does not already have one in the current environment) and assignment of a local name
- Allocation of memory for input-output buffers; in certain cases, input-output programs may be constructed for a channel, as specified for the transfer

3. Errors

- Conditions of opening incompatible with user rights
- Opening impossible due to constraints specified for sharing (e.g. constraints of the reader-writer type)
- Insufficient memory space for the local descriptor or for buffers

7.4.3.2 Closing

1. Interface specification

The only parameter to provide is the name of the file.

The effect of the operation is to prevent any further access to the file, while leaving it in a coherent and stable state, notably by making permanent any modifications carried out while the file was open.

2. Operations

The file descriptor is updated (assuming it was not updated as operations proceeded), so that modifications made while the file was open become permanent; the local descriptor is deleted and the local name is made reusable. The memory space taken up for buffers and input-output procedures is freed, if it was only allocated for the time the file was open. The file may be transferred to its original medium; if the medium is removable, a request for dismounting it may be issued.

Certain systems include the concept of a temporary file: this is a file known only by its local name. On closing such a file, the user must choose between two possibilities:

- Register the file, assigning an external name to it; the file is then saved.
- (By default) do nothing; the file is deleted.

3. Errors

No transfer (of the descriptor or file) may be underway when a file is being closed; this is to ensure the file remains coherent at the end of the operation.

7.4.4 Elementary access to information

The parameters for transfer primitives make it possible to specify:

- The 'access method' used, which determines the way the items being transferred are named (sequential access, direct access, by keys, etc.)
- Transfer synchronization (synchronous or asynchronous transfer); in cases of asynchronous transfer, the reactivation mode of the calling process must be specified
- The buffers used (specified by the user or provided by the FMS)

Elementary access (read or write) to a file record takes place in two stages:

- Determination of the physical address of the record taking its logical name as starting point; for this purpose, the methods described in section 7.2 are used
- Execution of the physical transfer; the address obtained in the previous stage is used, along with physical disk access primitives (as described in chapter 4)

7.5 File security and protection

7.5.1 Introduction

Files hold information managed by an operating system, including the information necessary to system management itself. It is therefore important to guarantee the integrity of data, including its integrity in case of software or hardware breakdowns, or of deliberate misuse. The classes of objectives and methods used can be distinguished. We shall use the term **security** for all the methods intended to ensure that any operation carried out on a file conforms to its specifications, even in cases of failure in the course of execution, and that the information contained in a file remains unaltered if no operation is carried out on it. The methods used are those which, more generally, provide for fault tolerance in the system; they are based on redundancy of information. We use the term **protection** for all the methods intended to specify usage rules and to guarantee that the rules are respected. An overview of the main protection methods was given in section 6.1.4, and applications were examined in section 6.4. They are based on the concept of access rights and on the existence of mechanisms making it possible to guarantee that operations conform to specified access rights. In what follows, we shall explain in turn the main methods used to provide for file security and protection.

7.5.2 File security

As we have just pointed out, the security of files is based on redundancy of information. That redundancy can be implemented in two ways: periodic saving of certain information, in order to restore an earlier state in case of deletion, and internal redundancy, making it possible to reconstruct information that has become incoherent as a result of a hardware or software fault, leading to partial corruption.

7.5.2.1 Internal redundancy and reconstruction

The principle underlying internal redundancy is to organize data structures in such a way that any information can be accessed in at least two distinct ways. This reduces the probability that accidental deletion of part of the information will lead to irremediable loss of the contents of a file.

The techniques currently used are the following:

- Double chaining (successor-predecessor) for files held on disk
- A pointer in each block to the block containing the descriptor, or the information that the block is free
- Inclusion within the descriptor of the symbolic name of the file and a pointer to the directory where it appears
- Duplication of part of the descriptor (e.g. in the first and last blocks of the file)

As example to illustrate internal redundancy techniques, we shall describe the underlying principle of file organization on a personal computer (the Xerox Alto; this form of organization was also adopted in the Xerox Pilot system).

A file is organized logically as a sequence of items of fixed size (256 bytes) called pages. A file page is the elementary unit of information that can be accessed. The design of the FMS is based on the following principles:

1. All data is regarded as 'absolute' or 'auxiliary'; absolute data should in principle be sufficient to define the FMS completely; auxiliary data is used to accelerate access.

2. If auxiliary information is used for access a validity check is always carried out using absolute data.

3. Auxiliary information can be reconstructed from absolute information.

The following functions are available:

- Create a file (which is initially empty)
- Add a page to the end of a file
- Delete the final page of a file
- Read or write any page in a file
- Delete a file

Files are named using an internal name *FV* which is the concatenation of a unique name *F* and a version number *V*. A page with number *N* in a file *FV* is named using its logical name *(FV,N)*. Any access to a file page uses its logical name.

Each page occupies a block on the disk. A block with physical address *AD* on the disk, which contains a page *(FV,N)* holds the following information:

- The disk number and the address *AD* of the page on the disk
- A header made up as follows:

F	unique name	absolute
V	version number	absolute
N	page number in the file	absolute
AP	address on disk of page $N-1$	auxiliary
AS	address on disk of page $N+1$	auxiliary

- The 256 bytes which make up the 'value' of the file page

External naming of files uses directories which are themselves files. Each entry in a directory, corresponding to a file, is an ordered triplet *(id,FV,AD)* where:

id is the file identifier
FV is the internal name of the file
AD is the address on disk of page 0 of the file

A file may belong to several directories; one of them is identified as the owner directory.

Any file includes an additional page, called the base page, identified by the number −1. This page contains;

- The file identifier
- The name of the owner directory and the address of its first page

Such information is absolute; the content of directories, on the other hand, is regarded as auxiliary.

The principle of active redundancy is implemented as follows.

a. Checking on allocation and freeing

A free block is characterized by a header filled with zeros. Such information is absolute; the disk occupation table (one bit per block, indicating whether the state is free or occupied) only plays an auxiliary role.

A page header can only be modified at one of two moments:

- During the first write operation after allocation; a check is carried out to ensure that the block is indeed a free block
- On freeing the block; a check is carried out that the *FV* number is that of the freed page, and the header is filled with zeros

b. Checking during access

The absolute name of a file page is *(FV,N)*; it is that name which is used to specify access. This is in fact an address, treated as auxiliary information and used for the physical access operation. Each time physical access takes place to a page, its header is consulted to check that the absolute name *(FV,N)* appearing in it is that of the page specified. The disk controller allows this operation to be carried out 'on the fly', without losing a disk rotation.

c. Reconstruction

The reconstruction operation makes it possible to reconstitute auxiliary data starting from absolute data, and in particular:

- To check that all links are valid, and to reconstruct those that have been deleted
- To reconstitute directories
- To reconstitute the disk occupation table
- To point out any inconsistencies that have been met

Reconstruction is carried out when the system is rebooted; it may also be requested if an inconsistency is detected during execution. The reconstruction algorithm works as follows:

1. Scan the whole disk, block by block; for each block with number *i*, proceed as follows:

- If its header is full of zeros, mark the block *i* as free in the occupation table
- Otherwise store *(FV,N,i)* in a table of blocks, held sorted on *FV,N*; check links and update them if necessary

2. Scan all the directories (directories have reserved *F* numbers); check that every directory contains a pointer towards page 0 of a file; if there are still uncatalogued files, create an entry for each of them in its owner's directory; if this directory does not exist, store the file in a directory of 'orphaned' files.

3. List the files that have not been reconstructed.

7.5.2.2 Periodic saves

One approach would be to save all the information contained in an FMS at regular intervals. Assuming information is saved to magnetic tape, at a throughput of $3{\cdot}10^5$ bytes/s, the duration of this operation is around one hour per Gigabyte, without taking account of magnetic tape handling; a total save per day is therefore possible for a few hundred Megabytes, but impractical for a bigger FMS.

Consequently, **saving by increments** is used in larger systems. A process reactivated at regular intervals scans the hierarchy of directories and copies to magnetic tape all files and directories modified or created since the last save. The scan takes place in top-down order, i.e. files are only saved after their ancestors. Restoration also takes place in a top-down way. Saving by increments can take place concurrently with normal activity on the system, on condition that files being modified are excluded from the current save.

To accelerate the restoration operation, a more complete save, called a **checkpoint**, is carried out less frequently than incremental saves. A checkpoint save is said to be **complete** if it covers all the previous checkpoint saves.

Order of magnitude figures for the frequency of saves and the length of time information should be held, for a large time-sharing system, are as follows:

save	period	time information held
incremental	a few hours	a few days
checkpoint	a week	3 months
complete	a month	a year

The information stored by this process is used in two ways:

- In response to an explicit request from the user, to restore an earlier state of a given file
- After a breakdown, using the procedure described below

In cases of breakdown, an attempt is first made to restore information for the FMS using internal redundancy, as indicated above. This operation provides us with a list of files likely to have been corrupted. One then carries out the following two stage procedure:

1. Restore files assumed to have been damaged, from incremental save tapes, moving backwards through time from the most recent. Once a file has been restored, it becomes useless to search for it any further, since its most recent state is available. This stage ends with rereading of the last checkpoint save.

2. If there are still files to be restored, we move further back through successive checkpoint saves until the last complete save (or until all the files in the list have been restored).

7.5.3 File protection

File protection uses the access list principle. An access list associated with a file contains, for each user of the system, the rights the user has over that file, i.e. all the operations the user is allowed to carry out. In practice, conventions are applied allowing the list to be shortened. We start by defining all the rights assigned by default to any user (the set may be empty); the access list then only contains users whose rights differ from the default set. Classification conventions also allow a set of rights to be associated with a group of users (project members, etc.), which shortens the list still further. The access list is used to check the validity of any operation on a file.

Example: Access lists in the Multics system. Rights associated with a file are *read, write, execute*; those associated with a directory are *access, extend, modify*. For example, to write to a file, a user must have the right to *access* the directory containing the file and the right to *write* to the file. A user whose name or whose project is not included in the access list has no default rights. Access lists may be modified by any user with the right to *write* (to a file) or to *modify* (a directory). Initial rights can be associated with a directory, i.e. rights assigned by default to any file or directory created within that directory: this, for example, lets a user automatically authorize all members of his own project to read his files, or to allow a particular user to read them, without having to specify such rights for each file individually.

7.6 Example: the Unix FMS

As an example of the principles we have been discussing, we shall now describe the file organization in the Unix system.

7.6.1 General characteristics: naming

The Unix user handles three types of files: ordinary files, directories and special files. Special files are the only direct means of accessing peripherals; their use will be described later. The only difference between ordinary files and directories is that the modification of the contents of directories is forbidden to users other than by means of special system commands. A Unix file takes the form of sequence of bytes; no other structure is provided by the FMS. The FMS makes no assumptions concerning the contents of ordinary files, whose interpretation remains the responsibility of the user.

The naming of files is based on the tree structure described in section 6.2.2. Identifiers are interpreted in the environment of the current directory; the special symbols . and .. respectively name the current directory and its father, in any environment other than the root. The symbol / names the root directory; any identifier beginning with a / is interpreted in the environment of the root. The same symbol, /, can be used as a separator in qualified names.

It is possible to create links towards a file. A (hand) defines a new name for the target file, which, unlike what happens in Multics, has the same status as its initial name. To maintain the tree-structured organization of directories, no link can be created to a directory. The deletion of the last link to a file automatically deletes the file.

7.6.2 Organization of data

7.6.2.1 Descriptors

In a directory, the entry corresponding to a file contains the file identifier and an internal name, which is the index of its descriptor in a general table associated with the storage device. The descriptor ('i-node' in the Unix terminology) contains:

- The file type (ordinary, directory, special)
- The name and group of the file owner (see section 7.5.3)
- Protection information
- Physical location information (see section 7.3.2.2)
- The size of the file, in characters
- Its creation, last access and last modification dates

There is a table of descriptors for each storage device (see section 7.6.2.4).

7.6.2.2 Physical location

Secondary memory is organized into blocks of fixed size (512 bytes). A 13-word table *T* is reserved in file descriptors for physical location information. Depending on the number of blocks *T* occupied by the file, one, two or three levels of indirection are used (see section 7.3.2.2):

- Words *T[0]* to *T[9]* contain the addresses of blocks 0 to 9 of the file (the latter being set to 0 if $t<10$).
- If $t>10$, the word *T[10]* contains the address of a 128-word location table, containing the addresses of the following blocks (10 to 137).
- If $t>138$, the word *T[11]* contains the address of a table giving the addresses of the 128 new location tables; it is therefore possible to go as far as $10+128+128^2=16,522$ blocks.
- Finally, if $t>16,522$, three-level indirection is used for the following blocks: the address of the primary table is in *T[12]*; this therefore takes us to a maximum size of $16,522+128^3-2,113,674$ blocks.

Note that the access time to information in a file is not uniform, but is faster in the beginning part of a file. Consequently, access time to the first 5,120 characters (10 blocks) does not depend on the size of a file. This property can be turned to good use, by putting the most commonly used information at the start of the file.

If there are several secondary memory devices, or volumes, for files, a separate table of descriptors is associated with each of them. Each is resident on a volume at a fixed address. The internal name of a file is an ordered pair (address of device, index of descriptor in the table).

7.6.2.3 Peripheral management

Peripheral devices are represented by special files, generally held together in a single directory *(/dev)*. Instead of location information, the descriptor of a special file contains a pointer to the descriptor of the device, which contains two indexes, called the major and minor indexes. The major index identifies the device type and points to the programs of its access primitives, shared by peripherals of the same type. The minor index identifies each device individually and allows access to its specific data, notably to the input-output buffer it uses.

7.6.2.4 Removable volumes

The management of removable volumes conforms to the principles described in section 6.2.3.2. The directory of a removable volume is organized exactly like the general directory. The logical mounting command *(mount)* allows the directory of a volume to be incorporated into the general directory, at any level and under a freely chosen name chosen at will. From that moment on, all files in the volume become accessible. The only restriction is that it is impossible to create links between different devices: a file on one volume is only accessible through the root of the directory of that volume, and that root does not point towards its father. This avoids the need to search for links during dismounting.

Assume that we want to incorporate a volume on a device associated with the special file */dev/name*, under the name *vol*, in the current directory. We proceed as follows, after physical mounting of the volume:

1. Create a directory named *vol*, which is initially empty.
2. Execute the command

```
mount /dev/type vol
```

This command has the effect of replacing the internal name associated with the directory *vol* by the name $(d, 1)$ where d is the address of the device for the volume (found from the descriptor for */dev/name*) and 1 is the index assigned, by convention, to the descriptor for the root in the descriptor table. As all access paths to file on the device go through the *vol* directory, linkage is correctly established.

On dismounting, a check is carried out before breaking the link, to ensure that all files in the volume have been closed.

7.6.3 Operations and use

7.6.3.1 Descriptor management; local names

For the sake of economy, only descriptors of open files are copied to main memory. These descriptors, referred to as active, are held in a single active descriptor table (ADT). A file may be simultaneously opened by several users. Each of them independently uses it by means of a read-write pointer specific to that user. The pointer cannot therefore be contained in the file descriptor, which must be unique: it is stored in a resident table, called the open file table (OFT). A new entry is created in it each time a file is opened, and several entries may name a file that has been simultaneously opened by several users. Apart from the read-write pointer, this entry contains the mode under which the file was opened and a pointer to an entry in the ADT (fig. 7.11).

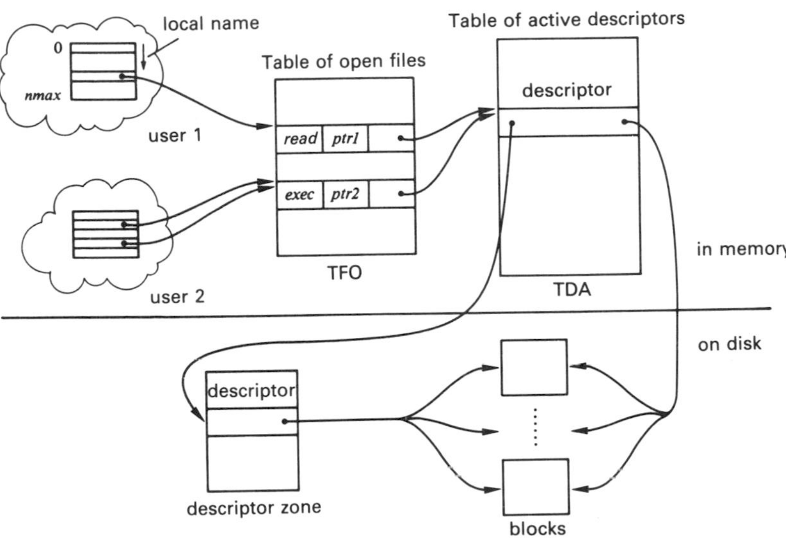

Fig. 7.11. File descriptors in Unix

Finally, to reduce the frequency of searches through directories and to simplify naming, a user can name a file using a **local name**. This name, which is an integer between 0 and *nmax* (*nmax* being of the order of 20) is allocated during the opening operation. It acts as index in a table of local names, held in a space specific to each user. Entries in this table are pointers to the OFT. It should be remembered (see section 6.2.3.1) that a local name is in fact a stream name, which may name either a file or a pipe.

Note that several local names, held by the same user, may name the same entry in the OFT (see primitive *dup* in section 7.6.3.2), and that several entries in the OFT may point to the same descriptor (this is the case of a file simultaneously opened by several users). In each entry of the OFT and the

ADT, a counter records the number of pointers to that entry; when that counter returns to 0, the entry is deleted. In the case of the ADT, the disk copy of the descriptor is then updated if it has been modified. The ADT therefore acts as a cache for descriptors (see section 9.7.1).

7.6.3.2 Access primitives

The access functions that we shall describe are primitives implemented by supervisor calls. They are used to implement operations available in the command language. Each primitive returns a result of integer type, which is used, in particular, to indicate errors.

---

open(filename, access mode)

Effect :opens the file in the specified access mode
Result :local name allocated (−1 in case of failure)

---

close(local_name)

Effect :breaks the association between the local name *locn* and the file (or pipe) associated with it
Result :success → 0, error → −1

The primitive *dup* (duplicate) makes it possible to create another local name for a file that is already open. it is used, in particular, to connect pipes, and also to determine whether a given local name is that of an open file.

---

dup(local_name)

Effect :if *local_name* is the local name of an open file, allocate another local name *local_name1* which is a synonym of *local_name* (naming the same file)
Result :success → *local_name1*, error → −1

Reading and writing take place from a current position, defined by a pointer. These operations automatically increment the pointer by the number of characters read or written. The primitive *lseek* allows the pointer to be moved explicitly.

---

read(local_name,buffer,nchar)

Effect :reads *nchar* characters from the file (or pipe) with local name *local_name* into zone *buffer*

Result :number of characters actually read (less than *nchar* if the end of file has been reached)

---

write(local_name,buffer,nchar)

Effect :write *nchar* characters from zone *buffer* to the file (or pipe) with local name *local_name*

Result :number of characters actually written

---

lseek(local_name,disp,orig)

Effect :displaces the read-write pointer by *disp* characters, from the position defined by *orig*:

0 → start of file

1 → current position of the pointer

2 → end of file

Result :the new current position (− 1 if error)

Note that the pointer may be displaced beyond the end of the file. The effect is to extend the file, with intermediate positions remaining unfilled; these 'gaps' take up no memory space.

7.6.3.3 File protection

File protection is provided for by access lists as outlined in section 7.5.3. There are three elementary access modes analogous to those defined in Multics: read, execute, write for a file; consult, access, modify for a directory.

For right checking, users are not individualized as in Multics, but divided into three classes: the owner of the file, members of a user group, all other users. The access list of a file therefore has a fixed size; it lists access rights attached to each of these groups, and can only be modified by the file owner or system administrator. An original characteristic of the protection system is that a file may change owner (its current owner may pass it on to another user); such transmission is made possible by the creation of links equivalent to the initial name (see section 7.6.1).

7.7 Bibliographic notes

Overall discussions on the organization of an FMS appear in texts on operating systems. These include, in particular, [Shaw 74 (chapter 9), Wilkes 75 (chapter 6), Habermann 76 (chapter 9), Peterson 83 (chapter 3)]. The hierarchical organization model for an FMS is described in [Madnick 69].

A general discussion of logical access methods (hashing and indexing) is given in [Ullman 80 (chapter 2)]; see also [Delobel 82 (chapter 7)]. The corresponding algorithms are studied in detail in [Knuth 73, Wirth 76].

Ideas on the implementation of security measures in an FMS are given in [Fraser 69 and 72, Wilkes 75]. The reconstruction algorithm in section 7.5.2.1 is described in [Lampson 74]; see also [Lockemann 68]. The principle of periodic saving in Multics is discussed in [Stern 74].

For case studies, consult [Ritchie 74, Thompson 78, Bach 86] for Unix, and [Daley 65, Organick 72] for Multics; see also the user manuals for these systems.

Exercises

Exercise 7.1

Propose data structures to implement file protection:

- As in Multics (access list (*<client name>, <list of rights>...*))
- As in Unix (*<owner rights>, <group rights>, <other rights>*)

Give outlines for:

- Right modification primitives (rights for execution of these primitives are specified in the directory which includes the file)
- Sequences for checking rights in the file access primitives

Exercise 7.2

Specify procedures for the allocation and freeing of secondary memory blocks and suggest data structures and program outlines for their implementation. Examine separately the case of a single allocation table and a table using cylinders.

Exercise 7.3

Using files in the Unix system and their access functions, suggest a means of implementing an indexed access method to records of fixed size.

Exercise 7.4

Using files from the Unix system and their access functions, suggest a means of implementing files with records of variable size:

- For sequential access
- For direct access

Exercise 7.5

Assuming that a hashing function is available whose interface is to be described, specify the necessary data structures for the implementation of a tree structured file directory. Give outlines of directory management programs for creation and deletion operations applied to files or directories.

Exercise 7.6

Assume a tree structured file directory system is available (see preceding exercise).

1. Modify the system to allow the creation of links, as specified in Multics, then as specified in Unix. In both cases, give program outlines for the primitives *create_link* and *delete_link*. Suggest a means of handling naming conflicts which may result from the use of these primitives.
2. Suggest a program for the primitives *add_name* and *delete_name* allowing management of multiple names for a file within a single directory.

Exercise 7.7

Describe the data structures and programs for file and descriptor management in the Unix system. Assume that primitives are available for main and secondary memory space management, and specify interfaces for them.

Exercise 7.8

In a file system on floppy disk, files are organized into lists of chained blocks. Files can be extended or shortened only from the end.

1. Giving the necessary data structures, write the program sequences to implement memory management in primitives *create, delete, add_a_block, remove_a_block*.
2. Introduce a minimum quantity of redundant information, to suggest a simple reconstruction algorithm allowing all or part of the contents of a floppy disk to be restored after a breakdown during execution of one of these primitives. You may wish to consider several solutions and evaluate their relative overheads, in space and in time, as well as their efficiency and the various assumptions concerning breakdowns (loss of the contents of a single file block, of several file blocks, or of part of the allocation table).

Exercise 7.9

Specify the algorithm for reconstructing the contents of a disk after a system breakdown, along the lines discussed in section 7.5.2.1.

Exercise 7.10

Describe a periodic file save algorithm, along the lines indicated in section 7.5.2.2. Examine, in particular, the possibility of reducing the volume of information saved.

Exercise 7.11

In a file management system, files may be shared between several users, and used simultaneously. A file may be deleted by the user who owns it. Nevertheless, if other users are using the file at the moment it is deleted, there are risks of inconsistency or of deadlock. Propose a solution making it possible to avoid such risks, and make the necessary modifications to primitives *open, close* and *delete*.

Chapter 8
Models for resource allocation

This chapter discusses the principles underlying resource allocation in computer systems. Two aspects will be considered:

1. The application of results from queueing theory to an analysis of a number of simple models of computer systems, notably for processor allocation
2. A study of methods making it possible to avoid deadlock, i.e. the situation where several processes within the system block each other, as a result of resources being allocated in an unplanned way

8.1 Introduction

8.1.1 Definitions

We shall use the term **resource** for any object which may be used by a process. All resources are therefore associated with access procedures, allowing them to be used, and with a set of rules for their use; examples of such rules have been given in chapter 4 (exclusive access, the reader-writer model, etc.). There is therefore no fundamental distinction between the concept of an object (as it was described in chapter 3) and the concept of a resource; the use of the two separate terms expresses a difference in connotation: we tend rather to talk of an object if we are interested in specifying the implementation of the object and its access functions, and of a resource if we are concerned with the problem of allocating it, as is the case in this chapter.

A resource is said to be **allocated** to a process if the process can use the resource, by means of access procedures. The acquisition of the resource by the process may be implicit or explicit. In the former case, the very existence of the process, or its transition to a certain state, makes it eligible to use the resource; in the second case, the request must be explicitly stated, in the form of a submission to an **allocator** of the resource. Allocators and requests may take various forms: for example, an allocator may be a process, to which requests are transmitted by sending messages; then again, it may be a monitor (see chapter 4) for which a particular procedure acts as a request transmitter. The reaction of an allocator to a request also take various forms: allocation of the requested resource, or refusal with or without blocking of the requesting process.

The use of a resource by a process may also end in several ways: explicit or implicit **freeing** of the resource by the process, or **preemption**, i.e. obligatory withdrawal of the resource by the allocator.

A resource is said to be **pooled** if it exists in several equivalent copies, so that a request can be equally well satisfied by allocating of one or other of them.

A few examples will help clarify these concepts.

Example 1: Processor. The 'access procedures' to the processor are defined by its instruction set and the contents of its status word; the processor is allocated to a process by loading its status word. There are no explicit requests: to submit such a request, a process would already have to be in possession of the processor being requested! A process is implicitly eligible for the use of the processor as soon as it moves into the 'ready' state. The allocator consists of two procedures, a dispatcher and a scheduler; the allocation algorithms will be considered in section 8.2.

Example 2: Main memory. The allocation of main memory is generally based on one of two distinct mechanisms.

a. Explicit allocation: this is the mechanism used to acquire a memory zone, either by a program in the course of its execution, or by the operating system prior to loading a program.

b. Implicit allocation: in this mode of allocation, the request is issued implicitly, at the moment an instruction is interpreted, in cases where the address transmitted by the processor is that of a location not allocated to the process. This mechanism underlies the implementation of virtual memory.

The allocation of main memory is studied in detail in chapter 9.

Example 3: Secondary memory. Secondary memory is allocated in pooled blocks of fixed size. Allocation and freeing may be explicit or implicit (e.g. the extension of a file leads to a request for a further block being issued). The allocation of secondary memory has already been considered, in chapter 7.

Example 4: Communication channel. If several processes are sharing the services of a common input-output device (e.g. a printer or a transmission line), requests are transmitted in the form of messages to a server process which manages that device. Each message contains the information necessary for the execution of the requested transfer. Messages are managed as a queue with or without priority; requests may or may not be blocking.

8.1.2 Problems of resource allocation

The aim of a resource allocation system is to satisfy requests fairly while maintaining acceptable levels of performance. If all processes have the same priority, allocation is **fair** if they are treated in the same way overall (e.g. mean waiting time is the same for all of them); if there are differences in priority between processes, the concept of fairness is difficult to define in general terms, but is expressed in the fact that the quality of service (measured for example by the reciprocal of the mean waiting time or by any other expression which is felt to be appropriate) is an increasing function of priority, and two processes of equal priority are treated in the same way. It has been found that there is a risk, in certain allocation algorithms, that a process may be made to wait indefinitely. This phenomenon, known as **starvation**, conflicts with the principle of fairness and has to be avoided.

If processes use several resources, two other undesirable phenomena may appear. **Deadlock** (already considered in chapter 4 when we dealt with the nesting of critical sections), is the indefinite blocking of several processes, each of which is waiting for resources to be freed by the other. An excessive level of demand for certain types of resources may lead to degradation in system performance, illustrated by the everyday phenomenon of **congestion** on roads or on telephone switchboards; analogous phenomena may occur in computer systems, and methods to overcome them are discussed in section 9.6.

The assumption made in this chapter is that allocation is centralized, so the algorithms implemented can immediately discover the state of allocation of all resources at any moment. Allocation in a distributed system, for which such knowledge cannot be obtained, poses specific problems that we shall not consider here (see [Lampson 81a] and our discussion of distributed systems in chapter 11).

The main tool for the quantitative study of resource allocation is the queueing model, for which the main ideas applicable to operating systems are summarized in section 8.2. These ideas are used in section 8.3 for a study of specific problems: processor allocation and disk transfer management. This is followed, in section 8.4, by an examination of more complete system models using the same concepts. The handling of deadlock, which uses other tools, will be the subject of a specific study in section 8.5.

8.2 Introduction to single queue models

The study of queueing models is an important field in applied mathematics, whose theoretical basis as well as its application to computer science have been studied in considerable detail. We shall merely mention the basic assumptions of the single queue model, and the main concepts derived from it. An introduction to queueing networks is given in section 8.4.1. For a detailed study of queueing models, the reader should refer to the bibliographic list given at the end of this chapter.

8.2.1 Presentation of the model

The model used for the allocation of a single resource is that of the single

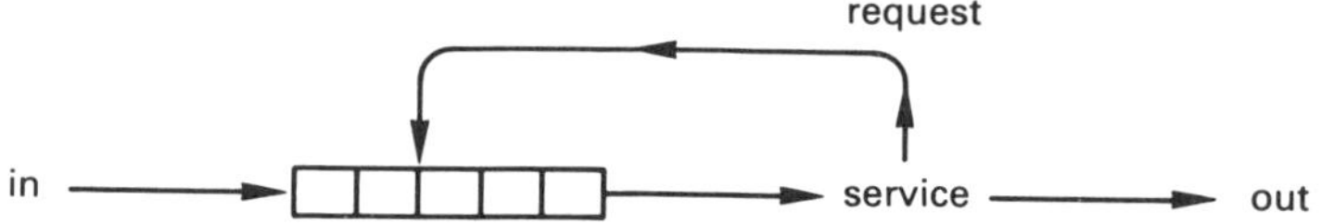

Fig. 8.1. A single-server queue

server queue, shown in fig. 8.1. Clients request a service which takes the form of exclusive use of a server for a certain time (the service time). The server can only serve one client at a time; clients arriving while the server is occupied wait in a queue. The server can therefore be treated as a resource with exclusive access, with the service time corresponding to the utilization time for the resource.

The times at which clients arrive and the length of service time they request are not generally exactly known in advance: these are random variables, defined by their distribution.

The model is therefore defined by three characteristics:

1. The distribution of client arrival times
2. The distribution of requests for service time
3. The policy for queue management

In this study, we shall limit ourselves to the simplest model of the distribution of arrival times, a Poisson distribution. This model has the advantage that it lends itself easily to calculation, while still representing fairly faithfully certain real situations. It allows identification of the main parameters for an allocation policy and will give an idea, at least in qualitative terms, of their influence. Some comments on the validity of the results obtained appear in section 8.4.4.

8.2.1.1 Distribution of arrival times

We say that the times at which clients arrive follow a **Poisson distribution**, with parameter λ, when:

- The probability that a client arrives during a small interval of time dt is equal to λdt
- The probability that more than one client arrives during this interval dt is negligible
- The probability that a client arrives is independent of the instant of observation and the previous history of arrivals

These properties allow a simple determination of the shape of the distribution function in the interval between successive client arrivals. Let $P0(t)$ be the probability that no client arrives during a time interval of duration t.

We then have:

$$P0(t+dt)=P0(t).(1-\lambda dt)$$

(this expresses the fact that no client arrives in interval t, no client in interval dt, and that these two events are independent). We can deduce

$$P0'(t)= -\lambda P0(t), \text{ with } P0(0)=1$$

and hence $P0(t)= exp(-\lambda t)$.

Now let $F(t)$ be the distribution function for the interval T between successive arrivals.

$$F(t)=Pr(T\leqslant t)$$
$$F'(t)dt=Pr(t<T\leqslant t+dt)$$

To define the event $(t<T\leqslant t+dt)$, we write that no client arrives during interval t, exactly one client arrives during interval dt, and that these events are independent:

$$F'(t)dt = P0(t).\lambda dt, \text{ with } F(0)=0$$

and hence

$$F(t)= 1-exp(-\lambda t)$$

Figure 8.2 represents this distribution function, called an **exponential distribution**.

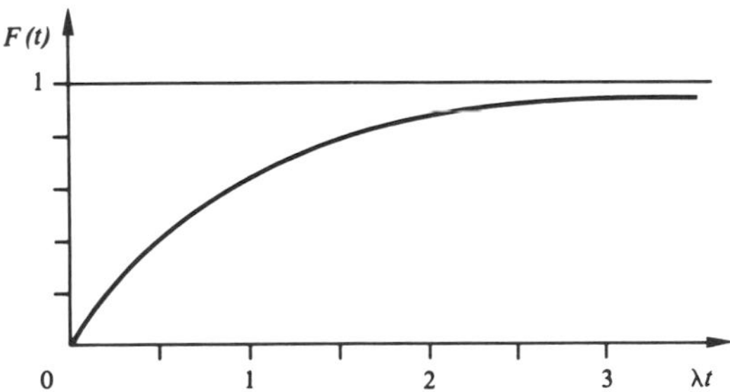

Fig. 8.2. Poisson process: distribution of interarrival intervals

The mean interval between arrivals is defined by

$$\text{mean interval between arrivals} = \int_0^\infty x.F'(x)dx = 1/\lambda$$

Finally, we have an important property: the process resulting from the superimposition of a set of processes with arrival times obeying independent Poisson distributions, with parameters λ_i, is itself a Poisson distribution, with parameter $\lambda=\Sigma\ \lambda_i$.

8.2.1.2 Distribution of service times

We assume that the service times *ts* requested by a client are independent random variables, defined by the same distribution function

$$B(t)=Pr(ts\leqslant t)$$

Two important characteristics of the service time distribution are the **mean service time**

$$ts=E(\overline{ts})= \int_0^\infty tdB(t)$$

and the **variance**

$$vs=Var(ts)= \int_0^\infty t^2dB(t)-(\overline{ts})^2$$

which measures deviation from the mean value.

Service times are often assumed to be exponentially distributed. This distribution, already introduced in section 8.2.1.1, is defined by:

$$B(t)=1-exp(-\mu t)$$

The mean value and variance of service times are then given by:

$$ts=1/\mu \quad vs=1/\mu^2$$

The exponential distribution is 'memoryless': if we observe a client during service, the distribution of service times remaining is independent of the service time already provided. The probability that the service ends between t and $t+dt$ is in fact equal to μdt independently of previous history.

In computer science applications, where we are interested in the distribution of execution times, we often find that the observed variance is greater than that given by an exponential distribution. We then use a **hyper-exponential** distribution, for which the distribution function is a weighted sum of exponentials:

$$B(t)=1-\sum_{i=1}^{k} a_i exp(-\mu_i t) \quad \text{with} \quad \sum_{i=1}^{k} a_i=1$$

We then have:

$$\overline{ts}=\sum_{i=1}^{k} a_i/\mu_i \qquad vs=2\sum_{i=1}^{k} a_i/\mu_i^2-(\overline{ts})^2$$

A hyper-exponential distribution makes it possible, with a suitable choice of the values of a_i and μ_i, to represent a population where the proportion of very long or very short service time requests is higher than would be expected using an exponential distribution.

8.2.2 Main conclusions

Assume

$$\varrho=(mean\ service\ time)/(mean\ time\ between\ arrivals)=\lambda\overline{ts}$$

This parameter characterizes the **traffic intensity** of the system. During a long period of time T, there will on average be λT jobs, and the mean quantity of work submitted to the system during this time T occupies the server for a time $\lambda T\ \overline{ts}=\varrho T$. If $\varrho>1$, the system receives on average more work than it can absorb, and the queue will lengthen indefinitely: the system is said to be **overloaded.**(1) We shall only consider cases where $\varrho<1$. In this case, it can be shown that a **stationary** operating mode exists, and we shall always assume that the system is in such a state, where all the quantities defined below are independent of time.

The operation of the system is characterized by the following quantities:

$\overline{Wq}$	mean waiting time for a client in the queue
$\overline{W}$	mean time the client remains in the system
$\overline{Nq}$	mean number of clients in the queue
$\overline{N}$	mean number of clients in the system
$p(n)$	probability that there are n clients in the system

(1) The case $\varrho=1$ is unstable, and is assimilated to that of overloading.

In stationary mode, whatever the service policy adopted, it can be shown that:

$$\bar{N}=\lambda\bar{W} \quad \text{(Little's formula)}$$

Moreover, we have

$$\bar{W}=\overline{Wq}+\bar{ts}$$

(the time spent in the system by a client is the sum of the time spent in the queue and the service time), from which we conclude

$$\bar{N}=\overline{Nq}+\varrho$$

This means that ϱ can be interpreted as the mean rate of occupation of the server; the probability that the server is idle (and therefore that the queue is empty) is $1-\varrho$.

The relations above make it possible to determine all the quantities $\bar{W}$, $\overline{Wq}$, $\bar{N}$, $\overline{Nq}$ as soon as any one of them is known.

We shall present two common server models and the main useful conclusions deriven from them, without demonstration.

1. Totally available server

We start by assuming that:

- The server is permanently available for service; the duration of switching between clients is zero.
- The behaviour of the server is independent of the length of the queue.

This model may be extended to the case where several identical servers operate in parallel; a client is dealt with by the first available server.

To specify the operating characteristics of such a system, we use a notation devised by Kendall:

<arrival distribution>/<service distribution>/<number of servers>

where the following abbreviations are used for the arrival and service distributions:

M :(for a Markov process), Poisson distribution for arrivals, exponential distribution for service times
D :deterministic distribution (non-random); e.g. arrivals at regular intervals, or constant service times
G :general distribution

We give the results for models M/M/1, M/M/c and M/G/1.

queue M/M/1	queue M/M/c
$\varrho=\lambda\overline{ts}$	we write $u=\lambda\overline{ts}$ and $\varrho u/c$
$\overline{NQ} = \varrho^2/(1-\varrho)$	$\overline{Nq}=\varrho C(c,u)/(1-\varrho)$
$\overline{N}=\overline{Nq}+\varrho=\varrho/(1-\varrho)$	$\overline{N}=\overline{Nq}+u$
$\overline{Wq}=\overline{Nq}/\lambda=\varrho\overline{ts}/(1-\varrho)$	$\overline{Wq}=\overline{Nq}/\lambda$
$\overline{W}=\overline{N}/\lambda=\overline{ts}/(1-\varrho)$	$\overline{W}=\overline{Wq}+\overline{ts}$
$p(n)=\varrho^n.(1-\varrho)$	
$Var(W)=[\overline{ts}/(1-\varrho)]^2$	$C(c,u)=\frac{u^c}{c!}/\left[\frac{u^c}{c!}+(1-\varrho)\sum_{n=o}^{c-1}\frac{u^n}{n!}\right]$

queue M/G/1

$\varrho=\lambda\overline{ts}$
$\overline{Nq}=\varrho^2(1+C^2_{ts})/2(1-\varrho)$, with $C^2_{ts}=Var(ts)/(\overline{ts})^2$
$\overline{N}=\overline{Nq}+\varrho=\varrho[1+\varrho(1+{}^2_{ts})/2(1-\varrho)]$
$\overline{Wq}=\overline{Nq}/\lambda=\varrho\overline{ts}[1+\varrho(1+C^2_{ts})/2(1-\varrho)]$
$\overline{W}=\overline{N}/\lambda=\overline{ts}[1+\varrho(1+C22_{ts})/2(1-\varrho)]$

The last relation above (in any of the four equivalent forms shown) is called the Pollaczek-Khintchin formula.

2. Walking type server

A more general behavior model is that of the walking type server, sometimes also called the Skinner model. The behavior of the server is described by the outline below:

```
loop
  if queue empty then
    wait (T)
  else
    serve client(ts);
    self-restore(rt)
  endif
endloop
```

Each service period (of duration *ts*) is followed by a 'restoration' period (of duration *rt*); moreover, if the server finds the queue empty, it waits a time T before it becomes available again. The variables *t, rt* and T are random; we write $S = st + rt$ and we assume that S and T are independent. This model makes it possible, in particular, to take account of the time the server needs to switch between clients; it will be valuable to us when we consider paging the disks (section 8.3.2).

The mean number of clients in the system is given by:

$$\bar{N} + \frac{(\lambda \acute{P})^3(2+A^3_P)}{2(1-\lambda\bar{S})} + \lambda \bar{ts} + \frac{\lambda}{T}\int_0^\infty t(1-F_T(t))dt$$

where $F_tT(t)$ is the distribution function for T and $C_s^2 = Var(S)/(s)^2$.

In the case where T is constant, we have

$$1 - F_T(T) = \begin{cases} 1 \text{ for } t \leqslant T \\ 0 \text{ for } t > T \end{cases}$$

and

$$\bar{N} = \frac{(\lambda\bar{S})^2(1+C^2_s)}{2(1-\lambda\acute{P})} + \lambda\left(\bar{ts} + \frac{T}{3}\right)$$

from which we can deduce $\bar{W}$ using Little's formula: $\bar{W} = \bar{N}/\lambda$.

8.2.3 Example application

A computer system consists of n identical installations, each of which can be treated as a server of the M/M/1 type, with characteristics λ and μ (fig. 8.3a). We shall examine the effect on the response time of the system, for constant processing power, of pooling resources.

- In the system show in fig.8.3b, the clients in the n queues are brought together into a single queue. The distribution of client arrials, resulting from a superimposition of Poisson distributions, remains a Poisson distribution, with parameter $n\lambda$. The system is of the M/M/n, with characteristics $n\lambda$ and μ.

- In the system shown in fig. 8.3c, the n servers in parallel are replaced by a single server, which is n times more powerful. The total processing power is therefore constant, but the mean service time for a job is divided by n: the system is of the M/M/1 type with parameters $n\lambda$ and $n\mu$.

We shall now calculate mean response times in cases a, b and c using the formulas in section 8.2.2 (the response time of a job is the time it stays in the system).

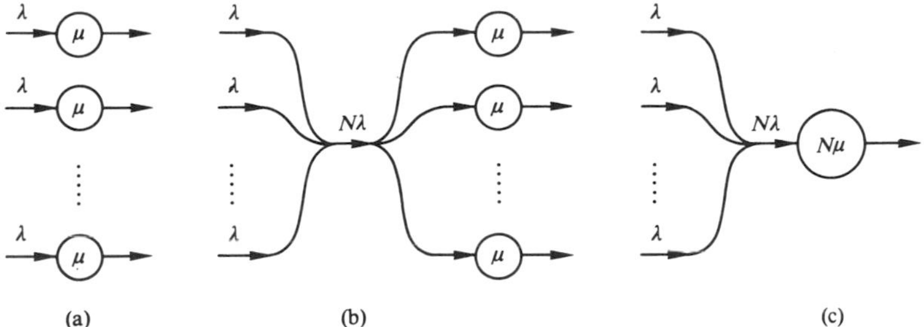

Fig. 8.3. Concentration of a system's resources

$\bar{W}\bar{a} = 1/\mu(2-\varrho$
$\bar{W}\bar{b} = 1/\mu + C(N, N\varrho)/N\mu(1-\varrho)$
$\bar{W}\bar{c} = 1/N\mu(1-\varrho)$

We have $\bar{W}\bar{c} = \bar{W}\bar{a}/N$, and it can be shown, by calculating $C(n, n\varrho)$, that $\bar{W}\bar{a} > \bar{W}\bar{b} > \bar{W}\bar{c}$. *By way of example, for* $N := 2$, $\varrho = 1$, our calculations will give $\varrho = 0.8$: $\bar{W}\bar{a} = 5$, $\bar{W}\bar{c} = 2.5$, $\bar{W}\bar{a}/2$.

This result shows the gain that can be obtained by **concentrating** resources. It can be interpreted intuitively as follows: in case *a*, a server may remain idle while clients are waiting in a queue for another busy server. This situation cannot occur in case *b*; but if servers are idle, their processing power is unused even when they could be applied to accelerate processing in busy servers. System *c* makes the best possible use of resources. Note that *b* and *c* have similar performance levels at heavy loads, when the probability of finding an idle server in *b* is negligible; but the system is then close to saturation.

8.3 Models for the allocation of a single resource

The results of the single server model can be directly applied to the allocation of a single resource. We shall consider two cases: processor allocation and management of exchanges with a paged secondary memory.

8.3.1 Application 1: processor allocation

8.3.1.1 Introduction

Processor allocation policies can be classified with reference to several characteristics.

1. Preemption or not

Preemption makes it possible to reallocate the processor before the active process has completed execution. It therefore allows the allocation policy to take account of:

- The priority of newly arrived tasks
- The time already used by the active process

2. Priority and means of determining priority

The priority of a process is an information allowing it to be distinguished from other processes when a choice has to be made (entry or exit from a queue, for example). The priority of a process may be defined in various ways:

- Fixed priority: defined *a priori,* as a function of the service time requested, etc.
- Priorty varying through time: a function of the elapsed waiting time, of the service already received, etc.

The main variable that we shall be considering is the mean response time; the parameters characterizing a request are those which determine the distribution of arrival time and of service times; these parameters are not always known, and it is therefore important to know the effect of their variation.

It is found in practice that users find delays increasingly difficult to tolerate the shorter the task they have submitted; this is as true for interactive work as for background work. Processor allocation policies are therefore aimed at *reducing the mean waiting time for the shortest jobs.* They differ according to the way they estimate the duration of jobs and according to the higher or lower privilege associated with jobs as a function of this estimated duration.

We shall start by describing the 'first come, first served' policy for which the mean waiting time of a task depends only on the load on the system and not on the service time requested. This policy will be used above all as a standard of comparison for the others described later.

8.3.1.2 First come, first served

The 'first come, first served' or 'first in, first out' (FIFO) policy uses a single queue, without priority or preemption. The active process executes until it is complete, and the next process at the head of the queue is then activated. A new arrival joins the end of the queue.

The results of the M/G/1 model can be directly applied. The mean response time is given by the Pollaczek-Khintchin formula:

$$\overline{W} = ts[1 + \varrho(1 + C^2_{ts})/2(1 - \varrho)],\ C^2_{ts} = Var(\overline{ts})/(\overline{ts})^2$$

Figure 8.4 shows the variation of the mean response time as a function of the load on the system and the variance in service time. Note:

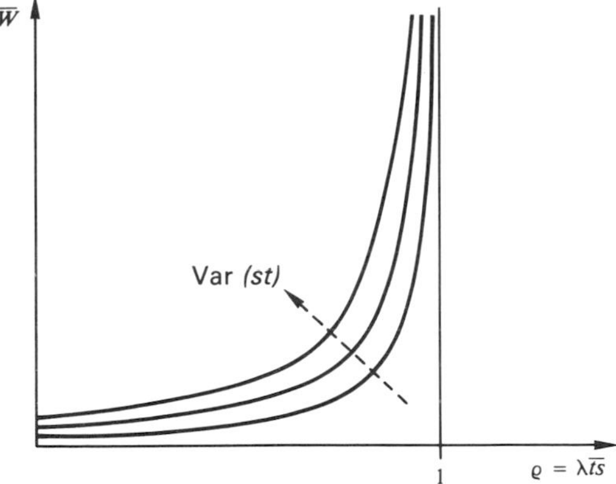

Fig. 8.4. Mean response times for a FIFO policy

- The rapid growth of response time as the system approaches saturation: a system is all the more sensitive to variations in load the more heavily it is loaded
- The influence of the **dispersion** of in service times on response times

These two effects reappear in all allocation policies

8.3.1.3 Shortest job first

In the 'shortest job first' (SJF) policy, jobs are ordered within the queue according to the service time they require, which is assumed to be known in advance, with the shortest jobs towards the front.

The mean waiting time is given as a function of the requested service time by the following formula:

$$\overline{Wq}(ts) = \frac{\lambda(\overline{ts})^2\,(1 + C^2_{ts})}{2[1-\varrho(ts)]^2} \quad \text{with} \varrho(ts) = \lambda\int_0^{ts} t\,dB(t)$$

Approximate formulas are:

- For low values of *ts*, where $\varrho(ts)$ is negligible:

$$\overline{Wq}(ts) \simeq \frac{\lambda}{2}(\overline{ts})^2(1 + C^2_{ts})$$

- For high values of *ts*, where $\varrho(ts)$ is close to $\lambda\overline{ts} = \varrho$:

$$\overline{Wq}(ts) \simeq \frac{\lambda(\overline{ts})^2}{2(1-\varrho)^2}(1 + C^2_{ts})$$

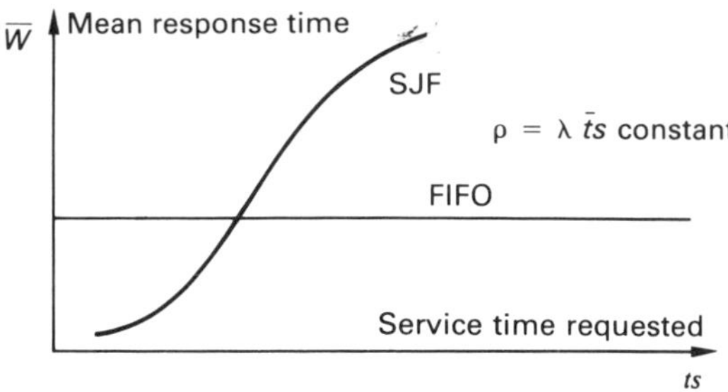

Fig. 8.5. Effect of the "shortest job first" policy

Figure 8.5 shows the general shape of the variation in response time as a function of the requested service time. Remember that for a FIFO policy, that time depends only on the traffic intensity, which we assume to be fixed. The figure highlights the privileged handling allowed to short jobs.

At a practical level, the SJF policy has two disadvantages: it leads to a risk of starvation for long jobs if the rate of arrival of short jobs is high, and it requires service times to be known exactly beforehand.

A means of avoiding the risk of starvation is to assign jobs a priority which grows with the length of time they are spent in the queue, with the initial priority being determined by their estimated service times. The HRN policy ('highest response ratio next') is based on this principle. The priority of a job, at time t, is given by:

$$p(t)=[W(t)+ts]/ts$$

where $W(t)$ is the time spent in the queue (i.e. $W(t)=t-ta$, where ta is the time the job arrived), and ts is its estimated service time. For equal waiting times, the shortest job has priority. In practice, priorities are recalculated at discrete moments and the queue is reordered if necessary.

The guiding idea underlying this algorithm is to share the processor fairly, attempting to maintain a constant value k for the ratio

$$W/ts=(Wq+ts)/ts$$

where W is the total time spent in the system by a job of duration ts. If this is achieved, everything takes place for each job as though it had exclusive access to a processor k times slower than the real processor. The HRN policy privileges short jobs, but the penalty paid by long jobs is reduced by the effect of using a variable priority.

The algorithms we shall now describe are also intended to provide for fair sharing of the processor, but do not require a priori knowledge of service times.

8.3.1.4 Round robin and derived models

In the **round robin** model, the processor is allocated in turn to all eligible processes for a fixed duration Q called a **time slice** or **quantum**. If a process ends or is suspended before the end of its time slice, the processor is immediately reallocated to the next. This policy is implemented by ordering processes into a circular queue; an activation pointer, which advances by a position each time a processor is reallocated, indicates the active process (fig. 8.6).

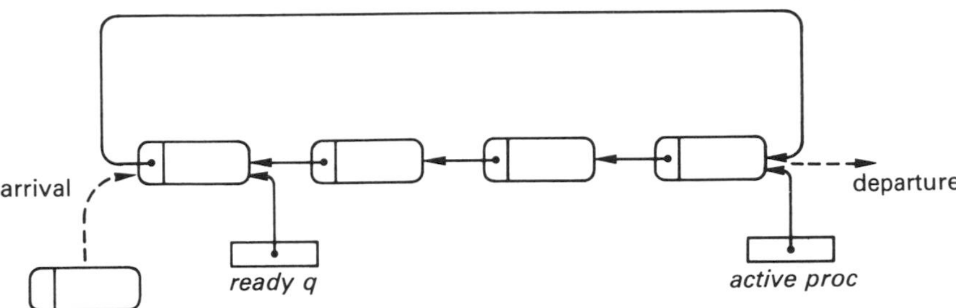

Fig. 8.6. Processor allocation: the round robin method

The round robin is an example of a policy with preemption. It can be regarded as an approximation to the 'shortest job first' policy in the case where the execution times of jobs are unknown beforehand. Let N be the mean number of eligible processes. A job which needs at least one time slice will be complete at the end of a time $N\,Q$; a job which requires k time slices will be complete at the end of a time NkQ. As will be shown in section 8.4.3, the round robin policy is well suited to interactive systems; the order of magnitude chosen for the time slice is such that most interactive requests are executed within a single time slice. The time slice should in any case be significantly larger than the processor switching time. These considerations mean that the usual values of a time slice are around between 10 and 100ms.

The round robin model is not easy to analyze; on the other hand, the limiting model obtained by letting the value of the timeslice tend towards 0 (and ignoring the processor switching time) is particularly simple. In this model, called the **shared processor** model, everything occurs as though each process had immediate access (without waiting) to a processor whose speed at any moment was that of the real processor divided by the current number of processes being served. It can be shown that the waiting time in the shared processor model is:

$$Wq(ts)=\varrho ts/(1-\varrho)$$

and the response time is:

$$W(ts)=ts/(1-\varrho)$$

The shared processor model therefore ensures that allocation is fair, with the time spent by any process within the system being proportional to the length of service it requires.

A refinement to the round robin model, intended to reduce service time still further for short jobs, is the multi-level round robin. This model includes n queues $Q_0, \ldots Q_{n-1}$. Each queue Q_i is associated with a timeslice q_i, whose value increase with i. A job in Q_i is only served if queues with numbers lower than i are all empty. If a job from Q_i has used up its timeslice without being terminated, it is added to queue Q_{i+1}; jobs from Q_{n-1} return to that queue. New jobs are added to Q_0 (fig. 8.7).

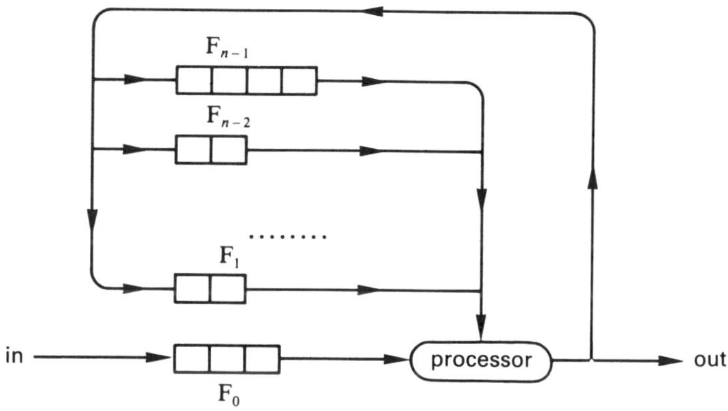

Fig. 8.7. Multilevel round robin

This policy increases the privilege granted to short jobs, compared with a SJF policy; like the latter, it runs the risk of starvation for long jobs, which can be avoided by the method described in section 8.3.1.2. Like the single round robin model, a limiting model can be defined, obtained by letting q_i tend towards 0 and n tend towards ∞, for which the mean waiting time can be calculated. Figure 8.8 shows the effects of the various policies examined so far.

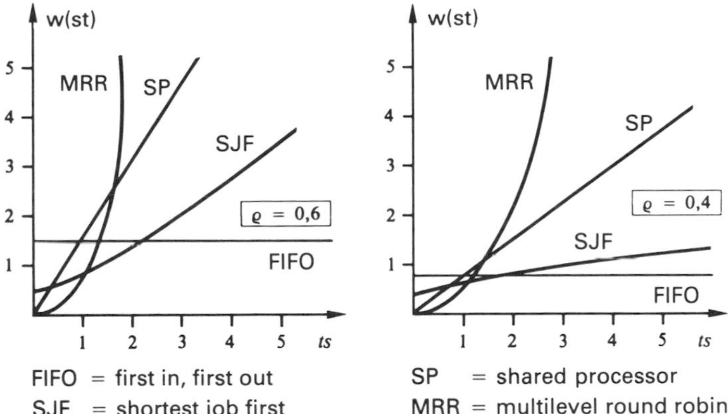

Fig. 8.8. Comparison of processor allocation methods (from [Coffman 68a])

It clearly illustrates the extent to which short jobs are privileged, as a function of the load on the processor.

8.3.2 Application 2: paging disk

We shall now consider the way in which exchanges between main memory and a fixed head disk are managed. Such a disk is organized into tracks and sectors and has a read-write head per track. Exchanges are managed by a server which receives transfer requests; requests concern the transfer of whole sectors, and specify the direction of the transfer, with an address in memory and an address on disk (track and sector). Our description is based on [Gelenbe 80].

We shall examine two policies for request handling:

1. Single queue. Transfer requests are stored in a single queue and handled on a firt come first served basis.

2. A queue per sector. A separate request queue is managed for each sector; the aim is to reduce mean waiting time by eliminating idle time. This requires that we know the current position of the disk.

These two policies are shown in figures 8.9a and 8.9b. A disk managed as shown in (b) is called a **paged disk**, as this modc of operation is commonly used for managing paging memories (see section 9.5).

We shall start by comparing the two policies, on the assumption that request arrivals follow a Poisson distribution and are uniformly distributed over the sectors. We shall write

λ for the mean rate of arrival of requests
R for the disk rotation time
n for the number of sectors per track

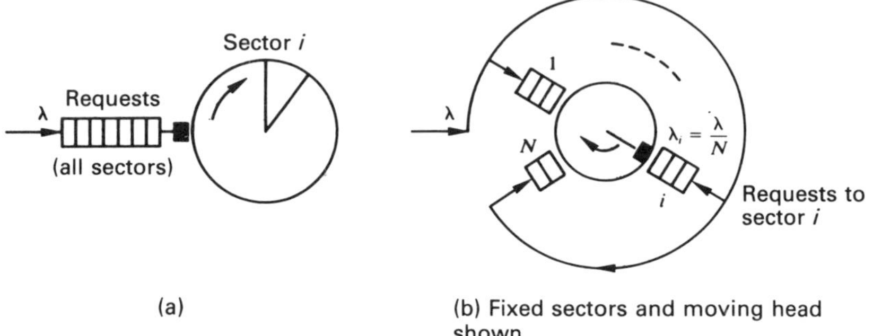

Fig. 8.9. Management of memory-disk transfers

The time a sector takes to pass under the head is therefore R/n.

1. Single queue for requests

Let us first build a model of the disk using an M/G/1 server, on the assumption that the duration of service can take any of n equally probable values:

$$R/n,\ 2R/n, \ldots (n-1)R/n$$

The mean service time *ts* is therefore:

$$\overline{ts} = \frac{1}{n} \sum_{i-1}^{N} \frac{iR}{n} = \frac{R(n+1)}{2n}$$

and the coefficient of variance is:

$$C_{ts}^2 = \frac{1}{(\overline{ts})^2} \sum_{i=1}^{N} \frac{1}{N}\left(\frac{iR}{N}\right)^2 - 1,\ 1 + C_{ts}^2 = \frac{2}{3}\left(\frac{2N+1}{N+1}\right)$$

The mean length of the queue, including the request being serviced, can be obtained from the Pollaczek-Khintchin formula:

$$\overline{N} = \lambda\overline{ts}\left[1 + \frac{\lambda\overline{ts}(1 + C^2_{ts})}{2(1 - \lambda\overline{ts})}\right]$$

and the mean service time is:

$$\overline{W} = \frac{\overline{N}}{\lambda} = \frac{R(N+1)}{2N}\left[1 + \frac{(2N+1)\lambda R}{3[2N - \lambda R(N+1)}\right] \quad (^1)$$

(1) This is only an approximate expression for low values of λ; if the queue is empty, we have $\overline{ts} = \frac{R}{2} + \frac{R}{n}$:

2. Paging disk

Each queue relating to a sector can be handled independently, using the Skinner model (walking type server), with

$$\lambda_i = \lambda/N \qquad ts = R/N,\ rt = (n-1)R/N$$
$$T = R \qquad S = ts + rt = R$$

This is because, once a request has been handled, the next in the queue must wait for the sector to come round again, during the next rotation; similarly, if the queue is empty, we have to wait for the next complete rotation. Applying for formula given in section 8.2.1.3, we find that the mean size of the queue for a sector is:

$$n\bar{N}_i = \frac{\lambda^2 R^2/N^2}{2(1 - \lambda R/N)} + \frac{\lambda R}{N}\left(\frac{1}{N} + \frac{1}{2}\right)$$

and therefore is the mean service time:

$$\bar{W} = \frac{\bar{n}_i}{\lambda_i} = \frac{\lambda R^2/N}{2(1 - \lambda R/N)} + R\,\frac{N+2}{2N}$$

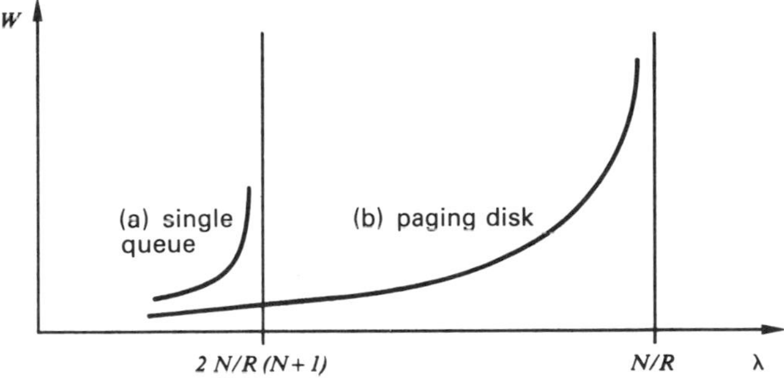

Fig. 8.10. Comparison of different approaches to memory-disk transfers

Figure 8.10 compares the two models for disk management.

A comparison of the saturation thresholds for the two policies makes it possible to quantify the advantage of using a paging disk. The saturation threshold is defined by $\varrho=1$. We therefore obtain:

for a single queue disk: $\lambda R.(n+1)/2n=1$
for the paging disk: $\lambda R/n=1$

The ratio of the critical thresholds for λ is therefore $(n+1)/2$; this ratio is a measure of efficiency of the paging disk per sector.

1. Open network

It can be shown that in this case each server behaves as though it were receiving a flow of arrivals following a Poisson distribution (though this is not in fact the case). All we have to do then is to calculate the distribution of mean throughput rates throughout the network, using the fixed transition probabilities and writing the throughput conservation equations as follows:

$$\Lambda_i = \lambda_i + \sum_{j=1}^{N} \varrho_{ji}\Lambda_j \quad \textit{for } i = 1,..N$$

The condition for the existence of a stationary solution is

$$\Lambda_i/\mu_i<1 \quad \text{for } i=1,\ldots N$$

Each server is treated individually using the M/M/c model.

2. Closed network

The combined probability $p(n_1,\ldots n_N)$ for a network with N servers and K clients is given by:

$$p(n_i, \ldots n_N)\frac{1}{G(K)} \sum_{i=1}^{N} (\Lambda_i/\mu_i)^{ni}$$

where the Λ_i are any solutions of the throughput conservation equations:

$$\Lambda_i = \sum^{N} s_{ji}\Lambda_j \quad \textit{for } i = 1,\ldots N$$

and $G(K)$ is a standardization constant such that the sum of the probabilities is equal to 1:

$$G(K) = \sum_{ki} \prod_{i=1}^{N} (\Lambda_i/\mu_i)^{ki}$$

$$k_i \text{ such that } k_1 + \ldots + k_N = K$$

The practical difficulty here is the calculation of $G(K)$. The formula above cannot be applied for this calculation and an algorithm involving recurrence has to be used (see bibliography in section 8.6).

The Jackson model was extended by Baskett, Chandy, Muntz and Palacios-Gomez to handle a larger class of service policies (BCMP network, see [Baskett 75]).

8.4 Models of operating systems

8.4.1 Queueing networks

The model of a single queue is useful for local representations of the behavior of part of the system, or in cases where a system can be assimilated as a whole to a single server. To represent a complex system, we use a network of queues covering serval servers; a client follows a path through the network submitting requests in turn to the different servers.

The general tool used to handle queue networks is simulation (see section 8.4.4). Nevertheless, analytic models may be used under some assumptions.

A **Jackson net** is characterized by the following assumptions:

- Each of the N stations in the network is a single server, or a set of identical servers in parallel; the service distributions are exponential.
- After having received service from station i, a client can ask for service from station j, or leave the network; transition probabilities are fixed.
- In an **open** network, the network is supplied from outside by several independent sources of clients, each of which obeys a Poisson distribution; in a **closed** network, the number of clients is fixed, and there are no exits or entrances.

Under these assumptions, it can be shown that the stationary solution for this model, if one exists, can be expressed in 'product form': the combined distribution of queue lengths for the various servers is the product of the probability distributions for the individual queues. The analytic approach adopted depends on whether the network is open or closed.

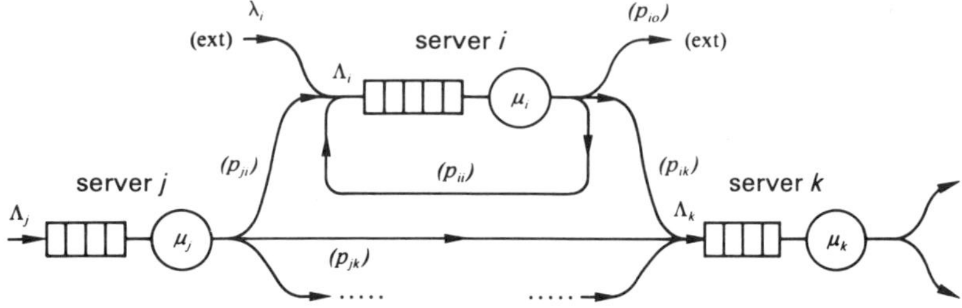

Fig. 8.11. Jackson network: notation

The notation used is as shown in fig. 8.11. Each station is marked with an index i $(i=1,2,\ldots N)$. Index 0 is used for the outside of the system. We write

Λ_i for the total rate of entry of clients to station i $(i=1,\ldots N)$

λ_i for the rate of entry from outside to the station i $(i=1,\ldots N)$

p_{ij} for the probability of transition towards station j on exit from station i $(j=0,\ldots N)$; p_{i0} is the probability of leaving the net on exit from station i

n_i for the mean number of clients waiting or being served at station i, under stationary conditions

μ_i for the mean service time at station i $(i=1,\ldots N)$

8.4.2 Application 1: a system with several servers

Consider the network shown in fig. 8.12.

Jobs are submitted from N independent terminals, whose mean behavior is identical. Each job requests the services of a processor P, and then those

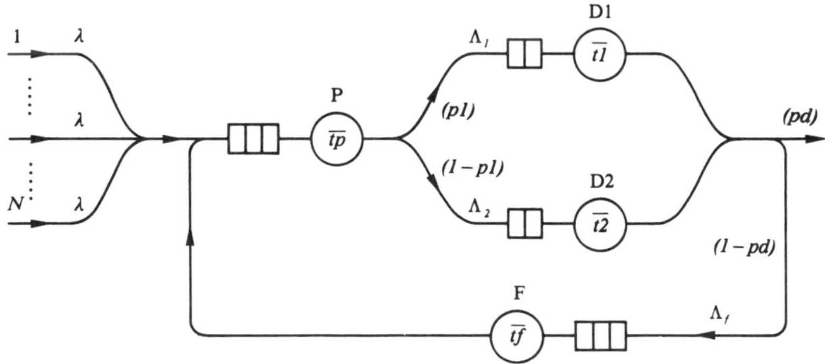

Fig. 8.12. Example of a queueing network

of an input-output device selected from D1 or D2, with probabilities p_1 and $1-p_1$. It can then terminate, with a probability p_d, or request consultation of a file on a server F and begin the cycle again.

We shall assume that the distributions for services P, D1, D2 and F are exponential (with means $\bar{t_p}$, $\bar{t_1}$, $\bar{t_2}$, $\bar{t_f}$), that the transition probabilities p_1 and p_d are fixed, and that requests issued by each terminal follow a Poisson distribution, with parameter λ. The Jackson network model can therefore be applied. The throughput conservation equations can be written (with the notation used in fig. 12):

$$\Lambda_p = N\lambda + \Lambda_f \qquad \Lambda_2 = (1-p_1)\Lambda_p$$
$$\Lambda_1 = p_1.\Lambda_p \qquad \Lambda_f = (1-p_d)\Lambda_p$$

From which we deduce the rate of arrival at entry point to each server:

$$\Lambda_p = N\lambda/p_d; \quad \Lambda_1 = p_1.N\lambda/p_d; \quad \Lambda_2 = (1-p_1)N\lambda/p_d; \quad \Lambda_f = (1-p_d)N\lambda/p_d$$

Each server can be treated as though it were M/M/1. Here are a few examples of the use of this model:

1. Let us assume first that:

$$N = 40$$
$$\lambda = 0.01\ s^{-1}$$

$$t_p = 0.8\ s \qquad p_1 = 0.6$$
$$t_1 = 0.3\ s \qquad p_d = 0.4$$
$$t_2 = 0.6\ s \qquad t_f = 1\ s$$

We find:

$$\Lambda_p = 1 \qquad \Lambda_2 = 0.4$$
$$\Lambda_1 = 0.6 \qquad \Lambda_f = 0.6$$

We can then determine $\overline{Nq}$ and $\overline{Wq}$ for each server, using the M/M/1 formulas. This allows us to calculate the loading levels:

$$\varrho_p = \Lambda_p.\overline{t_p} = 0.8 \qquad \varrho_2 = \Lambda_2.\overline{t_2} = 0.24$$
$$\varrho_1 = \Lambda_1.\overline{t_1} = 0.18 \qquad \varrho_f = \Lambda_f.\overline{t_f} = 0.6$$

The mean sizes of queues are given by $\overline{Nq} = \varrho/(1-\varrho)$:

$$\overline{Nq_p} = 4 \quad \overline{Nq_1} = 0.25 \quad \overline{Nq_2} = 0.32 \quad \overline{Nq_f} = 1.5$$

We can also calculate the mean waiting time of a job according to the number of cycles it requires in the system and whether it uses D1 or D2.

2. We can calculate the number of terminals which will saturate the system. To do so, we determine the value of N for which one of the ϱ becomes equal to 1. We find that for $N=50$, $\varrho_p=1$. The bottleneck is then caused by P. Conversely, we can calculate the increase in capacity necessary to absorb a different load.

8.4.3 Application 2: model of a time-sharing system

A simple model of a time-sharing system can be constructed as a closed network (fig. 8.13) where interactive users, whose number remains constant

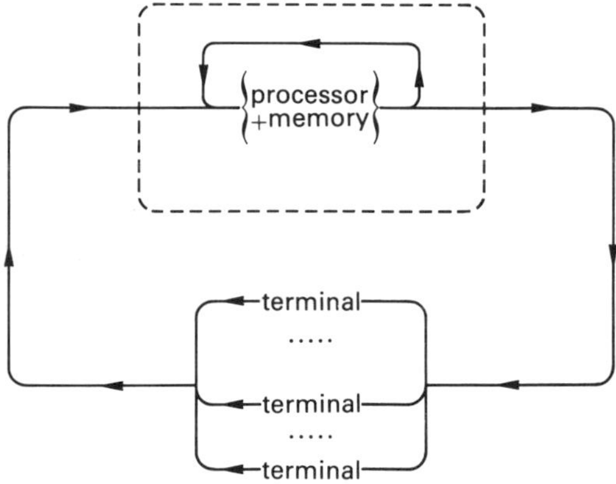

Fig. 8.13. Model of a time-sharing system

at N, submit jobs to a server including a processor, main memory and secondary memory. A process is associated with each user. We shall assume that the system is heavily loaded; under these conditions, only a subset of processes is allowed to use main memory. This subset changes as processes become suspended while waiting for users to respond to messages. As we shall see in chapter 9, the policy adopted for managing the processor-memory combination (selection of multi-programmed processes, exchanges with secondary memory) is intended to maximize the load on the processor. Without going into the details of this policy, we shall simply consider its overall effect, summarized by the mean value of ϱ.

The behavior of a process in the system can be summarized as follows:

```
loop
   thinking time; -- the user is typing a request
                  -- mean time: td
   response time  -- the system handles the request
                  -- mean duration: tn
endloop
```

Let ts be the service time requested, i.e. the mean processor time necessary to handle a request. The mean rate of handling requests is $\varrho/\overline{ts}$; assuming that any job submitted will ultimately be executed, this value is also that of the mean rate of submission of requests, λ. This rate can be calculated in another way: as the mean duration of a process cycle is $\overline{ta}+\overline{tr}$, each process will submit requests at a rate of $1/(\overline{ta}+\overline{tr})$; the total rate of submission is N times greater. This gives us

$$\lambda=\varrho/\overline{ts}=N/(\overline{tr}+\overline{ta})$$

and hence

$$\overline{tr}=N.\overline{ts}/\varrho-\overline{ta}$$

Remember that this result has been obtained on the assumption that the system is heavily loaded; it is therefore valid for high values of N. For low values, the processor becomes idle through lack of requests to execute, there is little interference between processes, and the value of the response time $\overline{tr}$ is close to $\overline{ts}$. These results are shown on fig. 8.14.

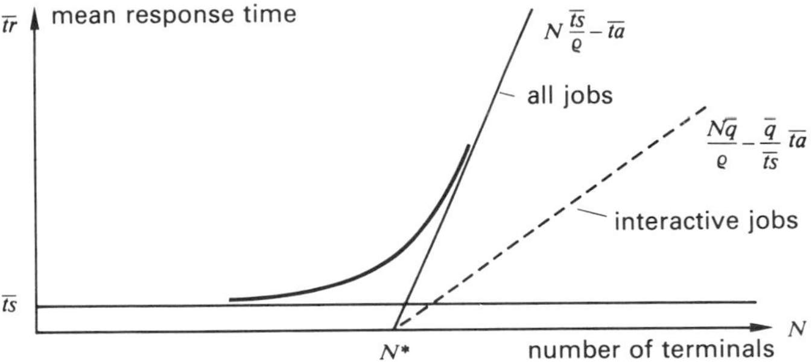

Fig. 8.14. Response times in a time-sharing system

Let N^* be the value of N corresponding to $\overline{tr}=0$, i.e.

$$N^*=\varrho.\overline{ta}/\overline{ts}$$

This value corresponds approximately to the saturation threshold of the system; beyond this number of users, the introduction of a further user increases the mean response time for all users by a value equal to $\overline{ts}/\varrho$.

It is worth repeating that the results above are based on the assumption that the policy adopted for managing memory and the processor maintains ϱ at a constant value (which we hope is high), and that this value remains independent of N. The methods to make this possible (and notably to avoid thrashing, i.e. a sudden collapse in ϱ and therefore an explosive increase in response time), are examined in section 9.6.

We can define the results of this model still further, by separating interactive requests, with a short execution time, from other requests. Assume that the processor is allocated using a round robin algorithm and that the value Q of the timeslice is selected in such a way that interactive requests are executed within a timeslice. Let $\bar{n}$ be the mean number of processes being currently served; the mean response time $\overline{ti}$ for an interactive request will then be $\bar{n}.\bar{q}/\varrho$, where $\bar{q}$ is the mean processor time used by a process once it is active ($\bar{q}<Q$, since certain requests terminate before the timeslice is used up). Little's formula gives us $\bar{n}$, the number of processes waiting for a request to be handled:

$$\bar{n}=\lambda.\overline{tr}, \text{ with } \lambda=\varrho/\overline{ts}$$

and hence

$$\overline{ti}=n.\bar{q}/\varrho=tr.\bar{q}/\overline{ts}$$

This result (see fig. 8.14), highlights the privileged way interactive processes are handled by the round robin algorithm.

8.4.4 Field of application of queueing models

8.4.4.1 Analytic models

A model based on queues is essentially a predictive tool, allowing:

- The evaluation, during the design stage, of the overall characteristics of a computer system
- The determination of critical parameters and possible bottlenecks
- The evaluation of the consequences of modifications made to design choices or operating conditions

The use of such a model is economical if its mathematical properties allow the application of precise and efficient algorithms to its solution. The possibility of working in this way is often obtained at the cost of making approximations, either in the system models, or in the solution algorithms for the model. It is generally estimated that a good specialist may obtain accuracy to within 10% on mean rates of job throughput and on rates of utilization of resources, and accuracy to within 30% on mean response times. Let us consider two fields of application.

1. Prediction of the capacity of a computer installation. Such a model can be used to determine the overall characteristics of an installation (speed and number of processors, memory capacity, input-output throughput, etc.) as a function of the estimated load and the performance levels desired. If the model is being used to predict the consequences of extending an existing configuration, it can be checked and calibrated using the results of measurements on the current installation. As load predictions are often fairly rough, the accuracy of an analytic model is sufficient for this type of application.

2. Assistance in the design of new architecture. In the design stage for a new hardware architecture, a model is useful to show the influence of various choices and to identify critical parameters. The design of input-output subsystems and memory hierarchies is a particularly suitable field for mathematical modelling.

If greater accuracy is needed, or if the conditions do not exist for the application of known models, we have to use simulation.

8.4.4.2 Simulation models

Compared with analytical models, simulation has the advantage of imposing no limitations other than those based on economic considerations, on the complexity of the model used. We can therefore represent a computer system or subsystem at a very fine level of detail, and obtain more accurate results. Simulation also has the advantage of providing results for transient modes while mathematical models generally only make it possible to deal with steady states.

Two simulation methods are used.

1. Trace-driven simulation. A **trace** is a record of variables changing through time, observed on an existing system that we want to study or improve. This trace is used to feed a determinist model of the system, whose parameters can be modified to evaluate their influence on system performance. Such models are applied first and foremost to the management of memory hierarchies (paging memories, caches; see section 9.7). The traces used are then reference chains (see section 9.2), i.e. sequences of memory addresses generated by the execution of a process.

2. Statistical simulation based on discrete events. This method uses models based on queueing networks, to which we apply discrete simulation methods used by specialized languages such as Simula. Simulated time advances through discrete values between significant instants, i.e. corresponding to a change of state in the system. A sequencing set (see section 4.4.5), modified dynamically during program execution, allows these instants to be ordered; to each of them is associated the sequence of actions to execute if the system is to move on to the next stage. There are integrated software packages specially adapted to handling models of computer system (see the references in section 8.6).

Input parameters for simulation are sequences of values derived from a random number generator whose distribution must be specified. We can also combine this method with the one above, feeding the system with traces.

The most difficult stage in the use of a simulation model is the interpretation of results. These can only be significant if their accuracy can be determined; statistical methods have been developed to make this possible (see the references in section 8.6).

8.5 Handling deadlocks

8.5.1 Presentation of the problem

An example of a deadlock has already been met in section 4.6.2.4: when two critical sections, corresponding to the use of two different resources, are nested in a different order for each process, there is a risk of indefinite blocking of each process, as each is occupying one resource while waiting for that allocated to the other.

Such a situation can be generalized to any number of processes and resources, if the following conditions are met:

1. The resources are used under mutual exclusion.

2. Each process must use several resources simultaneously, and acquires each resource as it needs them, without freeing those that it already posesses.

3. Requests for resources are blocking, and resoures cannot be preempted.

4. There is a set of processes $(p_0,...p_n)$ such that p_0 is waiting for a resource occupied by p_1, p_1 is waitng for a resource occupied by $p_2,...p_n$ is waiting for a resource occupied by p_0.

Example: Two process p_1 and p_2 are using two types of resources, r_1 and r_2. The system contains seven units of r_1 and six units of r_2. The respective quantities of r_1

and r_2 necessary for the execution of the processes are 6 and 3 for p_1, 4 and 5 for p_2. Consider the system in the following state:

	r_1	r_2
allocated to p_1	4	2
allocated to p_2	2	3
available	1	1

Whatever the order of execution of the processes, neither will be able to obtain all the resources necessary, if no resource is freed or preempted. Starting from this state of the system, deadlock is inevitable.

The problem of deadlock can be dealt with in two ways:

- By **prevention** (section 8.5.2):the resource allocation algorithm guarantees that deadlock cannot occur
- By **detection** and **cure** (section 8.5.3): no preventive measure is taken; deadlock is detected if it occurs, and the cure is to take the system to a state where processes are unblocked, generally at the price of losing some information

8.5.2 Prevention algorithms

8.5.2.1 A priori prevention algorithms

If nothing is known in advance concerning the requests processes will submit, prevention methods involve eliminating one of conditions 1 to 4 above.

The **global allocation** method is intended to eliminate condition 2: each process demands all the resource it needs as a block; it releases a resource as soon as it no longer needs it. This method means blocking resources in a non-productive way, and often means eliminating any real parallelism in execution; it should not, however, be rejected out of hand.

The **ordered classes** method is intended to eliminate the circular waiting situation (condition 4). Resources are divided into classes $C_1, C_2, \ldots C_m$. A process can only acquire a resource in class C_i if it has already acquired all the resources necessary in classes C_j, $j<i$. All processes therefore request their resources in the same order, that of the classes.

Assume that circular waiting takes place, i.e. that there are processes $p_0, p_1, \ldots p_{n-1}$ such that p_i is waiting for a resource r_i allocated to $p_{i \oplus 1}$ (the symbol $\oplus$ is used for addition modulo n). Let $c(r_i)$ be the number of the resource class of r_i. Since $p_{i \oplus 1}$ is waiting for $r_{i \oplus 1}$ and owns r_i we have $c(r_i) < c(r_{i \oplus 1})$ and consequently by transitivity $c(r_0) < c(r_0)$. Circular waiting is therefore impossible and deadlock is avoided.

8.5.2.2 Banker's algorithm

The prevention algorithm can be improved if we have information on the requests to be made on resources. If each process submits a **claim** in advance, i.e. an upper limit to its requests for each resource, the **banker's** algorithm makes it possible to avoid deadlock by reevaluating the risk at each allocation. This algorithm is based on the concept of a **safe state**: an allocation state is safe if, starting from that state, it is possible to have the system execute without deadlock under the most pessimistic assumption, that in which each process actually requests the maximum quantity of each resource provided. The banker's algorithm only allocates a resource if this allocation maintains the system in a safe state.

Let us consider a system including *n* processes and *m* classes of resources. Its state is represented by the following data structures:

```
Resource,Available  :array [0..m-1]of integer
Claim,Alloc         :array [0..n-1,0..m-1] of integer
```

where

Resource[j]:total number of resources in class *j*
Claim[i,j] :maximum number of resources of class *j* necessary to process *i*
Alloc[i,j] :number of resources in class *j* allocated to process *i* at any particular instant
Available[j]:number of resources available from class *j* at any given instant

By definition, at any given instant:

$$Available[j]=Resource[j]-\sum_{i=0}^{n-1} Alloc[i,j] \text{ for } j=0,\ldots m-1$$

The notation *A[i,*]* is used for the row vector *i* in matrix *A*. If *U* and *V* are two vectors with the same dimension *k*, we write, by convention:

$U \leqslant V$ **iff** $U[i] \leqslant V[i]$ for $i=0,\ldots k-1$
$U < V$ **iff**$U \leqslant V$ and $U <> 7V$

The system specifications require that:

$0 \leqslant Alloc[i,*] \leqslant Claim[i,*] \leqslant Resource$, for $i=0,\ldots n-1$
$Alloc[i,*] \leqslant Resource$
$Available \geqslant 0$ (the null vector)

These relations stipulate, for each class of resource, that a claim may not exceed the number of resources available, that the number of resources allocated to a process cannot exceed its claim, and finally that the system may not allocate more resources than it has in total. A system state is said to be **achievable** if it conforms to these specifications; we shall only consider achievable states.

Let A_0 be a state achievable by the system. Let us attempt to find a process p_i such that, if it were executed alone starting from state A_0, using all the resources specified by its claim, it could complete its execution. Such a process p_i must satisfy the following condition in state E_0:

$$Claim[i,*] - Alloc[i,*] \leqslant Available$$

Assuming that we find such a process, say p_{i0}, and that the we execute it until it terminates. It then frees all its resources, and the system moves into an achievable state E_1 defined by

$$Available_{E1} = Available_{E0} + Alloc[i_0,*]$$

The operation can then be repeated, looking for a new process p_{i1}, and so on for as long as possible. The sequence of processes obtained in this way is said to be safe. A system state is said to be **safe** if, starting from that state, it is possible to construct a complete safe sequence, i.e. one that includes all processes in the system.

From this definition, a system in a safe state cannot be deadlocked, since we can define an order of processes allowing them all to be executed. The converse can also be shown (see exercise), i.e. if a system is not deadlocked, it is in a safe state. The banker's algorithm is based on this property; it is executed each time a resource is requested by a process. Let *Request[i,j]* be the number of resources in class j requested, in the current state of the system, by process i.

```
if Alloc[i,j]+Request[i,j]>Claim[i,j] then
  <error>             -- total request>claim
else
  if Request[i,j]>Available[j] then
    <suspend p>
  else                -- simulate allocation
    <define new state by:
    Alloc[i,j]:=Alloc[i,j]+Request[i,j]
    Available[j]:=Available[j]-Request[i,j]>

  endif;
  if the new state is safe then
    <carry out allocation>
  else
    <restore original state>
    <suspend p >
  endif
endif
```

The core of this algorithm is the test for the safety of a state, which means attempting to construct a safe sequence. This is a combinatorial algorithm which *a priori* requires *n!* trials; but this number can be reduced to n^2 thanks to the following property (see exercise) which eliminates the need for backtracking after failure:

In a safe state, any safe sequence can be extended to become a complete safe sequence.

In other words, if an attempt to extend a partial safe sequence fails, the system state is not safe and there is no point in attempting to build another sequence.

Given this property, the safety test can be carried out by the following algorithm:

```
Currentavail:array[0..m−1]of integer;
Rest:           set of process;

Currentavail:=Available;
Rest:={all processes};
possible:=true;
while possible do
  find a p in Rest such that
    Claim[i,*]−Alloc[i,*]<Currentavail;
  if found then      --simulate execution of p
    Currentavail:=Currentavail+Alloc[i,*];
    Rest:=Rest−{p}
  else
    possible:=false
  endif
endwhile;
safe state:=(Rest=<empty>)
```

This algorithm can be simplified if there is only one class of resources (see exercise).

8.5.3 Detection and cure algorithms

The state reliability algorithm can be used to detect deadlocks, if the maximum demand *Claim[i,*]−Alloc[i,*]* for each process is replaced by the actual demand at any given time. If, under these conditions, it is impossible to find a complete safe sequence, the system is deadlocked. More precisely, the deadlocked processes are those which form the set *Rest*, at the end of the algorithm.

To resolve a deadlock, execution of the system has to be restarted; this can only take place by recovering resources already allocated. A simple-minded method is to destroy all deadlocked processes, starting with those whose cost of deletion is the lowest (according to a criterion which has to be defined), until execution can restart. This method is not without risk, if the deleted processes have left data in an inconsistent state. It is therefore preferable to save the state of processes periodically, defining **checkpoints** corresponding to states that are regarded as significant. In cases of forced withdrawal of resources from a process, it can be returned to the state corresponding to its last checkpoint.

The curing of deadlock by process deletion and return to an earlier state runs the risk of starvation, if the cost criterion selected always leads to the same process being chosen. Various methods have been proposed to solve this problem: a 'privilege' protecting its holder against forced deletion and which moves from process to process, or a cost factor that grows with the number of preemptions.

If preemption has been allowed, and it is possible without loss of information, a particular form of detection-cure can be used, continuous avoidance. This method is used in particular for distributed systems (see [Cornafion 81]).

8.6 Bibliographic notes

General texts on queueing theory, oriented towards computer applications, are provided by [Allen 78] and [Kleinrock 76a]. Texts specifically concerned with the construction and use of computer system models include [Kleinrock 76b (which is particularly oriented towards networks), Sauer 81, Gelenbe 80 and 82, Lavenberg 83, Lazowska 84]. Aspects concerned with performance measurement are dealt with in [Ferrari 78]. [Allen 75] is an overview of the use of queueing models for the study of computer systems, with numeric applications. A survey of the main aspects of performance evaluation (measurement, models and simulation) appears in [Heidelberger 84], which also gives a detailed bibliography.

Processor allocation algorithms are studied in [Coffman 68a and 68b, Muntz 75]. The HRN algorithm was introduced in [Brinch Hansen 71]. The Jackson model for queueing networks was introduced in [Jackson 63], and its extension to a wider class of servers (the BCMP model) appeared in [Baskett 75]. The time-sharing system model (section 8.4.3) is dealt with in [Kleinrock 76b]. The decomposition methods for queueing networks are described in [Courtois 77]. Algorithms for handling numerical processing of network models are discussed in [Buzen 73, Boyse 75]; see also the books mentioned above, notably [Allen 78, Lavenberg 83]. An example of a tool for simulating computer systems represented by queueing networks (QNAP) is described in [Merle 78].

A complete bibliography on deadlock problems is given in [Newton 79], and a survey of the problem in [Coffman 71], as well as in general texts on operating sytems, notably [Shaw 74, Crocus 75, Habermann 76a, Peterson 83]. The ordered class algorithm is described in [Havender 68]. The banker's algorithm was introduced in [Dijkstra 65a] and generalized in [Habermann 69]. A model based on graphs is discussed in [Holt 72].

Exercises

Exercise 8.1

A computer system operates as shown below:

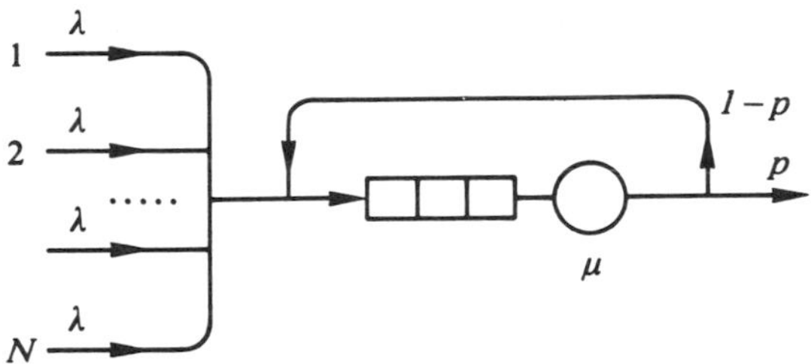

Each terminal behaves as though it were a source of requests obeying a Poisson distribution, whose service times are distributed exponentially. Calculate:

- The entry rate to the server
- The number of terminals which would saturate the system, for constant values of the other parameters

Exercise 8.2

A computer system operates as shown below:

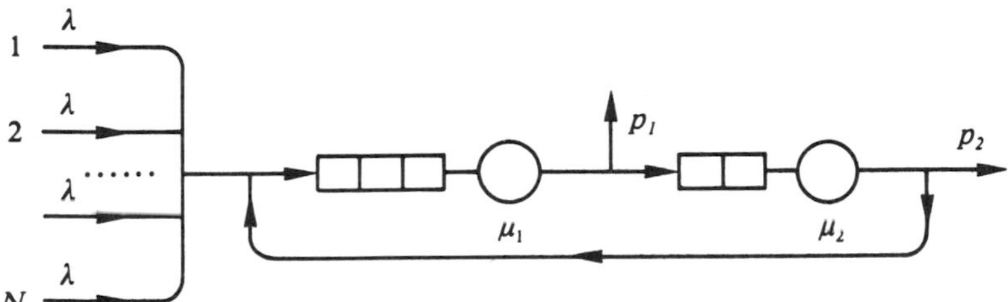

On the same assumptions as in the previous exercise, calculate:

- The rate of entry to the two servers
- The number of terminals which would saturate the system, for constant values of the other parameters
- The relation that must exist between system parameters for both servers to be equally loaded

Exercise 8.3

Show that the 'shortest job first' allocation policy minimizes the mean response time for a set of jobs. **Hint:** Consider the total execution time for a set of jobs under this policy, and then exchange the positions of two jobs.

Exercise 8.4

A file management system includes a primitive *extend(f,n)* which has the following effect: if there is enough space on the disk, extend the file by adding *n* pages to its end; otherwise suspend the calling process. The deletion of a file frees the pages it occupies. If several processes use this primitive, is there a risk of deadlock (given that the size of the disk is limited)? What solutions could be proposed to avoid it (modifying the primitives if necessary)?

Exercise 8.5

Jobs are executed in a multi-programming environment on a computer. Each job uses at most three magnetic tape units at a time; it requests them and frees them according to its requirements. A unit allocated to a job may not be preempted. The system has 10 tape units.

1. Show that there is a risk of deadlock if the tape units are allocated without restriction.

2. It is intended to avoid deadlock by reserving the three tape units beforehand, at the start of each job. How many jobs can execute simultaneously? Let T be the mean execution time of a job if it is alone; the cpu is active for only 20% of this time, and the rest of the time is used for input-output operations on tape. What is the mean throughput of jobs when the system is operating in its stationary mode, given that all tape units can operate in parallel?

3. It is observed that jobs use two tape units for most of the processing time, and that three units are needed for only about 5% of the time, towards the end of the job. Is a more efficient allocation policy than in 2) possible? Evaluate the gains obtained, in terms of mean throughput.

Exercise 8.6

Two cyclical processes p and q use two common resources A and B. Each process goes through a stage where it simultaneously requires both resources, which it requests one after the other as it needs them (as other processes may only need one of the resources), and which it frees entirely at the end of the stage. If the order in which resources are required is different for the two processes, can they be programmed in such a way as to avoid deadlock without preemption or global reservation?

Exercise 8.7

Consider a mono-programmed batch processing system with input-output buffers in memory, as outlined in exercise 4.13 (1). Memory zones acting as input and output buffers are allocated and freed dynamically, according to requirements, using a common zone of fixed size.

Identify the risk of deadlock and propose a policy avoiding it.

Exercise 8.8

Three processes share three unpooled resources, with exclusive access and without preemption. Using the procedures *allocate(resource)* and *free(resource)*, write program outlines for these processes:

- With a risk of overall deadlock for the three processes
- With a risk of starvation for only one of the processes, without deadlock

No process can use more than two resources.

Exercise 8.9

Show that, if a system is not deadlocked, a complete safe sequence of processes can be constructed.

Exercise 8.10

Show that, if a system is in a safe state, it is possible to extend any safe sequence of processes to make it a complete safe sequence.

Exercise 8.11

1. Show that, in a system with a single class of resources, a safe state is characterized by the following property: there is at least one process which can execute up to termination, satisfying all its requirements using the current set of free resources alone.
2. Deduce a safe allocation algorithm for a single class of resources.
3. Consider a system with several classes of resources. Show by means of an example that an unsafe state of the system can be regarded as safe for each class of resources considered in isolation from the others.

Exercise 8.12 [R.C. Holt]

Consider a system with a single class of resources, where units are allocated and freed one by one. Let n be the number of processes, m the number of units. The claim made by each process is less than or equal to m and the sum of all claims is less than $m + n$. Show that deadlock is impossible. **Hint:** Consider a state where all resources are allocated and show that it is safe (criterion from exercise 8.11).

Exercise 8.13

Write a detailed program for the allocation of resources using the banker's algorithm, introducing the necessary data structures.

Exercise 8.14

Show that, in the general case, the complexity of the banker's algorithm is of the order of $n^2.m$ where n is the total number of processes, and m is the total number of classes of resources.

Exercise 8.15

Complete the banker's algorithm on the assumption that processes may be created and deleted dynamically, and that a process can modify its claim. Identify the operations which will require special authorization from the resource allocation system.

Chapter 9
Memory management

This chapter is devoted to a study of the memory management function in an operating system. The concept of virtual memory stands at the heart of our discussion: it is the interface for the memory resource presented to users by the system. We shall examine the various basic techniques for the implementation of virtual memory using physical storage devices forming the installation's memory hierarchy. The applications of these techniques to the implementation of multiprogramming systems will be discussed in chapter 10.

9.1 Basic concepts of memory allocation

9.1.1 Virtual memory

9.1.1.1 Introduction and review

The concept of a virtual resource was introduced in chapter 4 to separate the problems of the use made of a particular resource from the problems of allocating that resource. For a virtual processor (or for a process, which comes down to the same thing) virtual memory is the medium used for all information that is potentially accessible. It is therefore, more precisely, the set of all locations whose addresses may be generated by the processor.

The allocation of memory involves implementing this virtual memory using physical storage devices such as main memory, disks, etc. In the final analysis, access by a process to information is concretely expressed in an access operation by a physical processor to a location in main memory addressable by that processor.

Memory allocation therefore involves the representation in memory of information manipulated by processes. The problem has already been considered in chapter 6, whose main results we shall review here, to set them clearly in the context of the present study.

The information accessible to a process is defined by:

- All the information it can name in its program, a set of **objects**
- All naming information, or **names**
- A mapping between names and objects

For a user writing a program in a high-level language, names and objects are defined by that language. These names and objects differ from those handled by the physical processor. The program must therefore undergo a series of transformations called **binding**. Binding involves a **translation** stage (mapping objects to memory locations and identifiers to the corresponding relative addresses), a **linkage editing** stage (linkage of programs that have been translated separately) and finally a **loading** stage (definitive establishment of addresses, so far defined to within one relocation operation).

In chapter 6, we considered a single user, and therefore left aside problems of competition for memory usage. It is to take that problem into account, and to separate it clearly from those associated with naming, that we shall define the concept of virtual memory. Memory, treated in chapter 6 as the end point of translation and linkage of programs, will therefore be regarded as virtual, and the aim of this chapter is to study how it can be concretely implemented in physical memory. We shall observe, furthermore, that the concept of virtual memory is useful even for a single user, who is freed by it from problems associated with the internal management of memory space (see the example in section 9.1.2).

The conceptual separation between naming and binding problems, on the one hand, and memory allocation problems on the other, is as shown below:

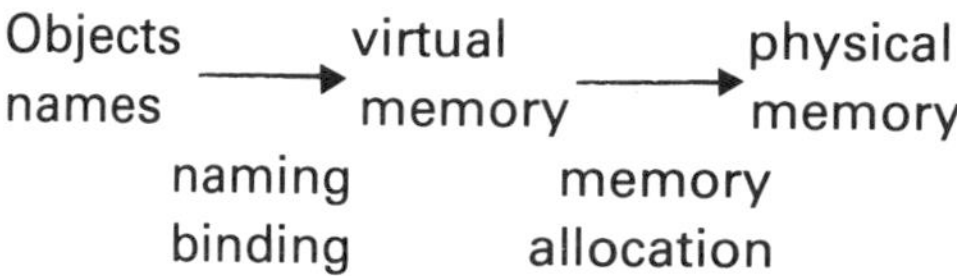

This distinction is not always easy to maintain. The concept of virtual memory is not simply a conceptual tool, but has been implemented on machines by physical address transformation devices, which respect the separation of functions more or less faithfully.

Note, finally, that the elementary concepts presented in chapter 6 (operation of a loader, etc.) remain valid in the case of a single program executed on a machine without an address transformation mechanism; virtual memory then becomes identical with physical memory.

9.1.1.2 Organization of virtual memory

The definition of virtual memory has to be made relative to a given machine architecture: it is the set of all locations named by addresses generated by a processor (here we are dealing with actual addresses, i.e. after indirection, indexation, etc.). Two forms of organization are commonly used:

1. *Linear virtual memory*. The virtual memory is a series of identical locations, organized sequentially and named by consecutive integers called virtual addresses. An object is represented in a location, or several consec-

utive locations; it is named by the virtual address of the first location. This organization is therefore identical to that of a physical memory.

2. *Segmented virtual memory*. The virtual memory is made up of a set of segments. A segment (see section 6.4.1) occupies a series of consecutive locations; its size may vary. A virtual address is therefore an ordered pair (segment number, displacement of the word within the segment), called a segmented address. An object, which may occupy all or part of a segment, is named by the segmented address of its first location.

Note: A linear virtual memory is a particular case of a segmented memory, using a single segment of fixed size.

Figure 9.1 illustrates these two forms of organization.

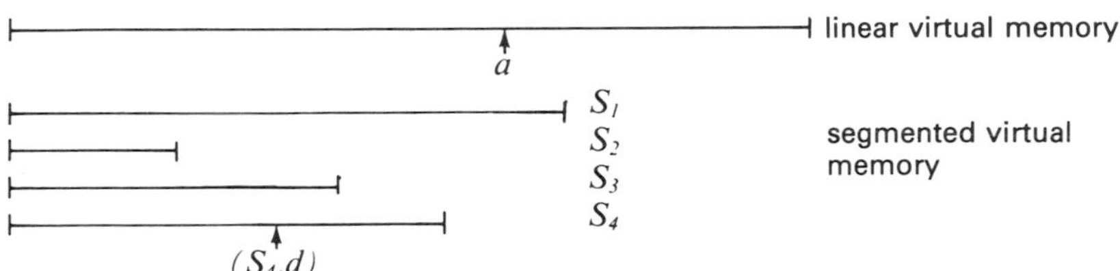

Fig. 9.1. Virtual memory organizations

In the rest of this chapter, we shall use the term segment more generally to indicate a contiguous zone in virtual memory, defined in logical terms, even if no segmented addressing mechanism is used.

9.1.2 Problems of memory allocation

The allocation of memory must allow a process to access an object defined in virtual memory, by loading that object within a reasonable time into main memory, which is the only type of memory which is directly addressable. A memory allocation policy must therefore provide a solution to the two following problems:

a. Establishing a *mapping between virtual addresses and physical addresses*

b. Implementing *physical memory management* (allocation of locations, information transfer)

If information is common to several users, two further constraints have to be introduced:

c. The need to *share* information between several users

d. Ensuring mutual *protection* of information belonging to different users

An example will help us illustrate aspects a and b, for the case of a single user.

Example: Overlay. A common method for executing a program whose size is greater than that of physical memory, is to break it down into sections, and to define configurations, or collections of sections, which can be held together in memory. Each section is permanently held in secondary memory and loaded into principal memory according to the configuration to be executed. A tree structure (fig. 9.2)

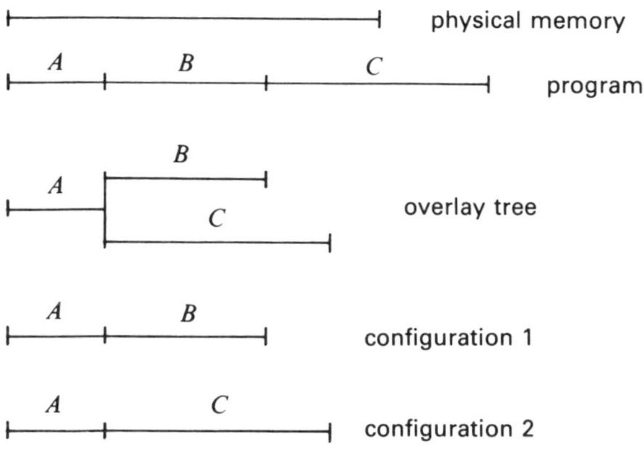

Fig. 9.2. Execution with overlay

makes it possible to reduce the number of transfers and to hold common information which is always present. This breakdown in effect carries out segmentation of the program, even if segmented addressing as such is not used.

In this example:

- The breakdown into segments is explicitly defined by the programmer who specifies the overlay tree.
- The correspondence between virtual and physical addresses is established once and for all by the loader, which produces absolute object segments, containing physical addresses.
- The memory zones assigned to segments are also allocated during loading.
- The transfer of segments between main memory and secondary memory is carried out, during execution of the program, by special instructions inserted into the program during loading.

In what follows, we shall distinguish between various ways of allocating memory.

1. **Static placement** — virtual-physical mapping established once and for all
   a. One program in memory at a time
   b. Sharing of memory between several programs
2. **Dynamic relocation** — virtual-physical mapping can vary through time

   Allocation of physical memory
   a. By **zones** (of variable size)
   b. By **pages** (of fixed size)

This classification defines the structure of this chapter. For each of these modes of allocation, we shall present the mechanisms necessary and the allocation policies used.

Allocation with dynamic relocation of programs (or dynamic allocation) is discussed in section 9.1.3. It will make it necessary to find out the behavior characteristics of programs, which are discussed in section 9.2. The underlying principles of static systems for program placement are described in section 9.3. Dynamic allocation will be discussed in the three following sections: 9.4 for allocation by zones of varying size, 9.5 and 9.6 for allocation by pages of fixed size. The hierarchical organization of memory and the management of information transfers between levels in this hierarchy will be discussed in section 9.7.

9.1.3 Dynamic allocation of memory

Two types of method are used, depending on whether the allocation unit is defined by logical divisions (contiguous memory zones, or segments) or by physical divisions (blocks of fixed size, or pages). In either case, a relocation mechanism must be available to allow a program, or part of a program, to be loaded into any zone or page.

The aim of a dynamic memory allocation policy is to ensure that at any moment the information necessary for the execution of the current instruction is immediately accessible to the processor, and is therefore in main memory. This goal cannot generally be permanently achieved: we usually try to reduce the probability that information is missing from memory when it is necessary (this event is called a segment or page **fault**). An allocation policy must specify the following (the term 'object' is used here for the chosen allocation unit, whether it is a segment or a page):

a. **When** should an object be loaded into main memory?
- When necessary (loading **on demand**)
- Before it is necessary (**pre-loading**)

b. **Where** should an object be loaded?
- If there is enough free space, into which locations should it be loaded (problem of **placement**)
- Otherwise, which object or objects should be sent back to secondary memory to make room in main memory (problem of **replacement**)

We shall use several criteria to evaluate and compare memory allocation algorithms.
- Criteria associated with usage of the memory resource, measured, for example, by the degree of wasted (or unusable) space
- Criteria associated with access to information, such as mean access time, or the rate of page faults
- More global criteria, characterizing the performance levels induced by memory allocation: the rate of use of the cpu, or the response time in an interactive system

9.2 Program behavior

The behavior of a program in its virtual space determines its requirements for physical memory. It is therefore worth getting to know the characteristics of that behavior, to improve the efficiency of dynamic memory management algorithms.

9.2.1 Behavior of programs in a linear virtual memory

Consider a program executing in a linear virtual memory containing all its instructions and data. Let us start with a few definitions:

1. The passage of time is measured by the execution of successive instructions: execution of an instruction defines a unit of time. This time is called virtual, as it applies to the fictional execution of the program on the assumption that it had all necessary resources available to it (memory and processor). In cases of shared resources, we could, for instance, reason in terms of a given program independently of the other programs.

2. The demand for memory is evaluated by dividing virtual memory into contiguous blocks of fixed size, made up of an integer number *np* of locations. Access to a location in a block is called **reference** to that block. Blocks are numbered using consecutive integers, making it possible to label references. Changing the value of *np* allows us to examine the behavior of a program at a more or less detailed level. At the most detailed level ($np=1$) we can monitor references instruction by instruction. The choice of the size

of block, for a given application, is dictated by the allocation unit for physical memory. In what follows, and unless we state otherwise, we shall use the term 'page' instead of 'block', as the results obtained from this kind of analysis apply above all to the management of paging memories (see section 9.6).

3. The behavior of the program, at the level of detail chosen, is defined by the sequence of page numbers that have been the subject of successive references during execution. This sequence is called the **reference string** for the program considered and the size of page selected.

Note: The execution of a single instruction can give rise to several distinct references: pages concerning the instruction itself, pages containing the operand or operands.

We shall examine two aspects of program behavior: the properties of reference strings behavior in restricted memory.

9.2.1.1 Properties of reference strings

Experience shows that reference strings in programs have common characteristics, which we shall describe first in qualitative terms.

1. *Non-uniformity*. Let n_i be the total number of references to page p_i. The distribution of the numbers n_i will not be uniform: a small fraction of pages will generally account for a large proportion of the total number of references. To give an idea of the order of magnitude, it is common to find that more than 75% of references concern less than 20% of pages.

2. *Locality*. Over a fairly short observation period, the distribution of references shows a certain stability: at a given instant, references observed in the recent past are generally a good approximation to references in the immediate future.

This locality property can be expressed more precisely using a program behavior model. In this model, which is merely a simplified representation of reality, the execution of a program is defined as a succession of 'phases' separated by 'transitions'. A phase i is characterized by a set of pages S_i and an interval of (virtual) time T_i. When the program enters phase i, it remains in it for a time T_i and its references will be mainly concentrated on pages belonging to S_i. It then undergoes a transition, during which references to pages are more broadly scattered, before it enters phase $i+1$. Phases are therefore period of stable and relatively predictable behavior, while transitions represent more erratic behavior.

Figure 9.3, drawn from [Hatfield 72], which represents the references observed during the execution of a program, gives an idea of the behavior of a real program.

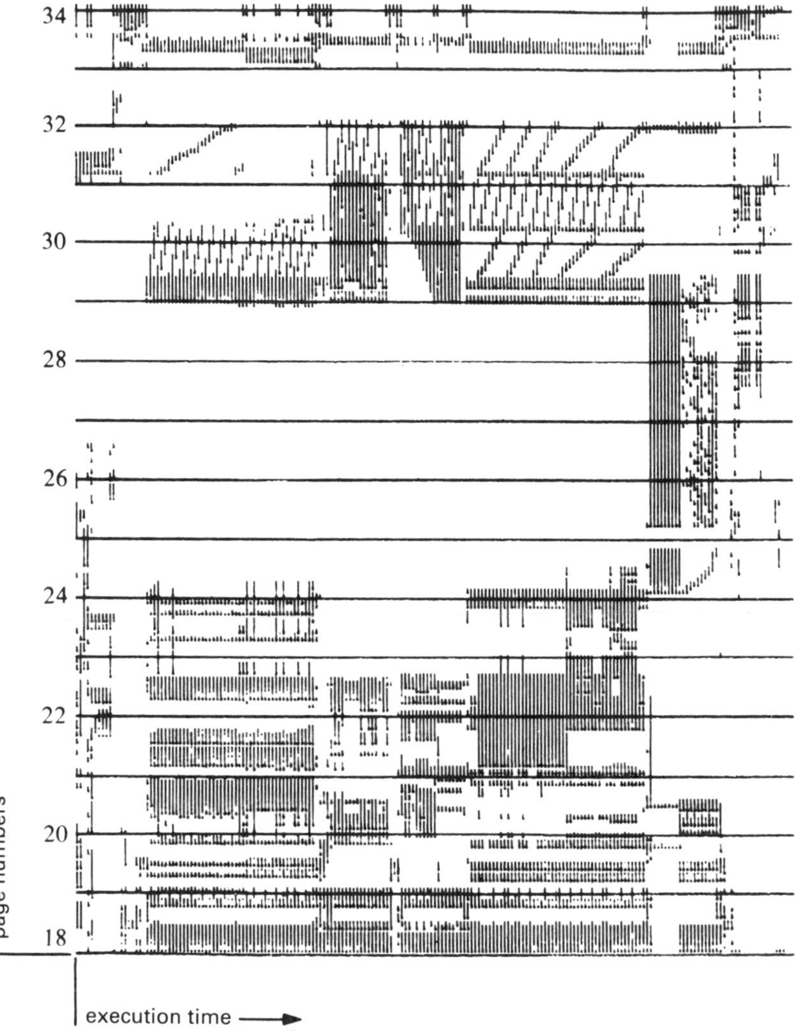

Fig. 9.3. References in a virtual memory program

Experience shows that transition periods represent only a small fraction of the total virtual time in the execution of a program (a few percent). They are nontheless important because of the scatter of memory requests to which they lead. Most virtual time is spent in phases of long duration (some tens or hundreds of thousands of instructions).

This type of behavior can be explained qualitatively by taking into consideration the fact that programs are often organized into procedures, each of which has a specific context, that data access operations are often concentrated (table scanning), and that programs include loops whose execution will also concentrate references.

The concept of a **working set** is also used to characterize the behavior programs and to attempt to predict it from observation. At any time t, the working set with window T, written $W(t, T)$, is the set of pages to which at least one reference has been made between instants $t-T$ and t (it should be remembered that we are dealing with virtual time). The locality property can be expressed by the fact that pages belonging to $W(t, T)$ have a higher probability than the others of being the subject of the next reference, at instant t, on condition that a suitable choice of the size T of the window is made. Assuming behavior on the phase and transition model, the size T must be selected to be less than T_i if the program is in phase i; during transition periods, the working set is renewed and cannot therefore be used as a basis for estimation. We shall return, in section 9.6.3, to the use of the concept of the working set.

9.2.1.2 Behavior in restricted memory

Another way of characterizing the behavior of a program is to study its performance as a function of the memory space allocated to it. A program is initially stored in secondary memory; at a given instant, only a subset of its pages is present in main memory. If the next reference is to a page missing from main memory, a **page fault** occurs, and the missing page is loaded into main memory (we say that pages are loaded **on demand**). If there is no space available, the page loaded must take the place of a page that is already present; the page to replace is determined by a **replacement algorithm**.

The behavior of a program in restricted memory, for a given replacement algorithm, is characterized by the sequence of its page faults if the program is being executed under the conditions described above. Experience shows that there are properties common to most programs and which are relatively independent of the replacement algorithm used: these properties therefore intrinsically characterize the behavior of programs. The influence of the replacement algorithm is examined in section 9.6.2.

The properties observed can be illustrated by two curves, showing program behavior for different sizes of main memory. The shape of these curves is representative of a type of behavior that is frequently met.

Figure 9.4 shows the mean interval between two successive page faults, an interval called the **lifetime**. This curve is S-shaped, with the section nearest to the approximating ax^k, with $1.5<k<2.5$, depending on the program. The point of contact with the tangent of highest gradient from the origin is often called the **knee**.

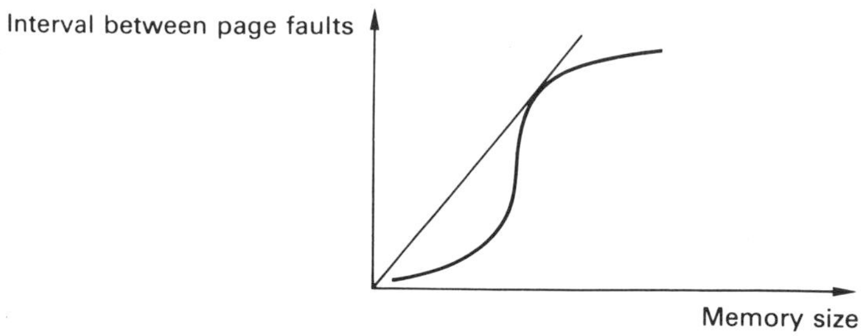

Fig. 9.4. Mean time between page faults in limited memory

Figure 9.5 represents the total number of page faults observed during the execution of a program. If the size of memory is reduced, we observe that the number grows slowly at first; below a certain size, growth becomes explosive.

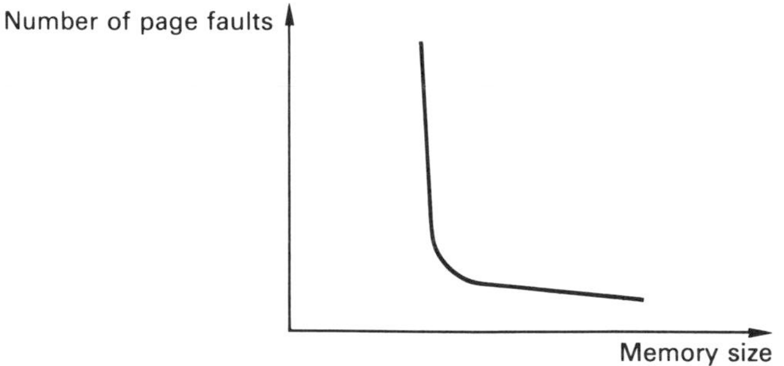

Fig. 9.5. Total number of page faults in limited memory

Note that figures 9.4 and 9.5 represent the same phenomenon from two points of view: below a certain memory size, the rapid growth of the number of page faults corresponds to the rapid fall in the mean interval between page faults.

9.2.2 Behavior of segmented programs

Let us now consider a program which is executed in a segmented virtual space. The concept of a reference string, introduced for a linear virtual space, can be transposed to segmented space, replacing references to pages by references to segments. In this way, we can study the distribution of references to different segments, as well as performances in limited memory with a 'segment on demand' policy. The concept of a working set can also be transposed (it becomes the set of segments to which reference has been most recently made), and again the locality property also applies for segment references.

An important characteristic to determine in a segmented memory system is the distribution of segment sizes. The division of programs and data into segments is in principle associated with a logical division. The measurements available, on the size of segments in segmented systems, or on the size of logical units (files) in non-segmented systems, suggest that the following two trends apply:

- The distribution of sizes can be approximately represented by a sum of exponentials (hyper-exponential distribution).
- Many segments are very small in size (typically the median size is of the order of a few tens of words).

By way of indication, figure 9.6, drawn from [Satyanarayanan 81], shows

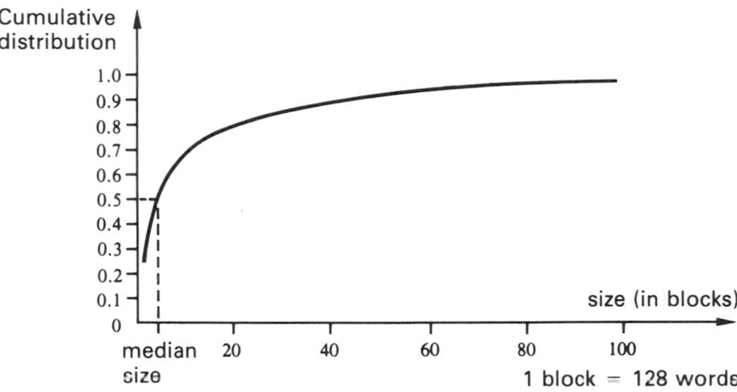

Fig. 9.6. Distribuion of the size of files in a system

the distribution of file sizes in a time-sharing system. This system does not use a segmented memory; however, files correspond to logical entities, like segments, and the distribution of their sizes gives an indication of the distribution of segment sizes.

9.3 Sharing of memory without relocation

9.3.1 Simple swapping

In the **swapping** method, a fixed memory zone is reserved for user programs (generally, this is the zone immediately following that occupied by the operating system). Programs are held on disk in absolute form (loading is carried out for each program as though it were the only one in the free zone). The whole program must be loaded into main memory, before execution. The allocation of the processor to programs therefore determines transfers.

In cases of processor preemption, the program under way has to be saved to disk before its successor is loaded.

Note: This mode of allocation can be compared to that used for overlays, where the operating system plays the role of the root of the overlay tree. Moreover, if a program is larger than the free zone, an overlay scheme can be used within that zone.

This pattern has the advantage of simplicity. Its main disadvantage is that it leaves the processor idle while transfers are taking place. It is therefore used on small installations if response time constraints are compatible with the duration and frequency of transfers. It is also the usual mode of operation for personal computers.

Local improvements make it possible to reduce the volume of information transferred and therefore the loss in time on the processor:

- When a program is saved to disk, only the parts modified are stored (in practice, this means the data zone).
- The 'onion skin' algorithm makes it possible to avoid transfers when a program is 'overlayed' by a smaller program: to restore the bigger program, only the part that has been overlayed needs to be reloaded.

Nevertheless, these improvements can only lead to small gains. It is more interesting to allow a program to execute while another is being transferred. This means simultaneously holding several programs in memory, either in part or in their entirety. This type of sharing is called **multiprogramming**. Multiprogramming without dynamic relocation is made possible by memory **partition**.

9.3.2 Memory partition

9.3.2.1 Fixed partition

In a fixed partition system, memory is statically shared between a fixed number of zones. The sizes and limits of these zones are defined during system start-up.

A fixed assignment to a zone is made for each program, which we assume to be contained within a single segment. Programs are held on disk in absolute form, and the addresses in each program are the physical addresses corresponding to its location in the zone assigned to it.

While a program is being transferred to or from its zone, another program may be executed in another zone; we obviously need an autonomous input-output processor (a channel or a DMA). Figure 9.7 shows the location of programs and an activity time trace for a fixed partition system.

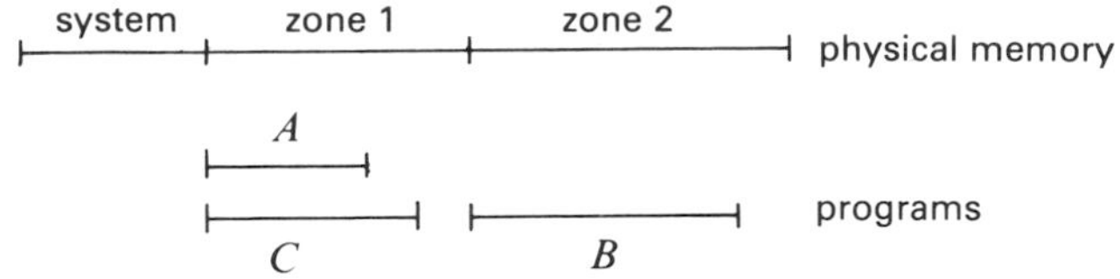

1) **Memory allocation**

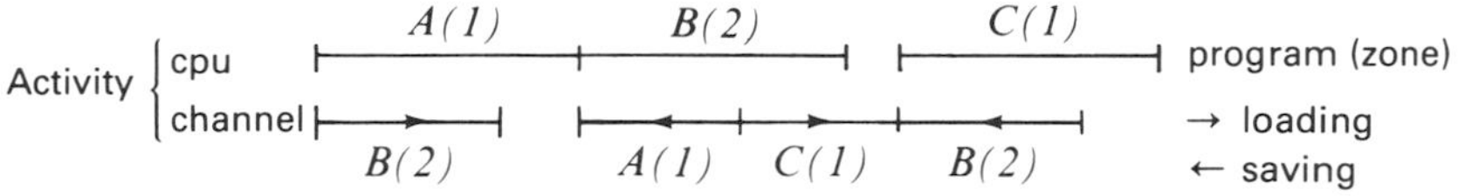

2) **Activity time graph**

Fig. 9.7. Fixed partition system

In practice, the activity pattern may be more complex, as each program may itself execute input-output. While this is happening, the processor will again be assigned to another program.

Fixed partition systems are commonly used on small or medium-sized installations where a very small number of interactive processes, or applications of the 'process control' type are running at the same time as background work. It makes it possible to define, during system start-up, zone sizes suitable to the different classes of programs. The response time for interactive jobs is limited by the ratio of execution time to transfer time, which itself depends on the extent of the zone multiplexing. This way of sharing memory is not particularly suitable to the execution of programs of very variable size.

The implementation of a fixed partition system is studied in section 10.1.

9.3.2.2 Variable partition

In a variable partition system, the division into zones is not determined once and for all, but is redefined at the end of execution of each program. The space freed at that time is shared among other programs. In consequence, the loading of a program (determination of addresses) can only take place at the last moment, when space is assigned to it. A program, once it has been loaded into memory, stays there until its execution is completed: there is therefore no dynamic relocation. Multiprogramming makes it possible to keep the cpu active during program loading, or during the input-output operations carried out by a program. This form of operation is suitable for batch processing of jobs, on a machine which has no dynamic relocation mechanism.

9.4 Dynamic allocation of memory by zones

9.4.1 Dynamic relocation mechanisms

The dynamic allocation of memory by zones of any size requires the use of a mechanism for the dynamic relocation of these zones. In chapter 6, we described two such mechanisms, whose underlying principles we shall examine here.

1. *Base registers* (see section 6.3.3.2). The location in physical memory of a single segment is defined by a pair of registers, called the base and limit registers. The base register *BR* contains the physical address of the origin of the segment; the limit register *LR* acts as a protection mechanism to prevent accidental access to locations outside the segment. For a virtual address *(BR, LR, d)* the following address computation is carried out for each access operation:

```
a:=BR+d;
if a≤LR then
  phys.addr:=a
else
  <error>      -- trap handled by the system
endif
```

2. *Segmentation* (see section 6.4.1). Segmentation may be regarded as an extension of addressing by base registers, which avoids the problems of reallocating these registers during changes of segments. Each segment is associated with a descriptor which contains, in particular, its origin address and its size; descriptors are held together in a table which is itself named by a special register. Calculation of the physical address corresponding to the segmented address *(s, d)* is as follows:

```
desc:=desctab[s];
if d<desc.size then
  phys.addr:=desc.orig+d
else
  <error>        -- trap handled by the system
endif
```

Any memory access operation requires another access operation, to read the descriptor. To improve access efficiency, one can use an accelerator device made up of an associative memory of small size (typically 8 or 16 entries), which holds the descriptors of segments which have been referred to most recently; the numbers of these segments are used as access keys. When access is made to memory, it is the associative memory that is searched first for the segment descriptor. It is only if that search fails that the segment table is consulted. The associative memory therefore acts as a cache (see section 9.7.1) for descriptors. The locality property ensures that there is a high level of success.

The dynamic relocation mechanisms we have been describing make it possible to locate a segment in any zone of main memory and to move it at minimal cost in terms of management (updating of the descriptor or of the base-limit registers). Segments can therefore be used as a main memory allocation unit, and consequently zones of variable size can be managed. We shall now describe the main allocation methods and their implementation in an operating system.

9.4.2 Allocation policies

The specification of a dynamic segment allocation policy must be able to answer the questions raised in section 9.1.3. Loading generally takes place on demand, because of the high cost in space and execution time associated with incorrect pre-loading. We still have to resolve the problem of placement (choice of a free zone) and that of replacement (choice of zones to free if no free zone is available).

9.4.2.1 Placement and replacement

Algorithms are defined by the way they represent free zones. Three methods are commonly used:

- Chaining of free zones in a list
- Subdivision of blocks ('buddy systems')
- Zones of predefined size

1. Chained free zones

The most common algorithms use chaining. Each free zone is associated with a descriptor which contains the address of its origin, its size and its chaining links. This descriptor is itself held in the zone (fig. 9.8). Assume we have to find a zone of size t. We explore the list of free zones; if the current zone is z, the possible criteria of choice are:

- *First free zone* ('first fit'). The first zone z such that $size(z) \geq t$ is selected. This choice is intended to speed up searching. The list is circular and searching starts from the latest zone allocated, to avoid a concentration of very small zones at the beginning of the list.
- *'Best fit'*. Zone z giving the lowest residue (zone remaining after alloca-

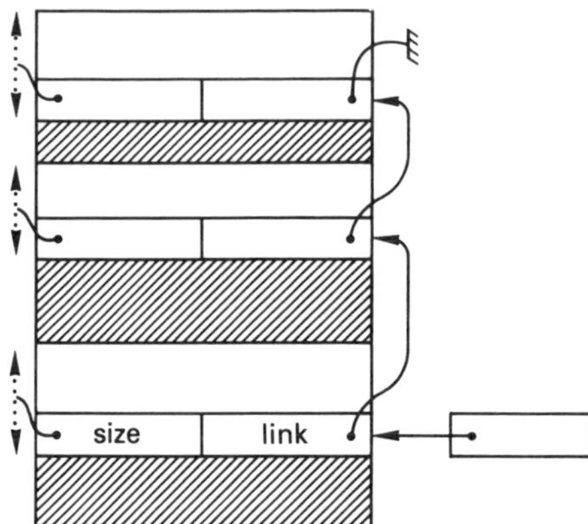

Fig. 9.8. Linked representation of free zones

tion) is selected; in other words, we choose z such that $size(z)-t$ is a minimum, which means scanning the whole of the list or holding it sorted by size. The aim is to make better overall use of memory; but there is a tendency towards fragmentation, i.e. to the proliferation of small zones which are hard to use.

- *'Worst fit'*. A zone z is chosen such that $size(z)-t$ is a maximum. The aim here is to avoid fragmentation.

In all three cases, a block of size t in zone z is allocated; the residue, if there is any, replaces the initial zone and descriptors are updated. A lower limit to the size of the residue is sometimes set, to reduce the total number of zones.

When a zone is freed, it is reinserted into the list and merged, it appropriate, with any neighbouring free zones. This merging is made easier if zones are doubly chained and stored in increasing address order.

The many studies on these algorithms (see the bibliography) show a choice between *first fit* and *best fit* must depend on the characteristics of the demand, *first fit* being more rapid if there is a wide spread of sizes required. The rate of use of memory is generally similar for the two algorithms. *Worst fit* is generally less advantageous than the other two algorithms.

Measurements on time-sharing systems have shown that most requests, in these systems, usually concentrate on a small number of generally low sizes. This observation explains why there has been interest in the two classes of algorithms described below:

2. *Allocation by subdivision ('buddy systems')*

In the buddy system method, the sizes of zones are quantified: they are expressed as multiples of a certain allocation unit and permited sizes are defined by a recurrence relation. Two common systems are:

- The binary system (1,2,4,8,...), $S_{i+1}=2S_i$
- The Fibonacci system (1,2,3,5,8,13,...), $S_{i+1}=S_i+S_{i-1}$

If there are not enough blocks of a given size S_i, a block of size S_{i+1} is subdivided, using the recurrence relation. For example, in the binary system, the subdivision of a block of size 8 creates two blocks of size 4; more generally, the subdivision of a block of size S_{i-1} creates two blocks of size S_i. In the Fibonacci system the subdivision of a block of size S_{i+1} *creates two blocks of size* S_i and S_{i-1}. The algorithm is applied recursively if there is no free block of size S_{i+1}.

We can regard any block of size $s>1$ as the concatenation of two blocks into which it can be divided; these blocks are called 'buddies'. The addresses of the origins of these blocks are defined as soon as we know how the free zone is initially located (fig. 9.9).

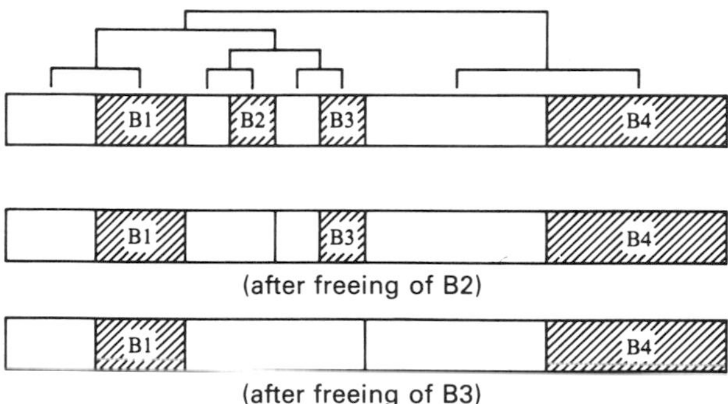

Fig. 9.9. Allocation of memory by binary buddy system

This mode of allocation has two advantages, if the distribution of the blocks S_i reflects that of demand:

- Searching for a free block of given size is fast.
- When a block is restored, it is easy to determine whether its buddy is free, as its address is known; if it is, the blocks are recombined (and the process iterates).

3. Pools of blocks of predefined size

If the characteristics of the demand for memory space are well known, and if most requests concern one of a series of well defined sizes, it is worthwhile using an *ad hoc* algorithm (unusual demands being handled by one of the preceding methods). For example, measurements on IBM VM/370 systems have shown that around 95% of requests were associated with ten particular sizes. The allocator uses ten stacks each of which contains blocks of one of these sizes; this avoids the need to scan chains in most cases. A 'first fit' algorithm handles cases of requests for sizes other than the ten standard sizes. Memory is periodically reorganized to resupply the stacks.

Whatever the algorithm used, the free space may become insufficient. Several remedies can then be considered:

- Freeing a zone by, if necessary, sending the information it contains back to secondary memory. In this case, a replacement criterion has to be defined. Replacement criteria for allocation by zones are the same as those used for allocation by pages, discussed in sections 9.6.2. and 9.6.3.
- Reorganize memory entirely by **compacting**, displacing occupied blocks in such a way as to make them contiguous. The free space remaining then itself becomes a contiguous zone. The displacement of information in memory is a long operation, whose cost is proportional to the volume of information displaced (see exercise); moreover, the task is complicated if the zones allocated contain absolute pointers, as they have to be updated (this is not the case, in principle, if addressing uses base registers or segments).
- In cases where blocks allocated may have become inaccessible, recover them by a garbage collection technique.

9.4.2.2 Use of allocation algorithms

In an operating system, memory allocation algorithms are used in two ways:

1. By the system itself, when allocating memory to jobs, or during the creation of processes, the reservation of input-output buffers, etc.

2. By users: the system provides primitives, in the form of supervisor calls, to request the allocation or freeing of memory. These are used, for example, by compilers for the management of dynamic variables.

For example, in a system using variable partition and dynamic relocation, a memory zone is allocated by the system as each job is considered. Depending on the addressing method used, a pair of values in base-limit registers, or an entry in the segment table, are assigned to the job. In the case of registers, their values are part of the job's context, and can be used to reload base-limit registers when the job is activated (fig. 9.10).

On certain machines, (e.g. DEC PDP-10), the (unmodifiable) program zones are separated from data zones for each job, with a separate base register for each zone. This configuration makes it possible to reduce the size of the zones allocated and of the information transferred (since program

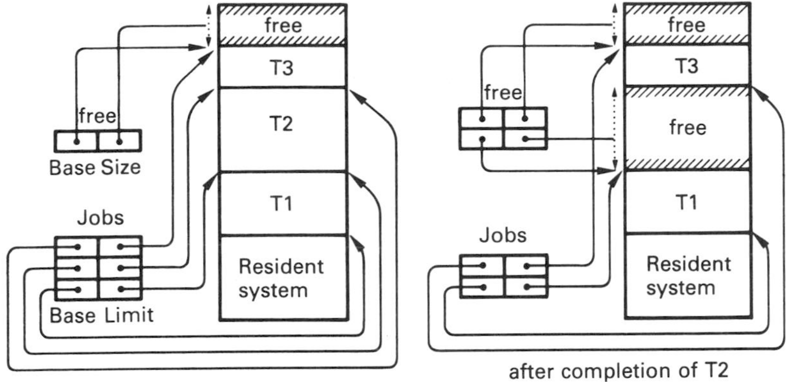

Fig. 9.10. Allocation of memory to jobs

zones do not need to be saved); it also allows programs to be shared between several jobs.

Certain systems (e.g. CDC, Univac) carry out compacting at the end of each job to ensure that free space is held as a single whole; the images of the base-limit registers or the segment table have to be updated each time a job is displaced (fig. 9.11).

9.4.2.3 *Conclusion*

By way of conclusion to this brief overview of memory allocation methods by means of zones, we should stress the fact that there is no optimal method, whatever the criterion chosen (memory usage, execution time, etc.) for all situations, and it is therefore vital to have a rough idea at least of demand characteristics, before an algorithm is chosen.

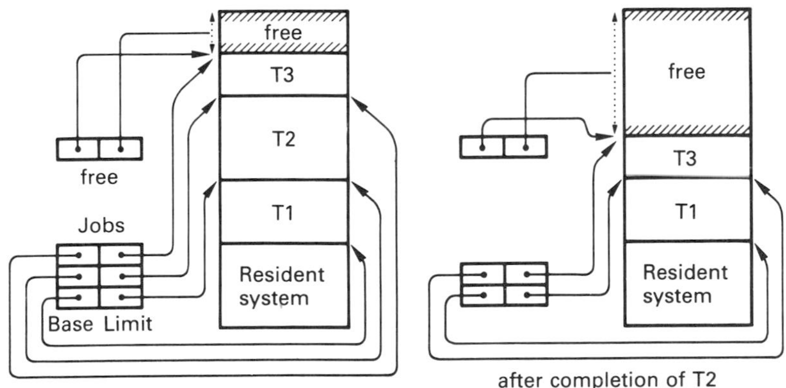

Fig. 9.11. Allocation of memory to jobs, with compacting

The limitations on allocation by zones are a result of the contiguity constraint on allocated zones; consequently, free locations are not pooled resources since, for example, a segment cannot be loaded into two disjoint free zones even if the total space is sufficient. The reorganization of memory is too costly an operation to be carried out frequently. The idea which led to the introduction of paging was that of pooling the memory resource by allocating it in units *of fixed size* which are not necessarily contiguous. The task then becomes one of resolving the addressing problem introduced (we need an equivalent of a base register for each allocation unit) and a compromise has to be found for the size selected for this unit.

9.5 Fundamental principles and mechanisms of paging

A paged virtual memory is divided into blocks of fixed size or **pages**, which are used as allocation units. Physical memory is itself divided into blocks the same size called **frames**. We shall consider in turn the paging mechanisms used for a linear virtual memory and for a segmented virtual memory.

9.5.1 Paging a linear memory

9.5.1.1 Simple paging

Figure 9.12 shows the general outline of a paged virtual memory.

The role of the box marked 'paging function' is to establish a correspondence between the addresses of pages in virtual memory and the addresses of frames in physical memory, in such a way that a page can be stored in any frame. Frames therefore become pooled resources whose management is simpler than that of zones of variable size.

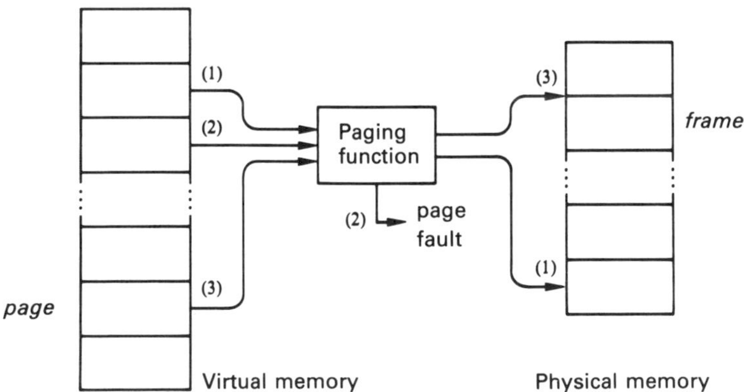

Fig. 9.12. Virtual paging memory

The number of locations in a page is always a power of 2. We shall write

$L = 2^l$ for the size (number of locations) in a page
$Npage = 2^p$ for the number of pages in virtual memory
$Nframe = 2^f$ for the number of frames in physical memory

A virtual address is then built up by concatenating a page number (p bits) and a location in the page (l bits). In the same way, a physical address is the concatenation of a frame number (f bits) and a displacement (l bits). Common page sizes are between 512 and 4096 bytes.

Given a virtual page number *page*, the paging function determines whether the page appears in physical memory, and if it does to find the number *frame* of the frame containing it. Efficiency considerations make it necessary to implement this function by hardware.

Historically, three techniques have been used in turn:

1. *Associative memory*. An associative memory, with an entry per frame, stores the number of the page each frame contains. This principle was used on the first paging machine (Atlas), which contained 32 frames (fig. 9.13a). Its very high cost has made its extension to larger memories prohibitive. The use of a small associative memory has however come back in favor, as an acceleration mechanism (see section 3 below).

2. *Memory Map*. A memory map is a set of registers, indexed by page numbers. Each register contains a presence indicator (1 bit) and a frame number, which is only significant if the bit is set to 1 (fig. 9.13b). The XDS Sigma 7 machine used this technique, with $p=8$ and $l=9$ (256 pages of 512 words). The use of a memory map only increases access time to memory by about 10% if no page fault takes place.

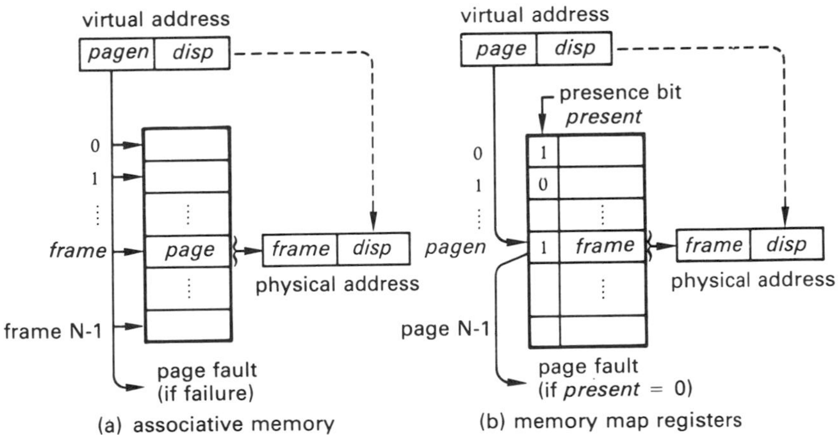

Fig. 9.13. First implementations of the paging function

3. *Page table in memory*. With the current trend towards increasing sizes of virtual memories (24 or 32 address bits), a memory map is again too costly. The most common implementation of the paging function uses a **page table** in main memory, indexed by a virtual page number (fig. 9.14).

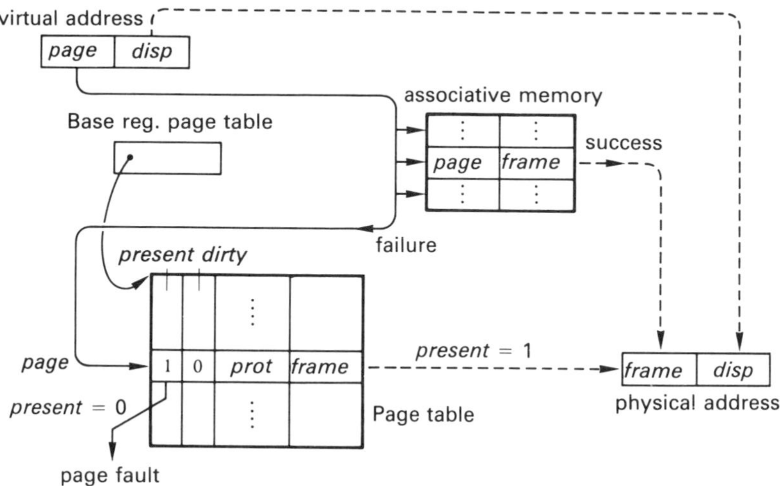

Fig. 9.14. Organization of a page table

Entry number *page* contains the following information:

- A frame number *frame*
- A presence indicator *present* (1 bit)
- A modification indicator *dirty* (1 bit)
- The access mode allowed (protection) *prot*

When memory access takes place, the correspondence between a virtual address and a physical address is established as follows:

```
virtual.addr:=(page,disp);
if present[page]=1 then  -- page in memory
  physical.addr:=(frame[page],disp)
else                     -- page not present
  <page fault handling>
endif
```

If a page is present:

- *dirty[page]* shows whether the page has been modified since it was loaded into memory (in that case, the page is called 'dirty'); this information is used by replacement algorithms (see section 9.6.2)

- *prot[page]* shows the allowed mode of access to the page; this information is used by protection mechanisms: unauthorized access causes trapping due to violation of protection

Access to a page now requires two references to memory, because the page table has to be consulted. To reduce mean access time, one once again uses the associative memory technique described in 1) but with a reduced size of memory (a few tens or hundreds of entries) in which ordered pairs *(page,frame)* collected during the most recent access operations are stored. Because of the locality property in programs (see section 9.2.1.1), there is a high probability (90 – 95% for common sizes) of finding the number of the page address, and therefore of determining its frame, using the associative memory. It is only in cases of failure that the page table is read; the associative memory is then updated, and the current ordered pair *(page,frame)* replaces the least recently used entry.

Note that a page table represents the contents of a particular virtual memory. If the operating system allows each process, or each user of the system, to define a separate virtual memory, it must manage a separate page table per process or per user. The pointer to the origin of this table then becomes part of the process or user context. Page tables are held in physical memory, in a zone reserved for the operating system. The problems of sharing information between virtual memories are considered in section 9.5.3.

Example: Paging on the DEC VAX 11/780. The virtual memory accessible to a process on the DEC VAX 11/780 is defined by a 32-bit address. 30 bits define the virtual space accessible to a user (21 bits for the page number, 9 bits for the displacement). The remaining two bits make it possible to define an extension to the virtual space used by the operating system.

Each entry in the page table for a process is made up of 32 bits:

<31>	:presence bit *present*
<30–27>	:protection *prot*
<26>	:write bit *dirty*
<25–21>	:field reserved for the operating system's use
<20–0>	:frame number *frame*

An associative memory stores the most recent ordered pairs *(page,frame)*.

9.5.1.2 Two-level paging

The tendency for virtual memory sizes to grow is coming up against the problem of overloading main memory with page tables, whose size increases in proportion to the memory itself. Two-level paging aims to solve this problem by restricting the page table only to those parts of virtual memory that are actually used.

In this approach, virtual memory is divided into hyperpages, which are themselves divided into pages. A virtual address now takes the form *(hyp,page,disp)*. The hyperpage number *hyp* allows access to a hyperpage table, each of whose entries includes a pointer to the page table for the hyperpage, which is restricted to pages actually being used. A 'size' field makes it possible to monitor this restriction. Page tables are used as in simple paging (fig. 9.15). An associative memory, which holds the most recent ordered triplets *(hyp,page,frame)*, is used to accelerate consultation (this requires two additional access operations to memory in case of failure).

Note that virtual memory remains linear: the last location in hyperpage $i-1$ has as successor the first location in hyperpage i. It is therefore a loose use of terms to refer to this approach as 'segmentation'. This division of virtual memory can, nonetheless, be used to simulate a segmented memory.

Example: Two-level paging was introduced on the IBM 360/67 and adopted on its successors in the IBM 370 series. Various combinations of page and hyperpage sizes can be chosen.

h	*p*	*d*
8	4	12
8	5	11
4	8	12
4	9	11

Two sizes of pages (2 or 4 kbytes) and two sizes of hyperpages (64 or 1024 kbytes) may be selected.

9.5.2 Paging a segmented memory

Paging of a segmented memory aims at making memory allocation to segments more flexible by removing the contiguity restriction for placement of a segment. An entry in the segment table contains not only information specific to the segment (size, protection, type) but also a pointer to the page table for that segment. As in the approaches above, an associative memory stores the most recent references (fig. 9.16).

Example: The Multics system uses allocation by pages for a segmented memory. Because of the sometimes large size and high number of segments, the page tables

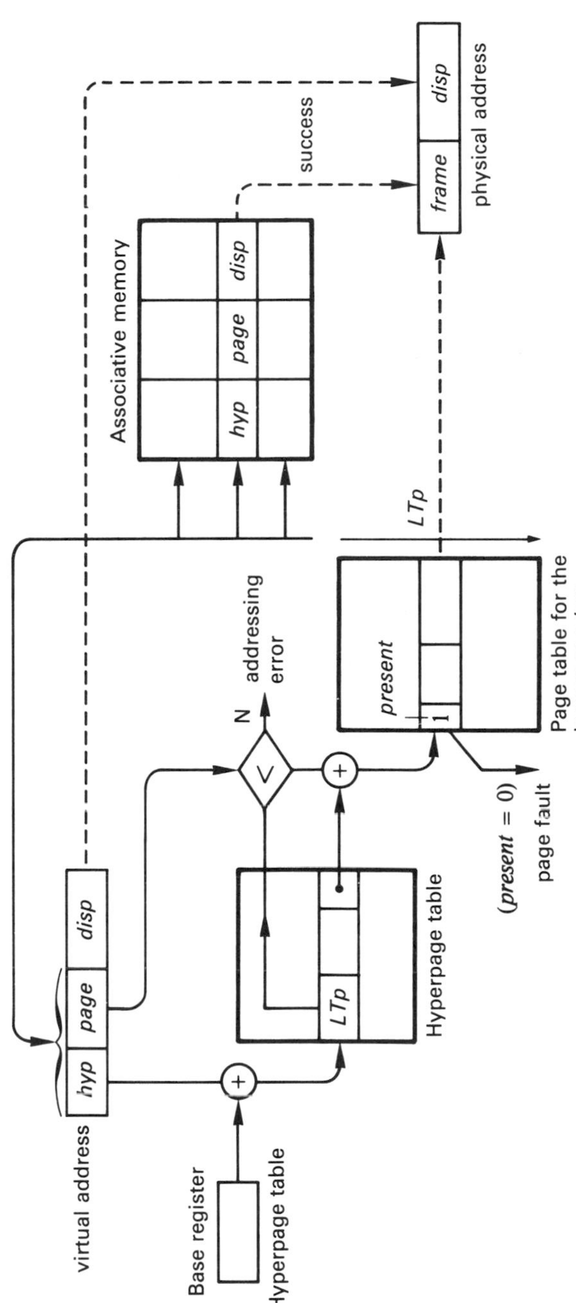

Fig. 9.15. Paging at two levels

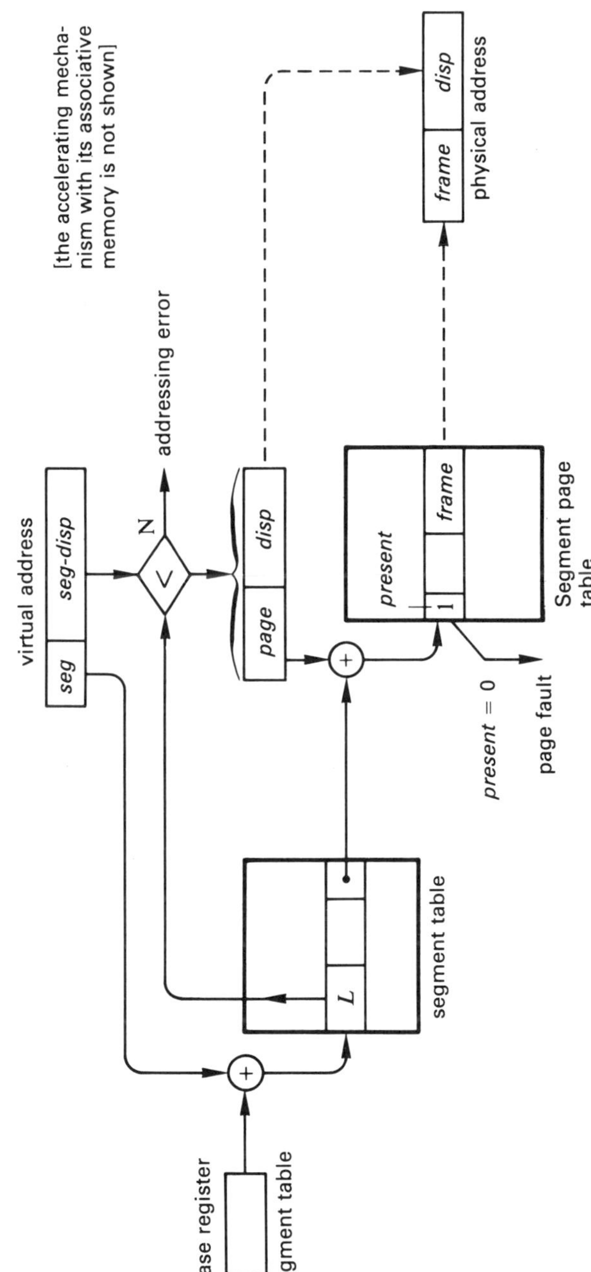

Fig. 9.16. Paging in a segmented memory

for segments, and the segment tables themselves, may be larger than a page, and therefore be paged themselves. The page table of a segment is held in main memory for as long as that segment is 'active' (i.e. the corresponding file is open for at least one process).

9.5.3 Implementation of paging

We shall consider the main mechanisms and data structures necessary to implement paging. The algorithms will be studied in section 9.6; a complete example of a paged virtual memory is given in section 10.2.

9.5.3.1 Page fault mechanism

Apart from translation of addresses as such (establishment of the *page-frame* correspondence), the access mechanism for a paged memory must carry out the following operations:

- Updating the write and use bits, if they exist
- Detection of page faults *(present[page]=0)*, which leads to a trap

The trap handling program for page faults must:

a. Find the missing page in secondary memory

b. Find a free frame in main memory; if no frame is free, it must free one by removing from memory the page it contains

c. Cause the page to be loaded into the frame above

Stage a) means that a mapping description must be available for each virtual memory. Its simplest form is that of a table indicating the secondary memory address of each virtual page. A segmented memory includes a table of this kind for each segment. Another form of description combines virtual memory and files: the contents of one or more files is associated with each virtual memory. The location of a virtual page in secondary memory is then determined by consulting the mapping table for a file one of whose elements it contains.

Example 1: In the Multics system, no distinction is made betwen a segment and a file: the mapping tables of segments describe the location of virtual pages in secondary memory.

Example 2: Access to files by association of their items with pages in a virtual memory is called **coupling**. An example of its implementation is given in chapter 10.

Stage b) uses a replacement algorithm (see section 9.6.2). This makes it necessary to store an occupation table in physical memory, which, for each occupied frame, gives the identity of the virtual page occupying it and supplementary information (protection, sharing, etc.).

9.5.3.2 *Sharing and protection of information*

The use of information shared between several virtual memories raises three problems:

- Naming: how to name shared information in a uniform way
- Physical sharing: how to ensure that shared information exists in a single copy
- Protection: how to ensure that rules (which may be applied selectively) governing access to shared information are respected

1. Naming of shared information

We shall distinguish the case of a linear virtual memory from that of a segmented virtual memory. Segmentation provides a simple solution to the problem of sharing (see chapter 6): the sharing unit is a segment, the name of a shared segment may itself be shared or selected independently by each process. In the case of a linear virtual memory, the name of an object is its virtual address. Two cases have to be distinguished depending on whether a virtual memory relocation mechanism exists.

- If such a mechanism exists (this is the case of a virtual memory with base registers), a shared object may be located at a different address in each virtual memory since base registers are specific to them.
- If such a mechanism is not present (as is more frequently the case), the loading of a shared object establishes its location once and for all, and it must be the same for all virtual memories. Fixed addresses defined by convention must therefore be reserved in each of them for every object that can be shared. This technique is used, in particular, for those parts of an operating system that are shared by all users.

2. Physical location of shared information

A page containing shared information may be loaded into any frame; the page tables of the virtual memories where this page appears therefore contain the same frame number, in the corresponding entry (fig. 9.17a).

In a segmented virtual memory, sharing applies to segments, and the page tables for shared segments are themselves shared. All the descriptors for a segment therefore contain not the address of the segment but that of its page table, which is unique (fig. 9.17b).

This sharing of page tables may also be implemented for a linear memory with two paging levels, if the hyperpage is being used as the shared unit. Note that sharing in this way still contains shared objects to be located at identical addresses.

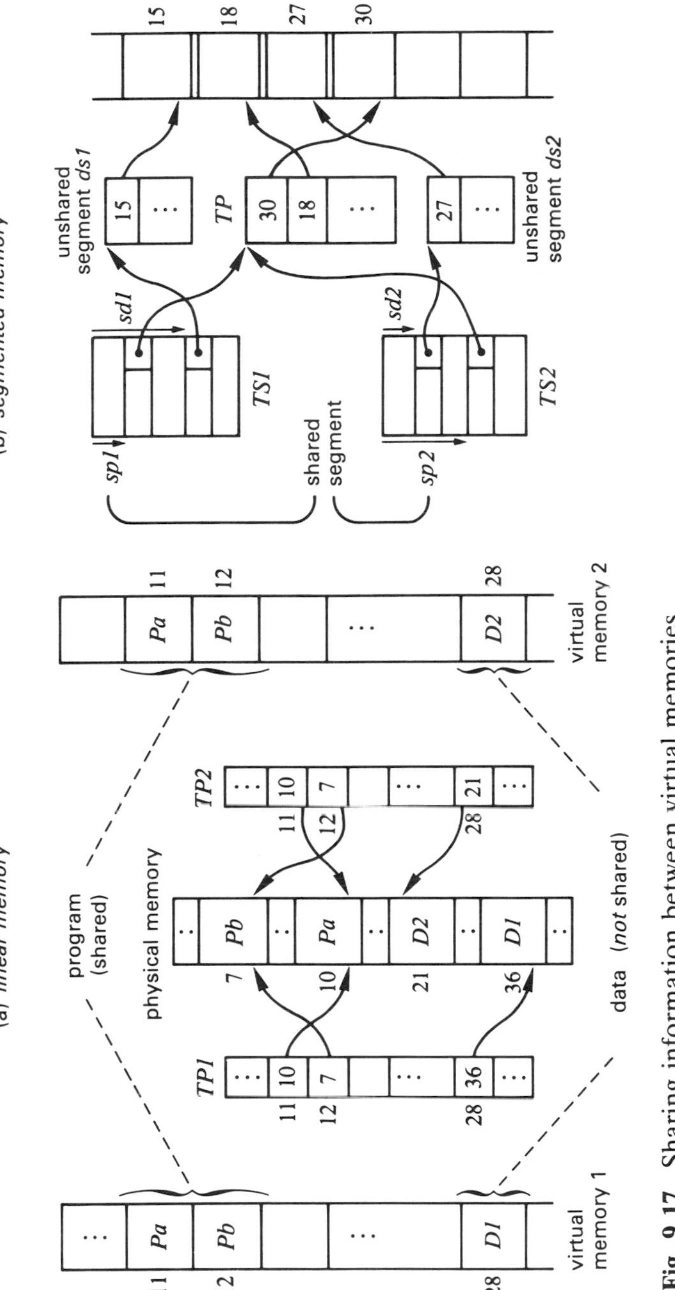

Fig. 9.17. Sharing information between virtual memories

3. Protection of shared information

If the sharing unit is a page, a shared page may be associated with different access rights in each of the virtual memories in which it appears. These rights are specified in the corresponding entry of the page table. If the sharing unit is a segment, selective protection will apply to the segment as a whole. Access rights to a segment for a process appear in the segment tables for that process. If individual access rights to pages in the segment are specified, they will appear in the page table shared by the user processes and are therefore shared by all the processes. They must therefore be compatible with the overall rights associated with the segment. Hyperpages are dealt with in exactly the same way as segments.

9.6 Management of a paged virtual memory

9.6.1 Allocation policy parameters

Allocation policies for paging memory can be classified according to several criteria. We shall assume that the system is multiprogrammed between several processes, each of which has its own virtual memory.

1. *Fixed or variable partition*. In a **fixed partition** policy, a fixed number of frames is assigned to each process; note that this number only remains constant for as long as the number of multiprogrammed processes is itself constant. In a **variable partition** policy, the number of frames assigned to each process varies through time. As all frames are equivalent, it is their number (and not their identity) which is the significant parameter.

2. *Paging on demand or pre-loading*. Paging **on demand** was defined in section 9.2.1.2: a page is only loaded into memory following a reference giving rise to a page fault. The policy which loads pages in advance, before any reference to information that they contain, is called **pre-loading**.

3. *Local or global replacement*. Page replacement takes place (see section 9.2.1.2) when a page is loaded into an occupied frame, i.e. a frame containing a page loaded previously and still liable to be used (the latter page is sometimes called the 'victim'). The replacement algorithm is said to be **local** or **global** depending on whether the victim is selected from amongst pages allocated to the process which triggers replacement or from all pages present in memory.

Before we study and compare the page replacement algorithms, we ought to mention criteria that are valid whatever the algorithm, and which are applied first. We shall not mention them again later.

1. 'Clean' or 'dirty' pages. All things being equal, it is always less costly to swap a page that has not been modified since it was loaded (a 'clean' page) rather than a modified page (a 'dirty' page). A clean page has a faithful copy

in secondary memory and does not need to be saved. The indicator *dirty[page]*, which is maintained automatically, makes it possible to apply this criterion.

2. Shared pages. A page used by one process alone should be swapped in preference to a page shared between several processes (see section 9.5.3.2).

3. Special status pages. In certain cases, we want to give a page a temporary special status protecting it against replacement. This occurs above all for pages used as input-output buffers for the duration of a transfer.

9.6.2 Fixed partition replacement algorithms

For fixed partition policies, we shall only consider local algorithms; we only need to consider a single process, to which a fixed number of frames, say N, is allocated. The execution of this process is defined by a reference string.

1. Description of the algorithms

We shall start by considering two algorithms that can be used as reference standards: the optimal algorithm, which assumes complete knowledge of the future behavior of a program, and a 'neutral algorithm', which makes no use of any information.

a. Optimal algorithm (MIN). For a given reference string, it can be shown that the following algorithm below minimizes the total number of page faults: when a page fault occurs, choose as victim a page which will not be referred to later, or if there is no such page, the page which will be referred to latest. This algorithm assumes a knowledge of the entire reference string; it is therefore impossible to apply in real time. It does, however, provide a reference standard against which to measure other algorithms.

b. Random selection. The victim is selected randomly (uniform distribution) from amongst all pages present in memory. This algorithm has no particular virtue, as it takes no account of the observed or predictable behaviour of the program; it is useful above all as a point of comparison.

c. Chronological order of loading (FIFO). This algorithm selects as victim the least recently loaded page. Its main advantage is that it is simple to implement: it is only necessary to maintain a FIFO queue of frame numbers into which successive pages are loaded.

d. Chronological order of usage (LRU, or least recently used). This algorithm attempts to approximate the optimal algorithm, using the locality property (see section 9.2.1.1). Its underlying principle is that, since the most recently used pages have a higher probability than the others of being used in the near future, a page that has not been used for a long time has a low probability of being used shortly. The algorithm therefore chooses as victim the page to which reference was least recently made.

The implementation of the algorithm requires that frames should be ordered according to the date of the last reference to the page they contain. For this to be possible, an item of information has to be associated with each frame and updated at each reference. This information may be a reference date; a more economical solution, but which is still expensive, is to use a counter incremented by 1 at each reference; the frame for which the counter has the lowest value contains the victim. As counters are limited in capacity, they have to be reset to zero each time one of them reaches its maximum capacity; this approach therefore only approximately implements the LRU principle. Because of its cost, this solution has only been used on experimental installations. If the size of the counter is reduced to a single bit, we obtain the next algorithm, whose cost is acceptable.

e. The FINUFO (first in not used, first out) algorithm. This algorithm is a very rough approximation to the LRU principle. A utilization bit U is associated with each frame, and is set to 1 each time a reference takes place to the page it contains. Frames are ordered in a circular queue and a pointer *ptr* points to the last frame loaded. The algorithm can then be written as follows:

```
ptr:=next(ptr);
while U[ptr]<>0 do
  U[ptr]:=0;
  ptr:=next(ptr)        -- in the frame queue
endwhile;
victim:=ptr;
```

The pointer advances until it reaches the first frame whose U bit is set to zero; frames met on the way, whose U bit is set to 1, are given a second chance: they are not selected as victim but their U bit is set to zero. This is also called the **clock** algorithm, since the movement of the pointer is analogous to that of a clock hand. The setting of the U bit to 1 when a reference is made can be left to a hardware or software device.

2. *Evaluation and comparison*

Many experimental studies (see bibliography in section 9.8) have provided evaluations of replacement algorithms. Figure 9.18, drawn from [Baer 80] gives the overall picture of the results obtained. We observe:

1. That algorithms can be classified in general, in order of decreasing

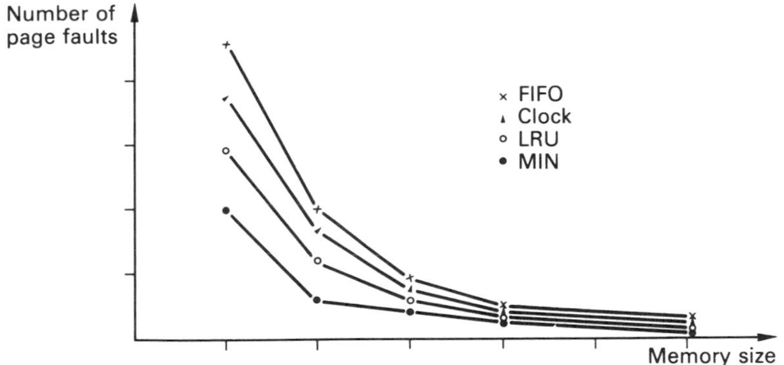

Fig. 9.18. Performance of replacement algorithms

performance, as follows: MIN, LRU, Clock, FIFO (the performance level of the FIFO approach is of the same order as random selection)

2. Memory size is very much more important a factor than the choice of a replacement algorithm; in other words, program performance can be improved much more significantly by increasing the number of frames allocated, rather than by refining the replacement algorithm, and this is all the truer the poorer the initial performance level is.

9.6.3 Variable partition algorithms; load control

The results above suggest that the best approach is to allocate a size of memory to each program that is suitable to its behaviour, and which must therefore be dynamically variable.

This can be attempted in two ways:

1. By using a variable partition algorithm
2. By using a global replacement algorithm, which means applying one of the algorithms studied for fixed partition to all the programs present

In both cases, we have to define the policy to apply in case of overloading, i.e. if the memory demand becomes excessive and leads to loss of performance. This is why we shall start by studying the behaviour of a system under extreme conditions. We shall then present variable partition algorithms based on local measurement of the behaviour of programs, and then control algorithms which use global criteria.

9.6.3.1 Instability and thrashing in a multiprogrammed system

In the first systems using paged virtual memories, it was found that beyond a certain level of load (measured, for example, by the number of interactive users), there was a sudden loss of performance. This phenomenon, called

thrashing, appears in a fall in processor usage and a major increase in page swapping; response times reach unacceptable values.

A qualitative explanation of thrashing makes it possible to identify its causes and to suggest remedies. Consider a paging memory system, multiprogrammed for a set of processes each of which corresponds to an interactive user. The physical memory is shared fairly between the processes, whose mean behavior is assumed to be identical; this distribution is implemented by a global replacement algorithm. Beyond a certain number of processes, the mean number of frames allocated to each of them falls below the threshold corresponding to the sudden drop in the 'lifetime' graph (see section 9.2.1). The overall probability of a page fault, which is inversely proportional to lifetime, then grows very rapidly with the number of processes.

Let us consider the effect of this growth on system performance. The mean level of activity of a processor is given by:

$$\varrho = t/(t+pT) = 1/(1+pS)$$

where t represents the mean execution time for an instruction, T is the mean time to handle a page fault, and p is the overall probability of a page fault occuring. The ratio $S=T/t$ is of the same order of magnitude of the ratio of the time taken to transfer a page from disk, to the time for main memory access; its value is between 1000 and 10,000. Given these values, we find that:

- Maintaining ϱ at a value close to 1 means maintaining the overall probability of a page fault occuring, p, at a very low value (of the order of $1/S$).
- A small increase in p leads to a sudden fall in ϱ: the system's behaviour becomes unstable.

This behavior is illustrated by fig. 9.19.

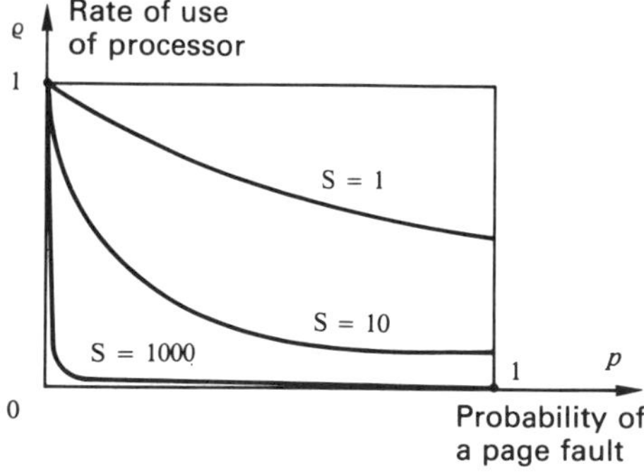

Fig. 9.19. Incidence of the rate of page faults on processor use

We saw in section 8.4.3 that the mean response time in an interactive system is associated with the rate of usage of the processor by the relation

$$\overline{tr}=N\overline{ts}/\varrho-\overline{ta}$$

The fall in ϱ therefore leads to a significant increase in response time.

The analysis above highlights the two factors in thrashing:

- Influence of the behaviour of programs in limited memory (growth of p as a function of the number of multiprogrammed processes)
- Influence of the memory hierarchy characteristics (fall in ϱ as p grows)

For given hardware and load characteristics, the **degree of multiprogramming** of the system (number of multiprogrammed processes) emerges as a determining factor. In what follows, we shall examine two ways of adjusting this parameter dynamically to avoid thrashing.

1. Implicitly, by providing each process present in memory with a number of frames appropriate for its observed behavior: this is the aim of variable partition replacement algorithms (section 9.6.3.2)

2. Explicitly, by acting directly on the degree of multiprogramming on the basis of a global view of the system's behavior: this is load control (section 9.6.3.3).

We shall end by making a few observations on the influence of the hardware characteristics of the system on its performance levels and its loading factor.

9.6.3.2 Variable partition replacement algorithms

If the number of frames allocated to a program is variable, the performance of an algorithm is defined by two quantities: the mean number M of frames occupied by the program and the mean number F of page faults per unit time. Mean values are evaluated throughout the execution of a program; the time unit used is the interval between two successive references to memory.

We have, furthermore, to start with a criterion making it possible to compare algorithms. For this purpose, two unit costs are defined:

- A time cost R: the cost of a page fault
- A space cost U: the cost of occupying a page in memory during a unit of virtual time

The cost of an algorithm is generally measured by a linear combination of time and space costs:

$$C=R.F+U.M$$

The relative importance of the time and space costs is determined by the ratio R/U. In the (M,F) plane, the performance of a given algorithm is defined by a curve with the shape shown in fig. 9.20.

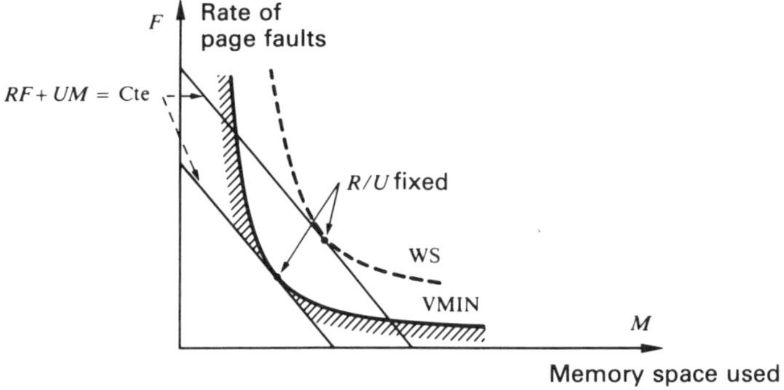

Fig. 9.20. Performance of variable partition algorithms

For a fixed value of R/U, the point of minimal operating costs is therefore defined by the point of contact between the algorithm performance curve used and the 'isocost' straight line $R.F+U.M=ct$.

For a variable partition, there is an optimal algorithm VMIN which plays the same role as MIN for a fixed partition; as with MIN, it cannot be implemented in real time and can only be used as a reference standard. It is constructed as follows:

After a reference to a page, the frame it occupies is immediately freed if and only if the page will not be referred to again during the next R/U units of time.

Implementable variable partition policies attempt to keep the memory size occupied by a program at any moment close to a minimum compatible with an acceptable rate of page faults. Two algorithms have been proposed to do this:

a. An algorithm based on the working set, or WS. A working set is maintained continuously for each process; when a page fault takes place, a page that does not belong to any working set present in memory is selected as victim. If no such page exists, frames are preempted from among those containing the working set for the lowest priority process (with priority determined externally, or by time of residence in memory). A process can only be an allocated memory if there are sufficient free frames to receive its current working set. The implementation of this algorithm requires that it is possible to identify the working set. Consequently, except in experimental implementations, it has only been applied approximately (see section 9.6.3.4 and chapter 10).

b. An algorithm based on the page fault frequency, or PFF. An indirect way of establishing that the number of frames allocated to a given process is sufficient is to measure its page fault frequency. The PFF algorithm is based on this principle; if this frequency is higher than an upper threshold, specified for each process, it receives a supplementary frame; conversely, frames are removed from it if its page fault frequency falls below a lower limit. The PFF algorithm requires only one usage bit per page and is therefore easier to implement than WS (see exercise).

Comparative studies (see section 9.8) have shown that WS and PFF policies give similar results, with performance levels in PFF apparently more sensitive than in WS to the size of the observation window.

9.6.3.3 Load control and configuration balancing

Overall load control involves acting on the degree of multiprogramming to maintain system performance levels within acceptable limits. For low or moderate load, multiprogramming increases the rate of usage of the processor by making use of idle time due to blocking or waiting time for pages; at heavy load, the reverse occurs, and this characterizes thrashing. This behavior suggests that there is an optimal value for the degree of multiprogramming, which maximizes the rate of usage of the processor for a given hardware configuration and load, and this has been confirmed in practice. An ideal load control algorithm would maintain the degree of multiprogramming close to that optimal value.

Several empirical optimization criteria have been proposed. They are all based on the same principle: an attempt to detect the onset of thrashing (by measuring the page fault rate) and to maintain the system just below this critical point.

Figure 9.21 shows how the rate of usage of the processor varies as a function of the degree n of multiprogramming. It should be borne in mind that

$$\varrho = 1/(1+pS)$$

where p is the overall probability of a page fault occuring in a unit of virtual time and S is the time taken to handle a page fault, using the same time unit. We shall write L for the overall lifetime (the mean period between successive page faults); an approximate value of p is given by $1/L$. At high values of n, p is high and pS is much greater than 1; ϱ is then close to $1/pS$, or L/S.

Figure 9.21 shows that the value of n such that $L=S$ is close to the optimum; the mean period between page faults is of the same order of magnitude as the duration of a transfer operation from disk. Two other

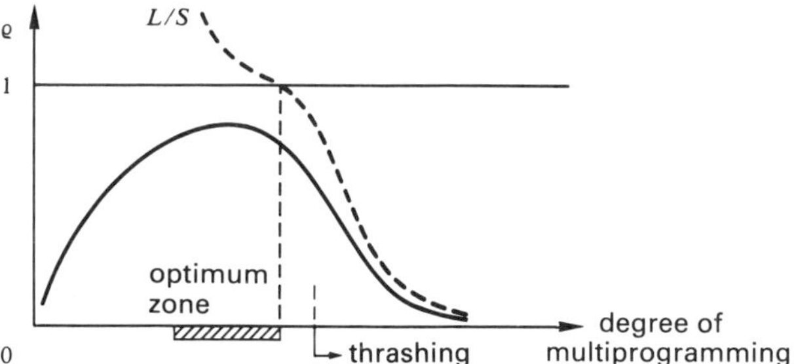

Fig. 9.21. Rate of processor use in a multiprogrammed system

equivalent formulations of the optimization criterion have been proposed:

- The '50% rule': the rate of use of the paging channel is close to 0.5
- The 'knee rule': the mean overall lifetime is that corresponding to the point of inflection on the lifetime curve (see section 9.2.1.2)

In practice, the number of page faults is measured periodically and this number is compared to thresholds determined empirically from measurements made on the system. If the upper critical value is exceeded, the degree of multiprogramming is reduced by 1: the lowest priority process, or the least recently loaded, must free the frame it occupies. Experience shows that it is worth allowing a certain margin to avoid violent oscillations caused by load control when the system is close to the critical threshold. This is made possible, in particular, by holding a reserve of free frames intended to absorb transient peaks in the page fault rate, and by introducing a delay time in the controller's reactions. A peak only causes a reaction if it uses up the reserve and if it lasts longer than the delay. The length of that delay and the size of the reserve have to be determined from observations in practice.

Load control allows the best possible use to be made of available resources for a given load. To handle a higher load, and to improve system performance, it may be necessary to improve hardware performance, by incorporating extensions or replacements. We then have to take care that the configuration remains balanced, to take full advantage of these gains in performance. Let V be the processor speed, M the size of main memory available and D the rate of exchanges with secondary memory. An empirical rule is to compensate for an increase in any one of these parameters, each time the configuration has changed, by an equivalent increase in one of the other two.

9.6.3.4 Examples

All current multiprogrammed systems include a mechanism for dynamic adjustment of the degree of multiprogramming, whether it uses one or other of the methods described above.

1. Systems using overall load control

Overall load control ('load leveling') was introduced on the experimental IBM M44 system; it is used, in particular, on the IBM 370 VM system. Its underlying principle is as described above: overloading of a system is detected by periodic measurements of paging activity, and the controller acts directly on the degree of multiprogramming.

2. Systems using an approximate estimate of the working set

Approximate estimates of the working set were introduced on the experimental EMAS system. They are used, in particular, in the VMS system on DEC-VAX. Estimates are more accurate on VMS: periodic measurements are used with the aim of determining dynamically the size of the working set for each process. The program for a process is only allowed into memory if there is sufficient free space to contain all its current working set. To avoid a process taking over the whole memory, an upper limit is fixed for each process. When that limit is reached, the process has to replace pages in its own memory space and cannot grow to the detriment of other processes. This method automatically reduces the priority of large programs. Starvation is avoided by handling admissions to memory in the order of arrival of their requests, and by fixing an upper limit to a process's residence time in memory.

9.7 Management of a hierarchical memory

9.7.1 Memory hierarchy

9.7.1.1 General characteristics

The information contained in the virtual memory of a system is distributed over a series of physical devices forming a **memory hierarchy**. In general terms, as we move away from the processor, we find that the characteristics of the devices are ordered in increasing size, in increasing access time and in decreasing cost per bit. Orders of magnitude for these characteristics are given in the table below.

	Size (bytes)	Access Time (s)	Relative cost per bit
Cache	10^3-10^4	10^{-8}	10
Main memory	10^6-10^7	10^{-7}	1
Bubble memory	10^6-10^7	$10^{-3}-10^{-4}$	10^{-2}
Fixed head disk	10^8	10^{-3}	$10^{-2}-10^{-3}$
Movable head disk	10^8-10^9	10^{-2}	10^{-3}
Magnetic tape	10^8-10^9	$10-10^2$	10^{-4}
Optical disk	10^{10}	10^{-1}	10^{-5}

Note:

- The capacities given for secondary storage devices are unit capacities (a system can contain several units).
- Optical disks, unlike other media, cannot be rewritten; they are used as a memory archive, accessed in read only mode after initial writing.

The ideal objective of a dynamic management policy for a memory hierarchy is to distribute information between devices in such a way that at any moment the information immediately necessary is directly accessible to the processor. In this way the properties of 'low-level' devices (high capacity and low cost) are combined with those of 'high-level' devices (rapid access). We have seen an example of the implementation of such a policy for the management of a paged virtual memory.

9.7.1.2 The cache

Consider two adjacent levels in a memory hierarchy. One may consider that information permanently resides at the lower level, while the memory management policy keeps at any time at the higher level the subset with the highest estimated access probability. This probability is usually estimated by the LRU algorithm on one of its variations. We then say that the higher level is used as a **cache** for the lower level. This term initially named a hardware device located at the highest level (i.e. between the processor and main memory); it is also used, by analogy, in a more general sense, including a software implementation. Here are three examples:

Example 1: The associative memory used to hold the most recent references in the paging system for a segmented memory operates as a cache for these references.

Example 2: The table of active descriptors in the Unix FMS (section 7.6) operates as a cache for file descriptors.

Example 3: The management of objects in the Plessey system (section 6.4.3) operates as a two-level cache for objects stored on disk. The first level is made up of the general descriptor table which stores the descriptors of objects named by at least one capability in memory. The second level is made up of capability registers, which contain descriptors of directly addressable objects.

A cache associated with a processor was first introduced in the IBM 360/85. This is a technique now very widely used: all main-frames, and a large number of medium-range computers (DEC-VAX, Apollo, etc.) now have such caches.

We shall describe the basic principle of a common form of organization of a cache (associative access by blocks) illustrated by the example of the IBM

370/165. The cache, with a total size of 8 Kbytes, is divided into 256 32-byte blocks; these blocks are organized into 64 'columns' of 4 blocks. The main memory is itself organized into columns of 32-byte blocks; a block is defined by its column number *c* and its row number *r*. A physical address byte *addr* appears in block *(c,r)* with

$$r = addr \textbf{ div } 2048 \text{ and } c = (addr \textbf{ mod } 2048) \textbf{ div } 32$$

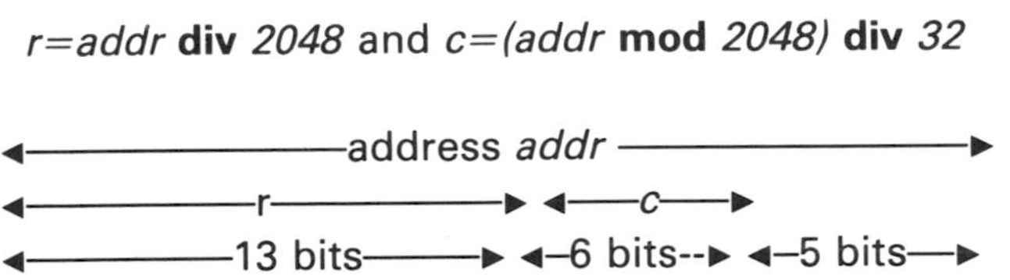

The memory block *(r,c)* can be loaded into one of the four rows of column *c* of the cache. For each column, the cache contains the following information (fig. 9.22):

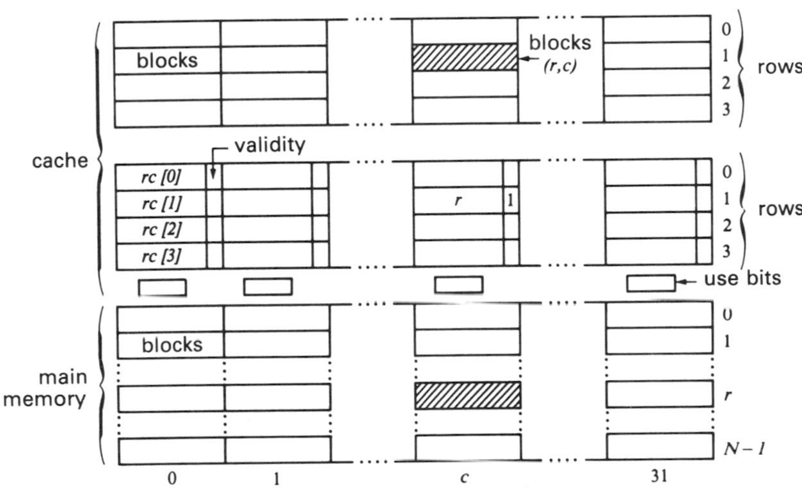

Fig. 9.22. Organization of a cache using associative access by blocks

- The contents of four memory blocks
- Row numbers *rc[i]* for these four blocks (*i*=0,1,2,3)
- Management information (use and validity bits)

During read access to a memory location, the physical address *addr* of the location, obtained by converting the virtual address, is transmitted to the cache. The values *r* and *c* are calculated as shown above; the value *r* is compared with the four values *rc[i]* associated with column *c*. If *r*=*rc[k]*, the block appears in the cache (row *k*, column *c*); it can therefore be read immediately, and the use bits are updated. Otherwise, the block is read into memory, and copied into column *c* of the cache, at row *k* determined by the replacement algorithm described below; *rc[k]* receives the value *r*. A write access takes place in an analogous way, but the block is simultaneously updated in the cache and in main memory ('write through'). Note that it is possible not to pass on the modification in memory until the modified block is swapped out (see exercises).

Replacement uses the LRU algorithm, implemented as follows. Each column of the cache is associated with a set of 6 bits *U[i,j]* organized into a triangle ($i,j=0,1,2,3;\ i+j<3$). When access takes place to a block in row *k*, the bits in *U[i,j]* on line *k* are set to 1 and those in column $3-k$ are set to 0. At any moment, the number *k* of the row to replace is such that line *k* of *U* contain only zeros and column $3-k$ of *U* contains only ones (either can be empty).

The operation of the cache may interfere with that of input-output. When a memory block, a copy of which exists in the cache, is modified by an input-output channel, the copy in the cache goes out of date. This problem could be solved by making all input-output operations pass through the cache. It is simpler to detect the inconsistency, by comparing the addresses of blocks affected by input-output activity with those of blocks present in the cache, and to mark the latter as invalid if necessary.

Let *ct* be the mean access time to the cache, *mt* the mean access time to memory, and *s* be the mean hit ratio (block present in the cache when access takes place). The mean access time to information by the process is given, as a first approximation, by

$$t=(1-s).mt+s.ct$$

This equation works for read only access, which is the most frequent type of access (around two thirds in common applications). For write access, the gain is smaller because of the need to write through to memory.

Experience shows that, for usual cache sizes (of the order of 1% of the size of main memory), and for common applications, the hit ratio is between 90 and 95%. The ratio *ct/mt* is of the order of 0.1: the advantage of using a cache is therefore obvious. The hit ratio measured confirms the locality property for most applications. The efficiency of the cache may be reduced if references are very scattered (as e.g. in some list processing applications).

9.7.1.3 File migration

The saving of files to an archive memory which is not directly accessible (magnetic tape) is made necessary by the limited capacity of disks. This problem is comparable to that of managing a paging memory, but there are two differences:

- The timescale is very different (measured in days rather than in milliseconds), and response time constraints are generally less severe.
- Units of variable size are used (files) rather than pages of fixed size.

For the latter reason, an algorithm of the LRU type, though often used, is not particularly suitable as it does not take into account the fact that it may be better to save a large file rather than a smaller file used less recently.

This effect can be taken into account by defining a cost function for a file f at a time t, using the product $L(f).[T(f)-t]$, where $L(f)$ is the current length of the file and $T(f)$ is the (future) date of the next reference to the file. The file to save first is the one whose cost function has the highest value.

The cost function above cannot be calculated in real time, and the algorithm used to implement it (called GOPT) is comparable to the MIN and VMIN algorithms for management of a paging memory. A simple approximation, based on the locality hypothesis which is shown to be reasonably accurate in practice, is to replace $T(f)-t$ by $t-rt(f)$, where $rt(f)$ is the date of the most recent reference to file f. More elaborate algorithms are based on more detailed predictions of the date of the next access operation; they can be used for repetitive applications, from which statistics concerning the use of files can be collected, allowing files to be classified by their usage characteristics (see the bibliographic notes).

9.7.2 Transfer management

9.7.2.1 Paging disk

A fixed-head disk has a read-write head for each track. The management of transfers for such a disk was examined in section 8.3.2. We saw the advantage of organization as a paging disk, with a separate request queue for each sector. Two practical aspects of this form of organization need to be mentioned:

- The time taken for the gap between two consecutive sectors to move under the read-write heads must be sufficient to allow a transfer operation to be launched. With an input-output channel, the launching of operations can be accelerated thanks to the chaining of commands: by taking the requests which are at the head of each non-empty queue, a command chain can be built up, which will be used for a complete rotation of the disk.
- The paging disk reorders requests, which are therefore not executed in the order in which they were issued. Care therefore has to be taken if the order of transfer operations is significant (writing and reading, or successive writes, to the same sector).

9.7.2.2 Moving head disks

A disk with a moving arm has a single read-write head per side of the disk. Radial displacement of the arm allows the head to be brought above the selected track. As well as the time taken to wait for the selected sector to come under the head, we have to take into account the time required for the radial movement of the arm from its current position. If the disk unit has several sides, all the arms carrying heads are linked; the set of tracks accessible without moving the arm is called a cylinder. The following policies have been considered.

1. First come, first served

In this policy, requests are handled in the order in which they arrive. There is no reason why the movement of the arm should be mimimal. The two policies below attempt to reduce this movement, which is the main factor determining access time (arm movements are slower than disk rotation).

2. Shortest seek time first

One heuristic which can reduce arm movements is, at the end of each transfer, to service the request whose track is closest to the current track.

This policy is analogous to the 'shortest job first' policy for processor allocation. It has the same disadvantage, which is the risk of starvation. It is possible to construct a request arrival sequence such that some requests will be indefinitely delayed. It can also be shown that the shortest seek time first policy is not optimal.

The need to avoid starvation led to the emergence of the following algorithms.

3. Scan

In the scan policy, the arm scans all tracks in a backwards and forwards movement. A request is handled when the head moves above the corresponding track. The regular movement of the arm avoids large-scale displacements which could occur in first come first served policies and avoids the risk of starvation in shortest seek time first.

Performance can be improved if the displacement of the head is limited to the most widely separated tracks for which requests are present.

A variant of this algorithm (called C-scan, for circular scan) treats tracks as though they were organized into a circle (the last track being the predecesor of the first). The arm therefore scans tracks and services all requests on the way through; its return to the starting position takes place without stopping. This variant aims to ensure that the distribution of request service times is uniform.

Systematic studies [Teorey 72] have shown the advantage of using scan or C-scan if loads are heavy. It is important here to know the loading characteristics before selecting an algorithm. Note too that careful placement of information can improve access performance: the sequential allocation of files, if possible, the organization of occupation tables by cylinders, storage of frequently used information in the middle zone of disks, can all help. Finally, certain moving head disks contain a few tracks equipped with fixed heads which can be used for frequently used information, such as file mapping tables.

9.8 Bibliographic notes

A review of virtual memory principles is given in [Denning 70]. A description of hardware organizations for memory appears in [Baer 80].

The intrinsic behavior of programs is studied in [Batson 76, Madison 76]. The behavior of programs in paging memories and improvements to this behavior are studied in [Brawn 68, Hatfield 71 and 72, Morrison 73]. The 'working set' model was introduced in [Denning 68]; a review of the results of its use, and a major bibliography of virtual memory management, appear in [Denning 80]. Statistics on the size and use of files in a time-sharing system are given in [Satyanarayanan 81].

An in-depth study of allocation by zones is given in [Knuth 73]. [Bays 77] presents a comparative study of certain common algorithms. An improved version of 'first fit' is given in [Stephenson 83]. Allocation algorithms by block subdivision ('buddy systems') are studied in [Peterson 77]. Examples of actual implementations of systems using allocation by zones are given in [Margolin 73, Bozman 84], which also gives numerous results of simulation and measurement.

The main replacement algorithms for fixed partition pages are compared in [Belady 66]. The optimal algorithm for variable partition is described in [Prieve 76] and the PFF algorithm in [Chu 76]. Adaptive algorithms for multiprogramming are studied in [Denning 76]; see also [Denning 80].

A model for the evaluation of memory hierarchies is given in [Mattson 70]. The principle of a cache is introduced in [Liptay 68]; a review and bibliography on caches appear in [Smith 82]. Algorithms on file migration are studied in [Smith 81]; an example of implementation appears in [Considine 77]. A comparative study of moving head disk management policies is given in [Teorey 72].

Exercises

Exercise 9.1

Assuming that procedures *loadsegment* and *flushsegment*, are available, with an interface to be specified, show what program sequences will have to be inserted into the segments of a program to be executed in overlay, to provide for memory allocation and for run time transfer management. Specify the information which has to be provided to the overlay loader to be able to insert the sequences, and the restrictions that have to be applied to references between segments.

Exercise 9.2

Write the memory allocation and freeing algorithms assuming that free zones are managed in chained blocks, implementing the three policies presented in section 9.4.1 (first fit, best fit, worst fit).

Exercise 9.3

Write the memory allocation and freeing algorithms for a 'buddy system':

a. Using a binary system
b. Using a Fibonacci system

Allocation requests should be satisfied using the free block of smallest size greater than that requested.

Exercise 9.4

Write the algorithm for allocating memory to jobs in a batch processing system, with zones of any size and dynamic loading. Base-limit registers are available. Specify the contents of the descriptor of a task and the operations to be carried out during loading and on termination of a job. Handle the cases of allocation both with and without compacting.

Exercise 9.5 [Knuth 73]

Assume that a memory allocation algorithm by zones operates, in steady state, with a more or less constant number of free zones (or 'holes'). Assume that a segment is allocated at one end of a hole, and that there is a probability p of filling the hole exactly. Caculate the ratio of the number of holes to the number of segments. Show that this ratio works out at 1/2 (the 50% rule) if $p=0$ (the allocation of a segment does not change the number of holes). **Hint:** Calculate the mean variation in the number of holes on allocation and freeing of a segment.

Exercise 9.6 [Denning 70]

Assuming the 50% rule, what is the minimal fraction f of memory that has to be kept free for the ratio between the mean size of a hole and that of a segment to be equal to or greater than a specific value? **Hint:** Note that f is the ratio between the total size of holes and the total size of segments.

Exercise 9.7 [Denning 70]

An operating system allocates memory by zones, sequentially and without reusing holes. When allocation becomes impossible, the whole of the memory is compacted. We write:

> M for the size of memory;
> t for the mean lifetime of a segment;
> S for the mean size of a segment;
> T for the time it takes to copy a word into memory;
> F for the mean proportion of free memory.

Calculate the percentage of the time taken for compacting, in steady state.
Hint: Note that in steady state a segment is created every t units of time; use this to deduce the time necessary to fill the free portion of memory, between two compacting operations.

Exercise 9.8

An operating system implemented on a segmented machine operates according to the 'segment on demand' principle. The addressing mechanism uses a segment table in memory; a segment is named by the displacement of its descriptor within that table. The memory is managed in zones of variable size; we assume procedures *allocate(zone)* and *free(zone)* are available, with parameters to be specified.

1. Propose a replacement algorithm; show what information has to be added to descriptors, and give a program outline for the segment fault handler.
2. Segments may be shared between several processors. How should sharing be taken into account in the algorithms above?

Exercise 9.9 [Belady 69]

Under certain conditions, the FIFO replacement algorithm behaves in a way contrary to what we would expect intuitively (Belady's anomaly): for a given reference string, the number of page faults increases with an increase in available memory size.

1. Construct a reference string C such that, for a certain size of memory N we have $Fault(C,N-1)>Fault(C,N)$ where $Fault(C,N)$ is the number of page faults generated by the execution of string C in a memory of N locations, with a FIFO replacement algorithm.
2. Show that the MIN and LRU algorithms cannot produce this anomaly. **Hint:** If $S(C,N)$ is the set of all the pages present in memory after execution of string C, show that $S(C,N)$ is included in $S(C,N+1)$.

Exercise 9.10 [Belady 66]

Prove that the MIN replacement algorithm is optimal for replacement with a fixed size partition.

Exercise 9.11 [Prieve 76]

Prove that the VMIN replacement algorithm is optimal for replacement with a variable size partition.

Exercise 9.12

Suggest an implementation of the PFF replacement algorithm described in section 9.6.3.2.

Exercise 9.13

A paging memory machine has a bit *U* per virtual page, automatically set to 1 when access takes place to that page. An instruction is available to reset to 0 all the *U* bits for all pages in a table of virtual pages (a separate table is associated with each multiprogrammed process).

Explain how this mechanism may be used to implement an overall replacement algorithm by approximate estimation of the working set. **Hint:** Use a process which is periodically reactivated; discuss how a period should be selected and how it can be fine-tuned if necessary.

Exercise 9.14

A virtual memory operating system includes a primitive *stickpage(nv)* whose effect is to protect the frame allocated to virtual page *nv* against replacement. The primitive *unstickpage(nv)* eliminates this protection.

1. What are the data structures necessary to implement these primitives?
2. Under what conditions would these primitives be useful? What risks do they lead to and what restrictions should be applied to their use?

Exercise 9.15

On certain machines, modifications affecting a data item present in a cache are not immediately reflected in memory, but only once the cache block containing them is reallocated. Discuss the advantages and disadvantages of this method compared to 'write through'.

Exercise 9.16

Show that the algorithm for the replacement of blocks in a cache, described in section 9.7.1.2, implements an LRU management policy. What is its advantages compared to an algorithm using a reference counter per block?

Exercise 9.17 [Hoare 74]

The management of a moving head disk is provided for by a monitor *disk* which has two entry points, procedures *request* and *free*. A process which has to access a track belonging to cylinder *c* must execute the sequence.

```
disk.request(c)
   <access cylinder c>
disk.free
```

Write the program of monitor *disk* to implement the following three management policies:

1. First come, first served
2. Shortest seek time first
3. Scan and C-scan

Hint: If necessary, use waiting with priority (section 4.4.6) to classify waiting processes in the order in which they must be served.

Exercise 9.18

By identifying a moving head disk with an M/M/1 server, evaluate the traffic intensity below which all request management policies are more or less equivalent.

Exercise 9.19

A moving head disk contains N cylinders, with access requests assumed to be uniformly distributed between them. Calculate the mean value of head displacements, as a number of cylinders. **Hint:** Note that the distances travelled by the arm will not be uniformly distributed.

Chapter 10

Structure of a multiprogrammed system

In this chapter, we shall show how the main methods examined so far can be applied to the construction of an operating system using multiprogramming. We shall consider two frequently encountered cases: a system with fixed memory partition, and a system with a virtual paged memory.

In both cases, we shall examine the main data structures (tables, queues, etc.) necessary for system management and the guiding principles of the algorithms used, laying particular stress on the overall organization of the system and on cooperation between processes forming it, as well as on the major decisions to be taken during system design. Many other forms of organization can be envisaged; we shall indicate in passing a few possible variants, while others appear in the exercises.

10.1 A partition system

10.1.1 Basic assumptions

1. Hardware

a. The machine is a monoprocessor.
b. The addressing mechanism uses relocation by means of base registers.
c. Secondary memory is a disk managed by a channel or a DMA.

2. System organization

a. The system is based essentially on time-sharing by a small number of users; each user is associated with a single process.

b. Main memory is shared as a fixed number of zones defined once and for all during system start-up; if this number is less than the number of users (which we assume to be the case), programs and data for processes which cannot obtain enough space in memory are stored on disk.

c. Exchanges between main memory and disk take place globally, by zones, using the swapping principle (see chapter 9).

10.1.2 System organization

10.1.2.1 States of processes

Let us start by examining the way memory is managed. The system is multiprogrammed between processes whose programs are loaded into specified zones in main memory (we shall simply say that processes are 'loaded'). Loaded processes are therefore in the ready state.

When a process p is blocked, the memory zone it occupies may be freed to make way for another process; the program and data for p are saved to disk; in this case, we say that process p has been 'swapped out'. When a swapped out process is restarted, it becomes a candidate for reloading into memory.

To avoid indefinite occupation of a memory zone by a process which is not involved in any input-output operation (and which therefore cannot be blocked), it is also possible to swap out a ready process after it has made sufficient use of the processor.

We shall assume that zones are of equal size, and that their size is sufficient to contain the program and data for a process. The use of base registers means that a process can be loaded into any zone: all that is required is that during activation of the process, base registers are loaded with the addresses where the program and its data are located.

Let us now examine the way in which the processor is allocated and the underlying principle for managing exchanges. The processor is allocated in turn to ready processes, using the round robin principle (see chapter 8). The active process may lose the right to use the processor for one of two reasons (see chapter 5).

1. Blocking: we assume that a process, in an interactive system, can only be blocked because it is waiting for a response from the user at the terminal.

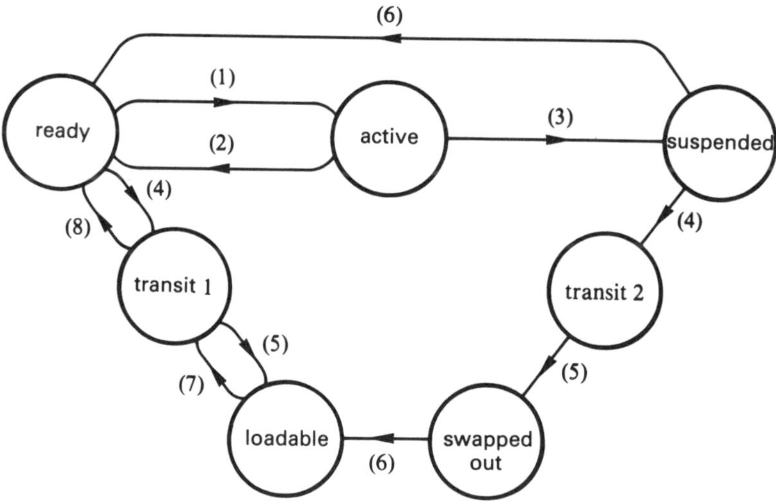

Fig. 10.1. A process cycle in a partition system

2. Preemption: to avoid starvation, we assume that the cpu is allocated for a duration less than or equal to a fixed timeslice.

A process becomes ready as soon as it is loaded into memory. It cannot be swapped out without having been activated. If the active process is blocked, it becomes a candidate for being swapped out; a decision on whether it should actually be swapped out or not depends on whether there are processes waiting to be loaded. A blocked process can be recovered if it is reactivated before being swapped out. A swapped process becomes a candidate for loading as soon as it is reactivated. Figure 10.1, which shows the cycle followed by a process, summarizes these points.

The table below shows the causes for the various transitions in fig. 10.1:

Transition	Operation	Triggering event
1	Processor allocation	(2) or (3) on another process
2	End of timeslice	Clock interrupt
3	Blocking	Prompt sent to terminal
4	Start of swap-out	(6) or end of disk transfer
5	End of swap-out	End of disk transfer
6	Reactivation	Response from terminal
7	Start of loading	(6) or end of disk transfer
8	End of loading	End of disk transfer

There are three important comments to be made on this table.

1. The events triggering a transition are always interrupts or supervisor calls: they are the 'entry points' of an operating system.

2. A process state transition may cause a transition in another process: freeing the processor leads to its reallocation to another process; the end of a transfer, which frees the disk-memory channel, allows another transfer operation to be launched.

3. Transit states were introduced so that transitions could be regarded as instantaneous: no event can take place 'during' a transition.

10.1.2.2 Input-output

We shall adopt the operating model for peripherals described in section 4.4.4.1: each peripheral is managed by a monitor whose entry points represent access functions.

1. Operation of the disk. A monitor *disk* has a single entry point

disk.exchange(req). The parameter *req* (request) is a record whose various fields specify the characteristics of the requested exchange:

req.mode	:read or write
req.zone	:memory zone number
req.dadd	:disk address
req.n	:number of bytes to transfer
req.p	:number of the loaded or swapped process

The zone number determines its memory address (see section 10.2.2.3).

A call to *disk.exchange* appears to be synchronous: on return from this procedure, the transfer has been carried out. In fact, there is a waiting period within the monitor, with the period end marked by an end of transfer interrupt.

2. Operation of terminals. Each terminal (identified by number *i* which also refers to the processes associated with that terminal) is made up of two distinct devices, the screen and keyboard. It is however managed by a single monitor *term[i]*, because of the interrelations between the two devices (echo on screen of characters entered through the keyboard). The monitor has two entry points:

term[i].output(out)

which displays on screen the contents of a line placed in an output buffer *out*;

term[i].prompt(out,in)

which displays a line (a prompt) placed in the output buffer *out*, and then reads a line into the input buffer *in*. A line is a sequence of characters entered through the keyboard, terminated by the character <CR> (carriage return); characters are displayed on the screen as they are entered.

Here again, procedures seem to be synchronous. The monitor disguises the interrupt handling caused by input and output of characters and also the waiting period inherent in procedure *prompt*.

As it is possible for the calling process to be swapped out while it is waiting, the execution of the transfer, in procedure *prompt*, is left to a resident process *transfer_term[i]* associated with each terminal *i*.

10.1.2.3 Data structures

The state of memory occupation is represented by a table which gives the following information for each zone, identified by its number *z*:

addr[z]	start of zone address
size[z]	size of zone (identical for all zones)
proc[z]	number of the process loaded in the zone (*nil* if the zone is not occupied).

The system manages a resident table of process state vectors; since processes are associated with terminals, this table can only take a fixed number of entries. For each process, numbered *i*, the table contains the following fields:

Stat[i]	process status word
Reg[i]	registers
Zone[i]	number of the zone in which the process has been loaded (*nil* if the process is not loaded)
Dadd[i]	address of the saved zone on disk
State[i]	state of the process
Length[i]	space occupied by the program and data
<chaining links>	

Ready processes are chained in a queue *ready_q*, managed in first come, first served mode; two procedures *add* and *remove* allow insertion and extraction of processes respectively. A pointer *active_proc* indicates the active process.

The dispatcher program (sequence *allocate_processor*) is as shown in chapter 5, with two further instructions:

```
set_clock(q)                          -- load time slice
BR:=addr[Zone[selected_proc]]         -- load base register
```

10.1.2.4 Structure and operation of the system

Apart from the monitors which manage peripherals and the process management kernel, the operating system is made up of the following programs:

- Programs responsible for disk management (monitor *disk* and process *transfer_disk*)

- Programs responsible for terminal management (monitors *term[i]* and process *transfer_term[i]*)
- The clock interrupt handling program

The process *transfer_disk* is a cyclical process operating on the client-server pattern. It receives transfer requests, and handles them in their order of arrival. It communicates with client processes by way of a mailbox managed by a monitor with two entry points:

reqqueue.deposit(req)
reqqueue.collect(req)

Before looking in detail at the *transfer_disk* process, we shall first consider exchanges with the terminal.

Monitor *term[i]* has the following outline:

```
term[i]:monitor
  begin
  var input_buffer[i],output_buffer[i]:line;
      c[i]:condition;

    procedure write;        -- internal procedure
    <displays on screen the contents of output_buffer [i]>
    procedure read;         -- internal procedure
    <fills input_buffer[i] from the keyboard>

  procedure output(out);
    output_buffer[i]:=out;
    write;

  procedure prompt(in,out);
    output_buffer[i]:=out;
    c[i].signal;
    in:=input_buffer[i];

  procedure exchange;
    c[i].wait;
    remove(i,ready_q);
    State[i]:=suspended;
    write;                  -- displays output_buffer[i]
    read;                   -- fills input_buffer[i]
    load(i)                 -- exchange complete
  end term[i]
```

We shall not go into detail concerning the bodies of procedures *read* and *write*, which drive the terminal controller and handle interrupts (see exercises). The process *transfer_term[i]* is as follows:

```
process transfer_term[i]

    loop
        term[i].exchange
    endloop
```

The buffers *input_buffer[i]* and *output_buffer[i]*, which are resident in memory, are permanently associated with terminal *i*. Exchanges with the terminal cannot make direct use of the buffers *in* and *out*, which are in the zone for process *i* and may therefore be flushed to disk.

Let us now look in detail at the procedure *load*.

```
procedure load(i);        --request to load process i
                          --make space if necessary
if State[i]=blocked then
   add(i,ready_q)
   State[i]:=ready        --process not yet swapped
else
   find_free_zone(z);
   if z=nil then          --no free zone, create one
      choose_swappable_process(k);
      prepare_swapout_request(k,req);
      reqqueue.deposit(req);
      z:=Zone[k]          --freed zone
   endif;
   prepare_load_request(i,z,req)
   reqqueue.deposit(req)
endif
```

Note that process *i* is 'recovered' if it has not yet been swapped out. Procedures *find_free_zone* and *choose_swappable_process* present no difficulty: the first provides the number of a free zone (*nil* if all are occupied); the second returns the number of a blocked process; if there are none, it provides the number of the least recently loaded ready process.

The request preparation procedures are written as follows:

```
prepare_swapout_request(i,req) --i = process to swap out
  case State[i] of
    ready:remove(i.ready_q);     --cannot be selected
            State[i]:=transit1;
    blocked:State[i]:=transit2;
  endcase;
  with req do
    mode:=write;
    zone:=Zone[i];
    dadd:=Dadd[i];
    n:=Length[i];
    p:=i
  endwith

prepare_load_request(i,z,req)    --load process i
                                 --into zone z
  State[i]:=transit1;
  proc[z]:=i;
  with req do
    mode:=read;
    zone:=z;
    dadd:=Dadd[i];
    n:=Length[i];
    p:=i
  endwith
```

For the system to operate correctly, requests have to be handled sequentially: the load request can only be executed once swap out has been completed.

We can now give the details of process *transfer_disk*.

```
process transfer_disk

  loop
    reqqueue.collect(req) --causes suspension if the queue is empty
    disk.exchange(req)    --execution of transfer
    acknowledge_req(req)--transfer complete
  endloop
```

The procedure *acknowledge_req* carries out the management operations necessary after execution of a transfer. These operations are different for loading and swap out.

```
acknowledge_req(req)

  i:=req.p                    --process number
  if req.mode=read then
    Zone[i]:=req.zone;
    State[i]:=ready;
    add(i,ready_q)
  else
    case State[i] of
      transit1:State[i]:=loadable;
      transit2:State[i]:=swapped out;
    endcase;
    Zone[i]:=nil
  endif
```

Finally, handling of the end of timeslice interrupt leads to reallocation of the processor to the next eligible process in the queue. Moreover, if there is a loadable process (this has to be a process which was swapped out while it was ready), procedure *load* issues a request for it to be loaded..

To ensure that the system's state variables remain coherent, all procedures handling these variables are executed under mutual exclusion, either in a monitor, or in the body of an interrupt handler or a supervisor call.

Various extensions to the simple system just described above are proposed in the exercises.

10.2 A paging virtual memory system

10.2.1 General organization

We shall now consider a paging virtual memory system. We shall start by describing its overall structure, and then go on to describe in detail the main decisions to be taken concerning the memory management policy adopted, before going into detail on algorithms and data structures.

10.2.1.1 Basic assumptions

1. Hardware

a. The machine is a monoprocessor.

b. The virtual memory is linear (single segment) and uses single-level paging, with a table of pages in memory.

c. Secondary memory is a disk managed by a channel.

2. System organization

a.The system is essentially used interactively (terminals), but will also handle background jobs of lower priority.

b. The allocation unit (job or user) is defined as an association between a single process and a single virtual memory.

c. The cpu is allocated in timeslices, using the round robin algorithm.

d. Memory is allocated by pages on request.

e. The degree of multiprogramming is monitored by a load control mechanism.

This overall pattern is representative of a large class of time-sharing systems. For example, the organization described here is approximately that of the VMS system on the DEC VAX computer [Levy 82], which itself has many features in common with the experimental system Esope [Bétourné 70]. The presentation below does not set out to describe a particular system faithfully: there are variants for the different algorithms, the most interesting of which are examined.

10.2.1.2 Memory management

Here we shall consider on the one hand the organization of virtual memory and the link between virtual memory and files, and on the other hand the policy adopted for managing physical memory and for load control.

1. Organization of virtual memory

We shall assume that the virtual memory is linear and there is no internal relocation mechanism (such as base registers). Executable programs (produced by a loader) therefore contain absolute virtual addresses and must be placed in fixed locations in virtual memory.

Files, the permanent information storage units, are held in secondary memory. To access information contained in a file, the file first has to be loaded into virtual memory. A priori, it is therefore possible to transfer information as necessary between files and virtual memory; this means that we operate as though we were working with a physical memory. In this mode of operation, there are consequently two types of information exchanges between main memory and secondary memory:

- Transfers due to paging, i.e. due to the representation of virtual memory pages by frames in physical memory. In general terms, each virtual memory then has an image of the disk, containing all the pages in that memory (at least for the pages used). At any moment, a subset of these pages is contained in the frames of physical memory. Transfers are controlled by the physical memory allocation mechanism.

- Transfers resulting from exchanges between files and virtual memory. These transfers are similar to input-output operations.

The coexistence of these two types of exchange poses delicate problems for avoiding interference. For example, if a file is being read, the virtual memory pages to which it has been copied must remain in physical memory until the end of reading: the frames they occupy must not be reallocated.

One way of avoiding these problems is to impose a single method of exchange between main memory and disk. In this method, all information is held permanently in a file, and every item of information is assigned a location in secondary memory. Files are broken down into items of the size of a page. To access an item in a file, it is associated with a virtual memory page, which in a sense forms an addressing window; at the same time, the page is marked as being 'absent'. The first time this page is accessed, the page fault mechanism detects its absence and causes the item to be loaded from the file in question. This method, whose implementation is described below, is called **coupling** or **file mapping**. It attempts, to a certain degree, to simulate segmented addressing (where files play the role of segments), without a segmenting mechanism.

2. *Physical memory management*

We shall define two levels for physical memory management: the management of frames at a constant level of multiprogramming (frame acquisition or swapping), and load control (adjustments to the degree of multiprogramming). Such control takes place by estimating the size of the working set for each process (see section 9.6).

We shall start by defining the current space for each process: this is the number of frames occupied by the process's pages at any moment. We assume that every page belongs specifically to a process; the case of shared pages will be examined separately. For each process, the current space can reach a maximum size specified by *npmax* (measured as a number of frames). While its current space has not reached that maximum, the process may require frames by selecting them from among the free frames; once the maximum level has been reached, there are two possible solutions:

a. The process may be required to carry out replacement within its current space.

b. The process may be 'swapped out' and its *npmax* readjusted.

Solution a. is that used in the VAX/VMS system: a process whose current space has reached the maximum size specified must free a frame at each new page fault. Freed frames are nonetheless recoverable in memory, as long as they have not been reallocated (see section 10.2.4.2). The system guarantees a minimum size for the stock of free frames, making it possible to smooth out peaks caused by rapid and temporary growth in the size of a working set. Primitives allow a process to modify its own *npmax*, within limits specified by the system.

Solution b is that used by the EMAS system. Each process belongs to a category characterized by a maximum memory occupation level *npmax* and a maximum memory residence time *tmax*. A process changes category as specified by fixed transition rules, according to its observed behavior. Categories associated with a high demand for resources are penalized by having a reduced priority for memory access.

In all cases, when a process is 'swapped out' from memory (i.e. it ceases to participate in multiprogramming) the system stores the composition of its current space; the process may not be reloaded into memory unless there are sufficient free frames to receive the pages of that current space. If necessary, frames are freed by swapping out one or several processes.

10.2.2 Job cycle

10.2.2.1 States of a process

The states of a process can be deduced from the resource allocation pattern above:

1. The allocation of a processor distinguishes between two states (active and ready), as indicated in chapter 5.

2. The allocation of memory makes it possible, in the first place, to distinguish between processes involved in multiprogramming (i.e. which have pages loaded into memory and are participating in processor allocation) and the others. The concern to ensure good use memory usage leads to its being used to hold only those processes likely to be executed, i.e. those which are not blocked. A more detailed analysis shows the need to distinguish two main causes of blocking in a time-sharing system.

- Waiting due to a page fault, whose duration is of the same order as a transfer between memory and disk
- Waiting due to user thinking time, whose mean duration (expressed in seconds) is very much greater than that of transfers between memory and disk

This leads to our distinguishing between processes waiting for a page, which conserve the pages already loaded into memory, and those blocked for another cause, whose pages are eliminated from memory. The corresponding states are 'page wait' and 'blocked'.

3. Finally, load control, which acts on the degree of multiprogramming, leads to defining a state, 'memory wait', which is that of a process which has not been blocked, but cannot be allowed into memory as there is insufficient space.

The pattern emerging from this analysis is shown in fig. 10.2.

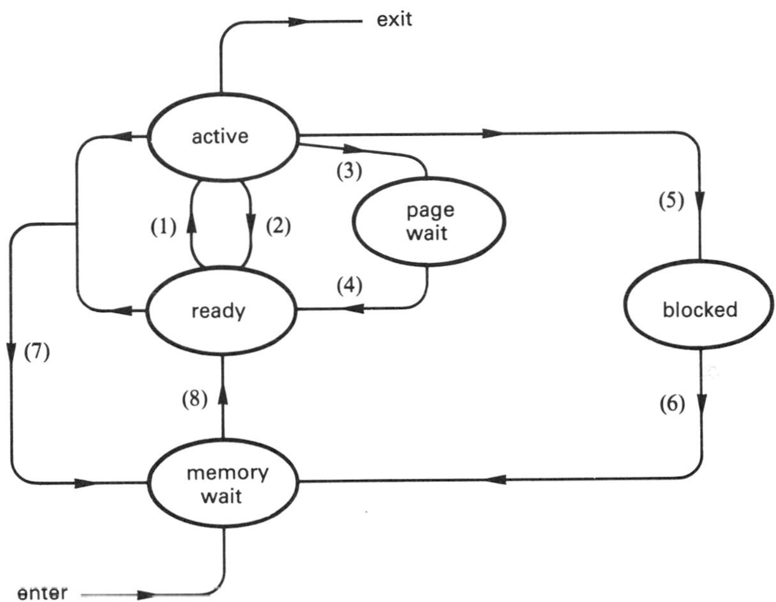

Fig. 10.2. A process cycle in a virtual memory system

10.2.2.2 Events and transitions

State transitions are always triggered either by an external event giving rise to an interrupt (clock, end of input-output, etc.), or by a call to the system kernel, programmed by the user (supervisor call) or triggered automatically (trap). Furthermore, one transition may cause another: for example, the suspension of an active process leads to a new process being selected, etc.

The various transitions between states can be classified by their causes:

Transition	Operation	Triggering event
1	Processor allocation	Clock interrupt
2		(1),(3),(5)
3	Paging	Page fault (trap)
4		Page return (interrupt)
5	Suspension	Supervisor call *(wait)*
6	Blocking Activation	Supervisor call *(signal)*
7	Memory flushing	(depends on control algorithm)
8	Memory loading	(6),(7),(5)

10.2.3 System data structures

10.2.3.1 Process table and queues

A process is named by a number assigned to it on its creation and which defines an entry in a process table, resident in memory. Each entry in the process table has the following fields:

- Storage zone of the status word
- Storage zone of registers
- Process state
- Chaining links in the queue

Two queues are defined:

- The queue for processes loaded in memory, or current processes (processes that are ready or waiting for a page). The active process is selected from amongst those eligible, using the algorithm described in section 10.2.4.1.
- The queue of processes which are waiting to be loaded into memory according to the algorithm described in section 10.2.4.2.

Global variables are also defined, which are pointers in the process table, and which indicate:

- The active process
- The head of the current process queue
- The head of the 'memory wait' process queue

10.2.3.2 File location tables

Each open file has a table which describes its physical location. This table is present in memory when the file is open; a pointer in the file descriptor allows it to be accessed. Each file is broken down into items of the size of a page, and the physical location of the file is defined by the addresses of these items. The location table contains a disk address for each file item and, if a copy of the item is present in memory, the number of the frame where it is loaded.

10.2.3.3 Virtual page tables

Each process has a table which describes the organization of its virtual space. This table is named by a base register (base of the page table) which is part of the context of a process and which is therefore loaded when the process is activated. This table has an entry for each virtual page *vp* containing the following fields:

```
presence bit            present[vp]
write bit               dirty[vp]
frame number            frame[vp]
page protection         prot[vp]
state of page coupling
    file number fn[vp]       (nil if page is not coupled)
    item number in[vp]
```

The fields *present[vp]* and *frame[vp]* are directly interpreted by the dynamic address translation mechanism, described in chapter 9 and which has the following form:

```
virtual address=(vp,d);      --(page no, displacement)
if present[vp]=1 then
   physical address:=(frame[vp],d)
else
   <page fault trap>
endif
```

Handling of page fault traps is discussed in section 10.3.4.2. It consists of checking whether the page is present in memory (we shall see that that may be true even if *present[vp]*=0), and to ask for it to be loaded from disk otherwise.

10.2.3.4 Physical page tables and queues

In the same way as for processes, states can be defined for memory frames, based on their allocation.

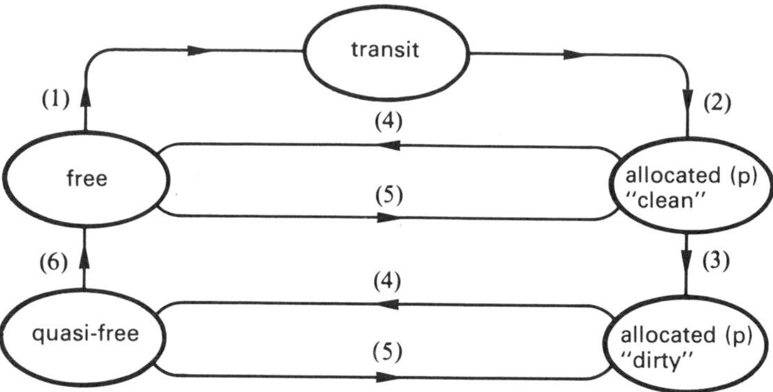

Fig. 10.3. State of locations

The first stage is to distinguish between a free frame and a frame allocated to a process *p*. This distinction is however insufficient, for two reasons:

1. The transfer time between disk and memory is high with respect to the instruction execution cycle; a frame is not therefore immediately usable after it is allocated (contents have to be loaded into it), but it is no longer free. The 'transit' state covers this situation.

2. It is useful to distinguish between frames whose contents have not been modified since they were last loaded (and which therefore have an exact copy on disk) and those which have been modified, whose disk copy is therefore out of date (or may not exist). This distinction applies equally to frames allocated to a process (which are classified as 'clean' or 'dirty') and to unallocated frames (which are classified as 'free' and 'quasi-free'). Figure 10.3 summarizes this discussion.

Transition	Event
1	Page fault (with allocation)
2	End of read from disk
3	First write
4	Freeing of memory
5	Page recovery
6	End of copy to disk

Each entry in the frame table contains the following fields:

- State of frame *state*
- Last item to which the frame was allocated *(FN,IN)*

- Last process to which the frame was allocated *p*
- Chaining links in frame queues *(succ,pred)*

10.2.4 Algorithms

10.2.4.1 Processor allocation

It should be remembered that the allocation of the processor involves two mechanisms: the dispatcher, which carries out the actual allocation (activation of the selected process) and the scheduler, which handles the sharing algorithm.

The dispatcher algorithm (procedure *allocate_processor*) is slightly different from the one described in chapter 5. The dispatcher is called at the end of each sequence executed under system control (interrupt program, trap handling, supervisor call), and allocates the processor to the first ready process in the current queue (remember that this queue is never empty). The process context, saved after its last transition into the active state or initialized after its creation, is loaded into the corresponding registers of the processor. This context includes, among other things, the base register of the page table; the virtual address transition mechanism therefore always acts on the virtual space of the active process. The scheduler, which handles allocation of the processor to eligible processes, is based on the round robin method (see section 8.3.1). This algorithm is implemented by:

1. Procedures for managing the current process queue; this is a queue managed on 'first come, first served' basis. It is useful to organize it as a circular queue, with a pointer *active_proc* indicating the active process. The procedure

add(p,current_q)

adds process *p* to the end of the queue (immediately before the active process); the function

next(p,current_q)

indicates the successor to *p*; the procedure

remove(p,current_q)

removes process *p* from the current process queue.

2. The handling of clock interrupts marking the end of a timeslice. The following operations are carried out:

handling end of timeslice interrupt:

```
set_clock(q)     --q = timeslice
allocate_processor
```

The dispatcher algorithm *(allocate_processor)* can be written:

```
p:=active_proc;
repeat
  p:=next(p,current_q)
until State[p]=ready;
active_proc:=p;
load_registers(reg[active_proc]);
load_psw (psw[active_proc]);
```

10.2.4.2 Page fault

A page fault takes place when the mechanism for access (using the page table) to a page *vp* of the selected process finds that the presence bit *present[vp]* is set to 0. This does not necessarily mean the corresponding page is absent from memory; it may in fact have been loaded, and then freed during an earlier activity sequence, and the frame containing it may still appear in the queue of free or quasi-free frames. If this is the case, the page should be recovered, and the process immediately moved into the eligible state. This reduces the number of transfers.

If the page is not present in memory, a frame has to be found in which to load it and a request has to be submitted for the corresponding transfer to be carried out; the format of requests and their handling will be examined later. The process moves into the 'page wait' state; it will become ready again once the missing page has been loaded (acknowledgement of the request).

The page fault handling algorithm can therefore be written:

```
page fault (virtual page vp, process p)

recover(vp);
if page absent then
  allocate_frame(frame);          --frame = number of the frame
                                           allocated
  prepare_request(req,read);  --update tables
  req_queue.deposit(req);
  State[p]:=page wait
endif;
allocate_processor;
```

The recovery algorithm consults the entry concerning the item associated with *vp* in the location table of the corresponding file. If the item is shown to be present, the frame containing it may be recovered; otherwise, the virtual page is missing. The recovered frame may be free, quasi-free, or (in the case of a shared file item) allocated to another process. Note that, in the latter case, the page may also be in transit; it will be marked 'present' in the location table (to prevent requests for it to be reloaded), but the process will not become ready until the request is acknowledged. This case is detected by consulting the physical page table.

The procedure *allocate_frame* allocates a frame to the requesting process and updates the tables in consequence:

```
remove(frame,free_queue);      --free_queue not empty
FN[frame]:=nil;
IN[frame]:=nil;
```

The file item previously contained in the frame now allocated is no longer accessible.

A request for a page transfer includes the following information:

- *m:* transfer mode (disk read or write)
- *fn:* frame number
- *dadd:* address of the page on disk
- *file,item:* identity of the item transferred
- *p:* identity of the requesting process

The procedure *prepare_request(req,mode)* constructs the request and updates the tables:

```
if mode=read then
  FN[frame]:=fn[vp];
  IN[frame]:=in[vp]
endif;
with req do
  m:=mode;
  fn:=frame;
  file:=FN[frame];
  item:=IN[frame];
  dadd:=<address of item(file,item)>;
endwith
state[frame]:=transit
```

The monitor *req_queue* manages the request queue. A call to procedure *req_queue.deposit* adds the transfer request to those already waiting.

Page transfer requests have two sources. Read requests are issued during page faults, as we have just seen. Write requests are issued in order to save the contents of a quasi-free frame before it is reallocated; the conditions governing the issue of such requests are discussed in the next section.

10.2.4.3 Management of main memory

We shall describe in turn the flushing and loading of a process into memory, and then the management of free frame queues. We shall start by presenting a general outline in which page transfers take place strictly on demand; we shall then go on to consider the possibility of anticipating transfers.

1. Swapping out a process

A process swap out is triggered by one of the following causes:

- Blocking or termination of the active process
- An action taken by the load control mechanism

If we write *p* for the swapped out process, the action to carry out is as follows:

- Chain the 'clean' frames occupied by *p* to the queue of free frames
- Chain the 'dirty' frames occupied by *p* to the queue of quasi-free frames
- *State[p]:=blocked* or *ready* or *nil* (depending on the cause of swapping)
- *remove(p,current_q)*
- *allocate_processor* (new active process)

2. Loading a process

It should be remembered that a process can only be loaded into memory if these are sufficient frames available to receive its current space. If loading has taken place for the first time, a default value is used for that space.

If pages are not pre-loaded, the 'loading' of a process into memory simply means inserting the process into the current process queue, without any transfer operation taking place, except transfer of the virtual page table if it is not resident in memory. The presence bits of all the pages in this table are reset to 0. When the process is activated, access to virtual pages leads by the page fault mechanisms to the allocation of frames and loading into memory of the necessary pages (or their recovery, if appropriate). The case of pre-loading will be examined later.

3. Management of available frames

The available frames include free and quasi-free frames, which are held in two separate queues. A free frame may be allocated immediately, but a quasi-free frame must first be saved to disk. It is therefore an advantage to have sufficient free frames to avoid delaying frame allocation after a page fault. This can be provided for by imposing by a lower limit on the number of free frames: if the number of frames falls below this limit (after allocating a frame), a request is prepared to save a number of quasi-free frames to disk, making them free immediately after the transfer. The appropriate parameters (minimum number of free frames, number of frames transferred, etc.) have to be determined by experience.

4. Anticipated transfers

In a policy based on supplying pages strictly on request, pages are transferred into main memory only when a page fault takes place; in the same way, a page is only copied to disk once the frame containing it is reallocated. Most systems use such a policy, at least for loading: experience suggests that, under normal operating conditions, the risk of losing performance by incorrect prediction is high (the cost of a page preloaded in error includes both memory space and transfer time). The VAX/VMS system, however, uses a form of preloading: when a page fault takes place, the missing page is not loaded alone, but is accompanied by a 'cluster' of nearby pages in virtual space; during saving, pages are also copied in clusters, if possible into contiguous locations on disk to accelerate transfers. The system's designers justify this approach on the basis of the small size of VAX pages. The size of page clusters is a system parameter (determined in practice and subject to variation depending on the virtual space considered).

10.2.4.4 Management of exchanges

Exchanges between memory and disk are managed by a separate process, which we shall call *disk_transfer*, with an algorithm along the following lines:

```
loop
  req_queue.remove(request_list);     --wait if queue is empty
  reorder(request_list);
  disk.exchange(request_list);        --await interrupt
  acknowledge(request_list)
endloop
```

The monitor *disk* is a peripheral management monitor analogous to that described in chapter 4. The procedure *disk.exchange* constructs the program for the channel corresponding to the execution of a list of requests. It then chooses execution of the program and suspends the calling process until the end of transfer interrupt is received. The process *disk_transfer* therefore has two waiting points, corresponding to the two monitor calls.

1. Waiting for the page transfer request to be deposited (procedure *remove* is blocking if the request queue is empty)
2. Waiting for reception of the interrupt indicating the end of transfer

To summarize, the process *disk_transfer* groups together pending requests if there are any, constructs the corresponding program for the channel, and starts its execution. If no requests are waiting, the process is suspended and waits for new requests to be deposited.

Note that requests are reordered to execute transfers in the order that disk sectors move under the read-write disks (see section 8.3.2); nevertheless, two transfers concerning the same frame must be executed in the order in which they have been requested, if one of them involves a write.

The procedure *acknowledge(request list)* carries out the following operations for each request executed:

- For pages to be read:

```
state[frame]                :=allocated(clean)
State[requesting.proc]      :=ready
```

- For pages being written:

```
state[frame]                :=free
```

This completes our general presentation of the system. The handling of various addition points is discussed in the exercises.

10.3 Bibliographic notes

Memory management techniques in multiprogrammed systems using virtual memory are illustrated using characteristic examples in the following studies: Multics [Bensoussan 72], Tenex [Bobrow 72], Esope [Bétourné 70 and 71], EMAS [Whitfield 73, Rees 82], VM 370 [Scherr 73, Auslander 81], VAX-VMS [Levy 82, Kenah 84].

Exercises

Exercise 10.1

Give the program for procedures *read* and *write* in monitor *term[i]* which manages input-output by lines on a terminal (section 10.1.2.2.):

1. With characters typed being simply echoed
2. With rudimentary editing facilities

The interface of the terminal controller is as specified in section 3.2.2.2 (procedures *input_char* and *output_char*).

Exercise 10.2

Supplement the programs requested in the preceding exercise by giving the program handling the character *BREAK*, which allows a user to take over control of a process directly.

Exercise 10.3

Specify the necessary data structures for managing free zones and context blocks in the fixed partition system described in section 10.1. Write the programs for procedures *find_free_zone* and *choose_swappable_process* specified in section 10.1.2.4.

Exercise 10.4

Assume you want to set up a fixed partition system on a machine with no relocation mechanism. A process is therefore preassigned to a zone during loading, and can only be reloaded into that zone.

Basing yourself on the general system outline described in section 10.1, construct the program for this system.

Exercise 10.5

Within the system described in section 10.1, a process which takes input from the terminal will never be blocked, and can never be swapped out, but occupies a zone permanently.

Modify the system to avoid that risk, specifying a maximum memory residence time for each process. Construct the new transition graph and modify the programs and data structures accordingly. **Hint:** The maximum residence time can be expressed as an integer number of timeslices. The corresponding checking procedure can therefore take place at the end of each slice.

Exercise 10.6

Modify the fixed partition system described in section 10.1 to take account of priorities assigned to processes, under the following two assumptions:

1. Priority only applies to processor allocation.
2. Priority applies to memory allocation as well (a ready process can be swapped out to make space for a higher priority process).

Exercise 10.7

The fixed partition system described in section 10.1 now contains three sizes of zones (large, medium or small).

1. Modify the system programs, on the assumption that a process is always loaded into a zone corresponding to the size of its program.
2. To increase system throughput, we shall allow a process to be loaded into a larger zone than it needs, if there are no swappable processes in a zone corresponding to its size. Modify the programs accordingly.
3. Under what conditions will the policy defined in 2) lead to a risk of starvation? How can that risk be avoided?

Exercise 10.8

We have to specify the necessary mechanisms for coupling files in virtual memory.

1. Specify the necessary data structures, including the file mapping tables (remember that a file is defined as a sequence of items of the size of one page).

2. Specify the effect and the parameters of a primitive *couple* which associates a file item with a virtual page. Examine the interaction between this primitive and other file access primitives. What protection mechanisms need to be implemented? Is a primitive *uncouple* necessary?

Exercise 10.9

In the virtual memory system described in section 10.2, input-output is managed by a system process which has its own virtual memory. Show how the programming of this process can be simplified using the coupling mechanism.

Exercise 10.10

In the virtual memory system described in section 10.2, we assume that the operating system is assigned a fixed zone in the virtual memory of each user. How can this arrangement be used:

- To ease communication between the user and the operating system
- To ease communication between two users by means of a mailbox

Exercise 10.11

How can the principle of the global allocation of memory to processes be modified to take account of sharing of certain pages by several processes in the system described in section 10.2?

Exercise 10.12

Suggest a way of implementing a restriction concerning the maximum time a process can be resident in memory, within the system described in section 10.2.

Exercise 10.13 [Whitfield 73, Rees 82]

This exercise concerns the load control method implemented in the EMAS system (see section 10.2.1.2). Each of the multiprogrammed processes is associated with a category, identified by a number. The following parameters are associated with each category:

npmax :maximum memory space occupied (number of frames)
Tmax :maximum memory residence time (number of timeslices)
prio :priority for admission to memory
trans_np :new category in case *npmax* is exceeded
trans_T :new category in case *Tmax* is exceeded

The 'transitions' *trans_np* and *trans_T* specify the number and new category assigned to the process if *npmax* or *Tmax*, respectively, is exceeded.

1. Suggest an experimental method to define parameters for categories. According to the type of job in question, what in your opinion is a 'reasonable' combination of *npmax* and *Tmax*? How should priorities and transitions be assigned? How can starvation be avoided?

2. The transitions specified allow a process to move into a category corresponding to a higher demand for resources. How should the inverse transitions be implemented (how can you 'demote' a process which is well below the maximum allocation levels for its category)?

3. Suggest an outline for the implementation mechanisms. Specify the necessary data structures, the handling of page faults and the handling of end of timeslice interrupts.

Chapter 11
Distributed systems

A **distributed computer system** is made up of a collection of computers and peripherals linked to each other by a communication system allowing them to exchange information. Depending on the nature of the communication system, and more precisely on the degree of interconnection it provides, we generally distinguish between **multiprocessors**, where communication generally uses a common memory, and **computer networks**. In common with general usage we shall use the word *distributed* only for the latter type of system. The design of such systems poses new problems, which have only been partially resolved to date, and is the subject of intense research and experimental work. This chapter is an introduction to a study of these problems.

11.1 Introduction

11.1.1 Why distributed systems?

Between 1970 and 1980, there was a major reduction in the cost of processors and memory, and a significant increase in their performance levels. The most obvious consequence of this development was the penetration of data processing into major areas of activity, in particular through microcomputers, whose power now exceeds that of the largest computers of 30 years ago. For many applications, a terminal with access to a time-sharing system can be replaced, at lower cost, by a microcomputer, which has the important advantage of being able to guarantee availability and good performance levels thanks to the independent management of its resources. Nevertheless, such a replacement does also have disadvantages:

1. The characteristics of microcomputers prevent their using applications with a high demand for in memory or cpu time.

2. The secondary memory of a microcomputer is of limited capacity and the risk of its contents being corrupted is significant.

3. Communication and sharing of data between users, allowed by time-sharing systems, are no longer possible.

These considerations explain the development of distributed systems interconnecting individual workstations and specialized servers by means of a high throughput communication network. Each client in such a system has access to a workstation on which he executes the bulk of his current jobs. Shared servers provide specialized services: reliable storage of large volumes of information, the use of powerful processors, high quality printer output, all of which are too costly to be provided individually to each client. The network allows clients to access servers and to communicate with each other.

This development was made possible by technical progress in data transmission, allowing the construction of reliable and efficient *communication systems* providing all the services necessary for the communication of information. Communication systems are described in section 11.1.2.

The considerations that led to the development of distributed computer systems can be summarized as follows:

- *Communication* needs leading most notably to the interconnection of existing applications, developed independently, to form a single integrated system.
- The desire to *increase availability* in a computer system, by allowing the immediate replacement of a failed component by an equivalent component: this mode of operations requires permanent communication between the system components and a software mechanism designed to handle reconfiguration and restarts in cases of accident.
- The desire to *share resources* by holding the most expensive resources in common, with the possibility of distributing load by program or data transfers.
- The desire to *adapt the structure of a computer system to that of the application it is handling*: this is notably the case of industrial process control systems (so called 'real time' systems) where it is common these days to associate one or several processors with each element of the system controlled; overall management of the whole system, as well as the availability considerations already mentioned, make communication between processors and appropriate software absolutely necessary.

It is interesting to note that the distribution of the elements of a system, for a given level of total processing power, is not the most economic solution, from the point of view of the usage made of that processing power: the effects of *concentrating resources* (see the example given in section 8.2.3) favour a centralized solution, from this strict point of view. Nevertheless, this economic aspect is no longer the only consideration at stake, as computing power is not as critical a resource today as it was in the past: considerations of availability or of adaptation to the structure of an application may lead to decentralizing the functionality of a system between a large number of specialized processors, accepting that some of them will be idle for most of the time. The concentration effect remains a factor, on the other hand, for large peripherals (file servers or printers) and for certain processors (large array processors), whose cost has fallen far less than that of current processors and main memories.

11.1.2 Characteristics of distributed systems

The major characteristics of distributed systems can be summarized as follows:

1. The absence of common memory means that it is impossible to define an overall state for the system by means of a set of shared variables. The absence of a common clock and the variations that may occur in message transmission times mean that two observers linked to two different elements of a system may have a different perception of the state of a third element and of the order of events occuring on it.
2. Distributed systems generally display a high degree of real parallelism.
3. Two factors increase the risks of failure compared to centralized systems: the high number of components, and the fact that the reliability of communication systems is generally lower than that of the computer systems they interconnect. Moreover, the specifications of distributed systems require a high level of availability. Consequently, mechanisms allowing the effects of failures to be reduced or eliminated (restart after breakdown, reconfiguration, etc.) play a major role in distributed systems.

11.1.3 Brief history of distributed systems

Distributed systems were implemented very early (at the end of the 50s) for surveillance systems (SAGE), or for reserving aircraft seats (SABRE system). These were specialized applications, where exchanges of data took place under the control of the application.

The end of the 60s saw the launching of projects on general wide area networks, the first of which was ARPANET. These projects gave rise to the development of packet switching techniques, and the first protocols, notably for file transfer, which were the basis of the earliest applications.

In the mid-70s, the experimental network developed at the Xerox Research Centre at Palo Alto (PARC) was something of a milestone, as it introduced several fundamental concepts: the principle of a high throughput local network, using a broadcasting bus (Ethernet), powerful individual workstations with bit-map screens, and client-server organization for access to shared resources such as files or printers. Other local area network techniques, using ring structures, began to emerge at the same time.

Apart from systems of the client-server type, the first distributed systems which appeared at the end of the 70s using local area networks were above all based on the interconnection of homogenous systems, notably Unix systems. Most of them simply extended the file management system; others introduced the creation and execution of remote processes.

The first integrated systems, designed to be distributed from the outset, appeared at the beginning of the 80s. Most were experimental systems, providing better knowledge of the problems associated with distribution, particularly reliability, synchronization and execution control, as well as resource allocation. Around 1985, several integrated distributed systems became available commercially, but many design problems have still to be resolved. At the same time, the reliability and performance levels of communications systems have improved, notably through the use of new communication techniques such as fibre optics and satellite transmission. Packet switching remains the technique used by nearly all commercial wide area networks. Work on distributed systems today intending to concentrate on defining fundamental concepts more closely (particularly for fault tolerance, security and languages for parallelism), and also on the development of very large-scale distributed systems (several thousand stations), built up by interconnecting local area networks. Finally, new types of systems with a high degree of parallelism, using a large number of processors interconnected by specialized links, are beginning to be explored.

This chapter is organized as follows: section 11.2 gives a brief overview of communication systems. The functions of a distributed operating system, and the main structures used, are described in section 11.3. The principal problems introduced by distribution are discussed in section 11.4; some of them are extensions of those posed by centralized systems, others are new. Finally, a few brief case studies of typical systems are given in section 11.5.

11.2 Communication systems

11.2.1 Functions of a communication system

We use the term **communication link** for a device which can be used for the transmission of information between two or more entities (physical devices, programs, processes, users, etc.). In distributed computer systems, communication links, like the systems themselves, are generally organized into a hierarchy of layers, on a similar model to that described in section 3.1. Each of these layers implements a particular level of abstraction, allowing communication between entities defined at that level. In what follows, we shall apply the term 'communication link' only to the medium used for the physical transmission of information, while more complex links built up at higher levels will be called **communication systems**.

The elementary communication operation is defined as the transmission of a data item, called a **message**, from a **sender** to one or more **receivers**. The basic primitives of the communication system are therefore:

send(message,receiver)
receive(message,sender)

Systems can be distinguished by the way the sender and receiver are named, the synchronization provided for by the primitives, the form of messages, the way that they are forwarded, how reliable transmission is, the nature and performance levels of links, etc. Various examples of communication primitives were discussed in section 4.4.3, for the particular case of communication between two processes.

Apart from these basic primitives, communication systems provide other functions, including:

- Making or breaking a permanent link between two partners (such a link, sometimes called a virtual circuit, makes it possible to transmit a stream of messages without having to name the receiver explictly)
- Transcoding of information (to ensure confidentiality or suitability for particular physical devices)

A communication system is characterized by:

- The services it provides, defined by the functional specifications of its interface
- Its performance levels: throughput, error rate (mean and deviation) and behaviour as a function of load

11.2.2 Interfaces and protocols

The **interface** of a communication system is defined, like interfaces for any system, by specifying the functions it provides to users. Such a specification forms a set of 'operating instructions' for the system, containing all the information necessary for its use, independently of how it is implemented.

The way a communication system's functions are implemented is called a **protocol**. A protocol is distinguished from a procedure by the fact that it involves at least two entities, the two communicating partners. In a hierarchically organized system, a protocol at level $i>1$ uses the interface provided by the communication system at level $i-1$. This protocol provides for communication between entities defined at level i; but this is in fact virtual communication, with actual communication taking place, for each partner, with entities defined locally at level $i-1$. In all cases, the physical transmission of information takes place at level 1, the base level.

Example: Figure 11.1 shows a simple communication system organized in three layers, each of which uses the interface of the immediately lower layer to implement its own functions. The message communication layer, built up over the physical communication interface, provides primitives making it possible to transmit messages of limited size between sites, defined by their physical location. These primitives are used by a file transfer protocol, which allows users to transmit files to each other, without knowing where they are. This protocol therefore implements the correspondence between user names and their physical addresses, as well as the

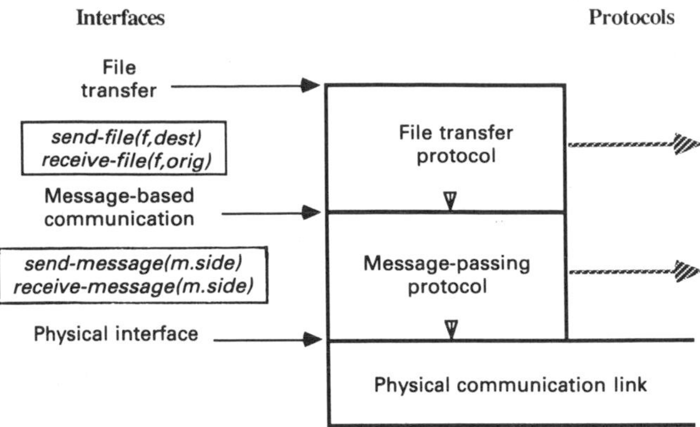

Fig. 11.1. A hierarchy of interfaces and protocols

decomposition of a file into elementary messages and their reassembly on arrival. The two functions may be separated into two distinct layers to allow other protocols to take advantage of the conversion service between names and addresses.

The advantages of such a hierarchical structure were presented in section 3.1:

- It provides a clear overall structure for the system, stressing precisely identified functions, and restricting information exchanges between levels to the bare minimum necessary.
- Functions are separated, allowing the operation of each layer to be independent from the internal structure of the others.

In the case of communication systems, a very important advantage is the possibility of defining **standardized interfaces and protocols** at each level. A new hardware device or a new subsystem may therefore be connected with an existing system, at any level, on condition that the standards applying to communication at that level are respected. Such standards have been defined by computer manufacturers, and by international standards organizations such as the ISO and CCITT.

By way of example, the ISO (International Standards Organization) has set up a reference model for describing interconnection between open systems (the 'Open Systems Interconnection' or OSI), which defines seven communication levels, whose functions we shall describe very briefly (see fig. 11.2):

1. **Physical layer**. Protocols at the physical level have the function of transmitting information (made up of a bit sequence) on the communication line. Standards must define the conventions for bit representation, for

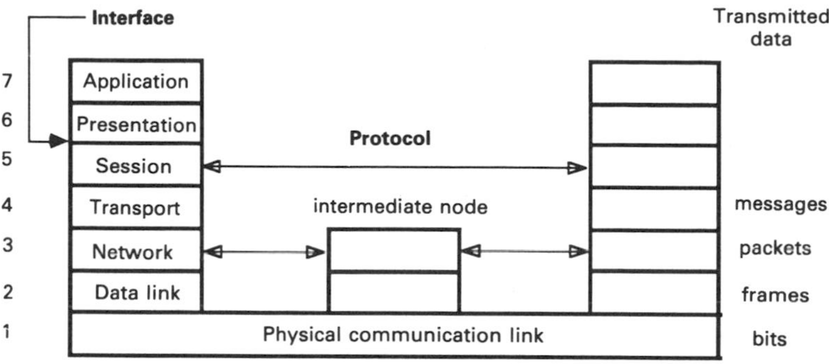

Fig. 11.2. The ISO reference model for Open Systems Interconnection

transmission synchronization, and for establishing or breaking communication; they also define physical interfaces.

2. **Data link layer**. The link protocols have the function of transmitting information with guaranteed maximal error rate, smaller than that of the physical layer (**error checking**), and to provide a **flow control** mechanism, allowing the receiver to influence the message transmission rate so that it matches his processing or storage capacity. At this level, messages are called **frames**. Apart from the raw information to be transmitted, a frame contains service information to allow error detection, the sequential numbering of frames, and flow control.

3. **Network layer**. The network protocols see to routing of messages between their origin and their destination. The problems to resolve are the choice of path, or **routing**, and **load control**, intended to avoid degradation in performance due to growth in traffic. Transmission units defined at this level are generally **packets** of fixed size, obtained by breaking messages down into smaller units.

4. **Transport layer**. Transport protocols have the function of transmitting (logical) messages between users. They see to decomposition of messages into packets and their reconstitution on arrival, as well as overall error and flow control. Unlike the lower levels, they provide for **end to end** communication, without using intermediate relays. The transport interface is the one seen by distributed application programmers who are not interested in the details of internal operations for message transmission.

Two types of service are generally provided by the transport interface:

a. The **virtual circuit** service, which makes it possible to establish a permanent link between communicating systems, analogous to continuous physical communication, on which messages can be transmitted with guaranteed reliability, preserving their order, and with flow ontrol facilities. The interface primitives are opening and closure of virtual circuits, and dispatch or reception of messages over a circuit.

b. The **datagram** service, which allows dispatching of individual messages, of limited size, between a transmitter and a receiver, without having to establish a link beforehand, and with reliability limited to that of the network layer. It is not guaranteed that the order of transmission of datagrams will be conserved.

Transport protocols are implemented, on each site, by a subsystem which is often called a **transport station**.

5. **Session layer**. Session protocols use the transport interface to establish and manage communication between two processes. They are responsible in particular for naming processes and, if necessary, for checking whether they are authorized to establish a link between themselves. This layer is sometimes identified with the transport layer.

6. **Presentation layer**. The presentation layer provides functions associated with the representation of the information transmitted. Examples of such functions are encryption and decoding of messages, to ensure that applications remain confidential; compacting of information, to reduce the volume of messages and therefore transmission times and costs; the definition of **virtual terminals**, generic models whose parameters allow them to be adapted to physical terminals with a wide variety of characteristics.

7. **Application layer**. The protocol that depends on the nature of the application. Examples of common protocols are: file transfer, remote access to a time-sharing system (remote login), electronic mail, transaction management (see section 11.4.4).

The CCITT X25 standard, widely used for wide area networks, defines standardized interfaces and protocols for levels 1, 2 and 3. The link protocol used by X25 is called HDLC (High-level Data Link Control).

The designer of a layered communication system must pay close attention to performance levels. Stacking up levels increases transmission time. Furthermore, certain functions are provided at several levels and may be redundant. Look again at the example of a file transfer protocol built on top of a message communication protocol. Each of these protocols may include a separate error checking mechanism: if the information transmitted is lost or corrupted, a copy is sent again. If the mean error rate is high, it is worth implementing error checking at the message level, as then only erroneous messages are retransmitted. If the error rate is very low (which is often the case in local area networks), it may be a good idea to carry out error checking only on the file as a whole (end to end checking): in the rare instances of errors, the whole file has to be retransmitted, but time and space are saved at the message level, by eliminating error detection at that level.

11.2.3 Classification of communication systems

Communication systems can be classified according to various criteria: topology, performance, functions, etc. Our presentation will distinguish them according to their degree of interconnection, generally correlated with geographic extent and performance levels. These criteria make it possible to define three major classes of system:

- Weakly or loosely coupled systems over long distances (more than 1km, up to 10,000 km and more): **wide area networks** or **long haul networks**
- Loosely coupled networks, over small distances (10 to 1000 metre): **local area networks**
- Tightly coupled systems, over very short distances (a few metres): **multiprocessors**

11.2.3.1 Wide area networks

A wide area network (fig. 11.3) is made up of a set of switching **nodes**, linked to each other by lines. Nodes are used for routing messages, and act as the entry points to the network. To use the network, a system (or **host**) must be connected to a node. The term **site** is used for all the installations geographically located at a node; the term is often used as a synonym of host. Lines linking nodes together may be cables, direct or satellite radio links, etc. Nodes are usually implemented by clusters of mini or microcomputers.

Two classes of networks can be distinguished according to the technique used for establishing a link between two hosts:

- **Circuit switching** networks: a physical link is established in each of the

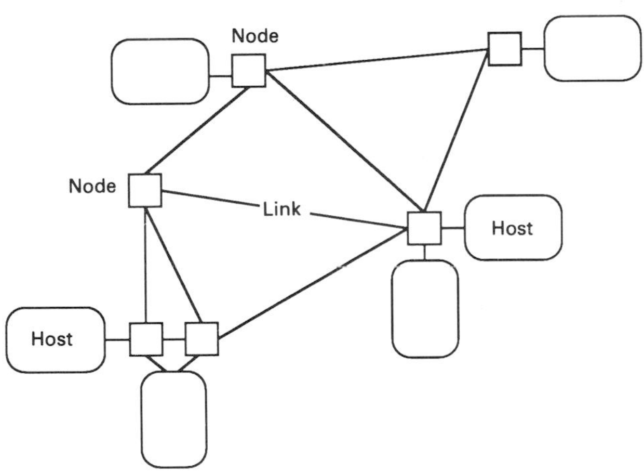

Fig. 11.3. A wide area network

intermediate nodes between the entry line and the exit line; the link lasts as long as the communication itself.

- **Data switching** networks: every line in a network can be shared by several simultaneous communications between different pairs of hosts. Sharing takes place by time multiplexing: messages belonging to independent communications may succeed each other on a given line. The vast majority of networks use this technique.

Amongst data switching networks we can distinguish:

- **Message switching** networks: the transmission unit is the logical message transmitted by one host and addressed to another.
- **Packet switching** networks: the transmission unit is a **packet** of fixed size. Messages are broken down into packets on transmission, and then built up again on reception.

Packet switching has numerous advantages, which is why it is very widely used:

- Breaking messages down into packets reduces the overall transmission time and the memory storage requirements at each node: each packet can be retransmitted towards its final destination as soon as it arrives at a node, without waiting for the rest of the message to arrive.
- Management of the buffer memories at nodes is simplified by the fact that packets are of fixed size.
- In cases of transmission errors, only the erroneous packet has to be transmitted, and not the whole message.

11.2.3.2 Local area networks

Local area networks have three characteristic properties:

- Their *small area they cover* (of the order of 10 to 1000 metres)
- Their *high throughput* (of the order of 1 to 100 Mbit/s)
- Their *integration*: a local area network is generally designed as a whole, and managed by a single organization

The most common local area networks can be divided into three classes, according to the allocation mode and the topology of the communication line: linear broadcasting networks with allocation by contention; token ring networks; slotted ring networks.

1. Linear networks with allocation by contention

This class of local area network is characterized by its topology (a linear communication line, made up of a coaxial cable or optical fibres) and its allocation mode. Figure 11.4 shows the layout of a local area network constructed around this kind of line.

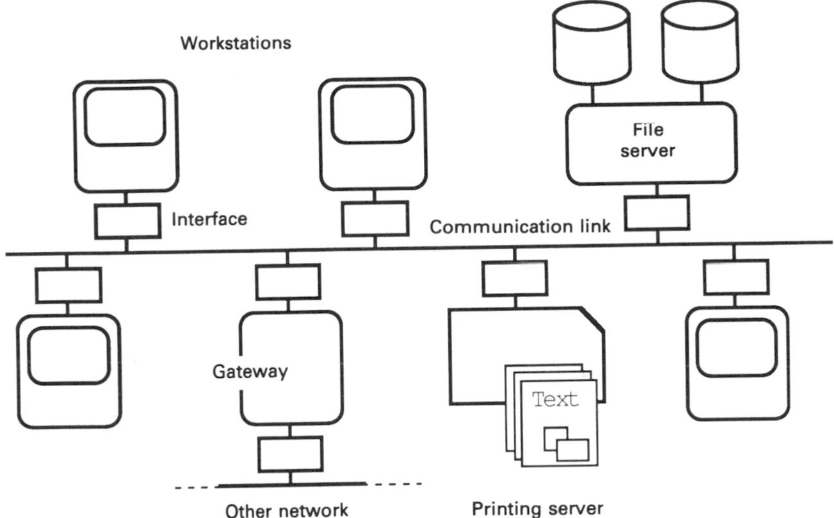

Fig. 11.4. A local area network

Line allocation is entirely decentralized. Messages (packets of fixed size) are broadcast to all hosts, which are permanently listening for them. Before transmitting a packet, a host waits for the line to be silent. Two or more hosts may then transmit simultaneously, which would lead to interference between messages. This phenomenon, called **collision**, is detected by all the senders, which receive their own messages and compare them, bit by bit, with those they transmitted. Transmission is then suspended, and the transmitter makes a new attempt after a waiting period, selected randomly to reduce the probability of a further collision. In cases of successive collisions, due to excessive load, the mean waiting time is increased, which has the side effect of allowing load control. Experience shows that, under common operating conditions, the probability of a collision occuring is in fact very small (of the order of 1%) and that the network remains lightly loaded most of the time.

A typical example of a network using this form of allocation (called CSMA/CD, for 'Carrier Sense, Multiple Access with Collision Detection') is the Ethernet network, initially developed at the Xerox Research Center. It operates at a throughput of 10 Mbit/s, with packets of 1500 bits. The interface between host and network (communicator) handles message coding, their collection by the addressee (by address recognition), and the line allocation protocol. Several branches of such a network can be linked by repeaters to form a tree structure.

2. Ring networks

In a ring network, messages travel in only one direction and are retransmitted by each node to the next. The receiver recognizes messages sent to it by their address, takes a copy of them, and retransmits them including an acknowledgement of receipt in them. After having gone all the way round the ring, a message is removed by its sender, if it has been received.

Two methods are used to allocate the line when a new message is transmitted.

a. Token ring. A message with a special configuration, called the **token** travels round the ring. Only the node which holds the token can transmit a message. It then transmits the token to its successor. A node which receives the token when it has nothing to transmit, passes it on.

b. Slotted ring. The information travelling round the network contains a number of message slots equipped with 'free' or 'busy' indicators. A node which receives a free slot can replace it with a message; the slot is then busy. Unlike the preceding case, several nodes can transmit simultaneously.

11.2.3.3 Multiprocessors

Multiprocessors generally use a common memory as their main form of communication. That memory is not necessarily formed by a single memory, but may itself be shared between several distinct units, with communication taking place by means of a bus interconnection. Each processor also generally has a local memory. The existence of a common memory makes it possible to define a global state for the system and therefore eliminates the problems met in the systems studied above.

A number of multiprocessors, most of them experimental, also use direct communication lines or channels, through which they communicate by way of messages.

11.3 Functions and structure of a distributed operating system

We can distinguish three main classes of distributed operating systems, depending on the extent to which functions associated with distribution are integrated into the operating system. This is not a rigorous classification and we have adopted it here mainly for the sake of our discussion. Case studies of representative systems are given in section 11.5.

11.3.1 Client-server systems

The client-server model of interaction, discussed in section 4.4.3.3 for the case of centralized systems, can be directly transposed to distributed systems. Historically, the first distributed systems were built on this model. A server is defined by its interface, which specifies the services it provides and the way it can be used. Clients call on these services, using the interface. All communication therefore takes place between a client and a server; a given site can play either role in turn.

For example, in a local area network such as the one shown in fig.11.4, there are two servers: a file server and a printer server. The clients are the processes executed on workstations. The file server stores a set of files, which may be private files held exclusively by certain users, or shared files. The basic primitives in its interface are transfer (in whole or in part) of a file from or to a workstation or another server. Each server is responsible locally for allocating the resources it manages; for example, the file server places requests into a queue, sees to file access synchronization, etc. A client can also request printing of a file stored on the file server. It transmits the print request to the file server, which itself plays the role of a client with respect to the printer server.

Communication between a client and a server uses two basic models: communication by messages, and remote procedure calls (see section 11.4.4). The inclusion of a machine in a distributed system of the client-server type can take place without any major modification to the operating system. Servers may be designed as centralized systems, but can also be implemented by the cooperation of several subsystems, using an approach analogous to that described in section 11.3.2.

By way of example, the organization of a file server is described in section 11.5.1.

11.3.2 Sharing resources by interconnection of homogeneous systems

In this type of system, the aim is to share a set of resources between distributed users, without placing them under the control of a single server. To simplify design, this kind of interconnection is only applied to homogeneous systems. Typically, the resources shared in this way are files, since the FMS is an easily isolated subsystem within an operating system, and file sharing can be the basis of other applications.

By way of example, we shall describe the operating principle of the 'Unix United' system implemented at the University of Newcastle-upon-Tyne to share files between a set of Unix systems. This system extends the file name space accessible in each of the host systems. To do so, the root of the directory of each host (initially named by a '/') receives a new name which names the host, and a new (virtual) root is introduced (fig. 11.5). The local naming system for files within a site (other than the root) remains the same; to access a remote site, the name of the site is used. For example (fig. 11.5), starting

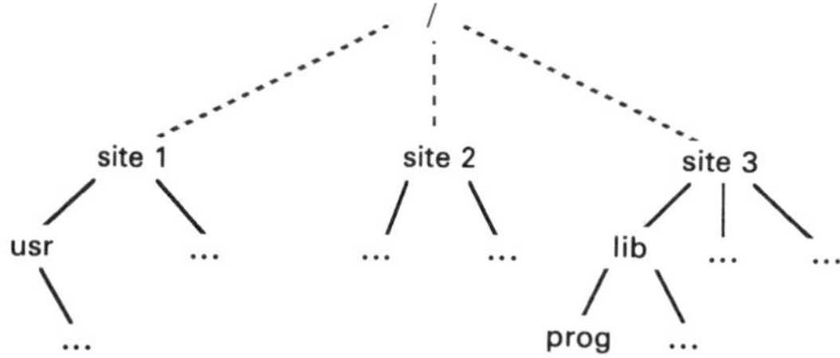

Fig. 11.5. File naming in Unix United

from the current directory *usr* on site *site1*, we can name a file on site *site3* by *../../site3/lib/prog*.

The principle underlying the implementation of this extension is simple, and uses decomposition into layers and the concept of an interface. On an isolated Unix system (fig. 11.6a) the user programs and the non-resident part of the system communicate by means of supervisor calls to the resident kernel. In interconnected systems (fig. 11.6b), a connection layer (the 'Newcastle Connection') is interposed, on each site, between the kernel and the non-resident system. It presents the upper layers with an interface identical to that of the kernel. Supervisor calls involving a remote site are intercepted by the connection layer, which communicates with the connection layers of other sites using remote procedure calls (see section 11.4.4), and allows access to files on these sites. Neither the kernel, nor the upper layers of the system are modified.

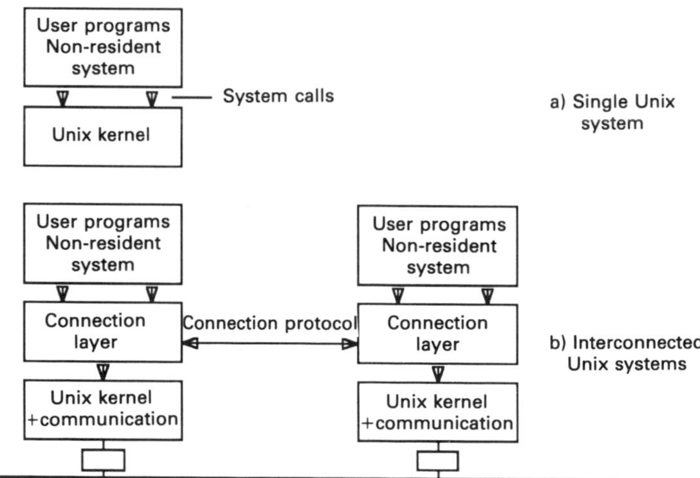

Fig. 11.6. Implementation scheme of Unix United

This system has the advantage of being simple to implement. Nevertheless, to name a remote file, we need to know the site where it is located: we say that naming is not 'transparent'. More complex systems (see section 11.5) allow transparent naming.

11.3.3 Integrated systems

In the systems we have been describing, functions associated with distribution are added to an existing system, whose overall structure remains broadly the same. The systems that we call 'integrated' are designed from the start to be distributed, and their basic functions (object naming, process management, virtual memory, etc.) take distribution into account. These basic functions are in general provided by a **distributed kernel** one copy of which is held on each site. These kernels communicate with each other, and the upper layers of a system call the local copy of the kernel at each site. Functions involving several sites are implemented by cooperation between the kernels of those sites.

Many experimental systems have been implemented to explore the design problems still posed (see the bibliography in section 11.6). An example of an integrated system, including global management of a virtual memory, is described in section 11.5.3.

11.4 Problems of distribution

In this section, we shall examine the main problems posed by the design of distributed operating systems. To do so, we use a simple model in which the system is made up of a collection of sites interconnected by a communication system. The system provides an interface at the transport level about which we make the following assumptions:

1. Any site may communicate with any other, by transmitting messages to it.
2. Communication is 100% reliable, without loss, duplication or corruption of messages (except in cases of breakdown or isolation of a site, see 4).
3. The order of messages is conserved between two sites.
4. A site can detect a breakdown on another site or a break in the link to that site.

These assumptions do not always apply: for example, the datagram service does not conserve the order of messages. For certain algorithms, we shall indicate the consequences of such violations.

11.4.1 Object naming

The general model presented in chapter 6 for object naming remains valid for distributed systems. We shall define two aspects here: the structure of the internal names of objects and the establishment of the correspondence between external and internal names.

11.4.1.1 Structure of internal names

It should be remembered that the internal name of an object is a unique name intended for the use of the operating system. Users handle external names.

We shall indicate the underlying principles of two methods used for the construction of internal names, for which there are other variants. Applications are discussed in the case studies in section 11.5.

1. Physical naming

<internal name>::= <site address><site local name>

This naming method is simple, and allows for immediate correspondence between the internal name and its address. Interpreted in its strictest sense, it does not allow migration of objects between sites. Nevertheless, if we choose to interpret the site address as a hint to the location of an object, migration becomes possible. To locate an object, it is then possible to use indirection (with objects remaining permanently managed by their site of origin) or use other information, such as associative tables managed as a cache; these methods are only economical if little object migration takes place.

2. Logical naming

<internal name>::=<server name><server local name>

In this naming method, all objects are managed by a (logical) server responsible for all operations on the object. A common implementation uses the server name as a **port name**. Remember (see section 4.4.3.2) that a port is a mailbox with which at most one receiver process can be associated. That process can play the role of server, to which requests are addressed in the form of messages sent to its port. This approach is more complex than the previous one, but has two advantages: it dissociates object naming from their physical location (which in particular allows them to migrate), and it makes it possible to modify dynamically the way a service is implemented. Consequently, a process associated with a port may be replaced, in cases of failure, by a backup process.

We still have to establish correspondence between a port name and a physical location. One method is to use a naming server, as in the interpretation of symbolic names (see section 11.4.1.2). Another method is to use capabilities (see section 6.4.3) managed by a distributed kernel. To access the port, a process must hold the appropriate capability. Capabilities can only be granted and interpreted by the kernel, by way of supervisor calls. When a process obtains a capability, it simply receives a local name allowing it to specify that capability with a local addressing space, without being able to access its internal structure, which contains the physical location and usage rights of the port it names.

11.4.1.2 Naming servers

Symbolic names, or identifiers, are those handled by users. They generally have a hierarchical structure, reflecting a logical organization. The correspondence between symbolic and internal names can be established in several ways:

1. Using the actual structure of the name: this is what happens, for example, in the Unix United system described in section 11.3.2, where analysis of a file name makes it possible to determine its site, and therefore the local directory which indicates its internal name. The logical structure of names then coincides, at least at the highest level, with physical structure.
2. By calling on a specialized server, called a **naming server**, which establishes the correspondence. That server is itself named by a fixed name, known in advance to all processes. It can be implemented in a centralized or distributed way. Centralized implementation poses no particular problems: the server manages a directory along the lines described in section 6.2. However, a breakdown on the site where it is implemented paralyses the whole system. It is therefore worth distributing the name service between several servers, using a logical name structure. Assume that this structure has two levels, i.e. <group name><local name>. Each of the servers between which the naming service has been distributed manages the directories for several groups; Conversely, the directory for each group is managed by at least two servers. Each server contains a table indicating, for each, the name of the servers containing a directory for that group. The servers themselves are named by universal names known to and interpreted by the whole system. To locate a name, a client turns to any server (e.g. the closest, or the least loaded) which provides the list of servers holding a directory for the requested group. The user can then select one of these groups, again on the basis of availability, load or proximity, to provide the information needed. This approach is used, in particular, in the Grapevine system [Birrell 82]. It can be extended to any number of levels. It requires the implementation of a protocol for managing duplicated information, to

ensure consistency between multiple copies of group directories and the server table.

Finally, location can be accelerated by maintaining local caches which store the correspondence between symbolic and internal names, for recent references. If this correspondence is variable (e.g. as a result of migrations), the information provided by the caches should only be interpreted as a hint.

11.4.2 Elementary synchronization methods

Synchronization in centralized systems can be provided by one of two basic mechanisms: access to shared variables (used for semaphores or monitors), and event scheduling in which a synchronization condition can be expressed by specifying an order for the events associated with synchronization points (see section 4.3.1). The first method cannot be used without a shared memory, the second method requires a common time reference, generally not available in a distributed system.

We shall present two methods which form the basis of many synchronization algorithms. The first makes it possible to define a total order on events in a distributed system, using 'logical clocks' synchronized by exchange of messages. The second is based on the use of a particular item of information, or privilege, moving between the various sites, which are organized into a virtual ring.

11.4.2.1 Logical clocks and timestamps

We assume that on any site in a distributed system, numbered *i*, we can define a precedence relation (written *precedes*$_i$) between two events local to that site. We then have to define a global precedence relation. Such a relation, written *precedes*, must have the following properties:

1. It must be compatible with local precedence relations. For any site *i* with two events (*a* and *b* local to the site) we must have:

$$a \textit{ precedes}_i\ b \Rightarrow a \textit{ precedes } b$$

2. It must respect the principle of causality for transmission of messages between two sites. For any message *m*:

$$\text{transmission}(m) \textit{ precedes } \text{reception}(m)$$

3. it must be transitive:

$$a \textit{ precedes } b \textbf{ and } b \textit{ precedes } c \Rightarrow a \textit{ precedes } c$$

To implement this relation, we define a **logical clock** HC_i for each site i, using integer values, which will date events on that site. This clock, initialized to zero, is incremented by one each time an event occurs on the site. The **date** of an event a on a site i is, by definition, the current value of C_i, written $C_i(a)$. Any message m transmitted by a site i bears a **timestamp** $E(m)$, which is its transmission date. A site j receiving a message m executes the following instruction:

$$C_j := \mathbf{max}(C_j, E(m)) + 1$$

The order of dates defines a total ordering relation between events. This order is not strict, as uncorrelated events, occuring at different sites, may have the same date. To obtain a strict ordering, we simply have to define an arbitrary order between sites, for example that of their numbers. Let a and b be two events taking place on site i and j respectively. We can then define relation *precedes* as follows:

$$a \text{ precedes } b \approx C_i(a) < C_j(b) \textbf{ or } (C_i(a) = C_j(b) \textbf{ and } i < j)$$

This is a strict total ordering, which meets properties 1, 2 and 3.

11.4.2.2 Mutual exclusion using timestamps

The mutual exclusion algorithm that we shall describe, developed by Ricart and Agrawala, is a direct application of event scheduling by timestamp. It is characterstic of a class of algorithm which applies a 'distributed queue', with a representation on each site. This queue is globally ordered by the logical time of entry requests.

The underlying principle of the algorithm is the following: a process which has to enter its critical section transmits a request for permission to enter to all the other processes, and awaits their response. A process can only enter its critical section once it has received a response from all the others. A process p_j which receives a request from a process p_i reacts as follows:

- If p_j is not in its critical section and has not asked for permission to enter it (*neutral* state), it responds immediately to p_i.
- If p_j has asked to enter its critical section (*cswait* wait), it only responds if p_i*'s* request is earlier (as defined by the global order based on the logical clocks) to its own request; otherwise, it delays its response, and records p_i*'s* request in its queue.
- If p_j is in its critical section (*cs* state), it delays its response to p_i until the end of its critical section (it then responds to all the requests waiting in its list).

The program executed on site i has the general form indicated in chapter 4:

```
prologue_i;
  <critical section>
epilogue_i
```

We shall give programs for the sequences *prologue*$_i$ and *epilogue*$_i$.

```
prologue_i:
  state:=cswait;
  m.type:=request;
  m.sender:=i;
  m.date:=H(i);
  add(m,list);             -- record the request locally
  broadcast(m);            -- broadcast to other sites
  sitesok:={i};            -- sites that have sent back a response
  while sitesok <> all sites do
    wait(message)
  endwhile;                -- agreement of all sites
  state:=cs;

epilogue_i:
  state:=neutral;
  for all m∈ list do
    send(response,m.sender);
    remove(m,list)
  endfor;

receipt of message m:

if m.type=request then
  case  state of
  cs    :add(m,list)
cswait: if m.date<m_i.date) then
        send(response,m.sender)
     else
        add(m,list)
     endif;
  neutral:send(response,m.sender);
  endcase
else        -- m.type = response
  if state <> cswait then
        <error>
  else
        sitesok:=sitesok ∪ {m.sender}
  endif
endif;
```

The entry of a process into its critical section requires $2(n-1)$ messages. If there are no breakdowns on sites or in the communication system, this algorithm implements mutual exclusion, without deadlock or starvation.

1. Mutual exclusion. If a site i, which has asked to enter its critical section, has received a response from all the others, then a) its request is the oldest (in the sense defined by the total ordering relation described in section 11.4.2.1) of all the requests that may be waiting; and b) all critical sections requested earlier have been completed. If a site j has itself sent an earlier request, or if it was in its critical section, it would not have sent a response to i. This global ordering of requests also guarantees that deadlock cannot take place: if two sites 'simultaneously' request entry to a critical section, their requests will be serialized by the global ordering relation, and the older will be satisfied first.

2. Absence of starvation. Any site i which has requested entry to a critical section will be able to enter it within a finite time (assuming that all critical sections last a finite time). When the critical sections asked for earlier have terminated, the request from i will necessarily become the oldest in the queue on each site. The algorithm is fair, as it ensures that processes execute their critical sections in the order of their requests.

Note that this algorithm will still work in cases where the communication system does not conserve the order of messages between two sites. In this case, the algorithm no longer guarantees that critical sections are executed in the order of their requests, but there will still be no starvation (see exercise).

The handling of breakdowns and protocols for removing and reinstating a site will also be discussed in the exercises.

11.4.2.3 Virtual ring and token passing

Another class of synchonization methods based on the movement of a particular information item, called a **token**, between sites organized into a **virtual ring**, defined by a system of site numbers selected by convention, from 0 to $n-1$. Messages move in the direction of increasing numbers. When the system is initialized, one and only one site has the token. The mutual exclusion algorithm is particularly simple:

```
wait(token,site_{i-1 mod n});
<critical section_i>
send(token,site_{i+1 mod n});
```

If a site receives the token, but does not have to execute a critical section, it sends the token immediately to its successor. We have already met this algorithm for allocating a line on a ring network (section 11.2.3.2). Its validity is based on the existence of a single token, and may fail due to breakdown on a site (at the moment that it holds the token) or of the communication system.

We shall not deal with the question of reconfiguring the virtual ring in cases of breakdown, or of removing or adding a site (see exercise). We shall only look at the method used to detect loss of the token and to regenerate it.

As the token moves in a continuous way around the ring, each site can detect its loss by using a watchdog timer; the length of the timeout will be based on knowledge of the maximum time it takes the token to move round the ring. The next step is to make sure that the token is not regenerated by several sites simultaneously, all of which have detected its absence.

This problem may be regarded as a particular case of a more general situation where one and only one process has to be selected from among several: it is the problem of **election**. As the choice of site selected is random, we choose, by convention, the site with the highest number. The Chang and Roberts algorithm uses 'filtering': each process initiating the selection procedure sends a message around the ring carrying its number. A process which receives such a message stops it if it has a lower number than its own, and itself becomes a candidate; otherwise it retransmits the message. Only the message from the process with the highest number will therefore complete a circuit and return to its sender, which will then be the selected process. This election algorithm can be used to choose a process that will regenerate a token if it is lost.

```
program for site i:
  detection of loss of token:
    candidate:=true;
    sendnext(election,i);

  receipt of message (election,j):
    choice
      j>i   :sendnext(election,j);
             candidate:=true;
      j<i   :if ¬ candidate then
                 candidate:=true;
                 sendnext(election,i)
             endif
      j=i   :regeneratetoken          --site i has been selected
    endchoice
```

Algorithms based on the transmission of a privilege can be presented in another way. We define the state of the site by a set of local variables, and allow site i read-only access to the state of its predecessor $i-1$ (modulo n). For example, the mutual exclusion algorithm below uses variable X_i {0,1} on each site P_i; site P_0 plays a particular role. We shall write ⊕ for addition modulo 2.

```
P0: X0:=0;
    loop
      wait (X0=Xn-1);
      <critical section0>
      X0:=X0 ⊕ 1
    endloop

Pi (i<>0): Xi:=0;
           loop
             wait (Xi=Xi-1⊕1);
             <critical sectioni>
             Xi:=Xi ⊕ 1
           endloop
```

The movement of the privilege round the ring is expressed by the advance of a 'wave front': by convention, an 'ordinary' site P_i (i<> 0) holds the privilege if it is immediately before the wave front. After a revolution, the wave front disappears; site P_0 then has the privilege (as in the initial state), and reforms the front at the end of its critical section.

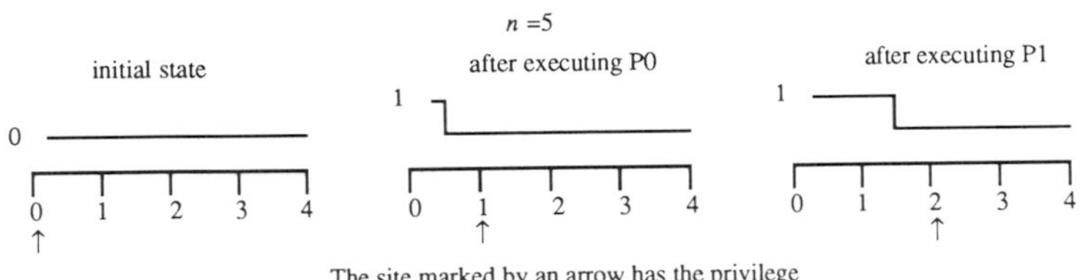

The site marked by an arrow has the privilege

This protocol can be made fault tolerant (see exercise).

11.4.3 Atomic actions and fault tolerance

The concept of an atomic action was introduced in section 4.2.1, for the case of an entirely reliable centralized system. We shall now extend this definition to the case of a distributed system, in which there may be faults. An **atomic action** is an operation (say A) which causes a set of objects (say S_A) to move from an initial to a final state within a finite time, and which is characterized by the following two properties.

1. The state of S_A is inaccessible to other actions during the duration of A (property of **indivisibility**).

2. In cases of a fault during the execution of A, the set S_A will return to its initial state (**restart** property).

In other words, at the end of an atomic action, the objects handled by this action are either in their initial state, or in their final state.

The concept of atomicity was initially introduced into database management systems, along with the concept of a transaction. We say that the state of a set of objects is **consistent** if it satisfies a set of relations called integrity constraints, which express semantic properties associated with a particular application. A **transaction** is an operation which takes a system from a consistent state to another consistent state. The property of atomicity makes it possible to execute transactions in parallel and to guarantee that the state of a system remains consistent in cases of failure.

Property 1) could be guaranteed by ensuring that transactions affecting common objects are executed in a critical section; this would have the same effect as executing the transactions in series. Property 2) could be guaranteed saving the initial state of S_A for the whole duration of the action, in order to be able to restore it in case of error. Our aim is to improve these approaches to the problem:

- By allowing concurrent access to objects, with the global effect being the same as that of indivisible actions executed in series
- By minimizing the volume and duration of storage of duplicated information
- By guaranteeing a high degree of reliability

We shall be concerned in turn with restart mechanisms after failures and with control of concurrent access.

11.4.3.1 Handling of failures

Two important preliminary comments need to be made:

a. The principle underlying the handling of failures is always based on **redundancy** (hardware, processing, information).

b. It is important to specify the assumptions made on the nature of the failures against which we hope to protect, and to be aware that no method will guarantee absolute reliability, but only a reduction in the probability of a particular type of damage in cases of the occurrence of a particular type of failure.

Note finally that a transaction can be voluntarily **aborted**, for example by the application of concurrent access control algorithms. Such cancellation is handled in the same way as an error, i.e. by restoring the initial state.

We shall first describe the principle underlying the implementation of atomic actions on a single site, and then its extension to atomic actions involving several sites.

We start by introducing a simple model to describe failures, defining three types of memory: main memory, secondary memory, and stable memory. Failures are classified in two categories: errors and disasters. The aim of failure handling is to guarantee that a system will operate correctly after an error; resistance to disaster cannot be guaranteed.

The basic operations are information transfer from or to secondary memory, and communication by messages between processors. The following are regarded as **errors**: failure of a processor with loss of its internal state; loss of the contents of main memory; incorrect reading or writing in secondary memory, if detected; isolated spontaneous corruption in secondary memory, if detected; loss or duplication of a message. The following are regarded as **disasters**: an undetected read error in secondary memory; spontaneous and undetected corruption of secondary memory; repeated and concentrated corruption of secondary memory.

These definitions can be made rigorous by specifying, using characteristic intervals of time and volumes of space, the meaning of the terms 'isolated', 'repeated' and 'concentrated'. An error is said to be 'detected' if its occurrence can be reliably observed by consulting an indicator.

Stable memory, by definition, can only be corrupted as a result of a disaster; no error can affect it. We shall not consider the construction of stable memories in detail here; see the bibliography in section 11.6, and exercise 11.4.

The techniques allowing consistent execution of transactions in the presence of failures were initially introduced in database management systems. They are based on the concept of **commitment**. The commitment of a transaction is a point of no return, separating the transaction into two stages. Before commitment, the effect of the transaction can be cancelled, and the initial state restored; after commitment, modifications are reversible and the transaction must be taken through to completion. Consider a transaction taking the system from an initial state S_I to a final state S_F. After a failure in the course of executing this transaction, the restart mechanism will take the system back to state S_I, or S_F, depending on whether the failure took place before or after commitment. Consequently, the commitment operation must itself be atomic, in the sense that no failure can occur 'during' commitment.

Two basic techniques, which are similar in underlying principle, are used to store restart information: a **log** and **shadow pages**.

1. *Log*. A log is a sequence of records maintained in chronological order and held in stable memory. Each record corresponds to an elementary modification executed by the transaction, and contains all the information needed to reconstruct the old value from the new, and vice-versa. A record is copied in stable memory *before* the corresponding modification is reflected in secondary memory. Commitment corresponds to writing the final record in the log. If a failure occurs before commitment, we have only to scan the log in inverse order and undo operations, record by record, deleting each record from the log as it is processed, by means of an atomic operation (one simply has to change a pointer). If a failure occurs after commitment, but before the last modification has been made to secondary memory, this operation may be restarted from the log held in stable memory. Note that failures can occur during the restart process, but its validity is not affected since the log is in stable memory and updating can be restarted from the first unprocessed record.

2. *Shadow pages*. We assume that the system's data is held in a paging memory. During the first stage of the transaction, modifications are not made to the original pages, which remain in their initial state, but to copies called shadow pages, stored in stable memory. Once all the modifications have been made, the transaction is committed. A second stage is to replace the original pages by the shadow pages. In cases of failure during the first stage, the shadow pages are freed. In cases of failure during the second stage, copying can be restarted as often as necessary, since the shadow pages will not have been corrupted.

We now have to extend these restart techniques to cases where several servers cooperate in a transaction. The principle is to nominate one server (e.g. the one that received the request) to act as transaction coordinator; the other servers are called slaves. Assume that we are using a log method. In the first stage, the coordinator asks the slaves to prepare their log, but without committing what they are writing; each slave informs a coordinator of the end of this stage. Once the coordinator receives all the replies, it orders the slaves to commit their actions; each slave informs the coordinator at the end of this stage. Once the coordinator has received all the replies, it commits its own actions, and the transaction is complete. Failure of a slave during the first stage detected is by the coordinator (using a watchdog timer); it then orders all the slaves to cancel their part of the transaction. Failure of the coordinator triggers a selection algorithm (see section 11.4.2.3) to name a new coordinator.

11.4.3.2 Concurrent access control

Let T_1, T_2,...,T_n be a set of transactions. By definition, the isolated execution of each transaction preserves the consistency of the system. The problem of controlling concurrent access can be expressed as follows: how to define an execution mechanism allowing the transactions T_i to execute in parallel while maintaining the consistency of the system.

Let *i*1,*i*2,...,*in* be a permutation of 1,2,...,*n*. The sequential execution:

$$T_{i1};T_{i2};...;T_{in}$$

maintains the system in a consistent state (as each intermediate state is consistent). For concurrent execution of the T_i transactions to be consistent, we only need its effects to be identical to that of sequential execution. Our concurrent access control method is to specify equivalence criteria and arrange execution of transactions in such a way as to apply these criteria. We shall describe the underlying principles of two such methods (the demonstration of their validity is left as an exercise).

1. Two-phase locking

In this method, read or write access objects (files, records, etc.), is protected by **locks** respecting the access rules defined by the readers and writers model (see section 4.4.2.2): access for writing must be executed under mutual exclusion, but several read accesses can be executed concurrently. Locking uses two primitives:

lock(object,mode), where *mode={read,write}*
unlock(object)

The rules for using these primitives are as follows:

a. A transaction cannot access an object unless it has previously locked it, in a mode compatible with that access.

b. A transaction may not lock an object that has already been locked (except to change its access mode from *read* to *write*).

c. All locks placed by a transaction must be removed once it is complete. An attempt at locking which is incompatible with the rules for readers and writers suspends the transaction which attempts to execute it.

A transaction is said to be **two-phase** if no locking operation follows an unlocking operation (if the transaction involves actions on several sites, a global ordering relation has to be defined using logical clocks). In other words, the transaction includes a phase in which objects are locked, followed by one in which they are unlocked. Under these conditions, it can be shown (see exercise) that concurrent execution of a set of two-phase transactions is equivalent to sequential execution and therefore preserves consistency.

Locking involves a risk of deadlock. A method to avoid that risk is described in section 11.4.5.

2. Optimistic method

The optimistic method is based on the execution of transactions in the hope that there will be no conflict; a transaction is only cancelled if it leads to conflict. This method has many advantages if the probability of conflict is low. Each transaction involves three successive steps, called preparation, verification and writing. In the preparation stage, the transactions are executed with modifications are written to shadow pages, along the lines described in section 11.4.3.1. In the verification stage, checks are made to ensure that consistency will be respected. If so, the shadow pages are made definitive through the writing stage. If not, the transaction is cancelled, and the shadow pages freed. To check on consistency, an ordinal number is assigned to each transaction, at the end of the preparation stage. The execution of a transaction T_j (with number j) maintains consistency if one of the following three conditions is true for all transactions T_i such that $i<j$:

a. end(write(T_i))<start(preparation(T_j))

b. Write(T_i) ∩ Read(T_j)=∅ **and** end (write(T_i))<start(write(T_j))

c. Write(T_i) ∩ Read(T_j)=∅ **and**Write(T_i) ∩ Write(T_j)=∅ **and** end(read(T_i))<end(read(T_j))

where the < sign is used to indicate precedence in logical time; Read(T_i) is used for the set of information read by transaction T_i, and Write (T_i) for the set of information written.

11.4.4 Management and structuring of distributed activities

In general terms, three classes of tools for structuring distributed activities can be distinguished, in increasing order of levels of abstraction:

1. Message communication primitives
2. Remote procedure calls (and their extensions)
3. Mechanisms based on objects

Messages are the fundamental tools for communication between processes executing on remote sites, and may therefore be used directly to describe the organization of distributed activities. Primitives for communication by means of messages are often regarded as providing a low level means of expression, which can lead to complex structures. This has led to the suggestion that messages should be used to build up higher level mechanisms.

A **remote procedure call** is a generalization of an ordinary procedure call to the case where the calling procedure and the called procedure are executed on different sites. This mechanism has the great advantage of providing a uniform way of structuring local and remote activities. Nevertheless, the precise specification and implementation of remote procedure calls have to be carefully considered, to take account of the risk of procedures ending incorrectly due to failure of the communication system or of one of the sites. There are various possible specifications:

a. Execution 'at least once': if execution halts normally, the called procedure has been executed once or several times.

b. Execution 'exactly once': if execution ends normally, the called procedure has been executed once and only once.

In neither case is a specification given for behaviour in response to an abnormal halt. A stricter constraint is the following:

c. Execution 'at most once': as b), but it is specified in addition that the call has no effect in cases of abnormal termination. The state before the call is restored.

A possible implementation of remote procedure calls (fig. 11.7) requires two service programs called **stubs**: *client_stub* on the calling site and *server_stub* on the called site. Let us start by describing normal behavior. The calling process executes, *client_stub*, which constructs a message containing the name of the called procedure and its parameters and sends it to the remote site. It then waits. Reception of the message on the remote site causes a service process to be activated. This process executes *server_stub*: it unpacks locally the procedure name and parameters from the messages

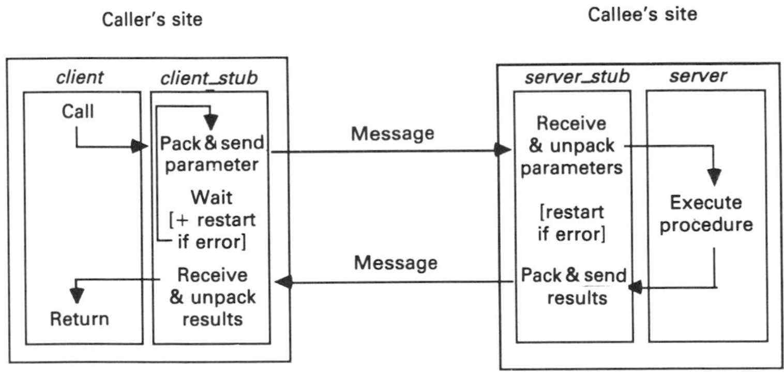

Fig. 11.7. Remote procedure call

executed the call locally, and sends the results back to the calling site. The calling process is reactivated by receipt of the message and collects its results.

Let us now examine error handling. Before being suspended, the calling process sets a watchdog timer; if results have not been returned within the preset period, the call is reexecuted; the maximum number of attempts is also predetermined. The problem is more complex on the called site. In a case of a 'once and once only' call, measures have to be taken to ensure that the called procedure is not executed twice. In case of loss of the return message and a second attempt by the caller, the called site must simply send the results again, and this means storing them. Furthermore, in cases of breakdown on the calling site, it must be able to delete any 'orphan' process resulting from incomplete calls to the called site. Finally, in cases of atomic execution, it has to be possible to restore the state before the call, in case of breakdown.

11.4.5 Resource allocation

The difficulty of allocating resources in a distributed system is a consequence of the impossibility of defining a global state. This problem can be solved in a variety of ways. For example, we shall discuss an algorithm for permanently avoiding deadlock, which uses a global order to resolve conflicts between transactions. An example of a conventional algorithm based on the reconstruction of a global state from partial information is given as an exercise.

An algorithm developed by Rosenkrantz , Stearns and Lewis avoids the risk of deadlock due to the use of locks in protocols, such as two-stage locking. **Conflict** occurs if a transaction (say T_i) attempts to lock a resource that has already been locked by another transaction (say T_j) in an incompatible mode. Conflict resolution is based on the assignment of priorities to trans-

actions. The algorithm guarantees, by cancelling a transaction if necessary, that transactions can only be made to wait for resources locked by a transaction of higher priority. Circular waiting is therefore avoided, and deadlock cannot take place.

At its creation, each transaction receives a timestamp, showing the value of the logical lock at the creation site. These timestamps define priorities. There are two variants of the algorithm depending on whether or not preemption can take place.

1. *Algorithm without preemption ('Wait-Die')*. If T_i is older than T_j, T_i waits; otherwise it is aborted.

2. *Algorithm with preemption ('Wound-Wait')*. If T_i is younger than T_j, T_i waits; otherwise, T_j is aborted.

An aborted transaction will be restarted later with the same timestamp, to avoid starvation. A transaction will inevitably become the oldest at some time, and this prevents its being aborted.

11.4.6 User interfaces

The subject of man-machine interfaces will be discussed in this chapter even though it is not strictly an issue for distributed systems. Nevertheless, the question has become particularly important with the appearance of workstations using sophisticated hardware interfaces, characterized by bit-map displays, and a direct naming device (the mouse). These workstations are most often used in local communication networks. Their user interface must therefore allow the greatest possible advantage to be taken of the hardware, while taking account, if appropriate, of aspects associated with the communication network.

A basic tool introduced for the construction of man-machine interfaces is the concept of a **window**. A window essentially implements a *virtual screen* defining a rectangular zone with which a user interface is associated. In the simplest case, this interface is a restriction on that of the physical screen and simply allows display and scrolling of text. More sophisticated systems make it possible to modify the size and position of windows, and to associate particular attributes with them affecting display modes and interactions with other windows. As with a screen, a window can be associated with a data stream, making it possible to display the contents of a file, the output stream produced by a process, etc. This association can be established dynamically.

That part of the system which implements window allocation, their display, and their user interface functions, is the **window manager**. At any time, the window manager must have a representation of the internal state of each window, i.e. of the position of the objects which are (virtually) displayed and the value of their attributes, and also of the overall state of the screen. That overall state is made up of the visible parts of windows, based on their positions and mutual relations (overlapping, main priorities) and of the internal state of each of them. Any modification of the contents of a window, its size, its position, or any other of its attributes means that the window manager has to recalculate the visible parts, and if necessary to redisplay the modified areas of the screen. Certain window manager functions (e.g. the global movement of a window) are now implemented on hardware devices for the more advanced terminals).

11.5 Case studies

These case studies are intended to illustrate the design principles we have been describing. File service is often an essential element in a distributed system; we shall discuss the principles involved in section 11.5.1. We shall then go on to describe two integrated distributed systems. In the Locus system (section 11.5.2), integration takes place at the level of the services accessible to users (files and processes), and an effort has been made to ensure that the system is resistant to failures. The Apollo/Domain system (section 11.5.3) illustrates the implementation of a distributed global virtual memory.

11.5.1 File serving

1. General characteristics

A distinction is generally made between two ways of providing file service in a distributed system. A first approach is to distribute file service over all sites, with processes on each site being able to access (if authorized) files on others. Such a service can be obtained by interconnecting existing file systems, or can be designed as a whole. In the second approach, one or more specialized **file servers**, acting independently or in cooperation with each other, provide access to files on a client-server basis. Finally, both approaches can be combined.

The first file servers were simple storage devices communicating with clients by means of file transfer protocols. They had two limitations: the transfer unit was a whole file (which meant that the client had to have a minimum storage capacity), and concurrent access to a file was impossible.

The main characteristics making it possible to define a distributed file service are the following:

a. Naming scheme. Certain servers manage symbolic names; others use only internal names, with the naming service being provided by a separate server. Symbolic naming patterns are generally hierarchical. Two important properties are transparency of access (uniform access mechanism for local or remote files) and transparency of location (the naming method is independent of the physical location of the objects named). A basic mechanism to implement these properties is to mount a group of files on a logical volume, which has a double linkage function (see section 6.2.3.2): providing a physical medium for this group of files, and allowing its logical insertion at a specified point in a naming hierarchy, or mount point. Depending on the system, mount points may be predefined (e.g. at the root of the local directory on the site), or they may be chosen freely.

b. Concurrent access control: implementation of atomic transactions, which may involve a single file, several files, or even several servers.

c. Access unit. The access unit may be an entire file; more commonly, servers allow access to pages or records. Many systems use local caches at the client site to speed up access.

d. Protection. As with naming, protection may be provided by the file server or by a separate server which assigns capabilities.

e. Availability. Availability is ensured by duplication of files, on different physical units. This duplication can be managed by the server or controlled by the client. The system must then see to mutual consistency of file copies (an analogous consistency problem is posed if multiple local caches are used).

2. Examples

An example of a file system built up by interconnection of existing system is Unix United, decribed in section 11.3.2. Remote access is transparent, but file names depend on their location. The access primitives are those of the Unix system, and there is no transaction mechanism. Another example of a distributed file system is that of the Locus system described in section 11.5.2. File names are independent of their location. Files may be duplicated, to increase their availability. A commitment operation allows atomic updating. The file access unit is the page; a cache storing recently accessed pages is used to speed up access. The communication protocol uses messages.

An example of a localized file server, accessible remotely by workstations on a local area network, is Alpine, implemented on a Xerox network, for general applications and for database management. It allows execution of atomic transactions, including transactions involving several servers. Files are not duplicated. The access unit is a page, and there is no local cache. The communication protocol uses remote procedure calls. Transaction management uses a log for transaction commitment or restart, and locks to manage concurrent access. Files are named by their internal names, defining a flat naming space; the correspondence between symbolic names and internal names is left to a separate name server.

11.5.2 Locus

Locus is a distributed operating system originally designed in the University of California at Los Angeles as a research project, on a DEC Vax network connected by Ethernet. A commercial version has also been developed.

1. General characteristics

The Locus system is a distributed version of Unix built not by interconnection of existing Unix systems, but by a complete rewrite of the Unix kernel. The aims of the system are a) to provide an integrated interface, where distribution (and possibly heterogeneity in hardware) is hidden from users; b) to ensure a high degree of availability and of fault tolerance.

The system's integration is expressed in a object naming system which is independent of physical location, and in facilities for remote process execution and for process migration between sites.

Availability is based on the mechanisms above and on file duplication; resistance to faults is obtained by implementing atomic transactions and by a restart mechanism allowing, in particular, the reconstruction of information after the network has been partitioned.

2. Distributed file system

In Locus, files are named using a hierarchical system, analogous to that in Unix, but covering the whole system. Naming is independent of location. Files may exist in multiple copies, and the FMS manages consistency beween copies. Finally, the FMS allows control of synchronization in concurrent access to files.

A file group (or logical volume) is the set of files corresponding to a subtree in the naming hierarchy. Groups are the basis of the file duplication system: every group can exist in several copies, each of which is entirely stored on a physical device local to a site, and contains the location information (descriptors, or *inodes* in the Unix sense) which define its physical location. For each group, a particular copy, called the primary copy, contains a copy of all the files in the group; the others may be incomplete. Nevertheless, the descriptor table always contains the locations for all the files in the group. The descriptor for a given file has the same displacement in this table for all copies of the group, and the file descriptors not present in the current copy contain the value *nil*. Finally, each group has a coordinating site (which does not necessarily contain a copy of the group) whose role will be described in detail below.

The internal name of a file, which is unique for all copies of the file, takes the form:

<group number, descriptor number>

A device containing a file group may be mounted on any site which can physically accept that device. Linkage is established using the *mount* command as described in section 6.2.3.2. A logical mounting table gives the internal name of the mount point of each group in the naming hierarchy and the number of the coordinating site for that group. This table is copied to each site and is updated, by broadcasting, during all mounting or dismounting operations, when a site is added or withdrawn, and if the network is reconfigured after an interruption. Each site in addition contains a local table of physical devices, establishing the correspondence between the group number and the physical device address, for devices currently mounted on the site.

Access to a file involves three sites, which are not necessarily distinct:

- The user site (US), which initiates the access request.
- The storage site (SS), which contains the copy of the file used for access.
- The current coordinating site (CCS), which sees to synchronization between accesses to the group to which the file belongs. This site knows the numbers of all the sites containing a copy of the group, and has a copy of the descriptors for the group on these sites.

We shall start by considering the elementary read and write operations for a single process, and then concurrent access control.

A request to open a file in read mode is sent by the US to the CCS (determined using the mounting table). Amongst the sites containing a copy of the file, the CCS chooses as SS the one with the most recent version (if appropriate), or otherwise the closest available site. This choice may require dialogue between the CCS and the site that may become the SS. Once the SS has been chosen the CCS transmits its identity to the US. Read requests are then sent directly by the US to the SS, specifying the internal name of the file and the logical displacement of the page to read. The SS allocates a memory buffer, into which it loads pages from its disk before transmitting them to the US. Several optimizations are possible to accelerate reading: a copy of the descriptor of an open file can be held in main memory in the SS, or the buffer may contain several pages, to accelerate sequential access after preloading.

For access in write mode, the CCS selects as SS the site containing the primary copy of the group. The copy of each page to modify is sent beforehand to the US (unless a completely new page is involved). Page exchanges between the US and the SS therefore take place in both directions, and each site maintains a buffer. Closure of the file leads to obligatory flushing of the remaining modified pages from the SS.

Access in write mode includes a commitment mechanism (see section 11.4.3.1) allowing a set of modifications to a file to be made atomic. This uses a shadow page mechanism. When a file page is modified for the first time (or a new page is first created), a shadow page on disk is allocated on the SS. The addresses of these pages are copied into the descriptor in main memory, and not to the copy on disk. If the write operation is cancelled, e.g. following a breakdown of the US, the shadow pages and descriptor in memory are freed. The commitment operation involves copying the memory copy of the descriptor to disk. Next the old pages have to be freed, all modifications have to be sent to other sites containing copies of the file, and the CCS has to be informed. The commitment mechanism is invisible to the US.

Let us now examine control of concurrent access to a file. To maintain compatibility with Unix, Locus allows two levels of sharing for data structures associated with a file (see section 7.6.3.1): sharing of the read/write pointer ('offset') and sharing of the descriptor ('inode').

a. Sharing of the pointer: at its creation, a process shares the read/write pointers to its father's open files. Several processes in a single family (possibly on separate sites because they were created remotely) can therefore share pointers, and any modification made by one of them must immediately be visible to all.

b. Sharing the descriptor: sharing of a descriptor is a consequence either of pointer sharing (by filiation), or of independent opening of a file by two processes (with different pointers).

In either case, sharing is governed by a token-based mechanism, under the control of a single manager process, located on the SS. In case a), mutual exclusion applies, without access restriction: a single token (or right to modify the pointer) is allocated in turn to requesting processes. In case b), the rule applied is the same as in the reader-writer model: several read tokens may be allocated, but only one write token. Possession of a token guarantees that the process has access to an up to date version of the file.

Determination of the internal name of a file from its symbolic name takes place by consulting directories, which are ordinary files. Searching begins either in the current directory, or in the root directory, whose internal names are known on each site. Concurrent access to directories is subject to no restrictions as modifications are atomic actions concerning one entry at a time.

3. Remote execution

A process may be created or executed remotely, or migrate during execution between homogeneous sites. The naming pattern for processes is extended to be able to name and locate processes on the network. A process is named by a unique number, a concatenation of its original site number (the number of the site when it was created) and a number local to that site. To find a given process, the system starts by looking for it locally (by looking up a hashing table), and then consults its original site. Each site maintains a table giving the current location of the processes created on it, and this table is duplicated on another site, defined beforehand, which replaces it in case of failure. To accelerate communication with its sons, each process maintains the list of sites where they are located.

Remote process creation ('remote forking') is based on the following principle: the father process transmits a creation request to the remote site, with all the information required to launch the execution of the son in particular a list of open files. Once that request has been accepted, the father is suspended and its image is transmitted to the sons site by paging on demand. Once that operation is complete, the father process is reactivated by a message containing the son's number.

The migration of a process begins by remote forking of a son process. Once the son has looaded its image, it takes the identity of its father by changing numbers. The father also changes identity; then it retransmits to its 'son' the signals it has received during the image transfer, and finally self-destructs. Migration is then complete.

4. Availability and resistance to failure

The possibility of holding multiple copies of files increases system availability. We shall briefly describe the failure handling mechanisms associated with the management of multiple copies.

The failure of a US site during file writing leads to cancellation of the operation and restoration of the previous state of the file. In cases of failure of an SS during reading, the coordinator will attempt to find a site in working order with another copy. In cases of failure of a group's coordinator, a new coordinator is named; it will have to consult all the other sites containing copies of the group to find out the state of all currently open files.

If a site containing a copy of a group of files is reinserted into the network after a breakdown, it has to update the state of the group. To do so, the system maintains a commitment counter for each group, which is incremented at each commitment after writing a file in the group. During commitment, the current value of the counter is stored in the file descriptor. Moreover, the system maintains three items of information in each copy of the group: a 'low water mark', a 'high water mark' and a list of the most recent commitments. The two marks contain values of the commitment counter: by definition, on the copy in question, all modifications earlier than the low water mark have already been made to files; the high water mark is the counter for the most recent commitment known locally. Note that, on the primary copy, the two marks coincide.

Updating a group after reinsertion is performed as follows: if its low-water mark is in the interval defined by the list of more recent commitments, the files modified by writes more recent than the low water mark are updated; if not, it is lagging too far behind, and the descriptors must be exhaustively searched to detect and update the modified files. If the primary site fails, another site takes its place; it must first consult all other sites containing copies of the file group to be informed of all known commitments.

11.5.3 Apollo/Domain

Apollo computers are individual workstations, principally designed for scientific applications, software production and computer assisted design. These workstations are designed to be linked together, and to servers, by a local area network using a token ring, operating at 12 Mbit/s. The Domain system provides for overall management of the network resources. We shall only consider the principles underlying the organization of the distributed virtual memory.

The organization of the virtual memory is based on the principle of **coupling** (see section 10.2.1.2): the system provides a 'flat' object space, which simulates a large one-level memory, distributed throughout the network. An object is made up of a set of pages (1 Kbyte). To access an object from a workstation, all or part of the object must be coupled (page by page) in the local virtual memory of the workstation. During the first access operation to a memory page coupled in this way, the corresponding page of the object is loaded (if necessary from a remote station); it is copied, if it has been modified, when the frame containing it is reallocated. Each of these local memories therefore operate as a cache with respect to the global object memory.

Each object is identified uniquely by a 64-bit internal name, formed by concatenating the name of its original site (the site on which it was created) and a timestamp local to that site. An object can migrate from its original site. The location algorithm for an object given its internal name uses the number of the original site and, if that is not sufficient, the information held by a 'hint manager'. Every program in the system which displaces an object, or which knows about a displacement (e.g. following mounting of a volume on a site) informs the hint manager. Furthermore, the location algorithm holds in a cache on each site the information concerning the most recent internal name-location associations made.

We can now describe the algorithm for handling page faults on a workstation. The mapping table for local virtual memory, for which there is a copy per process, takes the number of the virtual page where the fault occurred and determines the ordered pair *(id,np)*, where *id* is the internal name of the coupled object and *np* is the number of the page coupled in this object. The location algorithm above makes it possible to determine the site of residence of object *id*. If the object is local, everything takes place as in a centralized system: the missing page is loaded from the disk. If the object is on a remote site, the missing page is loaded by using a remote paging server, a copy of which is held on each site. Each site has a location table for local objects, which associates the internal names of objects on the site with their addresses on disk; consequently, only internal names have to be transmitted over the network, and not addresses on disk.

A consequence of using this access mode is that several copies of the same object may coexist in the virtual memories of the different sites (this situation is analogous to that of multiple caches on a multiprocessor). At the object level, the system provides an elementary version-handling mechanism based on timestamps, making it possible to manage concurrent access. Each object is associated with a timestamp, maintained on its residence site, which indicates the date of its last known modification. Moreover, each site holds the timestamps of objects whose pages it holds locally, and these timestamps are transmitted at any transfer of pages between sites. This makes it possible to detect violations of consistency: if a site has pages from an object, any new page read must have the same timestamp; if a page from an object is copied on its residence site, it can only be accepted if its timestamp is identical to the current timestamp; a new timestamp is then generated and sent to the site from which the write operation was executed. This mechanism is used at the virtual memory level to implement a reader-writer type approach.

11.6 Bibliographic notes

There are still few general works on the design principles for distributed computer systems. [Lampson 81a] is a basic reference; see also [Cornafion 81]. A collection of recent survey articles, principally concerned with conceptual questions, appears in [Paul 85]. Survey articles on distributed operating systems are [Rashid 85] and [Tanenbaum 85].

The monograph [Raynal 85] is a systematic description of the main classes of distributed algorithms; on this subject, see also [Schneider 85].

A basic reference work on communication systems is [Tanenbaum 81]. The specific problems of local area networks are discussed in [Hutchison 85], which includes case studies on the main networks used [Ethernet, rings]. The ISO/OSI reference model is discussed in [Zimmermann 80].

The management of names in distributed systems is discussed in [Watson 81]; examples of distributed name servers are described in [Birrell 82, Mullender 85a].

Event scheduling using logical clocks and timestamps was introduced in [Lamport 78], along with a mutual exclusion algorithm using timestamps. The algorithm described in section 11.4.2.2 is due to Ricart and Agrawala [Ricart 81]; there are a number of improved variants (notably [Carvalho 83, Ricart 83]).

The selection algorithm described in section 11.4.2.3 was developed by Chang and Roberts [Chang 79]. Other algorithms using the movement of messages around a virtual ring (regeneration of the token, selection, etc.) are described in [Raynal 85]. The principle of a privilege based on consultation of local variables is introduced in [Dijkstra 74]; see [Verjus 86] for a general study of this class of algorithms.

Transactions and two-stage locking were introduced in [Eswaran 76]; see also [Gray 78]. The optimistic handling of concurrent access was introduced in [Kung 81]; see [Mullender 85b] for an application to a file server. [Bernstein 81] is a survey article on concurrent access control methods. The implementation principle for a stable memory on disk and its use for atomic transactions are discussed in [Lampson 81b]. The use of a stable memory implemented in rapid access memory is described in [Banâtre 86].

[Lomet 78] gives an example of a distributed algorithm to prevent deadlock; a dynamic algorithm for avoiding deadlock is described in [Rosenkrantz 78]. An example of resource allocation in a distributed system is given in [Craft 83].

An implementation of the remote procedure call protocol is given in [Birrell 84]. Models based on objects for the structuring of distributed activities are described in [Almes 85, Liskov 85].

[Svobodova 84] and [Mitchell 85] are survey articles on file servers, which contain many references to descriptions of implementations. The Newcastle Connection is described in [Brownbridge 82] and the Alpine system in [Brown 85].

The Locus system is described in [Popek 85]; see also [Walker 83]. The management of virtual memory in Apollo/Domain is discussed in [Leach 83]. Other case studies describing experimental distributed operating systems are [Allchin 83] (Clouds), [Almes 85, Black 85] (Eden), [Cheriton 84] (the V kernel), [Liskov 85] (Argus), [Morris 86] (Andrew), [Mullender 85b] (Amoeba), [Needham 82] (the Cambridge distributed system), [Rashid 81 and 85] (Spice/Accent), [Zimmermann 81] (Chorus).

Exercises

Exercise 11.1 [Ricart 81]

Show that the Ricart and Agrawala mutual exclusion algorithm (section 11.4.2.2) remains valid if the communication system does not preserve the order of messages between two sites. What is the effect of such desequencing on the algorithm's performance?

Exercise 11.2

Complete the Ricart and Agrawala mutual exclusion algorithm so as to take account of the loss or reinsertion of a site.

Exercise 11.3

Give an algorithm for the loss or reinsertion of a site in a virtual ring. **Hint:** Organize the ring as a doubly chained list.

Exercise 11.4 [Lampson 81b]

This exercise examines the underlying principle for the implementation of a stable memory on disk. The disk is paged; reading and writing take place page by page. The following errors can occur: detected error during reading; undetected error during writing; spontaneous corruption ('decay'). To define the latter form of error more closely, we take a characteristic time T considered to be very long (with respect to the duration of a complete disk read) and make the following assumptions: probability that decay occurs more than once during a period of duration T is negligible; we know how to divide the disk into disjoint regions (e.g. by volumes) such that all the pages affected by a single occurrence of decay will be in a single region. Read errors are detected by a state indicator {*good*/*bad*}.

1.We define two operations *CarefulGet* and *CarefulPut* with the following specifications: after a *CarefulGet* either the page is in good condition and its value is correct, or it has to be regarded as corrupt; after a *CarefulPut* the page on disk will be in a correct state if no failure has taken place. Give the implementation principle for these operations, which define the interface of an abstract disk called *CarefulDisk*. **Hint:** On reading, declare a page corrupt after n failed attempts; on writing, check the result by rereading.

2. We shall now define a new abstraction, *StableDisk*, whose interface is defined by three operations: *StableGet, StablePut* and *Repair*. We represent a page of *StableDisk* by two pages of *CarefulDisk*, held in two disjoint regions (as defined to deal with spontaneous corruption). These operations have the following invariants between operations: not more than one of the two pages can be in the *bad* state; if both pages are in the *good* state, they contain the same values. The operation *Repair* is aimed to establish this invariant on initializing the system and to restore it after a failure. It is also carried out periodically (with a period less than T).

The *StableGet* read operation carefully reads the contents of a good page from the pair (at least one of them must be good). *StablePut* carries out two careful writes to the two pages in turn; the second write is only started once the first has been completed without error. *Repair* scans all the pairs of pages. If one is bad, it is overwritten with the contents of the other by means of *CarefulPut*. If both pages are good, with different values, one of them is written carefully over the other.

Show that these operations conserve the invariant defined above, despite the occurrence of errors. Deduce that the operation *StablePut* is atomic.

Exercise 11.5 [Eswaran 76]

Consider the parallel execution of a set of transactions $\{T_i\}$ which access a set of common objects. We say that a transaction T_j depends on transaction T_i for this execution, if there exists an object e such that one of the following conditions is met:

a. An action in T_i reads e and a later action of T_j modifies e

b. An action of T_j reads e and a later action of T_i modifies e

c. An action of T_i modifies e and a later action of T_j modifies e, without any other transaction modifying e in the meantime

This relation defines a dependency graph between the transactions. Show that:

1. A sufficient condition for two executions of the set $\{T_i\}$ to have the same effect is that they have the same dependency graph.

2. The graph corresponding to sequential execution is acyclic.

Deduce a sufficient condition for consistent execution of the set of transactions $\{T_i\}$.

Hint: For each object, examine the sequence of updating operations, noting that an update may depend on the value of objects consulted previously.

Exercise 11.6 [Eswaran 76]

Using the results of the previous exercise, show that two-phase locking (section 11.4.3.2) ensures consistent execution of a set of transactions. **Hint:** Transactions can be ordered by the start date of their second phase (first unlocking). Show that the dependence graph induced by execution is identical to that induced by sequential execution in the order defined in this way.

Exercise 11.7

This exercise concerns the optimistic method for concurrent access control.

1. Show that the validity conditions given in section 11.4.3.2 provide for equivalence between the execution of transactions and sequential execution.

2. In the algorithm described, the order number of the transactions is assigned at the end of the preparation stage. Another method would be to assign it on creation of the transaction. Compare the advantages of the two methods.

Exercise 11.8 [Lomet 78]

Consider an attempt to produce a distributed method for preventing deadlock, using claims. At the beginning of a transaction, a process declares the list of resources it intends to use (this is a claim). During a transaction, a process can only acquire a resource (by exclusive locking) if it appears in its claim. At the end of a transaction, all resources that it has locked are freed.

We define a relation *delays* between transactions, characterized by the following condition:

T_i *delays* T_j ~ there exists a resource locked by T_i
and belonging to the claim of T_j

1. Show that the presence of a loop in the graph for relation *delays* indicates that there is a risk of deadlock.

2. We assume that resources are distributed over several sites and that each site only knows of claims concerning the resources local to that site. Show, by way of an example, that a loop involving several sites cannot be detected on any of these sites using local information alone.

3. Assume a strict total ordering of transactions has been defined, by means of a relation written >. We write → for the relation defined by:

$$T_i \rightarrow T_j \sim T_i \textit{ delays } T_j \textbf{ or } T_i > T_j$$

Show that the presence of a global loop in the graph for relation *delays* leads to the presence of a **local** loop, on at least one site, in the graph for relation →. **Hint:** In the global loop, consider the transaction T which is 'greater than' all the others (as defined by $>$), and transaction U which *delays* T.

4. Deduce a deadlock prevention algorithm using only local information. Can starvation be avoided? **Hint:** Use timestamps to implement the relation $>$.

5. Extend the algorithm to cases where the resource sharing mode is that of the reader-writer model and not exclusive access.

Exercise 11.9

Compare the two variants Wait-Die and Wound-Wait of the deadlock avoiding method described in section 11.4.5, from the point of view of the frequency of cancellations. What, in your view, are the conditions of the applicability of each of these algorithms?

Bibliography

[Aho 77] Aho A.V., Ullman J.D., *Principles of compiler design*, Addison-Wesley, (1977)

[Allchin 83] Allchin J.E., McKendry M.S., Synchronization and recovery of actions, *Proc. Second Symposium on Principles of Distributed Computing* (ACM SIGACT/SIGOPS), Montreal, August 1983.

[Allen 75] Allen A.O., Elements of queueing theory for system design, *IBM Syst. J.*, vol. 14, 2 (1975)

[Allen 78] Allen A.O., *Probability, statistics and queueing theory with computer science applications*, Academic Press, (1978)

[Almes 85] Almes G.T., Black A.P., Lazowska E.D., Noe J.D., The Eden system: a technical review, *IEEE Trans on Software Engineering*, vol. SE-11, 1 (January 1985), pp. 43–59.

[André 83] André F., Herman D., Verjus J.P., *Synchronisation de processus parallèls: expression et mise en oeuvre dans les systèmes centralisés et distribués*, AFCET Monographs, Dunod, (1983). *Synchronization of parallel processes,* MIT Press, 1985.

[Andrews 83] Andrews G.R., Schneider F.B., Concepts and notations for concurrent programming, *ACM Computing Surveys*, vol. 15, 1 (March 1983), pp. 3–44

[Auslander 81] Auslander M.A., Larkin D.C., Scherr A.L., The evolution of the MVS operating system, *IBM J. of Research and Development*, vol. 25, 5 (1981), pp. 471–482

[Bach 86] Bach M.J., *The design of the Unix operating system,* Prentice-Hall (1986)

[Baer 80] Baer J.L., *Computer systems architecture*, Pitman, (1980

[Banâtre 86] Banâtre J.P., Banâtrc M., Lapalme G., Ployette F., The design and building of Enchère, a distributed electronic marketing system, *Comm. ACM,* col. 29, 1 (January 1986), pp.9–29.

[Banino 78] Banino J.S., Ferrié J., Kaiser C., Lanciaux D., *Contrôle de l'accès aux objets partagés dans un système informatique*, AFCET computer science monographs, ed. Hommes et Techniques, (1978)

[Banino 80] Banino J.S., Caristan A., Guillemont M., Morisset G., Zimmermann H., Chorus: an architecture for distributed systems, Research report no. 42, INRIA (November 1980) 68pp.

[Baskett 75] Baskett F., Chandy K.M., Muntz R.R., Palacios-Gomez F., Open, closed and mixed networks of queues with different classes of customers, *J. ACM*, vol. 22 (1975), pp 248–260

[Baskett 77] Baskett F., Howard J.H., Montague J.T., Task communication in Demos, *Proc. Sixth Symp. on Operating Systems Principles* (ACM-SIGOPS) (November 1977), pp. 23–31

[Batson 76] Batson A., Program behavior at the symbolic level, *Computer* (November 1976), pp. 21–26

[Bayer 78] Bayer R., Graham R.M., Seegmüller G. (ed.), *Operating systems — an advanced course*, Lecture Notes in Computer Science, vol. 60, Springer-Verlag, (1978)

[Bays 77] Bays C., A comparison of next-fit, first-fit, and best-fit, *Comm. ACM*, vol. 20, 3 (March 1977), pp. 191–192

[Belady 66] Belady L.A., Nelson R.A., Shedler G.S., An anomaly in space-time characteristics of certain programs running in a paging machine, *Comm. ACM*, vol. 12, 6 (June 1969), pp. 349–353

[Ben-Ari 82] Ben-Ari M., *Principles of concurrent programming*, Prentice-Hall, (1982)

[Bensoussan 72] Bensoussan A., Clingen C.T., Daley R.C., The Multics virtual memory: concepts and design, *Comm. ACM*, vol. 15, 5 (may 1972), pp. 308–318

[Bernstein 81] Bernstein P.A., Goodman, N., Concurrency control in distributed database systems, *ACM Computing Surveys*, vol. 13, 2 (June 1981), pp.185–221.

[Bétourné 70] Bétourné C., Boulenger J., Ferrié J., Kaiser C., Krakowiak S., Mossière J., Process management and resource sharing in the multi-access system Esope, *Comm. ACM*, vol. 13, 12 (December 1970)

[Bétourné 71] Bétourné C., Ferrié J., Kaiser C., Krakowiak S., Mossière J., System design and implementation using parallel processes, *Proc. IFIP Congress*, Ljubljana (August 1971)

[Birrell 82] Birrell A.D., Levin R., Needham R.M., Schroeder M.D., Grapevine: and exercise in distributed computing, *Comm. ACM*, vol. 25, 4 (April 1982), pp. 260–273.

[Birrell 84] Birrell A.D., Nelson B.J. Implementing remote procedure calls, *ACM Trans. on Computer Systems*, vol. 2, 1 (February 1984), pp.39–59.

[Black 85] Black A.P., Supporting distributed applications: experience with

Eden Operating Systems Review, vol. 19, 5 (December 1985), pp. 181–193.

[Bobrow 72] Bobrow D.G., Burchfiel J.D., Murphy D.L., Tomlinson R.S., Tenex, a paged time-sharing system for the PDP-10, *Comm. ACM*, vol. 15, 3(March 1972), pp. 135–143

[Bourne 83] Bourne S.R., *The Unix system*, Addison-Wesley, (1983)

[Boyse 75] Boyse J.W., Warn D.R., A straightforward model for computer performance prediction, *ACM Computing Surveys*, vol. 7, 2 (June 1975), pp. 73–93

[Bozman 84] Bozman G., Buco W., Daly T.P., Tetzlaff W.H., Analysis of free-storage algorithms — revisited, *IBM Syst. J.*, vol. 23, 1 (1984, pp. 44–66

[Brawn 68] Brawn B., Gustavson F.G., Program behavior in a paging environment, *Proc. AFIPS Fall Joint Computer Conf.*, vol. 33, Washington (1968)

[Brinch Hansen 70] Brinch Hansen P., The nucleus of a multiprogramming system, *Comm. ACM*, vol. 13, 4 (April 1970), pp. 238–241 & 250

[Brinch Hansen 71] Brinch Hansen P., An analysis of response ratio scheduling *Proc., IFP Congress*, Ljubljana (August 1971), pp 479–484

[Brinch Hansen 72a] Brinch Hansen P., A comparison of two synchronizing concepts, *Acta Informatica*, vol. 1, 3 (1972), pp. 190–199

[Brinch Hansen 72b] Brinch Hansen P., Structured multiprogramming, *Comm. ACM,* vol. 15, 7 (July 1972), pp. 574–578

[Brinch Hansen 73] Brinch Hansen P., *Operating system principles*, Prentice-Hall, (1973)

[Brinch Hansen 75] Brinch Hansen P., The programming language Concurrent Pascal, *IEEE Trans. on Software Engineering*, vol. SE-1, 2(June 1975), pp. 199–207

[Brinch Hansen 76] Brinch Hansen P., The Solo operating system: processes,monitors and classes, *Software — Practice and Experience*, vol. 6 (1976), pp. 165–200

[Brinch Hansen 77] Brinch Hansen P., *The architecture of concurrent programs*, Prentice-Hall, (1977)

[Britton 81] Britton K.H., Parker R.A., Parnas D.L., A procedure for designing abstract interfaces for device interface modules, *Proc. 5th International Conf. on Software Engineering* (ACM-IEEE), San Diego (9–12 March 1981)

[Brown 85] Brown M.R., Kolling K.N., Taft E.A., the Alpine file system, *ACM Trans. on Computer Systems*, vol. 3, 4 (November 1985), pp. 261–293.

[Brownbridge 82] Brownbridge D.R., Marshall L.F., Randell B., The Newcastle Connection — or UNIXes of the World Unite!, *Software Practice and Experience*, vol. 12, 12 (December 1982), pp.1147–1162.

[Bull 71] Bull G.M., Packham S.F.G., Time-sharing systems, McGraw-Hill, (1971)

[Buzen 73] Buzen J.P., Computational algorithms for closed queueing networks with exponential servers, *Comm. ACM*, vol. 16, 9 (September 1973), pp. 527–531

[Calingaert 82] Calingaert P., *Operatng systems elements: a user perspective*, Prentice-Hall, (1982)

[Campbell 74] Campbell R.H., Habermann A.N., The specification of process synchronisation by path expressions, in *Proc. Int. Symp. on Operating Systems*, Lecture Notes in Computer Science, vol. 16, Springer-Verlag (1974), pp. 89–102

[Carvalho 83] Carvalho O., Roucairol G., On mutual exclusion in computer networks, *Comm. ACM*, vol. 26, 2 (February 1983), pp.146–147.

[Chang 79] Chang E. J., Roberts R., An improved algorithm for decentralized extrema-finding in circular configurations of processors, *Comm. ACM*, vol. 22, 5 (May 1979), pp.281–283.

[Cheriton 79] Cheriton D.R., Malcolm M.A., Melen L.S., Sager G.R., Thoth, a portable real-time operating system, *Comm. ACM*, vol. 22, 2 (February 1979), pp. 105–115

[Cheriton 84] Cheriton D.R., The V kernel: a software base for distributed systems, *IEEE Software*, vol. 1, 2 (1984), pp.12–19.

[Chu 76] Chu W.W., Opderbeck H., Program behaviour and the page-fault-frequency replacement algorithm, *Computer*, vol. 9, 11 (November 1976), pp. 29–38

[Coffman 68a] Coffman E.G., Kleinrock L., Feedback queueing models for time-shared systems, *J. ACM*, vol. 15, 4 (October 1968), pp. 549–576

[Coffman 68b] Coffman E.G., Kleinrock L., Computer scheduling methods and their countermeasures, in *Proc. AFIPS Spring Joint Computer Conf.*, vol. 32, Thompson Book Co. (1968) pp. 11–21

[Coffman 71] Coffman E.G., Elphick, M.J., Shoshani A., System deadlocks, *ACM Computing Surveys*, vol. 3, 2 (June 1971), pp. 67–78 (reproduced in [Freeman 75], pp. 153–166)

[Coffman 73] Coffman E.G., Denning P.J., *Operating systems theory*, Prentice-Hall, (1973)

[Colin 71] Colin A.J.T., *Introduction to operating systems*, Macdonald (1971)

[Comer 84] Comer D., *Operating systems design: the ZINU approach,* Prentice-Hall (1984)

[Considine 77] Considine J.P., Myers J.J., MARC: MVS archival storage and recovery program, *IBM Syst.*, vol. 16, 4 (1977), pp. 378–397

[Conway 63a] Conway M.E., A multiprocessor system design, *Proc. AFIPS Fall Joint Computer Conf.* (November 1963), pp. 139–146

[Conway 63b] Conway M.E., Design of a separable transition-diagram compiler, *Comm. ACM*, vol. 6, 7 (July 1963), pp. 396–408

[Corbatò 69] Corbatò F.J., PL/I as a tool for system programming, *Datamation*, vol. 15, 5 (May 1969), pp. 68–76

[Corbatò 72] Corbatò F.J., Saltzer J.H., Clingen C.T., Multics — the first seven years, *Proc. AFIPS Spring Joint Computer Conf.* (1972) (reproduced in [Freeman 75], pp. 556–577)

[Cornafion 81] Cornafion, *Systèmes informatiques répartis*, Dunod, (1981) *Distributed Computer Systems: Communication, Cooperation, Consistency*, North-Holland (1985).

[Cosserat 75] Cosserat D., A data model based on the capability protection mechanism, *RAIRO-Informatique* (AFCET), vol. 9 (September 1975), pp. 63–78

[Courtois 71] Courtois P.J., Heymans F., Parnas D.L., Concurrent control with readers and writers, *Comm. ACM*, vol. 14, 10 (October 1971), pp. 667–668

[Courtois 77] Courtois P.J., *Decomposability: queueing and computer systems applications*, Academic Press, (1977)

[Craft 83] Craft D.H., Resource management in a decentralized system. *Proc. 9th ACM Symp. on Operating Systems Principles, SIGOPS Operating Systems Review*, vol. 17, 5 (December 1985), pp.11–19.

[Crocus 75] Crocus, *Systèmes d'exploitation des ordinateurs*, Dunod, (1975)

[Dahl 72] Dahl O.J., Hoare C.A.R., Hierarchical program structures, in *Structured Programming*, O.J. Dahl, E.W. Dijkstra, C.A.R. Hoare, ed., Academic Press (1972), pp. 175–220

[Daley 65] Daley R.C., Neumann P.G., A general-purpose file system for secondary storage, *Proc. AFIPS Spring Joint Computer Conf.*, pp. 213–229 (1965)

[Deitel 83] Deitel H.M., *An introduction to operating systems*, Addison-Wesley, (1983)

[Delobel 82] Delobel C., Adiba M., *Bases de données et systèmes relationnels*, Dunod, (1982)

[Denning 68] Denning P.J., The working set model for program behavior, *Comm. ACM*, vol. 11, 5 (May 1968), pp. 323–333

[Denning 70] Denning P.J., Virtual memory, *ACM Computing Surveys*, vol. 2, 3 (1970), pp. 153–189 (reproduced in [Freeman 75], pp. 204–256)

[Denning 76a] Denning P.J., Fault-tolerant operating systems, *ACM Computing Surveys*, vol. 8, 4 (December 1976), pp. 359–389

[Denning 76b] Denning P.J., Kahn K.C., Leroudier J., Potier D., Suri R., Optimal multiprogramming, *Acta Informatica*, vol. 7, 2 (1976), pp. 197–216

[Denning 80] Denning P.J., Working sets, past and present, *IEEE Trans. Software Engineering*, vol. SE-6, 1 (January 1980), pp. 64–84

[Dennis 65] Dennis J.B., Segmentation and the design of multiprogrammed systems, *J. ACM*, vol. 12, 4 (October 1965), pp. 589–602

[Dennis 66] Dennis J.B., Van Horn E.C., Programming semantics for multiprogrammed computations, *Comm. ACM*, vol. 9, 3 (march 1966), pp. 143–155

[Dijkstra 65a] Dijkstra E.W., Cooperating sequential processes, Tech. Rep. EWD-123, (1965) (reproduced in F. Genuys (editor), *Programming languages*, Academic Press, 1968, pp. 43–112)

[Dijkstra 65b] Dijkstra E.W., Solution of a problem in concurrent programming control, *Comm. ACM*, vol. 8, 9 (September 1965), p. 569

[Dijkstra 68] Dijkstra E.W., The structure of the THE multiprogramming system, *Comm. ACM*, vol. 11, 5 (May 1968), pp. 341–346

[Dijkstra 69] Dijkstra E.W., Notes on structured programming, Tech. Univ., Eindhoven (1969) (reproduced in *Structured Programming*, O.-J. Dahl, E.W. Dijkstra, C.A.R. Hoare, eds Academic Press, 1972, pp. 1–82)

[Dijkstra 71] Dikjstra E.W. Hierarchical ordering of sequential processes, *Acta Informatica*, vol. 1, 2 (1971), pp. 115–138

[Dijkstra 72] Dijkstra E.W., Information streams sharing a finite buffer, *Information Processing Letters*, vol. 1, 5 (October 1972), pp. 179–180

[Dijkstra 74] Dijkstra E.W., Self-stabilizing systems in spite of distributed control, *Comm. ACM*, vol. 17 (November 1974).

[DoD 83] DoD (U.S. Department of Defense), Reference Manual for the Ada Programming Language, the Pentagon, Washington, (1983).

[Eisenberg 72] Eisenberg M.A., McGuire M.R., Further comments on Dijkstra's concurrent programming control problem, Comm. ACM, vol. 15, 11 (November 1972), p. 999

[England 75] England D.M., Capability concept, mechanism and structure in System 250, *RAIRO-Informatique* (AFCET), vol. 9 (September 1975), pp. 47–62

[Eswaran 76] Eswaran K.P., Gray J.N., Lorie R.A, Traiger I.L., The notions of consistency and predicate locks in a data base system, *Comm. ACM*, vol. 18, 11 (November 1976), pp. 624–533.

[Fabry 74] Fabry R.S., Capability-based addressing, *Comm. ACM*, vol. 17, 7 (july 1974)

[Feiertag 71] Feiertag R.J., Organick E.I., The Multics input-output system, *Proc. Third ACM Symposium on Operating Systems Principles*, pp. 34–41 (1971)

[Ferrari 78] Ferrari D., *Computer systems performance evaluation*, Prentice-Hall, (1978)

[Ferrié 78] Ferrié J., Lanciaux D., Etude critique du système Plessey 250, in [Banino 78] (1978)

[Fraser 72] Fraser A.G., The integrity of a disc-based file system, in *Operating systems techniques*, C.A.R. Hoare, R.H. Perrott, eds, Academic Press (1972), pp. 227–248

[Fraser 79] Fraser A.G., Integrity of a mass-storage filing system, *Computer J*, vol. 12, 1 (February 1969), pp. 1–5

[Freeman 75] Freeman P., *Software systems principles*, Science Research Associates, (1975)

[Gelenbe 80] Gelenbe E., Mitrani I., *Analysis and synthesis of computer systems*, Academic Press, (1980)

[Gelenbe 82] Gelenbe E., Pujolle G., *Introduction aux réseaux de files d'attente*, Eyrolles, (1982)

[Graham 72] Graham G.S., Denning P.J., Protection — principles and practice, *Proc. AFIPS Spring Joint Computer Conf.* (1972)

[Graham 75] Graham R.M., *Principles of systems programming*, Wiley (1975)

[Gray 78] Gray J.N., Notes on database operating systems, in *Operating systems — an advanced course*, Lecture Notes in Computer Science no 60, Springer-Verlag (1978), pp.393–481.

[Habermann 69] Habermann A.N., Prevention of system deadlocks, *Comm. ACM*, vol. 12, 7 (July 1969), pp. 373–377 & 385

[Habermann 72] Habermann A.N., Synchronization of communicating processes, *Comm. ACM*, vol. 15, 3 (March 1972), pp. 171–176

[Habermann 75] Habermann A.N., Path expressions, Dept. of Computer Science, Carnegie-Mellon Univ. (June 1975) 34pp.

[Habermann 76a] Habermann A.N., *Introduction to operating system design*, Science Research Associates, (1976)

[Habermann 76b] Habermann A.N., Flon L., Cooprider L., Modularization and hierarchy in a family of operating systems, *Comm. ACM*, vol. 19, 5 (may 1976), pp. 266–272

[Habermann 83] Habermann A.N., Perry D., *Ada for experienced programmers*, Addison-Wesley, (1983)

[Hatfield 71] Hatfield D.J., Gerald J., Program restructuring for virtual memory, *IBM Syst. J.*, vol. 10, 3 (1971), pp. 168–192

[Hatfield 72] Hatfield D.J., Experiments on page size, program access patterns and virtual memory performances, *IBM J. Research and Development* (January 1972)

[Havender 71] Havender J.W., Avoiding deadlocks in multitasking systems, *IBM Syst. J.*, vol. 10, 3 (1971), pp. 168–192

[Heidelberger 84] Heidelberger P., Lavenberg S.S., Computer performance evaluation methodology, *IEEE Trans. on Computers*, vol. C-33, 12 (December 1984), pp. 1195–1220

[Hoare 72a] Hoare C.A.R., Towards a theory of parallel programming, in [Hoare 72b], pp. 61–71

[Hoare 72b] Hoare C.A.R., Perrott R.H., eds, *Operating systems techniques*, Academic Press, (1972)

[Hoare 78] Hoare C.A.R., Communicating Sequential Processes, *Comm. ACM,* vol. 21, 8 (August 1978, pp. 666–677.

[Holt 72] Holt R.C., Some deadlock properties of computer systems, *ACM Computing Surveys*, vol. 4, 3 (September 1972), pp. 179–196

[Holt 78] Holt R.C., Graham G.S., Lazowska E.D., Scott M.A., *Structured concurrent programming with operating systems applications*, Addison–Wesley, (1983)

[Holt 83] Holt R.C., *Concurrent Euclid, the Unix system and Tunis*, Addison-Wesley, (1983)

[Horning 73] Horning J.J., Randell B., Process structuring, *ACM Computing Surveys*, vol. 5, 1 (March 1973), pp. 5–30

[Horsley 79] Horsley T.R., Lynch W.C., Pilot: a software engineering case study, *Proc. 4th International Conf. on Software Engineernig* (ACM-IEEE) (September 1979)

[Howard 76a] Howard J.H., Proving monitors, *Comm. ACM*, vol. 19, 5 (May 1976), pp. 273–279

[Howard 76b] Howard J.H., Signaling in monitors, *Proc. Second International Conf. on Software Engineering* (ACM-IEEE) (October 1976), pp. 47-52

[Hutchinson 85] Hutchinson D., Mariani J., Shepherd D., eds, *Local area networks: an advanced course*, Lecture Notes in Computer Science no 184, Springer-Verlag (1985).

[Ichbiah 79] Ichbiah J.D. *et al.*, Rationale for the design of the Green programming language, *ACM SIGPLAN Notices*, Vol. 14, 6 (June 1979)

[Jackson 63] Jackson J.R., Jobshop-like queueing systems, *Management Science*, vol. 10 (1963), pp. 131–142

[Janson 85] Janson P.A., *Operating systems: structure and mechanisms,* Academic Press (1985)

[Jones 78a] Jones A.K., Protection mechanisms and the enforcement of security policies, in [Bayer 78], pp. 228–250

[Jones 78b] Jones A.K., The object model: a conceptual tool for structuring software, in [Bayer 78], pp. 7–16

[Kahn 81] Kahn K.C., Corwin W.M., Dennis T.D., D'Hooge H., Hubka D.E., Hutchins L.A., Montague J.T., Pollack F.J., Gifkins M.P., iMAX: a multiprocessor operating system for an object-based computer, *Proc. Eighth ACM Symp. on Operating Systems Principles*, pp. 127–136 (December 1981)

[Keedy 79] Keedy J.L., On structuring operating systems with monitors, *ACM Operating Systems Review*, vol. 13, 1 (January 1979), pp. 5–9

[Kenah 84] Kenah L.J., Bate S.F., *VAX/VMS internals and data structure*, Digital Press, (1984)

[Kessels 77] Kessels J.L.W., An alternative to event queues for synchronization in monitors, *Comm. ACM*, vol. 20, 7 (July 1977), pp. 500–503

[Kildall 81] Kildall G., CP/M: a family of 8- and 16 bits operating systems, *Byte* (June 1981), pp. 216–231

[Kleinrock 76a] Kleinrock L., *Queueing systems* (vol. 1: Theory), John Wiley, (1976)

[Kleinrock 76b] Kleinrock L., *Queueing systems* (vol. 2: Computer applications), John Wiley, (1976)

[Kleinrock 85] Kleinrock L., Distributed systems, *Comm. ACM*, vol. 28, 11 (November 1985), pp.1200–1213.

[Knuth 66] Knuth D.E., Additional comments on a problem of concurrent programming control, *Comm. ACM*, vol. 9, 5 (May 1966)

[Knuth 73] Knuth D.E., *The art of computer programming*, vol. 1: Fundamental algorithms, 2nd ed., Addison-Wesley, (1973)

[Kung 81] Kung H.T., Robinson J.T., On optimistic methods for concurrency control, *ACM Trans. on Database Systems*, vol. 6, 2 (June 1981), pp. 213–226.

[Lamport 74] Lamport L., A new solution of Dijkstra's concurrent programming problem, *Comm. ACM*, vol. 17, 8 (August 1974), pp. 453–455

[Lamport 78] Lamport L., Time, clocks and the ordering of events in a distributed system, *Comm. ACM*, vol. 21, 7 (July 1978), pp.125–133.

[Lampson 68] Lampson B.W., A scheduling philosophy for multiprocessing systems, *Comm. ACM*, vol. 11, 5 (May 1968), pp. 347–360

[Lampson 69] Lampson B.W., Dynamic protection structures, *Proc. AFIPS Fall Joint Computer Conf.* (1969)

[Lampson 71] Lampson B.W., Protection, *Proc. Fifth Annual Princeton Conf. on Information Science Systems* (1971)

[Lampson 73] Lampson B.W., A note on the confinement problem, *Comm. ACM*, vol. 16, 10 (October 1973), pp. 613–615

[Lampson 75] Lampson B.W., An open operating system for a single-user machine, *RAIRO-Informatique* (AFCET), vol. 9 (September 1975), pp. 5–18

[Lampson 76] Lampson B.W., Sturgis H.E., Reflections on an operating system design, *Comm. ACM*, Vol. 19, 5 (May 1976), pp. 251–265

[Lampson 80] Lampson B.W., Redell D.D., Experience with processes and monitors in Mesa, *Comm. ACM*, vol. 23, 2 (February 1980), pp. 105–117

[Lampson 81a] Lampson B.W., Paul M., Siegert H.J. (Ed.), *Distributed systems, architecture and implementations*, Lecture Notes in Computer Science, vol. 105, Springer-Verlag (1981)

[Lampson 81b] Lampson B.W., Atomic transactions, *in* [Lampson 81a], pp.264–265.

[Lampson 82] Lampson B.W., Fast procedure calls, *Proc. Symp. on Architectural Support for Programming Languages and Systems* (SIGPLAN Notices, vol. 10, 2) (March 1982), pp. 66–76

[Lauer 79] Lauer H.C., Satterthwaite E.H., The impact of Mesa on system design, *Proc. 4th International Conf. on Software Engineering* (ACM-IEEE) (September 1979)

[Lauesen 75] Lauesen S., A large semaphore-based operating system, *Comm. ACM*, vol. 18, 7 (July 1975), pp. 377–389

[Lavenberg 83] Lavenberg S.S., ed., *Computer performance modeling handbook*, Academic Press, (1983)

[Lazowska 84] Lazowska E.D., Zahorjan J., Graham G.S., Sevcik K.C., *Quantitative system performance — computer system analysis using queueing network models*, Prentice-Hall, (1984)

[Leach 83] Leach P.J., Levine P.H., Douros B.P., Hamilton J.A., Nelson D.L., Stumpf B.L., The architecture of an integrated local network, *IEEE Journal on Selected Areas on Communication* (November 1983), pp.842–856.

[Le Verrand 82] Le Verrand D., *Le langage Ada: manuel d'évaluation,* Dunod, (1982)

[Levy 82] Levy H.M., Lipman P.H., Virtual memory management in the VAX/VMS operating system, *Computer*, vol. 15, 3 (March 1982), pp. 35–42

[Levy 84] Levy H.M., *Capability-based computer systems*, Digital Press, (1984)

[Linden 76] Linden T.A., Operating system structures to support security and reliable software, *ACM Computing Surveys*, vol. 8, 4 (December 1976), pp. 409–445

[Liptay 68] Liptay J.S., Structural aspects of System 360/85: the cache, *IBM Syst. J.*, vol. 7 (1968), pp. 15–21

[Liskov 72] Liskov B.H., The design of the Venus operating system, *Comm. ACM*, vol. 15, 3 (March 1972), pp. 144–149 (reproduced in [Freeman 75], pp. 542–552)

[Liskov 85] Liskov B.H., The Argus language and system, *in* [Paul 85] pp.343–430.

[Lister 75] Lister A.M., *Fundamentals of operating systems*, Macmillan Press, (1975)

[Lockemann 68] Lockemann P.C., Knutsen W.D., Recovery of disk contents after system failure, *Comm. ACM*, vol. 11, 8 (August 1968)

[Lomet 78] Lomet D., Coping with deadlock in distributed systems, Report RC 7460, IBM T.J. Watson Research Center (September 1978).

[Lynch 74] Lynch H.W., Page J.B., The OS/VS2-2 system resources manager, *IBM Syst. J.*, vol. 13, 4 (1974), pp. 274–291

[Madison 76] Madison A.W., Batson A., Characteristics of program localities, *Comm. ACM*, vol. 19, 5 (May 1976), pp. 285–294

[Madnick 69] Madnick S.E., Alsop J.W., A modular approach to file system design, *Proc. AFIPS Spring Joint Computer Conf.* (1969), pp. 1–12 (reproduced in [Freeman 75], pp. 340–360)

[Madnick 74] Madnick S.E., Donovan J.J., *Operating systems*, McGraw-Hill, (1974)

[Margolin 71] Margolin B.H., Parmelee R.P., Schatzoff M., Analysis of free-storage algorithms, *IBM Syst J.*, vol. 10, 4 (1971), pp. 283–304

[Mattson 70] Mattson R.L., Gecsei J., Slutz D.R., Traiger I.L., Evaluation techniques for storage hierarchies, *IBM Syst. J.*, vol. 9 (1970), pp.78–117

[McKeag 76] McKeag R.M., Wilson R., *Studies in operating systems*, APIC studies in Data Processing, no. 13, Academic Press, (1976)

[Mealy 66] Mealy G.H., Witt B.I., Clark W.A., The functional structure of OS/360, *IBM Syst. J.*, vol. 5, 1 (1966), pp. 3–51

[Meinadier 71] Meinadier J.P., *Structure et fonctionnement des ordinateurs*, Larousse, (1971)

[Merle 78] Merle D., Potier D., Véran M., A tool for computer system performance analysis, in *Performance of computer installations*, D. Ferrari, ed., North Holland (1978), pp. 195–213

[Misra 81] Misra J., Chandy K.M., Proofs of networks of processes, *IEEE Trans. on Software Engineering*, vol. SE–7, 4 (July 1981), pp. 417–426

[Mitchell 79] Mitchell J.G., Maybury W., Sweet R., Mesa language manual, Tech. Rep. CS-79-5, Xerox Palo Alto Research Center (April 1979)

[Mitchell 85] Mitchell J.G., File servers, *in* [Hutchinson 85], pp. 221–259.

[Morris 86] Morris J.H., Satyanarayanan M., Conner M., Howard J.H., Rosenthal D.S.H., Smith F.D., Andrew: a distributed personal computing environment, *Comm. ACM*, vol. 29, 3 (March 1986), pp. 184–201.

[Morrison 73] Morrison J.E., User program performance in virtual storage systems, *IBM Syst. J.*, vol. 12, 3 (1973), pp. 216–237

[Mullender 85a] Mullender S., *Principles of distributed operating systems design*, Academisch Proefschrift, Vrije Universiteit te Amsterdam, Mathematisch Centrum (October 1985), 193 pp.

[Mullender 85b] Mullender S., Tanenbaum A., A distributed file system based on optimistic concurrency control, *Proc. 10th ACM Symp. on Operating Systems Principles, SIGOPS Operating Systems Review*, vol. 19, 5 (December 1985), pp. 181–193.

[Muntz 75] Muntz R.R., Scheduling and resource allocation in computer systems, in [Freeman 75], pp. 269–307

[Needham 82] Needham R.M., Herbert A.J., *The Cambridge Distributed Computer System*, Addison–Wesley (1982).

[Newton 79] Newton G., Deadlock prevention, detection, and resolution: an annotated bibliography, *ACM Operating Systems Review*, vol. 13, 2 (April 1979), pp. 33–44

[Organick 72] Organick E.I., *The Multics system: an examination of its structure*, MIT Press, (1972)

[Owicki 76] Owicki S., Gries D., Verifying properties of parallel programs: an axiomatic approach, *Comm. ACM.*, vol. 19, 5 (May 1976), pp. 279–285

[Parmelee 72] Parmelee R.P., Peterson T.I., Tillman C.C., Hatfield D.J., Virtual storage and virtual machine concepts, *IBM Syst. J.*, vol. 11 (1972), pp. 99–130

[Parnas 72a] Parnas D.L., A technique for software module specifications with examples, *Comm. ACM*, vol. 15, 5 (May 1972), pp. 330–336

[Parnas 72b] Parnas D.L., On the criteria to be used in decomposing systems into modules, *Comm. ACM*, vol. 15, 12 (December 1972), pp. 1053–1058

[Paul 85] Paul M., Siegert H.J. ed., *Distributed Systems: methods and tools for specification*, Lecture Notes in Computer Science no 190, Springer-Verlag (1985).

[Peterson 77] Peterson J.L., Norman T.A., Buddy systems, *Comm. ACM*, vol. 20, 6 (June 1977), pp. 421–431

[Peterson 81] Peterson G.L., Myths about the mutual exclusion problem, *Information Processing Letters*, vol. 12, 3 (June 1981), pp. 115–116

[Peterson 83] Peterson J., Silberschatz A., *Operating systems concepts*, Addison-Wesley, (1983)

[Popek 79] Popek G.J., Kampe M., Kline C.S., Stoughton A., Urban M., Walton E., UCLA Secure Unix, *Proc. AFIPS National Computer Conf.*, pp. 355–364 (1979)

[Popek 85] Popek G., Walker B.J. ed., *The Locus distributed system architecture*, MIT Press (1985).

[Presser 72] Presser L., White J.R., Linkers and loaders, *ACM Computing Surveys*, vol. 4, 3 (1972), pp. 149–167

[Prieve 76] Prieve B.G., Fabry R.S., VMIN — an optimal variable-space page replacement algorithm, *Comm. ACM*, vol. 19, 5 (May 1976), pp. 295–297

[Rashid 81] Rashid R.F., Robertson G.G., Accent: a communication-oriented network operating system, *Proc. Eighth Symp. on Operating Systems Principles*, ACM SIGOPS Review, vol. 15, 5 (December 1981), pp. 64–75

[Rashid 85] Rashid R., Network operating systems, *in* [Hutchison 85], pp.314–360.

[Raynal 84] Raynal M., *Algorithmique du parallélisme — le problème de l'exclusion mutuelle*, AFCET computer science monographs, Dunod, (1984). *Algorithms for mutual exclusion*, North Oxford Academic 1986

[Raynal 85] Raynal M., *Algorithmes distribués et protocoles*, Eyrolles (1985).

[Redell 74] Redell D.D., Fabry R.S., Selective revocation of capabilities, *Proc. IRIA International Workshop on Protection in Operating Systems*, Rocquencourt (July 1974), pp. 196–210

[Redell 80] Redell D., Dalal Y.K., Horsley T.R., Lauer H.C., Lynch W.C., McJones P.R., Murray H.G., Purcell S.C., Pilot: an operating system for a personal computer, *Comm. ACM*, vol. 23, 2 (February 1980), pp. 81–91

[Reed 79] Reed D.P., Kanodia R.K., Synchronization with event counts and sequencers, *Comm. ACM*, vol. 22, 2 (February 1979), pp. 115–123

[Rees 82] Rees D.J., Stephens P.D., The kernel of the EMAS 2900 operating system, *Software — Practice and Experience*, vol. 13 (1982), pp. 655–667

[Ricart 81] Ricart G., Agrawala A.K., An optimal algorithm for mutual exclusion in computer networks, *Comm. ACM*, vol. 24, 1 (January 1981), pp. 9–17.

[Ricart 83] Ricart G., Agrawala A.K., Authors' response to "on mutual exclusion in computer networks" by Carvalho and Roucairol, *Comm. ACM*, vol. 26, 2 (February 1983), pp. 147–148.

[Ritchie 74] Ritchie D.M., Thompson K., The Unix time-sharing system, *Comm. ACM*, vol. 17, 7 (July 1974), pp. 365–375 (latest edition in *Bell System Technical Journal*, vol. 56, 6, July-August 1978)

[Robert 77] Robert P., Verjus J.P., Towards autonomous descriptions of synchronization modules, *Proc. IFIP Congress* (1977)

[Rosen 69] Rosen S., Electronic computers: a historical survey, *ACM Computing Surveys*, vol. 1, 1 (March 1969), pp. 7–36

[Rosin 69] Rosin R.F., Supervisory and monitor systems, *ACM Computing Surveys*, vol. 1, 1(march 1969), pp. 37–54

[Saltzer 74] Saltzer J.H., Protection and the control of information sharing in Multics, *Comm. ACM*, vol. 17, 7 (July 1974), pp. 388–402

[Saltzer 75] Saltzer J.H., Schroeder M.D., The protection of information in computer systems, *Proc. IEEE*, vol. 63, 9 (September 1975), pp. 1278–1308

[Saltzer 78] Saltzer J.H., Naming and binding of objects, in [Bayer 78], pp. 99–208

[Satyanarayanan 81] Satyanarayanan M., A study of file sizes and functional lifetimes, *Proc. Eighth ACM Symp. on Operating Systems Principles* (SIGPLAN Notices, vol. 15, 5) (December 1981), pp. 96–108

[Sauer 81] Sauer C.H., Chandy K.M., *Computer systems performance modeling*, Prentice-Hall, (1981)

[Saxena 75] Saxena A.R., Bredt T.H., A structured specification of a hierarchical operating system, *ACM SIGPLAN Notices*, vol. 10, 6 (June 1975), pp. 310–318

[Scherr 73] Scherr A.L., Functional structure of IBM virtual storage operating system, part 2: OS/VS2-2 concepts and philosophies, *IBM Syst. J.*, vol. 12, 4 (1973), pp. 382–400

[Schmid 76] Schmid H.A., On the efficient implementation of conditional critical regions and the construction of monitors, *Acta Informatica*, vol. 6, 3 (1976)

[Schneider 85] Schneider F.B., Lamport L., Paradigms for distributed programs, *in* [Paul 85], pp. 431–480.

[Schroeder 72] Schroeder M.D., Saltzer J.H., A hardware architecture for implementing protection rings, *Comm. ACM*, vol. 15, 3 (March 1972), pp. 157–170

[Shaw 74] Shaw A.C., *The logical design of operating systems*, Prentice-Hall, (1974)

[Smith 81] Smith A.J., Long-term file migration: development and evaluation of algorithms, *Comm. ACM*, vol. 24, 8 (August 1981), pp. 521–532

[Smith 82] Smith A.J., Cache memories, *ACM Computing Surveys*, vol. 14, 3 (September 1982), pp. 473–530

[Stephenson 83] Stephenson C.J., Fast fits — new methods for dynamic storage allocation, *Proc. Ninth Symp. on Operating Systems Principles*, ACM Operating Systems Review, vol. 17, 5 (10–13 October 1983)

[Stern 74] Stern J.A., Backup and recovery of on-line information in a computer utility, Tech. Rep. MAC TR–116, MIT Lab. for Computer Science (1974)

[Stone 82] Stone H.S., *Microcomputer interfacing*, Addison-Wesley, (1982)

[Stoy 72] Stoy J.E., Strachey C., OS6 — an experimental operating system for a small computer, *Computer J.*, vol. 15, 2 & 3 (May & August) 1972)

[Svobodova 85] Svobodova L., File servers for network-based distributed systems, *ACM Computing Surveys*, vol. 16, 4 (December 1984), pp. 353–398.

[Tanenbaum 81] Tanenbaum A.S., *Computer Networks*, Prentice Hall (1981).

[Tanenbaum 85] Tanenbaum A.S., van Renesse R., Distributed operating systems, *ACM Computing Surveys*, vol. 17, 4 (December 1985).

[Tanenbaum 87] Tanenbaum A.S., *Operating systems: design and implementation,* Prentice-Hall (1987)

[Teorey 72] Teorey T.J., Pinkerton T.B., A comparative analysis of disk scheduling policies, *Comm. ACM*, vol. 15, 3 (March 1972), pp. 177–184

[Theaker 85] Theaker C.J., Brookes G.R., *A practical course on operating systems* Macmillan (1983)

[Thompson 78] Thompson K., Unix implementation, *Bell System Technical Journal*, vol. 56, 6 (July-August 1978), pp. 1931–1946

[Tsichritzis 74] Tsichritzis D.C., Bernstein P.A., *Operating systems*, Academic Press, (1974)

[Ullman 80] Ullman J.D., *Principles of database systems*, Computer Science Press, (1980)

[Verjus 86] Verjus J.P., Thoraval R., Dérivation d'algorithmes distribués d'arbitrage, *Technique et Science Informatiques*, vol. 5.1 (January 1986, pp. 37–47.

[Walker 83] Walker B., Popek G.J., English R., Kline C., Thiel G., The LOCUS distributed operating system, Proc. Ninth Symp. on Operating Systems Principles, *ACM Operating Systems Review*, Vol. 17, 5 (December 1983).

[Watson 70] Watson R.W., *Timesharing system design concepts*, McGraw-Hill, (1970)

[Watson 81] Watson R.W., Identifiers (naming) in distributed systems, *in* [Lampson 81a], pp. 191–210.

[Weizer 81] Weizer A.N., A history of operating systems, *Datamation,* vol. 27, 1 (jan. 1981), pp. 118–126

[Whitfield 73] Whitfield H., Wight A.S., EMAS — the Edinburgh multi-access system, *Computer J.*, vol. 18 (1973), pp. 331–346

[Wilkes 75] Wilkes M.V., *Time-sharing computer systems*, Macdonald, (1975)

[Wilkes 79] Wilkes M.V., Needham R.M., *The Cambridge CAP computer and its operating system*, Elsevier, (1979)

[Wirth 69] Wirth N., On multiprogramming, machine coding, and computer organization, *Comm. ACM*, vol. 12, 9 (September 1969)

[Wirth 76] Wirth N., *Algorithms + data structures = Programs*, Prentice-Hall, (1976)

[Wirth 82] Wirth N., *Programming in Modula-2*, Springer-Verlag, (1982);

[Wulf 81a] Wulf W.A., Levin R., Harbison S.P., *Hydra/C.mmp:an experimental computer system*, McGraw-Hill, (1981)

[Wulf 81b] Wulf W.A., Shaw M., Hilfinger P.N., Flon L., *Fundamental structures of computer science*, Addison-Wesley, (1981)

[Zimmerman 80] Zimmerman H., OSI Reference Model — the ISO model of architecture of Open Systems Inteconnection, *IEEE Trans. on Communication*, vol. COM-28 (April 1980), pp. 425–432.

[Zimmerman 81] Zimmerman H., Banino J.S., Caristan A., Guillemont M., Monsset G., basic concepts for the support of distributed systems; the Chorus approach, *Proc. Second International Conf. on Distributed computing Systems* (IEEE), Versailles (April 1981).

[Zimmermann 84] Zimmermann H., Guillemont M., Morisset G., Banino J.S., Chorus: a communication and processing architecture for distributed systems, Research report no. 328, INRIA (September 1984), 89pp.

[Zurcher 68] Zurcher F.W., Randell B., Iterative multi-level modeling — a methodology for computer system design, *Proc. IFIP Congress* (1968)

Index